ADVANCED
JAVA 1.1
PROGRAMMING

McGRAW-HILL
JAVA MASTERS
TITLES

Boone, Barry *JAVA Certification Exam Guide for Programmers and Developers.* 0-07-913657-5

Jenkins, Michael S. *Abstract Data Types in JAVA.* 0-07-913270-7

Morgenthal, Jeffrey *Building Distributed JAVA Applications.* 0-07-913679-6

Reynolds, Mark C. *Object-Oriented Programming in JAVA.* 0-07-913250-2

Rice, Jeffrey; Salisbury, Irving *Advanced JAVA 1.1 Programming.* 0-07-913089-5

Savit, Jeffrey; Wilcox, Sean; Jayaraman, Bhuvana *Enterprise JAVA: Where, How, When (and When Not) to Apply Java in Client/Server Business Environments.* 0-07-057991-1

Venners, Bill *Inside the JAVA Virtual Machine.* 0-07-913248-0

Advanced
Java 1.1
Programming

Jeffrey C. Rice
Irving Salisbury III

McGraw-Hill
New York • San Francisco • Washington, D.C. • Auckland • Bogotá
Caracas • Lisbon • London • Madrid • Mexico City • Milan
Montreal • New Delhi • San Juan • Singapore
Sydney • Tokyo • Toronto

McGraw-Hill

A Division of The McGraw-Hill Companies

Copyright © 1997 by The McGraw-Hill Companies, Inc. Printed in the United States of America. Except as permitted under the United States Copyright Act of 1976, no part of this publication may be reproduced or distributed in any form or by any means, or stored in a data base or retrieval system, without the prior written permission of the publisher.

1 2 3 4 5 6 7 8 9 0   DOC/DOC   9 0 2 1 0 9 8 7

P/N 052426-2
PART OF
ISBN 0-07-913089-5

The sponsoring editor for this book was Judy Brief and the production supervisor was Pamela Pelton. It was set in Vendome by North Market Street Graphics.

Printed and bound by R. R. Donnelley & Sons Company.

McGraw-Hill books are available at special quantity discounts to use as premiums and sales promotions, or for use in corporate training programs. For more information, please write to Director of Special Sales, McGraw-Hill, 11 West 19th Street, New York, NY 10011. Or contact your local bookstore.

Product or brand names used in this book may be trade names or trademarks. Where we believe that there may be proprietary claims to such trade names or trademarks, the name has been used with an initial capital or it has been capitalized in the style used by the name claimant. Regardless of the capitalization used, all such names have been used in an editorial manner without any intent to convey endorsement of or other affiliation with the name claimant. Neither the author nor the publisher intends to express any judgment as to the validity or legal status of any such proprietary claims.

To Rhonda.
—JEFFREY C. RICE

To my father, for always keeping me current with the computer industry and for shaping me into a hard-working individual.
—IRVING SALISBURY III

CONTENTS

Contents

PREFACE

Introduction

For programmers who are brand-new to Java, there is a wealth of information available to jump-start the learning process. In addition to numerous books that offer language primers and class-library descriptions, there are now Java language journals and magazines. New Web pages that offer tutorials and samples of code appear practically each day. Java users' groups that provide discourse on and support of Java are springing up world-wide. Finally, there are always the JavaSoft homepage at http://java.sun.com, the popular Gamelan homepage at http://www.gamelan.com, and the Java language usenet news group comp.lang.java. But for those who are beyond the language tutorials, there have been no resources focused solely on bridging the gap between simple applets and real-world applications. This book fills that void.

The development of this book was motivated by our experiences in talking and working with other Java programmers. We have chosen our topics based on code we have most often been asked how to write, topics that are applicable to real-world programming: creating reusable custom AWT widgets, extending the Java thread model, interacting with CGI programs, writing client/server applications, introducing new protocols, and creating file access control lists. To date, this book is the only single source that covers this spectrum of applications.

First and foremost, this book is about Java source code. Over 16,000 lines of Java sources were developed in the process of writing this volume, and the majority of that code is reprinted in its entirety in the chapters that follow. While the advent of the Web and CD-ROMs have made a convenient delivery mechanism for source code, there is still no substitute for hard copy. We feel strongly about providing a CD-ROM containing all our code, but we don't want to force our readers to access a CD just to refresh their memory as to how we have implemented reader/writer locks or priority queues.

To illustrate these topics we have picked examples that demonstrate Java programming techniques that are both important and generally useful. For portability, all examples are written to the core Java classes that are distributed with the JDK. We keep everything as simple and reusable as possible. In doing so, we expect our book to be both instructive and a real time-saver as you move to the next level of Java programming.

How to Use This Book

To a large degree, each chapter of this book is self-contained. Programmers wishing to dive into the details of multithreaded programming, for example, can jump right to Chap. 6. We do use many of our own classes throughout the book, however, and the chapters are organized such that classes used in one chapter will have been presented in a prior chapter. If you do move through the book nonsequentially, it should be possible to treat any classes as "black boxes" and refer back to their implementations later as needed. The book is divided into 10 chapters covering 10 different topic areas.

Chapter 1, "Introduction," presents our primary goal when writing Java classes—reusability—and the programming philosophies that guide us toward that goal. The material covered in this chapter should give you insight into our approach to Java programming.

Chapter 2, "Abstract Data Types," illustrates how the Java language can be used to create such general-purpose containers as linked lists, sorted linked lists, binary trees, and priority queues. These container classes are used throughout the rest of the book.

In Chapter 3, "Image Handling in JAVA," the Java image delivery model is explored, detailing how images are downloaded from remote hosts and how you can write classes that plug into the delivery model to access and manipulate raw image data.

The focus of Chapter 4, "Extending the Abstract Windowing Toolkit," is on extending Java's Abstract Windowing Toolkit (AWT). This chapter discusses the relationship between AWT user interface objects and their peers in the native windowing systems. This chapter also details both the JDK 1.0 and JDK 1.1 AWT event models and shows how to create custom AWT extension widgets.

Chapter 5, "Interapplet Communication," presents three techniques for allowing applets to communicate—through direct manipulation, through shared objects, or by using a server process as a message relay. The Remote Method Invocation (RMI) API is used to create an online chat service that illustrates applets communicating between browsers.

Chapter 6, "Multithreaded Programming," discusses the Java thread model and provides examples of how to implement traditional locking. Reusable classes that provide the functionality of reader/writer locks, semaphores, and barrier locks are provided as illustrations.

In Chapter 7, "Files and File I/O," an overview of the java.io package is provided. The details of extending the I/O stream model through custom filters are illustrated through a simple example of an extensible encryption filter. This chapter also steps through the applet authentication process required by browsers to allow applets to access files locally.

Chapter 8, "Network Programming," covers the Java socket-based model of network programming. A reusable, multithreaded, socket server framework is presented along with several example client-server applications built on that framework.

To facilitate seamless integration into the environment of Web browsers, Chapter 9, "Interaction with Browsers," discusses how applets can interact directly with the browser in which they run. The chapter also discusses applet- and widget-integration issues, a portable mechanism for creating protocol handlers, and interacting with CGI scripts.

The final chapter, "Security Managers," discusses the role security managers can play in Java applications and presents a SecurityManager subclass that implements Access Control Lists.

CD-ROM

The CD-ROM that accompanies this book contains all the source code presented here. In addition, it contains many applets and test programs that, while not discussed or presented in the text of the book, may be useful in demonstrating the capabilities of the classes elsewhere on the CD. At the base directory of the CD are a README file and index.html file that describe the contents of the CD in detail.

ACKNOWLEDGMENTS

We would like to offer our sincere thanks to the many people who made this book possible: To Lisa Swayne at Adler & Robin Books for her continuous encouragement, advice, and support. To Judy Brief and all the wonderful people at McGraw-Hill for their patience and assistance. To our reviewers, especially to Greg Waffen and Mikel Brown (yes Mikel, the book is finally out!). To Paul Pubst for his graphics work for the Web pages on the CD-ROM. To Dave Harms and Barton Fiske for a foot in the door. To Michael Peck for his moral support and friendship. To Joe Kosters for getting Jeff started with Oak and Webrunner back in 1994. To Clif and Barbara Rice and to Richard and Margaret Wright for lending a hand whenever needed.

Most of all, thanks to our families, without whose love, support, and encouragement this book would not have happened.

Introduction

By now you should be comfortable with the overall Java programming paradigm; the edit-compile-run-edit cycle should be second nature. After writing several applets or applications, it is likely that you have also started reusing classes from one project to the next. Indeed, a primary reason for using an object-oriented language like Java is to create reusable classes. However, the process of writing reusable classes may not be intentional or happening with appropriate forethought. Too often, classes are written without specific thought as to how they might be inherited and reused later. Typically, classes created in this ad hoc development style must be modified, perhaps even rewritten, before useful subclasses can be written.

Java as an object-oriented language is not a panacea. Unlike C++, where developers are free to mingle object-oriented with non-object-oriented programming, Java forces you to stay within the bounds of classes and objects. There are, however, no constraints within the language that guarantee reusability. Nothing can substitute for proper object-oriented design and software engineering. While it is beyond the scope of this book to cover all the subtleties of object-oriented design and programming, it is a goal of this book, and of this chapter in particular, to point out techniques, tools, and design philosophies that will help you to write better and more reusable and maintainable code.

This chapter has two areas of focus. The first is a discussion of the general design philosophies that characterize our approach to programming in Java. These philosophies have evolved through experience and have grown out of our attempt to attain a single overall goal: reusability. Assisting us in the pursuit of reusability are some practical resources, the discussion of which constitutes the second area of focus.

Design Philosophy

There are many qualities that distinguish good code: readability, maintainability, reliability, and reusability, to name just a few. Of these characteristics, we view *reusability* as paramount, for code that is written with this goal in mind typically encompasses the other qualities of good code. If you are writing a class that you know will be the foundation for later projects, you are likely to be more motivated to make it legible and error-free than if you are writing the class to be used only once.

To develop code that is reusable, we follow five design philosophies:

1. Keep it simple.
2. Keep it portable.
3. Keep it extensible.
4. Use packages.
5. Use interfaces.

Each of these tenets is described briefly in the following.

Keep It Simple

The first, and possibly most important, of our design philosophies is *keep it simple*. Implement functionality incrementally through inheritance, rather than create a monolithic class that does it all. Complex objects are harder to debug, harder to maintain, and harder to reuse than simple ones. The more complicated a class is, the more likely it is that a subclass will break some interaction between methods in the parent class by over-riding one of the parent's methods. With smaller, less-complex classes it is easier to avoid breaking the behavior of the parent unintentionally. Fur-thermore, by creating many small classes rather than fewer, more-complex classes, an inheritance tree with more nodes is created, providing more opportunities for inheritance and greater chances of creating a subclass that inherits just the right characteristics.

Keep It Portable

The growth in Java's popularity and in the number of Java licensees has been unlike anything in the computer industry to date. With so many operating system vendors providing Java Virtual Machines (VMs) native to their operating systems, there is an increased hazard of proprietary fea-tures and application programming interfaces (APIs) polluting the ubiq-uity of the Java platform. After all, it is in the best interest of an operating system company to find ways to make applications run only on its own OS, so that more end users will buy the operating system that runs the applications. Java licensees (such as SunSoft, Netscape, and Microsoft) are required to produce Java Virtual Machines that conform to the JavaSoft virtual machine specification. Java bytecodes will run on any VM that conforms to the specification. However, applications that use class libraries that rely on native methods will run only on operating systems to which the native methods have been ported. Applets that rely on native plug-ins or Active-X components risk being tied to a particular operating system. It is, therefore, in your own best interest to avoid using features that are not part of the Java Developer's Kit (JDK) core APIs, the standard API extensions (like JavaCommerce and JavaMedia), or that are not branded as "100% Pure Java."*

While there are prevalent desktop computer operating systems in the industry today, it is hard to know what the dominant runtime platform of tomorrow will be. Few could have predicted the growth of Java when it was first made public in the spring of 1995. Now, with Java-based thin-client computers, networked appliances, Java chip sets, and cellular phones with embedded Java VMs—all capable of running the same bytecodes—it is wise to avoid getting locked into a particular platform unnecessarily. Java applications and class files will be immediately reusable in these emerging markets, provided that the code has made use only of open APIs.

Finally, the JavaBeans specification is a good model to follow to assist in portability and reusability. Software that is written in Java and conforms to the Beans specification can be easily integrated in visual application builders running on any platform.

Keep It Extensible

Keeping designs extensible is probably the hardest design philosophy to adhere to, because it requires the most creativity and discipline. The creativity involves imagining code being used outside the context for which it was originally written. The discipline comes in making a ritual of the creativity exercise. It is far too easy to write an applet, class, or application just to solve a problem at hand. Unfortunately, the solution to today's problem may not lend itself easily to the challenges tomorrow brings. This is not to imply that you should attempt to solve all the world's problems in a scrolling-text applet. What is implied is that with a little forethought, your scrolling-text applet can be written such that someone could later inherit from it to create a scrolling URL-text applet. Without forethought, inheritance might be impossible. Programming for extensibility takes creativity and discipline and, like most things, gets easier with practice.

---

* Details on the "100% Pure Java" initiative can be found on the JavaSoft home page: http://java.sun.com.

Use Packages

Java packages are an extremely useful feature of the language, yet they are widely ignored by many beginning and intermediate Java programmers. This situation has arisen, in part, because most programmers cut their teeth on Java by creating applets, which are often contained in a single source file. Packages allow classes to be organized such that the classes within a common package can share information that is hidden from classes outside the package. This feature can be used to protect intrapackage class interaction from being accidentally or intentionally altered, and can make packaged classes more stable and predictable—all of which leads to more reusable code. Java packages also allow greater name-space resolution. Classes that are part of different packages may have the same name and still be referred to without ambiguity by using their fully package-qualified names (e.g., *test.a.MyClass* and *test.b.MyClass*). With less chance for name conflicts, classes in a package can be more easily used by others without concern that a name conflict will force a modification of the code.

Use Interfaces

Another Java feature that is underutilized by many beginning and intermediate Java programmers is *interfaces*. Java interfaces allow specification of an API; all classes that implement the interface conform to the API. Creating classes whose methods and constructors are passed arguments by interface, rather than by class name, affords much greater flexibility to those who reuse those classes. For example, you will see the *java.util.EventListener* interface used in several places throughout this book as a mechanism for providing asynchronous event notification. The fact that any class that implements the EventListener interface can register for notification makes the EventSource/EventListener notification model much more flexible and reusable.

Practical Resources

In developing this book, we availed ourselves of many resources to assist us in writing the classes we describe. Two in particular have been invaluable and bear mentioning. The first is a simple debugging method that you will see used throughout our code. This method can be incorporated into a general-purpose debugging class that follows. The second resource is the Java source code itself, both our own and that provided with the JDK.

A Debugging Class

As more sophisticated development environments have emerged, the availability of commercial-quality, graphical Java debuggers has rapidly increased. While any debugging environment with a user-friendly graphical user interface can be invaluable when developing applications, there are some challenges in debugging Java applets that cannot be met by debuggers. Because the environments in which an applet runs may vary in ways that are sometimes subtle and sometimes profound, debugging applets in a stable debugger environment is not always a guarantee that the applet will run in all Web browsers. For example, a development environment for applets may include the JDK's appletviewer or equivalent, which implements a different security policy than does Netscape's Navigator or Microsoft's Internet Explorer. Operations that work under appletviewer may cause security exceptions when the applet runs elsewhere. In situations like this, programmers must often resort to using the `System.out.println()` method for clues as to the cause of the problem.

One problem with `System.out.println()` is that it cannot be conveniently toggled. After several debugging messages are inserted in the code, once the problem is found the messages must be commented out or deleted to silence them. Furthermore, the identical debugging statements will often be reinserted at a later date if related problems are found. For this reason, many of our classes include a method called `dbg()`.

The `dbg()` method is a simple wrapper for `System.out.println()` that can be turned on or off by changing the value of a boolean instance variable, called `debug`, in the class. When `dbg()` is called, it is passed a String object that it will pass to `System.out.println()`, provided `debug` is set to *true*. The code for `dbg()` follows:

```
protected void dbg(String str) {
    if (debug) {
        System.out.println(this.getClass().getName() + ": " + str);
        System.out.flush();
    }
}
```

When the string is printed, it is prefixed by the name of the class that is calling dbg(). After printing the debug message, dbg() calls System.out.flush() to cause the data to be immediately printed. The following are typical messages from dbg():

```
ajp.threads.RWLock: Queues are empty...
ajp.threads.RWLock: Adding WRITER
ajp.threads.RWLock: 1 items in Writer queue.
ajp.threads.RWLock: releaseNextWriter waiting for 4 readers
```

In the classes that use the debug flag, it is typically set through an argument to the class's constructor, as shown here:

```
public RWLock() {
    this(false);
}
public RWLock(boolean debug)
    this.debug = debug;
    ...
}
```

This method of providing debugging information can easily be extended to a Debug class that includes the dbg() method, and perhaps even additional functionality. For example, Fig. 1.1 presents a Debug class that provides the added functionality of being able to dynamically set the output stream and provides support for levels of debugging messages. Because the dbg() method has been moved to a class, multiple Debug objects can be instantiated. This feature could be used to create one Debug object to write to System.out and another to write to a log file.* Furthermore, since the debugging is now implemented in a class, subclasses can be created that provide new features, like time stamps on each message.

There are two drawbacks to using a debug class versus a debug method within the class for printing the messages. The first drawback is that since the messages are coming from the Debug class, transparent printing of the class name is not supported. However, this feature could be added in a subclass by passing a reference to the instantiating object in the subclass's constructor. The second drawback is that there is a certain amount of overhead associated with the debug objects, as there may be multiple instances of them if multiple classes are being debugged. With minimal work, a static version of the class having less overhead could be created.

---

* We are assuming here, of course, that file access is allowed by the resident security manager.

Figure 1.1
The Debug class.

```java
package ajp.util;
import java.io.*;

/**
 * Generic class for doing debugging.
 * @version 1.3
 */
public class Debug {

    // Minimum level for debugging
    public static final int MIN_LEVEL = 0;

    // Maximum level of debugging
    public static final int MAX_LEVEL = 5;

    boolean debug;          // the debug flag
    PrintStream out;        // the stream to print to
    int debugLevel = 5;     // current debug level

    /**
     * Construct a Debug object with the debug going to System.out
     * and debugging turned on.
     **/
    public Debug() {
        this(System.out, true);
    }

    /**
     * Construct a Debug object with the debug going to a specified
     * PrintStream with debugging turned on.
     **/
    public Debug(PrintStream out) {
        this(out, true);
    }

    /**
     * Construct a Debug object with the debug going to a specified
     * PrintStream with a specified debug state.
     **/
    public Debug(PrintStream out, boolean state) {
        debug = state;
        this.out = out;
    }

    /**
     * Set the level of debugging to use.
     **/
    public void setLevel(int level) {
        if (level < MIN_LEVEL)
            level = MIN_LEVEL;
        else if (level > MAX_LEVEL)
            level = MAX_LEVEL;
        debugLevel = level;
    }

    /**
     * Turn the debugging on or off.
     **/
```

Figure 1.1
(*Continued*).

```
public void setDebug(boolean state) {
    debug = state;
}

/**
 * Send a string to the dbg method if level is
 * less than or equal to current debug level.
 **/
public void dbg(int level, String str) {
    if (level <= debugLevel)
        dbg(str);
}

/**
 * Send a string to the debug stream, if debugging is turned
 * on, regardless of current debugging level.
 **/
public void dbg(String str) {
    if (debug) {
        out.println(str);
        out.flush();
    }
}
}
```

Online Source

A resource available to anyone with the JDK is the full source code to all the Java core classes. It is hard to overemphasize the value of this resource. The JDK source package, provided in the *src.zip* file in the standard JDK distribution, is a wealth of information on how the Java classes work and how to write good Java code. It is also worth pointing out that the online documentation, while a valuable resource in its own right, is not always in sync with the sources. Since the online documentation is generated from comments embedded in the Java sources, and since the comments aren't always kept current with what is actually implemented, the source code should be used as the definitive guide. In addition to the online sources, the full source release for the JDK is available for free to individuals interested in research and evaluation.*

The ajp Packages

The code presented in the following chapters has been organized into a hierarchy of packages under the top-level package *ajp*. The classes have

---

* See the JavaSoft homepage at http://java.sun.com for details.

been placed in seven packages: *util, awt, interapp, threads, io, net,* and *security.* Each package directory has a Test subdirectory containing applets and applications that can be used to demonstrate the classes in the ajp packages. The packages are briefly defined as follows:

- *util*—A collection of general-purpose classes (see Chap. 2)
- *awt*—Extensions to the Abstract Windowing Toolkit (see Chaps. 3 and 4)
- *interapp*—Classes that support interapplet communication (see Chap. 5)
- *threads*—A package of high-level lock managers (see Chap. 6)
- *io*—Several file and I/O extension classes (see Chap. 7)
- *net*—A package of networking classes (see Chaps. 8 and 9)
- *security*—A file-access security manager (see discussion in Chap. 10)

The code presented in the following chapters has been altered slightly from the version that appears on the CD-ROM. To save space, most of the javadoc comments have been stripped out. In every other respect, the code in the ajp directory hierarchy on the CD-ROM is what appears in this book. Be sure to check the README file in the base directory of the CD-ROM for any errata or changes to the code. Also, be sure to read the copyright and legal files, which can be found in the base directory of the CD-ROM and through hypertext links in the file *index.html* on the CD-ROM.

Abstract Data Types

Introduction

Those who have programmed in C++ might immediately seek a rich library of general-purpose container classes in Java. *Container classes* are used to store and retrieve arbitrary objects and in C++ are commonly implemented using *templates*. While templates are not supported in Java because all objects inherit from the base class *Object*, it is easy enough to create classes that store and return arbitrary objects as instances of the Object class. And while Java does not have the automatic binding of return types that is supported by C++ templates, casting the object returned by a Java method achieves the same results.

There are several general-purpose container classes in the *java.util* package, specifically the *Hashtable, Vector,* and *Stack* classes. The utility of these classes is demonstrated by the fact that instances of them are peppered throughout the JDK source code. However, many common containers are absent from the JDK, such as linked lists, trees, and queues.

This chapter details four container classes that are used throughout this book: *LinkedList, SortedList, BinaryTree,* and *PriorityQueue.* The selection of these four classes as representative container classes was motivated largely by need. Many of the classes shown in subsequent chapters require container classes to store and organize objects. While classes already present in the java.util package could have in principle been used, there are times when a sorted linked list or binary tree presents a better solution to a problem than a vector or an array. The classes discussed in this chapter were originally created for this reason.

Although the selection of these four classes was pragmatic, taken as a whole they illustrate many features of the Java language that make it particularly well suited to the task of creating container classes.

Basic Containers

Fundamental to all container classes in Java is the principle that all objects derive from the base class *Object*. Through inheritance, every object is an instance of the Object class. Any object can be cast to Object and can be passed to a method that takes an instance of Object as an argument. The *Vector* class is a typical example of an Object container. The Vector method `elementAt()` returns the object that was stored at the index passed as an argument. The object is returned as an instance of Object. When using elementAt() the programmer must cast the returned object to the appropriate class:

```
MyClass myClassObject = null;
Object obj = vector.elementAt(x);
if (obj instanceof MyClass) {
    myClassObject = (MyClass)obj;
}
```

If the object returned by elementAt() is not of the expected class, an exception is generated when the object is cast to an incompatible class. For this reason, it is best to check the validity of the cast by using instanceof before casting (as is shown in the preceding), or at least to catch the exception:

```
MyClass myClassObject = null;
Object obj = vector.elementAt(x);
try {
    myClassObject = (MyClass)obj;
}
catch (ClassCastException e) {}
```

Basic container classes need only provide methods for storing and retrieving the objects they contain. A minimal container class might be:

```
public class Bag {
    private Object obj;

    public Object emptyBag() {
        Object tmp = obj;
        obj = null;
        return tmp;
    }

    public void fillBag(Object obj) {
        this.obj = obj;
    }
}
```

In the Bag class, the object is stored in a private instance variable, obj, and can be retrieved only through the emptyBag() method. Likewise, obj can have its value changed only through the fillBag() method. The simplicity of the Bag class makes it seem almost trivial; however, it is actually not very far removed from the Node class that is the foundation of several of the container classes in this chapter.

The container classes presented in the pages that follow fall into two categories: lists and organizers. *List classes* are collections of connected containers that require the programmer to directly control the insertion and removal of objects. The classic linked lists and tree structures fall into the category of lists. A user of a typical linked list must traverse the list to an appropriate point, then insert or remove the object at the chosen point in the list. *Organizer classes* are also aggregations of connected containers; however, unlike lists, organizers themselves manage the insertion and removal of objects. Different organizers set different policies for insertion; they can enforce them by not allowing the programmer direct access to the containers. Sorted lists, binary trees, and queues are all examples of organizers. A programmer using an organizer simply passes an object to the organizer. The organizer will determine where in its internal structure of containers the object should be stored.

List Classes

All containers classified as lists implement the *List interface* that is shown in Fig. 2.1. The List interface specifies an API for managing and traversing lists. Since List is an interface, it is possible to define many classes which implement the API. Methods that utilize lists of containers can be written independent of the list implementation, as long as they restrict their interaction with the list to the methods in the List interface. Furthermore, since the interface defines only the signature of the methods, it is possible to implement many traversal schemes and many types of lists.

The names of the methods in the interface suggest certain aspects of an implementation. For example, the only method for getting an object out of a List is through the getCurrent() method. The name of the getCurrent() method implies that Lists must have a notion of what constitutes a "current" element on the list. The current element is determined by explicit positioning through one of the *go* methods (e.g., goFirst(), goForward(), goBack(), and so on). The names of the methods for insertion and removal also suggest a relationship to the current item on the list: insertBefore(), insertAfter(), and removeCurrent(). Note that no methods in the API specify the use of any low-level container class. A class could implement the List interface and actually store the object internally on a Vector, Hashtable, or array. However, all the lists implemented here use the Node class as a basis for storage.

THE Node CLASS. The *Node* is a basic container class that supports multidirectional links to other Node objects. There are no methods in the Node class, just instance variables and a single constructor (see Fig. 2.2). The instance variables reference the object stored by the Node and up to

```
package ajp.util;

/**
 * An interface to support List classes.
 * @version 1.3
 **/
public interface List {

    /**
     * Insert an object after the current list item.
     * Throws an OffListException if the insertion point is off the list.
     **/
    public void insertAfter(Object toInsert) throws OffListException;

    /**
     * Insert an object before the current list item.
     * Throws an OffListException if the insertion point is off the list.
     **/
    public void insertBefore(Object toInsert) throws OffListException;

    /**
     * Insert an object as the last item on the list.
     * If list is empty, item inserted will be the first and last item.
     **/
    public void insertLast( Object toInsert );

    /**
     * Insert an object as the first item on the list.
     * If list is empty, the item will be the first and last item.
     **/
    public void insertFirst( Object toInsert );

    /**
     * Remove the last object on the list.
     * Throws an OffListException if the cursor is off the list.
     **/
    public void removeLast() throws OffListException;

    /**
     * Remove the first object on the list.
     * Throws an OffListException if the cursor is off the list.
     **/
    public void removeFirst() throws OffListException;

    /**
     * Remove the current object from the list.
     * Throws an OffListException if the cursor is off the list.
     **/
    public void removeCurrent() throws OffListException;

    /**
     * Change the cursor to the first item on the list.
```

Figure 2.1
The List interface.

```
     **/
    public void goFirst();

    /**
     * Change the cursor to the last item on the list.
     **/
    public void goLast();

    /**
     * Move the cursor forward one item in the list.
     * Throws an OffListException if the cursor is off the list.
     **/
    public void goForward() throws OffListException;

    /**
     * Move the cursor back one item in the list.
     * Throws an OffListException if the cursor is off the list.
     **/
    public void goBackward() throws OffListException;

    /**
     * Get the current object on the list.
     * Throws an OffListException if the cursor is off the list.
     **/
    public Object getCurrent() throws OffListException;

    /**
     * Is the cursor off the list?
     **/
    public boolean offList();

    /**
     * Is the list empty?
     **/
    public boolean isEmpty();

    /**
     * Returns the number of objects on the list.
     **/
    public int numItems();
}
```

Figure 2.1
(Continued).

four adjacent Node objects, located up, down, left, and right, relative to the current Node. When a Node is created, it is passed an object that the Node is to store. The constructor stores the object reference in the variable value. Figure 2.3 shows a visual representation of a Node object.

It is important to point out that the Node class, along with all the other base container classes presented here, implements the *java.io.Serializable* inter-

```
package ajp.util;

/**
 * A Node object is the building block for many data storage
 * types.  This node has references to four other nodes, providing
 * many different traversal possibilities, from LinkedLists to Graphs.
 * It is used to store an Object.
 *
 * For speed reasons, the nodes links are updated directly.  Any class
 * using a Node must be placed in the same package to have access to
 * these features.
 *
 * @version 2.3
 */
class Node implements java.io.Serializable {
    static final long serialVersionUID = 4800401753573512246L;

    // The next Node in the chain.
    Node left;

    // The previous node in the chain.
    Node right;

    // The node above me.
    Node up;

    // The node below me.
    Node down;

    // The object this node stores.
    Object value;

    /**
     * Create the Node with an Object inside it.
     **/
    Node(Object obj) {
        value = obj;
        left = null;
        right = null;
        up = null;
        down = null;
    }
}
```

Figure 2.2
The Node class.

face. The Serializable interface declares no methods, so there are no additional methods in the Node class because of the interface it implements. By declaring the Node class *Serializable*, we have indicated that the class can be serialized, that is, saved to an object output stream using the Java serialization API that is part of the JDK 1.1. This will allow, for example, Java Beans

Figure 2.3
A Node object.

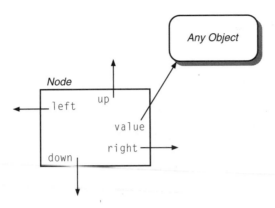

that use the container classes presented in this chapter to save their state, including any objects stored in the container classes they use.

There are two steps to ensuring that classes can be serialized. First the class, or a parent class it inherits from, must implement the Serializable interface. Second, the class must make sure that any instance variables for which serialization would be inappropriate (for example, a variable used to temporarily store an image reference), or impossible (a variable that is a reference to an object with a native implementation), be declared transient.

The variable serialVersionUID in the Node class is used by the serialization API to cope with the fact that a Node serialized today and saved to a file could be restored at a later date when the class definition has changed. The utility program serialver, which is included with the JDK, generates a unique long integer value that is assigned to the serialVersionUID variable and is used to prevent out-of-date serialized objects from being restored in a context in which the class definition has changed.

The Node class is a member of the package *ajp.util,* as are all the other classes presented in this chapter. The class, its instance variables, and the constructor are all package-private, which allows other classes in the ajp.util package to manipulate a Node directly, while classes outside the ajp.util package cannot. Applications can only use the Node class indirectly through the other classes of the ajp.util package.

THE LinkedList. The only List class shown here is an implementation of the classic doubly linked list called *LinkedList.* The LinkedList class implements the List interface and, as with any List implementation, the user of a LinkedList must manage the positioning, insertion, and removal of the objects contined within the list. Internally, the LinkedList class uses Node objects as containers. When an object is inserted into the LinkedList, a Node is instantiated and given a reference to the object to be stored. The Nodes and left and right links are then set so that the Node assumes a place on the list. Figure 2.4 shows a LinkedList with five nodes. The left instance variable is set to *null* on the first Node in the chain; the right instance variable is set to *null* on the last. The LinkedList class uses four instance variables of type Node to assist in traversing, inserting, and removing Nodes. The variables `first` and `last` always point to the beginning and end of the list respectively. The variable `cursor` is a reference to the current Node on the list during traversals or searches. The other Node reference within the class, `forEachCursor`, will be discussed later in this section.

A LinkedList is traversed using code such as the following:

```
LinkedList list;
...
for (list.goFirst(); !list.offList(); list.goForward()) {
    Object o = list.getCurrent();
    ...
}
```

Each time `goForward()` is called, the LinkedList resets its `cursor` variable to the next item on the list. If the cursor is off the end of the list, a call to `goForward()` will cause an *ajp.util.OffListException* object to be thrown. Thus, not shown in the preceding code is a `try` block around the loop, or a method declaration indicating that the method containing the loop throws OffListException.

The LinkedList implementation is shown in Fig. 2.5. Several aspects of its implementation bear examination and are discussed below. Figure 2.6 shows an applet that gives an interactive, graphical representation of a

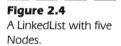

Figure 2.4
A LinkedList with five Nodes.

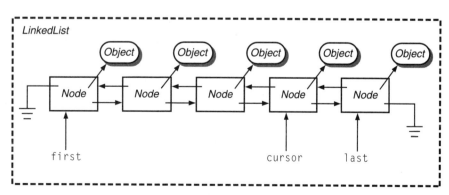

```
package ajp.util;

/**
 * A doubly linked list class.
 * @version 2.4
 **/
public class LinkedList implements List, java.io.Serializable {
    // number of items in this list
    int numItems;

    // first Node in list
    Node first;

    // cursor for list
    Node cursor;

    // last Node in list
    Node last;

    // the cursor to use with forEach method
    Node forEachCursor;

    /**
     * Create an empty LinkedList
     **/
    public LinkedList() {
        first = null;
        cursor = null;
        last = null;
        numItems = 0;
    }

    /**
     * Insert an object into the first position in the list
     * and set cursor to this item.
     **/
    public synchronized void insertFirst(Object someObject) {
        Node newNode = new Node(someObject);

        // if list is empty, we have to set the last item also
        if(isEmpty()) {
            first = newNode;
            cursor = newNode;
            last = newNode;
        }
        else {

            newNode.right = first;
            first.left = newNode;
            first = newNode;
            cursor = newNode;
        }
```

Figure 2.5
The LinkedList
implementation.

```
            numItems++;
    }

    /**
     * Insert an object into the last position in the list
     * and set cursor to this object
     **/
    public synchronized void insertLast(Object someObject) {
        Node newNode = new Node(someObject);

        // if list is empty then just insertFirst
        if (isEmpty()) {
            insertFirst(someObject);
        }
        else {
            last.right =newNode;
            newNode.left = last;
            last = newNode;
            cursor = newNode;
            numItems++;
        }
    }

    /**
     * Insert an object into the list after the current cursor location
     * and set cursor to this new item
     *
     * @param Object to insert
     * @exception OffListException if cursor is off the list
     **/
    public synchronized void insertAfter(Object someObject)
                                        throws OffListException {
        Node newNode = new Node(someObject);

        // if list is empty, same as insertFirst
        if (isEmpty()){
            insertFirst(someObject);
        }
        // if cursor at last item, same as insertLast
        else if (cursor.equals(last)) {
            insertLast(someObject);
        }
        // otherwise put item after the cursor
        else if(!offList()) {
            newNode.right = cursor.right;
            cursor.right.left = newNode;
            cursor.right = newNode;
            newNode.left = cursor;
            cursor = newNode;
            if(cursor.left.equals(last)) last = cursor;
            numItems++;
        }
        else {
```

Figure 2.5

(*Continued*).

```
                    throw new OffListException();
        }
    }

    /**
     * Insert an object into the list before the current cursor location
     * and set cursor to this new item
     **/
    public synchronized void insertBefore(Object someObject)
                                          throws OffListException {
        Node newNode = new Node(someObject);

        // first see if this is an empty list or if we are at the first item
        // in the list.
        if (isEmpty() || cursor.equals(first)) {
            insertFirst(someObject);
        }
        // otherwise put item after the cursor
        else if (!offList()) {
            goBackward();
            insertAfter(someObject);
        }
        else {
            throw new OffListException();
        }
    }

    /**
     * Remove the first item from the list
     * and set the cursor to the new first item in list
     **/
    public synchronized void removeFirst() throws OffListException {
        if (isEmpty()) {
            throw new OffListException("Cannot remove when list is empty");
        }
        // first see if we only have one item in the list
        else if (first == last) {
            first = null;
            last = null;
            cursor = null;
        }
        else {
            first.right.left = null;
            first = first.right;
            cursor = first;
        }
        numItems--;
    }

    /**
     * Remove the last item in the list and set
     * cursor to the new last item in the list
     **/
```

Figure 2.5

(Continued).

```
    public synchronized void removeLast() throws OffListException {
        if (isEmpty()) {
            throw new OffListException("Cannot remove when list is empty");
        }
        // see if we only have one item in list
        else if (first == last) {
            removeFirst();
        }
        else {
            last.left.right = null;
            last = last.left;
            cursor = last;
            numItems--;
        }
    }

    /**
     * Remove the current item the cursor is pointing to and set the
     * cursor to the next item in the list
     **/
    public synchronized void removeCurrent() throws OffListException {

        if (offList()) {
            throw new OffListException("Cannot remove when cursor is off");
        }
        else if(cursor.equals(first)) {
            removeFirst();
        }
        else if(cursor.equals(last)) {
            removeLast();
        }
        else {
            cursor.left.right = cursor.right;
            cursor.right.left = cursor.left;
            cursor = cursor.right;
            numItems--;
        }
    }

    /**
     * Get the object stored in the list pointed to by the cursor.
     **/
    public synchronized Object getCurrent() throws OffListException {

        if (offList()) {
            throw new OffListException("Cannot get item if cursor is off");
        }
        return cursor.value;
    }

    /**
     * See if the cursor is offList() i.e. not valid
     **/
```

Figure 2.5

(*Continued*).

```
public synchronized boolean offList() {
    return (cursor == null);
}

/**
 * See if the list is empty.
 **/
public synchronized boolean isEmpty() {
    return (first == null);
}

/**
 * Place the cursor on the first item in the list
 * Note: if the list is empty, this will still set the cursor
 * to offList()
 **/
public synchronized void goFirst() {
    cursor = first;
}

/**
 * Set the cursor to the last item in the list
 * Note: if the list is empty, this will set the cursor offList()
 **/
public synchronized void goLast() {
    cursor = last;
}

/**
 * Move the cursor to the next item in the list.
 * If the cursor is on the last item in the list, this
 * will set the cursor to offList().
 **/
public synchronized void goForward() throws OffListException {
    if (offList()) {
        throw new OffListException("Cannot go to next item in list " +
                                   "if cursor is offList()");
    }
    cursor = cursor.right;
}

/**
 * Move the cursor back one in the list.
 * If the cursor is on the first item in the list, this
 * will set the cursor offList().
 **/
public synchronized void goBackward() throws OffListException {
    if (offList()) {
        throw new OffListException("Cannot go back " +
                                   "if cursor is offList()");
    }
    cursor = cursor.left;
}
```

Figure 2.5

(Continued).

```
/**
 * Find an object in the list.  Will set the cursor to the
 * item if found.  Otherwise cursor will be off
 */
public synchronized void find(Object obj) {
    try {
        Node i;

        boolean found = false;
        for (i=first; i != null; i = i.right) {
            if (i.value.equals(obj)) {
                found = true;
                cursor = i;
                break;
            }
        }
        if (!found) {
            cursor = null;
        }
    }
    catch(OffListException e) {
        System.out.println("INternal errorin find " + e);
    }
}

/**
 * Remove object, if found. Resets cursor to item before the found item.
 * If not found, cursor will be off.
 *
 */
public synchronized void remove(Object obj) {
    try {
        find(obj);
        if (!offList()) {
            removeCurrent();
        }
    }
    catch(OffListException e) {
        System.out.println("Serious internal error in remove(obj) " + e);
    }
}

/**
 * Gives the item the iterator stopped on when using forEach method.
 * This will only be valid if forEach method hit a false response.
 *
 * @return Object iterator stopped on or null if it didn't stop.
 */
public synchronized Object forEachItem()  {
    Object o = (Object)null;

    if (forEachCursor != null) {
        o = forEachCursor.value;
```

Figure 2.5
(*Continued*).

```
          }
      return o;
  }

  /**
   * Iterate over all items on the list using the passed object's
   * forEach() method as the operation to perform.
   * This method will continue across the list as long as the forEach()
   * method returns true.  If forEach() returns false, the iteration
   * is stopped and a pointer to the item it stopped on is kept.
   **/
  public synchronized void iterate(ForEach f) {
      Node i;

      forEachCursor = null;

      for (i = first; i != null; i = i.right) {
          if (f.forEach(i.value) == false) {
              forEachCursor = i;
              break;
          }
      }
  }

  /**
   * See how many items are in the list
   **/
  public synchronized int numItems() {
      return numItems;
  }
}
```

Figure 2.5
(*Continued*).

LinkedList. The sources for this applet can be found on the CD-ROM that accompanies the book.

Within the LinkedList's implementation, two methods of traversal are possible. First, public methods provided by the class can be used. The body of the `find()` method implemented this way would take the following form:

```
try {
    for( goFirst(); !offList(); goForward() ) {
        if ( getCurrent().equals(obj)) {
            found = true;
            break;
        }
    }
    if (!found) {
        cursor = null;
    }
} catch (OffListException e) { }
```

Figure 2.6
A *LinkedList* test
program.

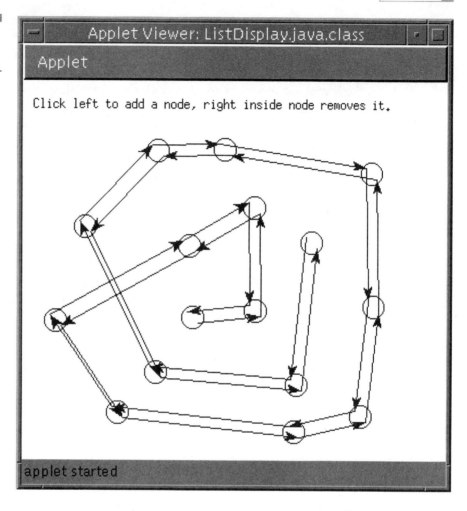

While this implementation is clear, it is not terribly efficient—executing four method invocations for each iteration of the loop. By implementing find() such that the nodes are accessed directly, there is only one method call per iteration:

```
for (Node i = first; i != null; i = i.right) {
    if (i.value.equals(obj)) {
        found = true;
        cursor = i;
        break;
    }
}
if (!found) {
    cursor = null;
}
```

Another interesting feature of the LinkedList implementation is the `iterate()` method. With many linked-list implementations, users of the lists end up writing a great deal of code to traverse a list, performing the same operation on each element encountered. Since this traverse-and-execute model is so common, the LinkedList class provides a method, `iterate()`, that does the work for the programmer.

The `iterate()` method is passed an object that implements the For-Each interface. The *ForEach interface* (see Fig. 2.7) simply defines a method, `forEach()`, which takes an object as an argument and returns a boolean.

As the list's `iterate()` method traverses the linked list, each object on the list is passed to the ForEach object's `forEach()` method. If the `forEach()` method returns *false*, the traversal is stopped and the LinkedList's `forEachCursor` (the fourth Node variable mentioned earlier) is set to the current node in the traversal. If the `forEach()` method returns *true*, the traversal continues with the next node in the list. The item pointed to by the `forEachCursor` can be retrieved by calling the LinkedList's `forEachItem()` method. Both the `iterate()` and `for-EachItem()` methods are specified in the *Iteration interface* shown in Fig. 2.8. The Iteration interface is implemented by the LinkedList class.

The `forEach()` method can be used in one of two ways: either to perform an operation on all objects on a list, or to perform an operation that attempts to locate a particular item. For example, take an implementation of a RaceCar class:

```
public RaceCar {
    public int speed;
    public void start() {
    ...
    }
}
```

Figure 2.7
The ForEach
interface.

```
package ajp.util;

/**
 * An interface for doing iterations on lists.
 * @version 1.3
 */
public interface ForEach {
    /**
     * The method to be executed for each item on the list.  If the
     * method returns false, the iteration will stop on that item.
     **/
    public boolean forEach(Object obj);
}
```

Figure 2.8
The Iteration
interface.

```
package ajp.util;

/**
 * An interface to support iterating over container classes.
 * @version 1.4
 */
public interface Iteration {

    /**
     * Starts the iteration.
     **/
    public void iterate(ForEach f);

    /**
     * The Object the iteration stopped on.
     **/
    public Object forEachItem();

}
```

Next consider a class, RaceTrack, that contains a LinkedList of all RaceCars involved in a race. To start all the cars in the list, the RaceTrack could implement the ForEach interface:

```
public RaceTrack implements ForEach {
    LinkedList cars;
    ...
    public void addCar(RaceCar r) {
        cars.insertFirst(car);
    }
    public boolean forEach(Object o) {
        if (o instanceof RaceCar) {
            RaceCar r = (RaceCar)o;
            r.start();
        }
        return true;
    }
    void startRace() {
        cars.iterate(this);
    }
}
```

The RaceTrack builds up its LinkedList through the addCar() method. Eventually, when the startRace() method is called, the Race-Track object passes itself as an implementor of the ForEach interface to the list's iterate() method. The list then traverses the list of RaceCars, passing each instance to the RaceTrack's forEach() method, causing the RaceCars to be started.

If a car ran out of gas during the race, the RaceTrack could remove the RaceCar that had stopped with a slightly modified forEach() method:

```
int mode;
boolean ret = true;
public boolean forEach(Object o) {
    if (o instanceof RaceCar) {
        RaceCar r = (RaceCar)o;
        switch(mode) {
        case START:
            r.start();
            break;
        case FIND_STOPPED:
            if(r.speed == o)
                ret = false;
            break;
        }
    }
    return ret;
}
```

The new variable, mode, is used to give the iterations different meanings. When the mode is equal to the constant *START,* the iterate() method will start all the cars. When mode is set to *FIND_STOPPED,* iterate() will traverse the list until it finds the first stopped RaceCar; then it stops, setting the forEachCursor on the item that stopped the iteration. The RaceTrack class can use this feature to eliminate stopped RaceCars:

```
void removeStopped() {
    mode = FIND_STOPPED;
    cars.iterate(this);
    Object o = cars.forEachItem();
    while(o != null){
        cars.remove(o);
        cars.iterate(this);
        o = cars.forEachItem();
    }
}
```

One final note on iteration: The LinkedList class provides methods for traversing the list one element at a time. When writing multithreaded programs, care must be taken not to change the state of the list in one thread while the list is being traversed by another. While all the methods in the class that modify the list are synchronized, the list is not protected by the monitor between method invocations. One way to prevent corruption of the list is to wrap the iteration in a synchronized block:

```
synchronized(list) {
    list.goFirst();
    while(!list.offList()) {
        ...
        list.goForward();
    }
}
```

Another way to protect lists from simultaneous access is to use the `iterate()` method where appropriate. Since `iterate()` is synchronized, and since the entire list is traversed within the method, the list cannot be modified by another thread calling other methods of the object. In situations where the each-element, front-to-back traversal provided by `iterate()` is not appropriate, traversing within a synchronized block is suggested.

Organizer Classes

The LinkedList class provides a flexible implementation of a doubly linked list with iteration. With the LinkedList class, the burden is on the programmer using the class to maintain the list. Insertions, removals, and accessing elements all require explicit positioning of the list's cursor. *Organizer classes* are containers that manage the placement of the objects within the container without programmer intervention. An organizer will determine where to place an object based on some algorithm it implements and will return objects in a pattern dictated by the algorithm. For example, a simple *stack* is an organizer. Stacks do not typically allow for explicit positioning of objects but rather implement a first-in-last-out (FILO) insertion and removal pattern.

The organizer classes presented here fall into two broad categories: full organizers and limited removal organizers. *Full organizers* are classes that implement the Organizer interface, as will be described shortly. *Limited removal organizers* are classes that have the general characteristics of an organizer but don't implement the Organizer interface, primarily because they allow only very specific patterns of removal. The full organizers used in this book are *SortedList* and *BinaryTree*. A limited removal organizer used in later chapters is a *PriorityQueue.**

Objects that are to be inserted into containers that implement the Organizer interface must themselves implement a specific interface, *Comparable*, as is shown in Fig. 2.9.

Through the three Comparable methods, objects can compare themselves to like objects. It is through the comparison methods that Organizer objects are able to determine where to insert objects into the Organizer's internal storage. The Organizer interface is shown in Fig. 2.10.

---

* See the Reader/Writer lock implementation in Chapter 4.

```
package ajp.util;

/**
 * An interface for creating classes that can be compared.
 * @version 2.2
 */
public interface Comparable {

    /**
     * Is the current Comparable object less than another.
     **/
    boolean isLessThan(Comparable compObj);

    /**
     * Is the current Comparable object greater than another.
     **/
    boolean isGreaterThan(Comparable compObj) ;

    /**
     * Is the current Comparable object equal to another.
     **/
    boolean isEqualTo(Comparable compObj) ;
}
```

Figure 2.9
The Comparable
interface.

The addItem() and removeItem() are used to store to and retrieve Comparable objects from Organizers. The find() method will return an Object that matches (typically one for which the isEqualTo() method returns true) the Comparable object passed as an argument. The elements() method acts much as the method of the same name in the Vector class; it returns an Enumeration object that allows the Organizer to be traversed one element at a time using the methods hasMoreElements() and nextElement().

SortedList. The first Organizer, the SortedList, is a specialized list that stores Comparable objects according to a lexically ascending order defined by the lessThan() method. The SortedList is built upon a LinkedList by default, but it can actually use any object that implements the List interface as its means of storage. The SortedList class has four constructors:

1. public SortedList()
2. public SortedList(List list)
3. public SortedList(boolean ascending)
4. public SortedList(List list, boolean ascending)

```
package ajp.util;
import java.util.Enumeration;

/**
 * An interface to support organizer classes.  An Organizer
 * is a Container that controls the order the items are
 * stored in and the order in which they are retrieved.
 * @version 2.2
 */
public interface Organizer {

    /**
     * Adds a Comparable item to this Organizer.  The actual way the object
     * is added depends on the organizer and cannot be controlled by the
     * user.
     **/
    public void addItem(Comparable object);

    /**
     * Find and remove all occurances of this object
     **/
    public void removeItem(Comparable object);

    /**
     * Find the first occurance of this object and return that object
     **/
    public Object find(Comparable object);

    /**
     * Returns an enumeration of the elements. Use the Enumeration methods on
     * the returned object to fetch the elements sequentially.
     */
    public Enumeration elements();

}
```

Figure 2.10
The Organizer
interface.

In the first form of the constructor, a LinkedList object is instantiated and later used to store the objects for the SortedList. In the second form, the List passed as an argument is used. Since the list internal to SortedList is accessed only by the methods in the List interface, the implementation allows another List object to be used. Thus, if a better List implementation is created, the SortedList class need not change; the improved List can just be passed to the SortedList's constructor. This illustrates one of the benefits of using interfaces to specify an API. The forms of the constructor that take a boolean will create a monotonically increasing list if the value of the argument passed is *true*. By default, SortedLists arrange their contents in ascending order.

A SortedList object accepts Comparable objects for insertion. To store non-Comparable objects in a SortedList, a wrapper must be created that either extends or encapsulates the object to be stored. For example, to store simple Java Strings in a SortedList, a class that encapsulates String and implements the Comparable interface must be created.* Figure 2.11 shows an example of a String wrapper class.

The SortedList sorts objects into ascending or descending order as the objects are inserted. An object being inserted is compared against the others on the list using either the isLessThan() or isGreaterThan() method of the Comparable object. The new object is inserted in front of the first node for which the comparison returns *true*.

A simple class for testing Organizers is given in Fig. 2.12. This test class is used as a tool for benchmarking various Organizer implementations. The OrganizerTest class has a runTest() method which generates a number of randomly generated CompString objects and adds them to an Organizer. After adding all the items, the organizer's contents are printed to standard output, one object is removed from the organizer, and the contents are printed again.

A SortedList can be tested by instantiating a OrganizerTest object, passing it a SortedList object, then calling the runTest() method of the OrganizerTest object:

```
import ajp.util.*;
public class SortedListTest {
    public static void main(String args[]) {
        OrganizerTest ot = new OrganizerTest();
        SortedList list = new SortedList();
        ot.runTest(5, list);
    }
}
```

The output generated by running this application is shown in Fig. 2.13.

In its implementation, the SortedList is about as simple a usable Organizer as is possible. It implements the methods in the Organizer and adds only the methods numItems() and isEmpty() (see Table 2.1). Within the SortedList is a List object. The SortedList class controls access to the List such that all insertions and deletions keep the contents of the list in

---

* The String must be encapsulated rather than subclassed because *String* is defined as a final class.

Figure 2.11
The CompString
class from
OrganizerTest.java.

```java
import java.util.Random;
import java.util.Enumeration;
import ajp.util.*;

class CompString implements Comparable {
    public String s;

    CompString(String s) {
        this.s = new String(s);
    }

    public String toString() {
        return s;
    }

    public boolean isLessThan(Comparable compObj) {
        boolean ret = false;

        if (compObj instanceof CompString) {
            ret = (s.compareTo(((CompString)compObj).s) < 0);
        }
        return ret;
    }

    public boolean isGreaterThan(Comparable compObj) {
        boolean ret = false;

        if (compObj instanceof CompString) {
            ret = (s.compareTo(((CompString)compObj).s) > 0);
        }
        return ret;
    }

    public boolean isEqualTo(Comparable compObj) {
        boolean ret = false;

        if (compObj instanceof CompString) {
            ret = (s.compareTo(((CompString)compObj).s) == 0);
        }
        return ret;
    }
}
```

either ascending or descending order. The implementation of the Sort-edList is shown in Fig. 2.14.

When the SortedList's elements() method is called, it returns a *List-Enumerator* object. The ListEnumerator class is an inner class of SortedList and is a wrapper around the SortedLists internal LinkedList. The List-Enumerator inner class functions as an adaptor, providing the hasMoreElements() and nextElements() methods of the Enumeration interface. This implementation detail is similar to the way the Java Vector class provides for enumeration. Since the enumeration is contained in a separate class that is accessible only to the SortedList class, users can use

```
public class OrganizerTest {
    String letters = "ABCDEFGHIJKLMNOPQRSTUVWXYZ";
    Random rand;

    public OrganizerTest() {
        rand = new Random(4242);
    }

    public void runTest(int count, Organizer org) {
        CompString str;
        CompString save = null;

        for (int i = 0; i < count; i++) {
            String s = "String "
                        + letters.charAt(Math.abs(rand.nextInt() % 26))
                        + letters.charAt(Math.abs(rand.nextInt() % 26))
                        + letters.charAt(Math.abs(rand.nextInt() % 26))
                        + letters.charAt(Math.abs(rand.nextInt() % 26));

            str = new CompString(s);

            System.out.println("Created String " + str);
            if (i == count/2)
                save = str;   // save one to remove later
            org.addItem(str);
        }

        printOrg(org);

        System.out.println("\nRemoving String " + save);
        org.removeItem(save);

        printOrg(org);
    }

    static void printOrg(Organizer org) {
        System.out.println("\nEnumeration");
        Enumeration e = org.elements();
        while(e.hasMoreElements()) {
            System.out.println("\tItem: " + (CompString)e.nextElement());
        }
    }
}
```

Figure 2.12
The OrganizerTest
class from
Organizer.java.

enumeration only by calling the SortedList's `elements()` method. This allows the SortedList and ListEnumerator classes to ensure that the list's cursor is reset to the start of the list prior to enumeration.[*]

---

[*] Inner classes are a feature of the JDK 1.1 and above. For older versions of the JDK, the ListEnumerator class would be broken out as a separate class accessible only to the ajp.util package.

Figure 2.13
The SortedListTest
output.

```
$ java SortedListTest
Created String String KFET
Created String String DXJG
Created String String FLDD
Created String String MFFM
Created String String BNUC

Enumeration
        Item: String BNUC
        Item: String DXJG
        Item: String FLDD
        Item: String KFET
        Item: String MFFM

Removing String String FLDD

Enumeration
        Item: String BNUC
        Item: String DXJG
        Item: String KFET
        Item: String MFFM
```

It is reasonable to use a SortedList when the number of objects to be inserted in the list is small. However, as the length of the list grows, so does average traversal time, since all traversals are linear from the start of the list. When a sorted organizer is needed that will be very dynamic and potentially very large, a binary tree is a better choice.

A BinaryTree. The BinaryTree class presented here is a fairly traditional binary search tree implementation. Rather than encapsulating a

TABLE 2.1

Public API of the
SortedList Class

Method signature	Purpose
synchronized void addItem(Comparable object)	Adds an item to the SortedList
synchronized void removeItem(Comparable object)	Removes an item from the SortedList
synchronized Object find(Comparable object)	Finds an object on the SortedList
synchronized void start()	Prepares the SortedList for traversal as an enumeration
boolean hasMoreElements()	Returns *true* if the enumeration has more objects that can be retrieved
synchronized Object nextElement()	Gets the next object in the enumeration
synchronized int numItems()	Returns the number of items on the list
synchronized boolean isEmpty()	Returns *true* if there are no items on the list

```
package ajp.util;
import java.util.Enumeration;

/**
 * A class that implements a sorted Linked List of Comparable
 * objects.  Utilizes a List object under the hood to store the objects
 * in.  Any object that conforms to the List interface can be passed in
 * to be used as the underlying container.
 * @version 2.3
 */
public class SortedList implements Organizer, java.io.Serializable {
    // order of list, increasing ir true
    boolean ascending;

    // the List object I will use under the hood
    List list;

    /**
     * Create a SortedList object with a specific implementation of a List
     * and a specified order of sorting.
     **/
    public SortedList(List list, boolean ascending) {
        this.list = list;
        this.ascending = ascending;
    }

    /**
     * Create an ascending SortedList object with a specific
     * implementation of a List and an increasing sorting order.
     **/
    public SortedList(List list) {
        this(list, true);
    }

    /**
     * Create a SortedList object with the default LinkedList implementation
     * and an increasing sorting order.
     **/
    public SortedList() {
        this(true);
    }

    /**
     * Create a SortedList object with the default LinkedList implementation
     * and a specified sorting order.
     **/
    public SortedList(boolean ascending) {
        this(new LinkedList(), ascending);
    }

    /**
     * Adds a Comparable item to this SortedList.  It will be placed in the
```

Figure 2.14
The SortedList
implementation.

```
             * list as specified in the sorting order.
             **/
            public synchronized void addItem(Comparable object) {
                try{
                    boolean inserted = false;
                    if (ascending) {
                        for (list.goFirst(); !list.offList(); list.goForward()) {
                            if (object.isLessThan((Comparable)list.getCurrent())) {
                                list.insertBefore(object);
                                inserted = true;
                                break;
                            }
                        }
                    }
                    else {
                        for (list.goFirst(); !list.offList(); list.goForward()) {
                            if (object.isGreaterThan((Comparable)list.getCurrent())) {
                                list.insertBefore(object);
                                inserted = true;
                                break;
                            }
                        }
                    }
                    if (!inserted) {
                        list.insertLast(object);
                    }
                }
                catch(OffListException e) {}
            }

            /**
             * Find and remove all occurances of a specific object. Will
             * set the cursor position to the element after the one removed
             * if found.  This needs to be taken into consideration when performing
             * traversals because traversals use the cursor position.  If not
             * found, cursor will be set to off.
             **/
            public synchronized void removeItem(Comparable object) {
                try {
                    while (find(object) != null) {
                        list.removeCurrent();
                    }
                }
                catch(OffListException e) {}
            }

            /**
             * Find the first occurance of this object and return that object.
             * Also sets the cursor to this object if found, otherwise will set
             * it off.  This needs to be taken into consideration when performing
             * traversals because traversals use the cursor position.
             **/
            public synchronized Object find(Comparable object) {
```

Figure 2.14

(Continued).

```
            Object obj = null;
            try {
                  for (list.goFirst(); !list.offList(); list.goForward()) {
                        if (object.isEqualTo((Comparable)list.getCurrent())) {
                              obj = list.getCurrent();
                              break;
                        }
                  }
            }
            catch(OffListException e) {}

            return obj;
      }

      /**
       * Returns an enumeration of the elements. Use the Enumeration methods on
       * the returned object to fetch the elements sequentially.
       * Warning! Do not modify the list while enumerating.
       */
      public Enumeration elements() {
            return new ListEnumerator();
      }

      /**
       * See how many items are in the list
       **/
      public synchronized int numItems() {
            return list.numItems();
      }

      /**
       * Is the list empty?
       **/
      public synchronized boolean isEmpty() {
            return list.isEmpty();
      }

      class ListEnumerator implements Enumeration {

            ListEnumerator() {
                  list.goFirst();
            }

            /**
             * Are there any more elements in this SortedList?
             **/
            public boolean hasMoreElements() {
                  return !list.offList();
            }

            /**
             * Get the next element which is the current cursor
             * position and move the cursor one forward.
```

Figure 2.14
(Continued).

```
          **/
      public synchronized Object nextElement() {
          Object ret = null;
          try {
              ret = list.getCurrent();
              list.goForward();
          }
          catch(OffListException e) {}
          return ret;
      }
   }
}
```

Figure 2.14
(*Continued*).

List, the BinaryTree manages the Nodes directly. A parent Node's right and left instance variables track its right and left children in the tree. The Node on the left contains a Comparable object that is less than the object contained by the parent Node. The Node on the right contains a Comparable object that is greater than the parent's Comparable object.

The BinaryTree class implements recursive traversals to add, remove, and find objects in the tree. Recursion starts at the root node of the tree and descends downward, descending to the right if the object being installed is greater than the object at the current Node and descending to the left if the object being installed is less than the object at the current Node. To illustrate the recursion, consider the tree shown in Fig. 2.15a. Each circle on the tree represents a Node that contains a Comparable object. The object is represented by the number in the circle. The state of the tree as it is shown is the result of the objects being installed in a random order. Assume the next node to be installed is *60*. Figure 2.15*b* shows the path taken to install *60* on the tree. First, an install method is called and is passed *60* and the root node of the tree. Since the root contains *30*, which is less than *60*, the install method calls itself, passing *60* and the right child of the root node, *80*. Again, *60* is compared to the current node, but this time is found to be less than *80*, so the recursion continues with *60* being passed to the left node, *50*. From *50* the recursion continues to *70* on the right. At the node containing *70*, the recursion stops since there are no further nodes; *60* is installed on the *less-than* side of *70*.

Binary search trees provide a reasonable solution to the problem of linear traversals suffered by linked lists. As long as objects are not already in order and the tree is reasonably well balanced, search times will be much improved over SortedLists; in the worst possible case, when objects are

Figure 2.15
(a) A binary tree.
(b) The path of
recursion for a new
node inserted into
a binary tree.

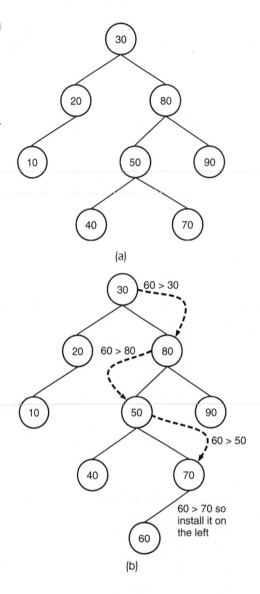

(a)

(b)

inserted in order, traversal times will be the same. In the preceding example, four nodes had to be traversed to install *60*. On a SortedList, with the same initial contents, six nodes would have to be examined before *60* could be installed.*

---

* Recall that the SortedList installs an object once it finds a node containing an object greater than the object being installed. Thus *10, 20, 30, 40, 50,* and *70* would all have to be examined before *60* would be installed.

The challenge in implementing a SortedList in the context of the classes and interfaces presented thus far is that ideally, the BinaryTree class should be plug-and-play compatible with the SortedList class. The difficulty is in the Organizer interface. To make BinaryTrees and SortedLists interchangeable, both must implement the same interfaces. SortedList supports the Organizer interface, which includes a mechanism for enumeration. Unfortunately, enumerating through an object designed for recursive traversal is difficult. Implementing the Enumeration `nextElement()` method requires diving down into the tree to find the next item, returning from the many recursive method calls, then returning the object found—a very expensive process. Another solution might be to have a separate thread descend through the tree, set a cursor on the current Node, and then wait for another thread to tell it to proceed. Somehow the thought of a multithreaded binary tree seems a bit heavy-handed. Still another solution is to provide for nonrecursive traversal, essentially creating a standard linked list out of the tree's nodes.

Since the Node class contains up and down Node references that have thus far been unused, there is the potential to organize the same nodes in multiple ways just by using different links. As the Nodes are installed on the tree, their *up* variable is used to reference the node above them. That leaves the *down* variable, which is used to point to the Node containing the next larger Comparable object. During installation of the Nodes in the tree, the Nodes containing both the next larger and next smaller Nodes are encountered.* By remembering these Nodes, the *down* pointers can be linked up once the new Node is installed, and an in-order linked list can be created.

In addition to providing the Organizer interface, the BinaryTree class also supports the Iteration interface. Since there are several ways to traverse a binary tree, the implementation of the iterate() method can process the nodes of the tree in order, preorder, or postorder. When iterating in order, the left child of each node is processed, then the node itself, then the right child. Preorder iteration implies processing the node first, then the left and right children. During postorder iteration, the left and right nodes are processed first, then the parent node is processed. The order of processing during an iteration is determined by a flag that is set with the `setOrder()` method and queried with the `getOrder()` method. These two methods are the only public methods in the API not specified by the interfaces that the BinaryTree implements (see Table 2.2).

---

* You may wish to try a few numbers on Fig. 2.15 to verify this.

TABLE 2.2

Public API of the
BinaryTree Class

Method signature	Purpose
synchronized void addItem(Comparable object)	Adds an item to the BinaryTree
synchronized void removeItem(Comparable object)	Removes an item from the BinaryTree
synchronized Object find(Comparable object)	Finds an object on the BinaryTree
synchronized void start()	Prepares the BinaryTree for traversal as an enumeration
boolean hasMoreElements()	Returns *true* if the enumeration has more objects that can be retrieved
synchronized Object nextElement()	Gets the next object in the enumeration
synchronized int numItems()	Returns the number of items on the list
synchronized boolean isEmpty()	Returns *true* if there are no items on the list
synchronized void setOrder(int order)	Sets the traversal order to in-order, preorder, or postorder
synchronized int getOrder()	Returns an integer representing the current order of traversal
synchronized void iterate(ForEach f)	Executes the forEach() method of the object passed once for every item in the tree
synchronized Object forEachItem()	Returns a reference to the item the iteration stopped on

The implementation of the BinaryTree is presented in Fig. 2.16. While most of the class is straightforward, the removeNode() method bears particular note. The basic idea behind removing a node from the binary search tree is to move one of the child nodes up to take the position of the parent, then take the other child and reinstall it below the promoted child node. In principle this is easy; however, maintaining the ordered list created through the Node's down variables adds a complication to the implementation.

Figure 2.17 illustrates the state of the BinaryTree during removal of a node. In Fig. 2.17*a* the same tree described earlier is shown, this time with the down references depicted as dark arrows. When the node *50* is to be

```java
package ajp.util;
import java.util.*;

/**
 * A binary search tree class that supports iteration and enumeration.
 * Instances of the BinaryTree class can be traversed in order using
 * either the iterate() method or the inorder() method.
 *
 * Also provided are methods for preorder and postorder recursion
 * through the tree.
 * @version 2.3
 **/
public class BinaryTree implements Organizer, Iteration, java.io.Serializable {

    // Indicates a preorder traversal.
    public static final int PREORDER  = 0;

    // Indicates a postorder traversal.
    public static final int POSTORDER = 1;

    // Indicates a in-order traversal.
    public static final int INORDER   = 2;

    // The root of the tree
    private Node root = null;

    // The Node that caused the iteration to stop
    private Node forEachCursor = null;

    // The Node find() stopped on
    private Node findCursor = null;

    // The Current node during iteration by enumeration
    private Node cursor = null;

    // Used during remove to adjust down link
    private Node firstNode = null;
    private Node largerNode = null;
    private Node smallerNode = null;

    private int order = INORDER;

    /**
     * Create an empty binary tree.
     **/
    public BinaryTree(){ }

    /**
     * Add a comparable object to the binary tree.  The object
     * is inserted in ascending order based on a standard definition
     * of its isLessThan() method.
     **/
    public synchronized void addItem(Comparable c) {
```

Figure 2.16
The BinaryTree class.

```
            largerNode = null;
            smallerNode = null;

            if (root == null) {
                root = new Node(c);
                firstNode = root;
            }
            else
                installNode(c, root);
        }

        /**
         * Remove a comparable object from the binary tree.  Note that the
         * Comparable object passed as an argument does not have to be the
         * same object as the one that is removed from the tree, it
         * just has return true from the isEqualTo() method.
         **/
        public synchronized void removeItem(Comparable c) {
            if (root != null)
                removeNode(c, root);
        }

        /**
         * Find a comparable object in the binary tree.  Note that the
         * Comparable object passed as an argument does not have to be the
         * same object as the one that is found on the tree, it
         * just has return true from the isEqualTo() method.
         **/
        public synchronized Object find(Comparable c) {
            findCursor = root;
            return (findNode(c, root)) ? findCursor.value : null;
        }

        /**
         * The actual find method.  Finds a match to the comparable object
         * recursing from n.  Returns true if it is found.  Sets findCursor
         * to the node that matches.
         **/
        private boolean findNode(Comparable c, Node n) {
            boolean ret = false;
            if (n == null || c == null) {
                return false;
            }

            Comparable nodeObj = (Comparable)n.value;

            if (c.isEqualTo(nodeObj)) {
                findCursor = n;
                ret = true;
            }
            else if (findNode(c, n.right)) {
                ret = true;
            }
```

Figure 2.16
(Continued).

```
        else if (findNode(c, n.left)) {
            ret = true;
        }
        return ret;
    }

    /**
     * The actual install method.  Installs the coparable object
     * recursivly from n.
     **/
    private void installNode(Comparable c, Node n) {
        Comparable nodeObj = (Comparable)n.value;
        Node newNode;

        if (c.isLessThan(nodeObj)) {
            largerNode = n;
            if (n.left == null) {
                newNode = new Node(c);
                n.left = newNode;
                newNode.up = n;
                newNode.down = largerNode;
                if (smallerNode == null) {
                    firstNode = newNode;
                }
                else {
                    smallerNode.down = newNode;
                }

            }
            else {
                installNode(c, n.left);
            }
        }
        else if (c.isGreaterThan(nodeObj)) {
            smallerNode = n;
            if (n.right == null) {
                newNode = new Node(c);
                n.right = newNode;
                newNode.up = n;
                newNode.down = largerNode;
                smallerNode.down = newNode;
            }
            else {
                installNode(c, n.right);
            }
        }
    }

    /**
     * Find the node at the end of a chain of right links.
     **/
    private Node farthestRight(Node n) {
        while (n.right != null) {
```

Figure 2.16
(Continued).

```
                n = n.right;
        }
        return n;
    }


    /**
     * Find the node at the end of a chain of left links.
     **/
    private Node farthestLeft(Node n) {
        while (n.left != null) {
            n = n.left;
        }
        return n;
    }


    /**
     * Moves up the tree looking for a down pointer that points to
     * the Node n.  Used for adjusting the down pointers for
     * object removal.
     **/
    private Node findPrevious(Node n) {
        Node start = n;
        Node ret = null;
        n = n.up;
        while (n != null) {
            if (n.down == start) {
                ret = n;
                break;
            }
            n = n.up;
        }
        return n;
    }


    /**
     * The removal of nodes from the tree is fairly involved.  The
     * basic idea is to move the node's right child as the farthest
     * right point of the chain under the node's left child.  The
     * trick is to adjust the down Nodes so that the inorder
     * enumeration stays valid.
     *
     * The removal descends recursively to find the matching node,
     * then makes all the link adjustments.  There is a great deal of
     * special handling for degenerate cases (no left child, no right
     * child, etc.)
     **/
    private boolean removeNode(Comparable c, Node n) {
        boolean ret = false;
        Comparable nodeObj = (Comparable)n.value;

        if (c.isEqualTo(nodeObj)) {
            /* Recursion stops here.  Now that the node is found
             * do the removal.  Three top level cases, this is the
```

Figure 2.16

(Continued).

```
                          * root node, this is a left child, this is a right child.
                          */
                if (n.up == root) {  // this is the root node
                    if (n.left == null) {  // no left node
                          root = n.right;    // move right node up.
                          firstNode = root; // reset firstNode for enumeration.
                    }
                    else if (n.right == null) { // no right node
                          root = n.left;  // just slide the left branch up.
                    }
                    else {   // two children of the root node.
                          // find the largest child on the left branch
                          Node tmp = farthestRight(n.left);
                          tmp.right = n.right; // move the right child
                          tmp.down = n.down;   // adjust the down pointer
                          n.right.up = tmp;    // adjust the up pointer on the
                                               //  right child
                          root = n.left;       // make left child new root node
                    }
                }
                else if (n.up.left == n) {
                    /* A left node to be removed.  There are four cases:
                     * no children, a right child but no left, a left
                     * child but no right, and both a left and a right child.
                     */
                    if (n.left == null && n.right == null) {
                          // no children -- adjust down pointer of previous
                          Node tmp = findPrevious(n);
                          n.up.left = null;
                          if (firstNode == n) {
                              firstNode = firstNode.down;
                          }
                          else {
                              tmp.down = n.down;
                          }
                    }
                    else if (n.left == null) {
                          // right only.
                          Node tmp = findPrevious(n);
                          // move right child up to current position
                          n.up.left = n.right;
                          n.right.up = n.up;
                          // adjust down pointer or reset firstNode
                          if (firstNode == n) {
                              firstNode = firstNode.down;
                          }
                          else {
                              tmp.down = n.down;
                          }
                    }
                    else if (n.right == null) {
                          // left only
                          Node tmp = farthestRight(n.left);
```

Figure 2.16
(Continued).

```
                            n.up.left = n.left;
                            n.left.up = n.up;

                            /* make furthest right child point to removed
                             * nodes "down" node.
                             */
                            tmp.down = n.down;
                    }
                    else {
                            // two children
                            Node tmp = farthestRight(n.left);
                            n.up.left = n.left;
                            tmp.right = n.right;
                            tmp.down = n.down;
                            n.left.up = n.up;
                            n.right.up = tmp;
                    }
            }
            else {
                    /* A right node to be removed.  There are four cases:
                     * no children, a right child but no left, a left
                     * child but no right, and both a left and a right child.
                     */
                    if (n.left == null && n.right == null) {
                            // no children
                            n.up.right = null;
                            n.up.down = n.down;
                    }
                    else if (n.left == null) {
                            // right only
                            n.up.right = n.right;
                            n.right.up = n.up;
                            n.up.down = n.down;
                    }
                    else if (n.right == null) {
                            // left only
                            Node tmp = farthestRight(n.left);
                            n.up.right = n.left;
                            n.left.up = n.up;
                            tmp.down = n.down;
                    }
                    else {
                            // both left and right
                            Node tmp = farthestRight(n.left);
                            n.up.right = n.left;
                            tmp.right = n.right;
                            tmp.down = n.down;
                            n.left.up = n.up;
                            n.right.up = tmp;
                    }
            }
            ret = true;
    }
```

Figure 2.16
(*Continued*).

```
            else if (c.isGreaterThan(nodeObj)) {
                 if (n.right == null)
                      ret = false;
                 else
                      ret = removeNode(c, n.right);
            }
            else if (c.isLessThan(nodeObj)) {
                 if (n.left == null)
                      ret = false;
                 else
                      ret = removeNode(c, n.left);
            }
            return ret;
      }

      /**
       * The real preorder traversal method. Recurses through the tree.
       **/
      private boolean preorder(ForEach f, Node n) {
            if (n != null) {
                 if (f.forEach(n.value) == false) {
                      forEachCursor = n;
                      return false;
                 }

                 if (preorder(f, n.left) == false) {
                      return false;
                 }

                 if (preorder(f, n.right) == false) {
                      return false;
                 }
            }
            return true;
      }

      /**
       * The real postorder traversal method. Recurses through the tree.
       **/
      private boolean inorder(ForEach f, Node n) {
            if (n != null) {
                 if (inorder(f, n.left) == false) {
                      return false;
                 }

                 if (f.forEach(n.value) == false) {
                      forEachCursor = n;
                      return false;
                 }

                 if (inorder(f, n.right) == false) {
                      return false;
                 }
```

Figure 2.16
(Continued).

```
        }
        return true;
}

/**
 * The real inorder traversal method. Recurses through the tree.
 **/
private boolean postorder(ForEach f, Node n) {
    if (n != null) {
        if (postorder(f, n.left) == false) {
            return false;
        }

        if (postorder(f, n.right) == false) {
            return false;
        }

        if (f.forEach(n.value) == false) {
            forEachCursor = n;
            return false;
        }
    }
    return true;
}

/**
 * Set the order of traversal.  Can be either PREORDER, POSTORDER,
 * or INORDER.
 **/
public synchronized void setOrder(int order) {
    switch(order) {
    case PREORDER:
    case POSTORDER:
    case INORDER:
        this.order = order;
        break;
    }
}

/**
 * Returns the order of traversal.
 **/
public synchronized int getOrder() {
    return order;
}

/**
 * Iterate over all items on the tree using the passed object's
 * forEach() method as the operation to perform.  This method
 * will continue across the list as long as the forEach() method
 * returns true.  If forEach() returns false, the iteration is
 * stopped and a pointer to the item it stopped on is kept.
 **/
```

Figure 2.16
(Continued).

```
    public synchronized void iterate(ForEach f) {
        forEachCursor = null;

        switch(order) {
        case PREORDER:
            preorder(f, root);
            break;
        case POSTORDER:
            postorder(f, root);
            break;
        case INORDER:
            inorder(f, root);
            break;
        }
    }

    /**
     * Gives the item the iterator stopped on when using forEach method.
     * This will only be valid if forEach method hit a false response.
     **/
    public synchronized Object forEachItem()  {
        Object o = (Object)null;

        if (forEachCursor != null)
            o = forEachCursor.value;
        return o;
    }

    /**
     * Returns the enumeration of the elements on the list.
     **/
    public Enumeration elements() {
        return new BinaryTreeEnumerator(this);
    }

    class BinaryTreeEnumerator implements Enumeration {
        BinaryTree tree;

        BinaryTreeEnumerator() {
            cursor = firstNode;
        }

        /**
         * See if there are more elements to Enumerate over
         **/
        public boolean hasMoreElements() {
            return (cursor != null);
        }

        /**
         * Returns the next element of the enumeration. Calls to this
         * method will enumerate successive elements.
         **/
```

Figure 2.16
(*Continued*).

```
        public Object nextElement() {
            Node tmp = cursor;

            if (tmp == null) {
                return(null);
            }
            cursor = cursor.down;
            return(tmp.value);
        }
    }
}
```

Figure 2.16
(*Continued*).

removed, the appropriate left, right, and up references of the bordering nodes must be adjusted. In addition, the down nodes of the next smaller node must be corrected. Conceptually, the process begins by moving *70*, the right child of *50*, below *40*, the left child of *50* (see Fig. 2.17*b*). Since *70* will be greater than any node under *40*, it must be positioned at the farthest right position under *40*. The method *farthestRight()* will traverse the right links of a node and its children and return the last one in the chain. Next, the down links must be adjusted (Fig. 2.17*c*). The down reference of *40* is set to point to the same node as *50*'s down link. Finally, *40* is moved into the position on the tree occupied by *50* by resetting the left variable in *80* and the up variable in *40* (Fig. 2.17*d*).

Although the scenario for removing a node just described may seem fairly easy, there are several special cases that require special handling. Beyond the cases where one or the other child is null, there are cases when the down reference that points to the node being removed does not belong to an adjacent node. For example, in Fig. 2.17, look at the down link between nodes *30* and *40*. If *40* is removed, node *30* must be found by traveling up the tree until a down reference that matches *40* is found. The method `findPrevious()` performs this function. Once the reference is found, the link can be changed appropriately.

Priority Queues

The only queue implementation in the JDK is a first-in-last-out queue, the *Stack* class. While there are no first-in-first-out (FIFO) queues provided as part of the standard Java class libraries, implementing a FIFO queue is not hard. A FIFO class can be constructed using a Java Vector to store the objects in the queue, for example. The problem with using a Vector is that

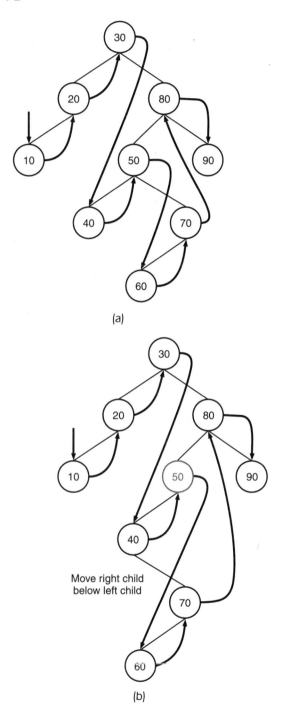

■■■ ■■■ ■■■ ■■■
Figure 2.17
The removal of a
node from a binary
tree: (a) the tree
before the removal;
(b) the right child is
moved below the left
child.

(a)

Move right child
below left child

(b)

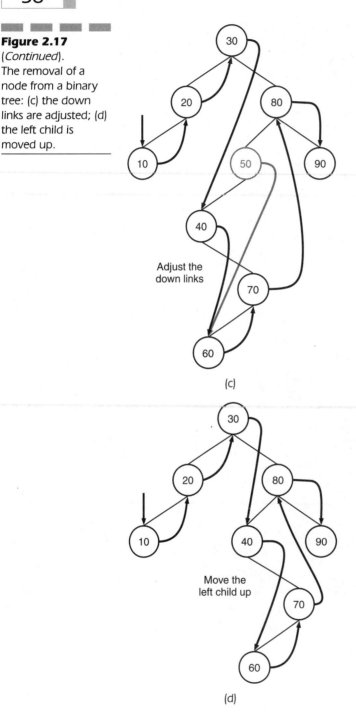

Figure 2.17
(*Continued*).
The removal of a
node from a binary
tree: (c) the down
links are adjusted; (d)
the left child is
moved up.

Adjust the
down links

(c)

Move the
left child up

(d)

for applications where the numbers of insertions and deletions are large, the performance of the Vector class is poor in comparison to linked lists (see the section titled "Performance Considerations" at the end of this chapter). Therefore, the queue class presented here, a *priority queue*, is built on top of a List.

Priority queues are sorted queues that insert objects in decreasing order according to an integer priority and remove objects from the queue, highest priority first and lowest priority last. For items inserted into the queue at the same priority level, the priority queue becomes a FIFO queue. Priority queues are useful whenever it is necessary to prioritize access of multiple objects to a single resource. For example, assume an order-processing application is implemented in Java. Purchase-order objects are delivered to the application asynchronously via a network connection, perhaps as e-mail messages, and must be processed one at a time. If the orders are delivered faster than they can be processed, some mechanism for queueing the orders is needed. Orders could be queued on a first-in-first-out basis, but it may make more sense to process the big orders first.* Using a priority queue, the incoming orders could be queued as to total dollar amount. Large, high-priority orders would be placed at the front of the queue, while smaller, low-priority orders would be placed later in the queue. Since objects can only be removed from the front of the queue, the largest orders would always be processed first.

IMPLEMENTATION.   Since queues are easily implemented on top of lists, and since a priority queue has much in common with a sorted list, the PriorityQueue class utilizes a SortedList to store objects. The API for the PriorityQueue class is simple; its six methods are shown in Table 2.3. The methods provide basic functionality, adding to and removing from the queue.

Because the internal storage mechanism for a priority queue is a SortedList, and since SortedLists store objects that implement the Comparable interface, the PriorityQueue must use Comparable objects. To insulate users of a PriorityQueue from the Comparable interface, the PriorityQueue wraps the object to be stored and its priority in an inner class, *PriorityItem*, which implements the Comparable interface.

The PriorityItem's `isGreaterThan()` and `isLessThan()` methods are used for inserting into the queue, so both methods return a boolean based on a comparison of the priority instance variables. The `isEqualTo()` class is used as the basis for removing objects from the PriorityQueue so

---

* The technical term for this is *cherry-picking.*

TABLE 2.3

Public API of the
PriorityQueue Class

Method signature	Purpose
synchronized void insert(Object item, int priority)	Inserts the item in the queue at the given priority level
synchronized Object peekHead()	Returns a reference to the object at the head of the queue
synchronized Object popHead()	Removes the object at the head of the queue and returns a reference to it
synchronized int numItems()	Returns the number of items in the queue
synchronized boolean isEmpty()	Returns *true* if the queue is empty
synchronized void dumpTo(OutputStream out)	Prints the contents of the queue to the specified output stream

it compares the actual PriorityItem objects, rather than their priorities, which might not be unique.

The PriorityQueue class itself is just a wrapper around the underlying SortedList. Objects are inserted using the SortedList's addItem() method. The SortedList does the work of locating the proper place in the list to insert the object. The only way to remove an item from the queue is through the popHead() method which saves a reference to the first item on the SortedList, then removes it from the list. The two operations are combined under the protection of the queues monitor to prevent another thread from modifying the queue between getting the reference and removing the object. The PriorityQueue and PriorityItem implementation are shown in Fig. 2.18.

Performance Considerations

One of the two motivating reasons behind the development of the container classes presented in this chapter is *performance*. There are scenarios where the performance of JDK container classes can be unacceptable. These scenarios involve random insertion into Vector objects.

The JDK Vector class uses an array of Objects to store data. The array is initially allocated to a specified size; then, as items are added to the vector, the array is grown as needed. The method of growing the array is to allocate another array that is a specified increment larger than the first and then to copy the original elements over to the new array using System.arrayCopy().

```
package ajp.util;

import java.io.*;
import java.util.Enumeration;

/**
 * A PriorityQueue class.  Items are added according to
 * their priority, with higher priority items being added to the
 * front of the queue.  Within the same priority, items are added with
 * a basic first in first out mechanism.
 *
 * @version 2.3
 **/
public class PriorityQueue implements java.io.Serializable {

    // the Sorted List used under the hood
    private SortedList list;

    /**
     * Create the PriorityQueue
     *
     **/
    public PriorityQueue() {
        // Create the SortedList in descending order
        list = new SortedList(false);
    }

    /**
     * Insert an item into the list with the given priority
     **/
    public synchronized void insert(Object item, int priority) {
        list.addItem(new PriorityItem(item, priority));
    }

    /**
     * Peek at the head of the queue
     **/
    public synchronized Object peekHead() {
        Enumeration e = list.elements();
        PriorityItem p = (PriorityItem)e.nextElement();
        return (p == null) ? null : p.getItem();
    }

    /**
     * Remove the head of the queue and return the item
     * removed.
     **/
    public synchronized Object popHead() {
        Object ret = null;

        Enumeration e = list.elements();
        PriorityItem p = (PriorityItem)e.nextElement();
```

Figure 2.18
The PriorityQueue
class.

```
            if (p != null) {
                list.removeItem(p);
                ret = p.getItem();
            }
            return ret;
    }

    /**
     * See how many items are in the queue
     **/
    public synchronized int numItems() {
            return list.numItems();
    }

    /**
     * Is the queue empty
     **/
    public synchronized boolean isEmpty() {
            return list.isEmpty();
    }

    /**
     * Dump the items and priorities out to a stream
     **/
    public synchronized void dumpTo(OutputStream out) throws IOException {
            DataOutputStream d = new DataOutputStream(out);

            Enumeration e = list.elements();
            while (e.hasMoreElements()) {
                PriorityItem p = (PriorityItem)e.nextElement();
                d.writeChars("Priority: " + p.getPriority() +
                            " Item: " + p.getItem() + "\n");
            }
            d.flush();
    }

    /**
     * Inner class to wrap the items passed to the priority Queue
     **/
    class PriorityItem implements Comparable {

        private int priority;   // The priority of the item

        private Object item;    // The item itself.

        /**
         * Create the PriorityItem.
         **/
        PriorityItem(Object obj, int priority ) {
            item = obj;
            this.priority = priority;
        }
```

Figure 2.18
(*Continued*).

```
            /**
             * Get the current item in the node.
             **/
            public Object getItem() {
                return item;
            }


            /**
             * Get the priority of this item.
             **/
            public int getPriority() {
                return priority;
            }


            /**
             * Is the current PriorityItem less than another.
             **/
            public boolean isLessThan(Comparable compObj) {
                boolean ret = true;
                try {
                    ret = (priority < ((PriorityQueue.PriorityItem)compObj).priority);
                }
                catch (Exception e) {}
                return ret;
            }


            /**
             * Is the current PriorityItem object greater than another.
             **/
            public boolean isGreaterThan(Comparable compObj) {
                boolean ret = true;
                try {
                    ret = (priority >
                            ((PriorityQueue.PriorityItem)compObj).priority);
                }
                catch (Exception e) {}
                return ret;
            }


            /**
             * Is the current PriorityItem object equal to another.
             **/
            public boolean isEqualTo(Comparable compObj) {
                boolean ret = true;
                try {
                    ret = this.equals((PriorityQueue.PriorityItem)compObj);
                }
                catch (Exception e) {}
                return ret;
            }
        }
    }
}
```

Figure 2.18
(Continued).

TABLE 2.4

Performance
Comparison of
Vector and
LinkedList Classes*

Class	Add element to end	Get element	Time, mm:ss Remove element from front
Vector	0:0.406	0:0.236	0:44.925
LinkedList	0:0.663	0:0.713	0:0.475

*Tests performed using JDK 1.1 with no just-in-time (JIT) compiler running on a 90-MHz pentium processor. The applications TestList.java and TestVector.java were used and can be found on the CD-ROM.

The performance problem with the Vector class occurs when elements are removed. Since the underlying storage object is an array, when an object is removed from the array all elements of the array above the object must be copied down one position. This is a costly operation compared to element removal in a linked list. To illustrate the point, Table 2.4 summarizes execution times of several comparable List and Vector operations under the JDK 1.1. While overall performance is similar for most operations, removing items can be several orders of magnitude more expensive for Vectors in the worst case.

SUMMARY

The Java language provides a rich environment in which classical abstract data types can be constructed. While Java does not possess the C language's explicit pointers, typically used to implement such data types as linked lists, and while there are no templates as there are in C++, container classes can be built using the Object class to store references to objects and instance variables to reference other containers. This chapter, rather than attempting to be a comprehensive guide to constructing abstract data types, focuses on four specific containers: the LinkedList, the BinaryTree, the SortedList, and the PriorityQueue. These classes are presented not as replacements for the standard Java container classes such as Vector or Hashtable, but rather as complementary tools for the Java programmer's tool box.

Image Handling
in Java

Introduction

The Java programming environment presents a unique platform for dealing with image data. Because Java has been targeted at the World Wide Web and since images are so central to the content on the Web, image support has always been integral to the Java core. Supporting images within the Java runtime is a challenge, however. Images accessed by a Java applet may reside on a remote Web server separated from the applet by several low-speed links. Requests for images from within a Java program may take inordinately long periods of time to fulfill. To allow applets to continue running while image data is being transferred, the Java image delivery model provides for asynchronous downloading of images with a notification scheme that informs applications when the data is ready.

To their great credit, the designers of the Java core class libraries have made the libraries easy enough to use and feature-rich enough that the majority of Java programmers will never need to delve into the details of creating images. Indeed, for those whose requirements stop at creating and displaying GIF and JPEG files, the Graphics and Image classes of the `java.awt` package provide ample functionality. However, for those who wish to directly manipulate image data, or who need precise control over the delivery of images to their Java applications, the classes in the `java.awt.image` package must be more fully understood.

This chapter explores the details of the *image delivery model*—the process by which image data is brought into the Java environment from local or remote sources and translated into a Java Image object. To illustrate the model, and to demonstrate its flexibility, extensions are discussed that interpose on image delivery to allow for direct manipulation of the image data, and that provide an alternate scheme for tracking the downloading of image data.

The Java Image Production Model

There are three roles in the production of images in Java: the *producer* of the image, the *consumer* of the image, and the *observer* of the image. Each image has one producer, one or more consumers, and zero or more observers. The three roles correspond directly to interfaces defined in the `java.awt.image` package:

1. ImageProducer
2. ImageConsumer
3. ImageObserver

Every java.awt.Image object has an *ImageProducer* that is responsible for generating the image's data. The ImageProducer generates image data and delivers it asynchronously to *ImageConsumer* objects in an incremental fashion, notifying any registered *ImageObservers* as each block of image data is delivered.

To a great degree, programmers are sheltered from the ImageProducers, ImageConsumers, and ImageObservers since images are typically created using higher-level methods, such as the `getImage()` method from either the `java.applet.Applet` class or the `java.awt.Toolkit` class. When `getImage()` is called, a reference to an Image object is returned that can be rendered using the `drawImage()` method of the Abstract Windowing Toolkit (AWT) *Graphics* class. The Image object has associated with it an ImageProducer that will generate the image's data. The ImageProducer, however, does not immediately start production of the image data. Usually, image production begins when data from the Images is first referenced—by passing the image to the `java.awt.Graphics.drawImage()` method, for example. Once the data is required for rendering, the ImageProducer will begin delivering the image data and eventually the full image can be displayed. The asynchronous delivery of the image to an applet or application is implemented through the ImageObserver interface.

ImageObserver

The ImageObserver interface specifies one method:

```
public boolean imageUpdate(Image img, int infoflags,
                           int x, int y, int width, int height)
```

As an ImageProducer generates a block of data* and delivers it to the ImageConsumer, it also calls the `imageUpdate()` method of any registered ImageObservers. The `imageUpdate()` method provides for asynchronous updates as more image data is produced. Before discussing each of the arguments passed to `imageUpdate()`, let's look at how the ImageObserver interface is used by the AWT.

---

* Each block of data is typically an array of bytes representing the pixels in one row of the image.

The AWT Component class implements the ImageObserver interface. Thus, every AWT user interface object, as well as the Applet class, includes an `imageUpdate()` method. To see how the `imageUpdate()` method is used, consider a simple `paint()` method that draws an Image in an applet:

```
public void paint(Graphics g) {
    g.drawImage(someImage, x, y, this);
}
```

The fourth argument to drawImage(), `this`, is a reference to an ImageObserver—the applet itself. The first time the applet's `paint()` method is called, the image has not been downloaded so there is no pixel data in the Image object. The call to `drawImage()` is passed a reference to the empty Image which, behind the scenes, triggers the Image-Producer to begin downloading the image. After the first block of image data is generated, the applet's `imageUpdate()` method is called by the ImageProducer and is passed a reference to the partially filled image. The `imageUpdate()` method inherited by the Applet class calls `repaint()` each time the ImageProducer sends more data. The call to `repaint()` triggers an asynchronous call to `paint()`, which calls `drawImage()` again. This time, however, the Image object contains some image data that can be drawn. The call to `drawImage()` causes the available data, a small slice of the image, to be drawn in the applet. Since `drawImage()` again passes the applet as the ImageObserver, the cycle of generating more data and notifying the applet when the next block is ready is repeated over and over, until the entire image has been delivered. The asynchronous, piecemeal delivery of image data creates the effect of images slowly being painted on the screen. While this painting behavior is acceptable for some applications, there are times when it is preferable to have the whole image downloaded before rendering it on the screen. The ImageObserver interface can be utilized directly—or indirectly, through a class such as `java.awt.MediaTracker`—to avoid displaying images before they have been completely downloaded.

There are several reasons why `imageUpdate()` may be called by the ImageProducer. Sometimes `imageUpdate()` is called because more image data has been delivered. The method is also called when the delivery of the image data is complete. Each time `imageUpdate()` is called, the reason is encoded in the second argument passed to the method, the *infobits* flag. Table 3.1 summarizes the values that can be ORed into infobits. The remaining arguments passed to imageUpdate are used differently depending on the value of *infobits*.

The `imageUpdate()` method can be overridden in an Applet or Component to directly monitor the progress of downloaded images. For

TABLE 3.1

Flags to `image-Update()`

Flag	Meaning
ABORT	Image production has been stopped.
ALLBITS	All image data has been produced and is available.
ERROR	An error has occured in production of the image data.
FRAMEBITS	A single frame of a multiframe image is completed.
HEIGHT	The height of the image is available.
PROPERTIES	The properties of the image are now available.
SOMEBITS	More pixels are available to be drawn.
WIDTH	The width of the image is available.

example, because the image data is delivered incrementally, the height and width of the image are not known by the Image object until the entire image has been downloaded. Because the dimensions of the image are not known, the Image's `getHeight()` and `getWidth()` methods return −1 until the entire image has been delivered. By overriding `imageUp-date()`, the width and height can be checked when the ImageProducer indicates that the image dimensions are available:

```
public boolean imageUpdate(Image img, int infoflags,
                           int x, int y, int width, int height) {
    if (infoflags & (HEIGHT|WIDTH)) {
        //can now call getHeight() & getWidth()
        ...
    }
    return super.imageUpdate(Image img, int infoflags,
                             int x, int y, int width, int height);
}
```

While overriding the `imageUpdate()` method does provide a mechanism for interacting with the delivery of images, a more convenient approach is to use the *MediaTracker* class.

The AWT MediaTracker class is used to initiate image preparation on demand, rather than waiting for the first request for image data to start the transfer. One use of the MediaTracker class allows applets to block until an entire image has been prepared. Once control is returned to the caller, the image being tracked can be displayed without the incremental painting previously described. The MediaTracker actually uses the method `java.awt.Toolkit.prepareImage()` to register itself as an ImageObserver with the ImageProducer. When the `imageUpdate()` method is called and the *ALLBITS* flag is set, control is returned to the applet waiting for the image being produced.

One drawback to the MediaTracker is that there is no callback mechanism when image delivery is complete. Applications must either block until an image is downloaded using the MediaTracker's `waitForID()` or `waitForAll()` methods, or they must periodically check the status of images being tracked by calling `checkID()` or `checkAll()`. An alternate means of tracking the downloading of images is implemented by the *ImageFetcher* class, which also illustrates the use of the ImageObserver interface.

The ImageFetcher Class

The most significant difference between the ImageFetcher class and the MediaTracker class is that the ImageFetcher class provides for asynchronous callbacks when an image is completely downloaded. The JDK's delegation event model is used to facilitate this callback scheme. The ImageFetcher class acts as the *source* of ImageDeliveryEvent objects which will be sent to registered *listeners*—objects implementing the ImageDeliveryListener interface. The basic model is illustrated in Fig. 3.1.

After an ImageFetcher object has been created, ImageDeliveryListener objects can register with the ImageFetcher. Once the image has been downloaded and is ready to be displayed, the ImageFetcher creates an ImageDeliveryEvent object which contains a reference to the image. The ImageDeliveryEvent is then dispatched to all registered listeners through the `imageReady()` method specified by the ImageDeliveryListener interface.

Objects are registered with an ImageFetcher through the ImageFetcher's `addImageDeliveryListener()` method. When the listener's `imageReady()` method is called, a reference to the image can be obtained via the `getImage()` method on the ImageDeliveryEvent object dispatched to the listener. For example:

```
class ImageDisplay extends Applet implements ImageDeliveryListener
{
    ...
        ImageFetcher imf = new ImageFetcher("cj.gif");
    ...

    public void imageReady(ImageDeliveryEvent evt) {
        Image img = evt.getImage();
        // display the image!
        ...
    }
}
```

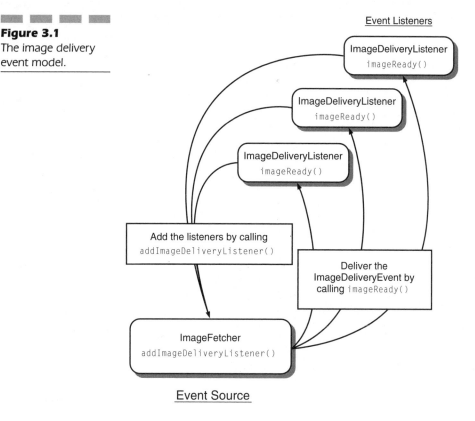

Figure 3.1
The image delivery
event model.

IMPLEMENTATION. The notifications supported by the Image-Fetcher are central to its functionality. The ImageDeliveryEvent class, shown in Fig. 3.2, consists of several instance variables and accessor methods that must be used to retrieve them. The fact that ImageDeliveryEvent extends the java.util.EventObject class, and that it uses a `getVariable()` naming scheme for all its instance variables, allows the ImageDelivery-Event and the ImageFetcher that uses it to be easily integrated into AWT-derived classes and Java Beans. Two types of images are supported through the ImageDeliveryEvent class: standard *java.awt.Image* objects and *ajp.awt.RawImage* objects, which will be discussed later in this chapter.

As previously mentioned, the ImageDeliveryListener interface defines one method, `imageReady()` as is shown in Fig. 3.3.

Both the ImageDeliveryEvent class and the ImageDeliveryListener interface are part of the ajp.awt.event package.

The implementation of the ImageFetcher class is shown in Fig. 3.4. Unlike the MediaTracker class, which can be used to track multiple

```
package ajp.awt.event;

import java.awt.Image;
import java.util.EventObject;
import ajp.awt.RawImage;

/**
 * A class representing image delivery events.
 * @version 2.1
 **/
public class ImageDeliveryEvent extends EventObject {
    static final long serialVersionUID = -6661487026005888714L;

    /**
     * Flag indicating that the event represents the
     * delivery of a raw image.
     **/
    public static final int RAW_IMAGE = 1;

    /**
     * Flag indicating that the event represents the
     * delivery of a standard Java image.
     **/
    public static final int STD_IMAGE = 2;

    // The image.
    protected Image img;
    // The raw image
    protected RawImage raw;
    // The type of image this event represents.
    protected int imageType;

    /**
     * Created an event object from representing the delivery of the
     * specified image.
     **/
    public ImageDeliveryEvent(Image img) {
        super(img);
        this.img = img;
        imageType = STD_IMAGE;
    }

    /**
     * Created an event object from representing the delivery of the
     * specified raw image.
     **/
    public ImageDeliveryEvent(RawImage raw) {
        super(raw);
        this.raw = raw;
        imageType = RAW_IMAGE;
    }
```

Figure 3.2
The ImageDelivery-
Event class.

```
  /**
   * Returns a handle to the delivered image.
   **/
  public Image getImage() {
      return(img);
  }

  /**
   * Returns a handle to the delivered raw image.
   **/
  public RawImage getRawImage() {
      return(raw);
  }

  /**
   * Returns a value indicating the type of image this event represents.
   **/
  public int getType() {
      return imageType;
  }
}
```

Figure 3.2
(Continued).

images, the ImageFetcher tracks only one image per instance. If it is necessary to track multiple images, multiple ImageFetchers need to be created. There are three forms of the constructor, each of which takes a different specification of an image as its sole argument. The forms of the constructor that take a String or a URL object instantiate an Image and pass it to the constructor that takes an Image as its argument. The image preparation is started immediately in the constructor by calling the default toolkit's `prepareImage()` method. If `prepareImage()` returns `true`, the image has already been loaded and is ready for display.

Figure 3.3
The ImageDelivery-
Listener interface.

```
package ajp.awt.event;

import java.util.EventListener;

/**
 * An interface supported by Objects wishing to receive notification
 * of image delivery.
 * @version 2.1
 **/
public interface ImageDeliveryListener extends EventListener {
    /**
     * Called when the image is ready (i.e. downloaded.)
     **/
    void imageReady(ImageDeliveryEvent evt);
}
```

```
package ajp.awt;

import java.awt.image.*;
import java.awt.*;
import java.util.*;
import java.net.URL;
import java.io.Serializable;
import ajp.awt.event.*;

/**
 * A class for retrieving images.  Provides asynchrounous notification
 * of image delivery through the Observer/Observable model.  Each
 * ImageFetcher is associated with one image -- Multiple images must
 * use multiple ImageFetchers.
 *
 * @version 2.2
 **/
public class ImageFetcher implements ImageObserver, Serializable {
      static final long serialVersionUID = 4190222774754113709L;

      // Chain of event listeners.
      private ImageDeliveryListener imageDeliveryListener;

      // The image being fetched.
      protected Image theImage;

      boolean debug = false;

      /**
       * Create an Image Fetcher.
       **/
      public ImageFetcher(Image someImage) {
            this.theImage = someImage;
            if (Toolkit.getDefaultToolkit().prepareImage(
                theImage, -1, -1, this)) {
                imageDone(theImage);
            }
      }

      /**
       * Create an Image Fetcher.
       **/
      public ImageFetcher(String pathname) {
            this(Toolkit.getDefaultToolkit().getImage(pathname));
      }

      /**
       * Create an Image Fetcher.
       **/
      public ImageFetcher(URL location) {
            this(Toolkit.getDefaultToolkit().getImage(location));
      }
```

Figure 3.4
The ImageFetcher
class.

```java
    /**
     * Notify the listeners that the image is ready.
     **/
    void imageDone(Image img) {
        processImageDeliveryEvent(new ImageDeliveryEvent(img));
    }


    /**
     * Notification hook for the ImageProducer.  This method is
     * called whenever the status of the image being produced
     * changes.
     **/
    public boolean imageUpdate(Image img, int flags,
                               int x, int y, int w, int h) {
        boolean status = true;

        if ((flags & (FRAMEBITS|ALLBITS)) != 0) {
            dbg("Image is here.");
            imageDone(img);
            status = false;
        }
        else if ((flags & (ABORT | ERROR)) != 0) {
            imageDone((Image)null);
            status = false;
        }
        return status;
    }

    /**
     * Add a listener to this fetcher.
     * @param l the listener who will be notified when the image is delivered.
     **/
    public
    synchronized void addImageDeliveryListener(ImageDeliveryListener l) {
        imageDeliveryListener =
                    AJPEventMulticaster.add(imageDeliveryListener, l);
    }

    /**
     * Removes the specified imageDelivery listener so that it no longer
     * receives imageDelivery events from this fetcher.
     **/
    public
    synchronized void removeImageDeliveryListener(ImageDeliveryListener l) {
        imageDeliveryListener =
                    AJPEventMulticaster.remove(imageDeliveryListener, l);
    }

    /**
     * Processes imageDelivery events by
     * dispatching them to any registered ImageDeliveryListener objects.
     **/
```

Figure 3.4

(*Continued*).

```
    protected void processImageDeliveryEvent(ImageDeliveryEvent ev) {
        if (imageDeliveryListener != null) {
            imageDeliveryListener.imageReady(ev);
        }
    }
}
```

Figure 3.4
(*Continued*).

In this case the `imageDone()` method is called, which creates an Image-DeliveryEvent object and passes it to the `processImageDelivery-Event()` method.

The final argument to the `prepareImage()` method is a reference to an ImageObserver, in this case the ImageFetcher object itself. When `prepareImage()` completes the preparation of the image, it will call the ImageObserver's `imageUpdate()` method, passing it a flag that has either the `ALLBITS` or `FRAMEBITS` portion of the flag set. When this happens, `imageDone()` begins the notification of any registered ImageDeliveryListener objects.

The mechanism by which listeners register and deregister with the ImageFetcher is through the `add/removeImageDeliveryListener()` methods. The mechanics of this registration will be discussed in Chap. 4.

ImageProducer

ImageProducers do the actual work of providing image data to ImageConsumers. Image data is delivered in arrays of bytes via the ImageConsumer's `getPixels()` method. ImageProducers are not instantiated directly but, rather, are accessed through the reference returned by an Image's `getSource()` method. The methods supported by the Image-Producer interface are described in Table 3.2.

Of the methods in the API, probably the most useful is the `start-Production()` method. Since `startProduction()` initiates delivery of the image data, it can be used by an ImageConsumer to start the downloading of an image synchronously:

```
class MyConsumer extends ImageConsumer {
    Image img;
    ...
    img.getSource().startProduction(this);
}
```

TABLE 3.2

Methods Supported by the ImageProducer Interface

Method signature	Description
`void addConsumer(ImageConsumer c)`	Registers the ImageConsumer with the producer
`boolean isConsumer(ImageConsumer c)`	Returns *true* if the consumer passed already registered with this producer
`void removeConsumer(ImageConsumer c)`	Unregisters the consumer with this producer
`void requestTopDownLeftRightResend (ImageConsumer c)`	Requests that the producer resend the data by columns, rather than by rows
`vod startProduction(ImageConsumer c)`	Registers the consumer and starts production of the image data

While the `startProduction()` method gives the consumer direct control over when the data transfer from ImageProducer to ImageConsumer begins, the data is still transferred asynchronously, with the usual notifications sent to any registered observers.

ImageConsumer

The *ImageConsumer* interface supports receipt of images from an Image-Producer. The methods in the ImageConsumer API are described in Table 3.3. Of the methods in the API, the most important for image delivery are the two `setPixels()` methods. As image data is generated by the ImageProducer it is delivered to the consumer via `setPixels()`. For example, in both the Netscape Navigator and the HotJava browser, a 50-row by 60-column image will be delivered to a consumer in 50 calls to `setPixels()`, each call delivering 60 pixels of data.

When `setPixels()` is called, the ImageConsumer must save the pixel data, which usually involves copying the incoming data into an array of bytes or integers. The consumer can be designed to manipulate the image data on the fly, possibly performing filtering or color conversion as the data is saved.[*]

---

[*] There are actually two ways to filter the image data. One way is to modify the pixels in the ImageConsumer; the other is to utilize the *FilteredImageSource* class. The Filtered-ImageSource class is discussed later in this chapter in the "Image Filtering" section. An example that uses image filtering is presented in Chap. 4 in the discussion of the *Image-Button* class.

TABLE 3.3

Methods Supported by the ImageConsumer Interface

Method signature	Description
`void imageComplete(int status)`	Called when either the image delivery is complete or when there is a change in status.
`void setColorModel(ColorModel cm)`	Sets the color model used when constructing the image pixels.
`void setDimensions(int width, int height)`	Sets the width and height attributes of the image. These dimensions are used to create an appropriately sized array to store the image pixels.
`void setHints(int flag)`	Lets the consumer know the order in which the pixels will be delivered.
`void setPixels(int x, int y, int w, int h, ColorModel cm, byte pixels[], int off, int scansize)`	Sets the pixels passed in the byte array. The pixels represent the image data in the rectangle defined by the x, y, w, and h parameters.
`void setPixels(int x, int y, int w, int h, ColorModel cm, int pixels[], int off, int scansize)`	Same as the above method, except that the data is passed in an integer array.
`void setProperties(Hashtable props)`	Sets a list of properties associated with this image.

The `setDimensions()`, `setHints()`, `setProperties()`, and `set-ColorModel()` methods are all called by the ImageProducer prior to the delivery of any image data. After all rows of the image data are delivered, the ImageProducer will call the `imageComplete()` method, at which point the consumer should remove itself from the list of consumers registered with the ImageProducer.

Extending the Image Delivery Model

To best understand the workings of the image delivery model, it is helpful to see how the model can be extended. The extension presented here is called *ImageGrabber*. The purpose of the ImageGrabber class is to provide a mechanism for directly accessing the raw pixel data associated with an image. In addition, the class provides a notification mechanism that will inform an object using an ImageGrabber both when the image is downloaded and when the raw pixel data is available for use.

The raw image data provided by the ImageGrabber class is represented by a class called *RawImage* (shown in Fig. 3.5), which provides information about the height, width, and color model associated with the image. The class provides accessor methods for the various image attributes, as well as an accessor, `getBytes()`, that returns an array containing the pixel data.

The ImageGrabber class is a subclass of the ImageFetcher class discussed earlier in this chapter and, as such, implements the ImageObserver interface. Thus, ImageGrabber objects can be used just as ImageFetchers are used, since they both provide for notification of image delivery to ImageDeliveryListeners. In addition, the ImageGrabber class implements the ImageConsumer interface and interposes on the delivery of image data by the producer.

Instances of the ImageGrabber class can be created with any of its three constructors which parallel the constructors in the ImageFetcher class:

1. `public ImageGrabber(Image someImage)`

2. `public ImageGrabber(String pathname)`

3. `public ImageGrabber(URL location)`

Like the ImageFetcher, the constructors allow the specification of an image as either an Image object, a pathname, or a URL. Registered ImageDeliveryListener objects will be notified when the image is delivered, as is the case with the ImageFetcher. However, the ImageGrabber also provides notification when the raw pixel data is available by sending an ImageDeliveryEvent object containing a reference to a RawImage object. An ImageDeliveryListener can handle both callbacks by implementing an `ImageReady()` method that checks the event type, filtering for Image and RawImage:

```
public void imageReady(ImageDeliveryEvent e) {
    switch(e.getType()) {
    case ImageDeliveryEvent.STD_IMAGE:
        Image img = e.getImage();
        // draw the image.
        break;
    case ImageDeliveryEvent.RAW_IMAGE:
        RawImage raw - e.getRawImage();
        // use the raw pixel data
        break;
    }
}
```

```
package ajp.awt;

import java.awt.*;
import java.awt.image.*;
import java.util.Observable;

/**
 * An abstract representation of the raw pixel data associated with an image.
 *
 * @version 2.2
 **/
public class RawImage implements java.io.Serializable {
      static final long serialVersionUID = -433463662606462460L;

      // The dimension of the image.
      private Dimension dim;
      // The pixels.
      private byte theArray[];
      // The color model for this Image
      private ColorModel model;
      // An image constructed from the pixels
      private Image image;

      /**
       * Create a RawImage.
       **/
      public RawImage(int width, int height) {
          this(new byte[width*height], width, height,
               Toolkit.getDefaultToolkit().getColorModel());
      }

      /**
       * Create a RawImage.
       **/
      public RawImage(byte arr[], int width, ColorModel cm ) {
          this(arr, width, arr.length/width, cm);
      }

      /**
       * Create a RawImage.
       **/
      public RawImage(byte arr[], int width, int height, ColorModel m) {
          theArray = arr;
          dim = new Dimension(width, height);
          model = m;
          image = Toolkit.getDefaultToolkit().createImage(
                  new MemoryImageSource(width, height, model,
                                        theArray, 0, width));
      }

      /**
       * Returns the Image associated with the RawImage.
       **/
```

Figure 3.5
The RawImage class.

```
        public Image getImage() {
            return image;
        }

        /**
         * Returns the bytes associated with the RawImage.
         **/
        public byte[] getBytes() {
            return theArray;
        }

        /**
         * Returns the size of the image.
         **/
        public Dimension getSize() {
            return new Dimension(dim.width, dim.height);
        }

        /**
         * Returns the width of the image.
         **/
        public int getWidth() {
            return dim.width;
        }

        /**
         * Returns the height of the image.
         **/
        public int getHeight() {
            return dim.height;
        }

        /**
         * Returns the ColorModel associated with the RawImage.
         **/
        public ColorModel getColorModel() {
            return model;
        }
}
```

Figure 3.5
(Continued).

The remaining methods defined in the ImageGrabber class are those required by the ImageConsumer interface: setDimensions(), setHints(), setProperties(), and setColorModel(). The implementation is shown in Fig. 3.6.

The two forms of the ImageGrabber's constructor that specify the image as either a pathname or URL create an Image object and pass it to the third form of the constructor, as was the case in the ImageFetcher class. Immediately after calling the parent class's constructor, the Image-

```
package ajp.awt;

import java.awt.image.*;
import java.awt.*;
import java.net.URL;
import java.io.ByteArrayOutputStream;
import java.util.Hashtable;
import ajp.awt.event.ImageDeliveryEvent;

/**
 * A class for retreiving images and the associated raw pixel data.
 *
 * @version 2.2
 **/
public class ImageGrabber extends ImageFetcher implements ImageConsumer {
    static final long serialVersionUID = -1327644559987206620L;

    // The pixel data
    byte[] pixels;

    // The dimensions of the image
    int width;
    int height;

    // The color model associated with the image
    ColorModel model;

    // The producer of the image
    ImageProducer producer;

    // A stream to store the bytes in as they are delivered.
    ByteArrayOutputStream stream;

    /**
     * Create an ImageGrabber.
     **/
    public ImageGrabber(Image someImage) {
        super(someImage);
        producer = someImage.getSource();
        producer.startProduction(this);
    }

    /**
     * Create an ImageGrabber.
     **/
    public ImageGrabber(String pathname) {
        this(Toolkit.getDefaultToolkit().getImage(pathname));
    }

    /**
     * Create an ImageGrabber.
     **/
```

Figure 3.6
The ImageGrabber
class.

```
    public ImageGrabber(URL location) {
        this(Toolkit.getDefaultToolkit().getImage(location));
    }


    /**
     * Set the size of the image being consumed.
     **/
    public void setDimensions(int width, int height) {
        this.width = width;
        this.height = height;
        stream = new ByteArrayOutputStream(width * height);
    }

    /**
     * Set the properties.  Not used by ImageGrabber.
     **/
    public void setProperties(Hashtable props) {
    }

    /**
     * Set the color model of the image being consumed.
     **/
    public void setColorModel(ColorModel model) {
        this.model = model;
    }

    /**
     * Set the hints for this image.  Not used by ImageGrabber.
     **/
    public void setHints(int hints) {
    }

    /**
     * Sets the pixels in the image.  Only bytes are supported.
     * This will be called by the ImageProducer for all of the
     * pixels in the image.
     **/
    public void setPixels(int x, int y, int w, int h,
                          ColorModel model, byte pixels[],
                          int off, int scansize) {
        stream.write(pixels, off, pixels.length - off);
    }

    /**
     * Sets the pixels in the image.  Only bytes are supported.
     * This method is not implemented.
     **/
    public void setPixels(int x, int y, int w, int h,
                          ColorModel model, int pixels[],
                          int off, int scansize) {
    }
```

Figure 3.6
(Continued).

```
    /**
     * Notification hook for the ImageProducer.
     * Called when no more image data needs to be sent.
     **/
    public void imageComplete(int status) {

        if (status == STATICIMAGEDONE) {
            rawImageDone(new RawImage(stream.toByteArray(), width,
                                      height, model));
            producer.removeConsumer(this);
        }
    }

    /**
     * Notify the observer that the raw image is ready.
     **/
    void rawImageDone(RawImage raw) {
        processImageDeliveryEvent(new ImageDeliveryEvent(raw));
    }
}
```

Figure 3.6
(*Continued*).

Grabber gets a reference to the ImageProducer and calls its `startPro-duction()` method. Before actual production of the image starts, the producer will call the ImageGrabber's `setDimensions()` method. In `setDimensions()` the ImageGrabber creates a *ByteArrayOutputStream* into which it can write the bytes and, once the image delivery completes, extract a byte array. The stream essentially buffers the pixels in the order they are delivered and then allows them to be extracted as an array. Using ByteArrayOutputStream is significantly faster than maintaining a byte array and copying the byte array passed to `setPixels()` one element at a time. In fact, for a 2,000- by 1,500-pixel image, using a ByteArrayOutputStream is more than twice as fast.[*]

When the producer completes the transfer of the image data, the ImageGrabber's *imageComplete()* method is called. If the status flag passed to `imageComplete()` is *STATICIMAGEDONE*, indicating that the entire image transfer is complete, the ImageGrabber converts the byte array into a RawImage object and passes the RawImage object to any Listeners through an ImageDeliveryEvent object. Finally, after the Listeners have

---

[*] On a 40-MHz SPARCStation 10 using version 1.0.2 of the JDK, copying the byte array takes around 15 seconds. Using the ByteArrayOutputStream takes approximately 6 seconds.

been notified, the ImageGrabber removes itself from the list of registered Consumers maintained by the ImageProducer.

The use of the ImageGrabber class is almost identical to that of the ImageFetcher. Figure 3.7 shows a simple applet that delays painting an image until it has received notification that the image has been delivered. Notice that in the `ImageReady()` method shown in Fig. 3.7, nothing is done with the RawImage that is received. In the following section this example is extended to use the raw image data to rotate the image prior to display.

Image Rotation

An important feature of the ImageGrabber class is that it provides a handle to the raw pixel data. Thus far nothing has been shown to indicate how this data can be used, however. To remedy this situation, and to show the usefulness of the ImageGrabber class, this section presents a simple rotation scheme that manipulates pixel data. Central to this image rotation is a helper class called *RawImageRotator.*

The RawImageRotator class implements a simple translation of pixels from one position to another based on a rotation around the center of the image. The class consists of two static methods that allow RawImage objects to be rotated and an Image or a new RawImage object to be returned. The two methods in the class's API are described in Table 3.4.

The RawImageRotator class is designed to be used in conjunction with the ImageGrabber. Figure 3.8 extends the example presented in Fig. 3.7 to utilize the RawImageRotator class to rotate an image in an applet. The applet adds a `processMouseEvent()` method that causes the image to be rotated by 10 degrees each time the mouse is clicked. When the `process-MouseEvent()` method is called, the applet passes the raw image data to the `createRotatedImage()` method, saving the reference to the returned image in the Image variable that is displayed when the applet is repainted.

The implementation of the RawImageRotator class is shown in Fig. 3.9. The actual rotation of the image pixels is done in the second `rotate()` method. The rotation implemented is very simple and is intended as an example of how to manipulate image data as arrays of bytes. The rotation does not attempt to interpolate points in the rotated image that are not mapped from the original image due to rounding errors. The result is that a rotated image may have "holes" or points in the image that correspond to the background color, rather than to the correct color from the original image. The rotation creates an array that is large enough to hold the entire

```
import java.applet.*;
import java.awt.*;
import ajp.awt.*;
import ajp.awt.event.*;

/**
 * A simple test Applet for the ImageGrabber class.  Uses the grabber
 * to load the image and associated pixels, but does not do anything
 * with the pixels.
 **/
public class GrabberTest extends Applet implements ImageDeliveryListener {
     Image im;
     ImageGrabber grabber;
     RawImage raw = null;
     int rot = 0;
     boolean loaded = false;

     public void init() {
         im = getImage(getCodeBase(), "images/Duke.gif");
         grabber = new ImageGrabber(im);
         grabber.addImageDeliveryListener(this);
     }

     /**
      * imageReady() is called both when the Image is ready and when the
      * pixel data is ready.
      **/
     public void imageReady(ImageDeliveryEvent e) {
         switch(e.getType()) {
         case ImageDeliveryEvent.STD_IMAGE:
             System.out.println( "Image is prepared.");
             loaded = true;
             repaint();
             break;
         case ImageDeliveryEvent.RAW_IMAGE:
             System.out.println( "RawImage is prepared.");
             raw = e.getRawImage();
             break;
         }
     }

     /**
      * Draw the Image to the screen.
      **/
     public void paint(Graphics g) {
         if (loaded)
             g.drawImage(im, 0, 0, this);
     }
}
```

Figure 3.7
An applet that
demonstrates the use
of the ImageGrabber
class.

TABLE 3.4	**Method signature**	**Description**
Public Static Methods of the RawImageRotator Class	`Image createRotatedImage(RawImage img, double angle)`	Returns an Image object representing the pixels of `img` rotated clockwise by angle degrees about the center of the image
	`RawImage rotate(RawImage img, double angle)`	Returns RawImage object representing the pixels of `img` rotated clockwise by angle degrees about the center of the image

rotated image, rather than cropping the rotated image to fit inside the dimensions of the original image.

The `rotate()` method first calculates the width and height of the rotated image. Figure 3.10 shows the geometry of the rotation. Once the size of the image that is needed to hold the rotated image is determined, a new RawImage is allocated to store the rotated pixels. Then the array of bytes in the RawImage is set to a specified *fill* value. After the array is initialized, the geometric transform is applied to each pixel in the original image and the original pixels are stored at the calculated offset into the new byte array. The rotation transform applied to the pixels is a two-dimensional shift-and-rotate. Although the pixels are stored in one-dimensional arrays, each pixel in the array has an x and y coordinate on the two-dimensional image. The image rotation involves shifting the x and y coordinates of each pixel to the origin, rotating the point about the origin, then shifting the point back by the same value used to move it to the origin. After the new x and y coordinates are calculated, the coordinates are translated into an offset into the byte array of the rotated image. Since a rounding error in translating x and y coordinates into an offset into the byte array could cause an exception to be thrown, a *try* block is wrapped around the assignment of the original pixels into the new array.

Double Buffering

Double buffering is a technique to optimize the rendering of images to a computer's display. Using graphics primitives to draw directly to an on-screen object is slow in comparison to manipulating image data in memory. The overhead of calling through several layers of libraries and accessing the hardware for each line, point, or character drawn can slow the visual performance of an application noticeably. By creating an off-

```
import java.applet.*;
import java.awt.*;
import java.awt.event.*;
import ajp.awt.*;

/**
 * An applet that loads an image and allows it to be rotated by 10
 * degrees each time the mouse is clicked in the applet.  Uses the
 * RawImageRotator class.
 **/
public class Rotator extends GrabberTest {

    public Rotator() {
        enableEvents(AWTEvent.MOUSE_EVENT_MASK);
    }

    protected void processMouseEvent(MouseEvent e) {
        switch(e.getID()) {
        case MouseEvent.MOUSE_RELEASED:
            if (loaded) {
                RawImage newRaw;
                rot += 10;
                im = RawImageRotator.createRotatedImage(raw,
                                                 (double)(rot%360));
                repaint();
            }
            break;
        }
    }
}
```

Figure 3.8
An application that
demonstrates the use
of the RawImage-
Rotator class.

screen buffer to draw into, then copying the entire off-screen image to the display with one call to a graphics library at an appropriate time, significant performance improvements can be achieved.

Double buffering is not built into AWT Components like *Canvas, Applet,* and *Panel.* If you want to use double buffering in an applet or application, you must do it yourself—which is unfortunate, since double buffering is so commonly used. To illustrate how double buffering can be incorporated into Components, the following section presents a double-buffered canvas. Examples of double-buffered Applet and Panel subclasses are presented on the CD-ROM that accompanies this book. These additional classes follow the same model as the double-buffered Canvas sub-

```
package ajp.awt;

import java.awt.*;
import java.awt.image.*;

/**
 * A class of static methods for rotating RawImages and returning either
 * RawImages or java.awt.Images that contain the resultant rotated image.
 *
 * @version 2.1
 **/
public class RawImageRotator {

    // Cannot be instantiated.
    private RawImageRotator() {
    }

    /**
     * Traverse the array and set the bytes to a specified value.
     **/
    protected static void setBytes(byte arr[], byte b) {
        if (b == -1)
            b = 0;
        for (int i = 0; i < arr.length; i++)
            arr[i] = b;
    }

    /**
     * Create and return an Image that contains the data in the
     * RawImage rotated by the specified number of degrees.
     **/
    public static Image createRotatedImage(RawImage img, double angle) {
        byte theArray[] = img.getBytes();
        RawImage raw = rotate(img, angle);
        return raw.getImage();
    }


    /*
       The idea here is to allocate a new array large enough to handle the
       rotated image, which will most likely be larger than the old image,
       execept for the degenerate cases of rotations by 90, 180, 270 and 360
       degrees.

       The method is to deal with the one-dimensional byte array as if it
       were a 2-D rectangle.  Each point in the 1-D array is translated to an
       X and Y coordinate with [0, 0] located at the top left of the image.
       The points are then translated relative to moving the image's center
       point to the origin.  The point is then rotated, then translated back
       relative to the *new* image's center point.  Finally the X and Y
       coordinates of the point are translated into an offset into the new
       byte array and the original byte value is copied into the new location.
```

Figure 3.9
The RawImage-
Rotator class.

```
    */


/**
 * Rotate the data stored in <tt>bytes</tt> about the center point.
 * The resulting ImageBytes object will likely be of different size.
 **/
public static RawImage rotate(RawImage img, double angle) {
        int height = img.getHeight();
        int width = img.getWidth();
        Dimension dim = img.getSize();
        byte theArray[] = img.getBytes();
        ColorModel cm = img.getColorModel();
        RawImage newRaw;
        byte newArray[];
        Point newCenter = new Point(0, 0);

        Point oldCenter = new Point(0, 0);

        oldCenter.x = dim.width / 2;
        oldCenter.y = dim.height / 2;

        double sinAngle = Math.sin(angle * Geometry.DEGREE2RAD);
        double cosAngle = Math.cos(angle * Geometry.DEGREE2RAD);

        width  = (int)(Math.abs(dim.width * cosAngle) +
                        Math.abs(dim.height * sinAngle) + 0.5);
        height = (int)(Math.abs(dim.width * sinAngle) +
                        Math.abs(dim.height * cosAngle) + 0.5);

        newCenter.x = width / 2;
        newCenter.y = height / 2;

        newRaw = new RawImage(new byte[width * height], width,
                                height, img.getColorModel());
        newArray = newRaw.getBytes();

        // init the array to something...
        setBytes(newArray, theArray[0]);

        for(int i = 0; i < theArray.length; i++) {
            double xx, yy;
            int x = i % dim.width;

            int y = i / dim.width;

            // Shift origin over to center point of original image.
            x -= oldCenter.x;
            y -= oldCenter.y;

            // Do the rotation.
            xx = x * cosAngle - y * sinAngle;
            yy = x * sinAngle + y * cosAngle;
```

Figure 3.9
(Continued).

```
            // Move it back to be centered at the new image's center.
            x=(int)(xx + newCenter.x);
            y=(int)(yy + newCenter.y);

                try {
                    newArray[y * width + x] = theArray[i];
                }
                catch (ArrayIndexOutOfBoundsException e) {
                    // Our calculations might be off a bit...
                }
        }

        return newRaw;
    }
}
```

Figure 3.9
(*Continued*).

class. The techniques used to embed the double buffering are the same in all three classes.*

A Double-buffered Canvas

The *BufferedCanvas* class provides double buffering in a subclass of `java.awt.Canvas` with little change in the overall API to the Canvas. When a BufferedCanvas is added to a Container, it creates an off-screen Image object that is used for double buffering. Associated with the off-screen Image is a Graphics object that is used to draw into the Image. The BufferedCanvas provides a method `getHandle()` that returns a reference to the off-screen Graphics object. To utilize a BufferedCanvas code for drawing into an on-screen image,

```
public void paint(Graphics g) {
    g.drawLine(x1, y1, x2, y2);
}
```

would be converted to something like:

```
public void drawIt() {
    Graphics g = bufferedCanvas.getHandle();
```

---

* The double-buffered Panel class is used extensively to illustrate the use of lightweight AWT components in Chap. 4.

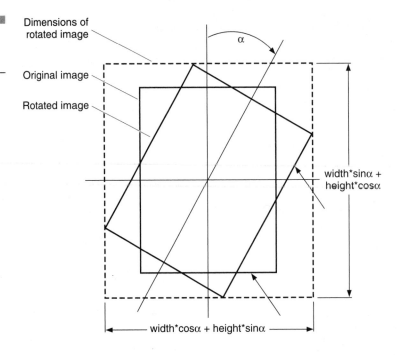

Figure 3.10
The geometry of an
image rotation.

```
    g.drawline(x1, y1, x2, y2);
    ...
    g.dispose();
}
```

In the preceding code sample, the actual drawing was moved out of the `paint()` method because the BufferedCanvas class provides its own `paint()` method that copies the off-screen image to the on-screen Graphics object. It is also worth noting that in the `drawIt()` method, the Graphics object's `dispose()` method is called when the object is no longer needed. This optimization is recommended whenever you extract a Graphics object from a Component.

The source code of the BufferedCanvas class is shown in Fig. 3.11.

Two aspects of the implementation bear particular notice. First, the BufferedCanvas implements the ComponentListener interface and, in the constructor, adds itself as a listener for any component events that occur on itself. This is done so that the BufferedCanvas will receive notification of any resize events. Any time the Canvas is resized, the off-screen image will be resized to match the Canvas dimensions. Second, the `paint()` method of the BufferedCanvas takes care of drawing the off-screen image to the on-screen Canvas. All the programmer needs to do to get the benefits of double buffering is to use the BufferedCanvas class and utilize the Graphics object returned by `getHandle()` for all drawing.

```
package ajp.awt;

import java.awt.*;
import java.awt.event.*;

/**
 * A double-buffered Canvas.   Encapsulates the double-buffering.
 *
 * @version 2.11
 **/
public class BufferedCanvas extends Canvas implements ComponentListener {
    static final long serialVersionUID = -7836541673933191710L;

    // The off screen Image
    private Image offImage;

    // debug flag
    private boolean debug = false;

    /**
     * Create the buffered canvas.
     **/
    public BufferedCanvas() {
        this(false);
    }

    // Create the canvas, setting the debug flag.
    public BufferedCanvas(boolean debug) {
        this.debug = debug;
        addComponentListener(this);
    }


    /**
     * Create a new off screen image at the current size of the canvas.
     **/
    protected void createBuffer() {
        int w = getSize().width;
        int h = getSize().height;

        Image newImage = createImage(w, h);
        if (offImage != null) {
            Graphics g = newImage.getGraphics();
            g.setClip(0, 0, w, h);
            // draw the off-screen image to the sreen.
            g.drawImage(offImage, 0, 0, null);
            g.dispose();
        }
        offImage = newImage;
    }
```

Figure 3.11
The BufferedCanvas
class.

```
/**
 * Invalidate the off-screen image.
 **/
public void invalidate() {
    super.invalidate();
    offImage = null;
}

/**
 * Retrieves a reference to the off-screen image.
 **/
public Image getOffScreenImage() {
    return offImage;
}

/**
 * Retrieves a reference to a Graphics object associated
 * with the off-screen image.
 **/
public Graphics getHandle() {
    return getOffScreenImage().getGraphics();
}

/**
 * Overridden to prevent filckering
 **/
public void update(Graphics g) {
    paint(g);
}

/**
 * Paint the Canvas.
 **/
public void paint(Graphics g) {
    // create and off-screen image if needed.
    if(offImage == null) {
        createBuffer();
    }
    g.drawImage(offImage, 0, 0, null);
}

/**
 * Clear the off-screen image.
 **/
public void clearGraphics(Color color) {
    if (offImage != null) {
        Graphics offG = offImage.getGraphics();
        if (offG != null) {
            Color c = offG.getColor();
            offG.setColor(color);
            offG.fillRect(0, 0, getSize().width, getSize().height);
            offG.setColor(c);
```

Figure 3.11

(*Continued*).

```
                        offG.dispose();
                }
        }
    }

    // Required component listener methods...

    /**
     * The panel has been resized.  Create a new off-screen buffer.
     **/
    public void componentResized(ComponentEvent e) {
        createBuffer();
        repaint();
    }

    public void componentMoved(ComponentEvent e) {
    }

    public void componentShown(ComponentEvent e) {
    }

    public void componentHidden(ComponentEvent e) {
    }

}
```

Figure 3.11
(*Continued*).

A Double-buffered Image Canvas

The BufferedCanvas class provides a convenient way to perform double buffering. A logical extension of the BufferedCanvas is a double-buffered canvas specifically designed for displaying an image. The *ImageCanvas* class is designed to extend the BufferedCanvas by incorporating an ImageGrabber object that can track the downloading of images and provide access to the raw image data. The Image displayed in the Canvas can optionally scale to fit the canvas as it resizes.

Figure 3.12 shows the ImageCanvas implementation. The class itself is reasonably straightforward. The ImageCanvas class both extends the BufferedCanvas and implements the ImageDeliveryListener interface. By inheriting from the BufferedCanvas class the ImageCanvas can double-buffer images. The ImageDeliveryListener interface enables ImageCanvas objects to be notified when images are downloaded.

The constructor for the ImageCanvas class takes three forms:

```
package ajp.awt;

import java.awt.*;
import java.awt.event.*;
import java.net.URL;
import ajp.awt.event.*;

/**
 * A double-buffered canvas for displaying Images.
 *
 * @version 2.5
 **/
public class ImageCanvas extends BufferedCanvas
                         implements ImageDeliveryListener, ComponentListener {

    static final long serialVersionUID = -7063851855128202887L;

    // The image displayed in the canvas.
    Image theImage;

    // Is the image loaded?
    boolean loaded;

    // Have the pixels been grabbed?
    boolean grabbed;

    // The raw pixels.
    RawImage raw;

    // Is the image scalable?
    boolean scalable;

    /**
     * Create an ImageCanvas.
     **/
    public ImageCanvas(Image someImage) {
        this(someImage, false);
    }

    public ImageCanvas(Image someImage, boolean debug) {
        super(debug);
        grabbed=false;
        loaded=false;
        theImage = someImage;
        scalable = false;
        ImageGrabber g = new ImageGrabber(someImage);
        addComponentListener(this);
        g.addImageDeliveryListener(this);
    }
```

Figure 3.12
The ImageCanvas
class.

```
/**
 * Create an ImageCanvas of the image at the specified pathname.
 **/
public ImageCanvas(String pathname) {
    this(pathname, false);
}

public ImageCanvas(String pathname, boolean debug) {
    this(Toolkit.getDefaultToolkit().getImage(pathname), debug);
}

/**
 * Create an ImageCanvas of the given URL.
 **/
public ImageCanvas(URL location) {
    this(location, false);
}

public ImageCanvas(URL location, boolean debug) {
    this(Toolkit.getDefaultToolkit().getImage(location), debug);
}

/**
 * Sets the flag indicating whether or not the image should be scaled
 * on resize.
 **/
public void setScalable(boolean scale) {
    scalable = scale;
}

/**
 * Called by ImageGrabber when the image is ready.
 **/
public void imageReady(ImageDeliveryEvent e) {
    dbg("imageReady() called. Type = " + e.getType());
    switch(e.getType()) {
    case ImageDeliveryEvent.RAW_IMAGE:
        dbg("Grabbed Raw image...");
        raw = e.getRawImage();
        grabbed=true;
        break;
    case ImageDeliveryEvent.STD_IMAGE:
        dbg("Grabbed Std image...");
        Graphics g = getHandle();
        if (g != null) {
            if (isScalable()) {
                g.drawImage(theImage, 0, 0,
                            getSize().width, getSize().height, this);
            }
            else {
                g.drawImage(theImage, 0, 0, this);
            }
            loaded=true;
```

Figure 3.12

(Continued).

```
                    repaint();
                    g.dispose();
                    break;
            }
        }
    }

    /**
     * Returns true if the image is scaled on resize.
     **/
    public boolean isScalable() {
        return scalable;
    }

    /**
     * Is the image loaded?
     **/
    public boolean isLoaded() {
        return loaded;
    }

    /**
     * Called by the Container whenever it is resized. This method
     * redraws the image to the appropriate size.
     **/
    public void componentResized(ComponentEvent e) {
        createBuffer();
        if (isScalable()) {
            Graphics g = getHandle();
            if (g != null) {
                g.setClip(0, 0, getSize().width, getSize().height);
                g.drawImage(theImage, 0, 0, getSize().width,
                            getSize().height, this);
                g.dispose();
            }
        }
        repaint();
    }
}
```

Figure 3.12
(*Continued*).

1. `public ImageCanvas(Image someImage)`

2. `public ImageCanvas(String path)`

3. `public ImageCanvas(URL location)`

The image passed to the constructor by reference, pathname, or URL will be displayed in the canvas. In the constructor, the image is passed to an ImageGrabber object that initiates the downloading of the image. When the image delivery is complete, the `ImageReady()` method is called by the ImageGrabber and the `loaded` flag is set, indicating that the image is available for display.*

Image Filtering

When images are passed from producer to consumer, the Java image delivery model provides for filtering the image data on the fly. Image filtering is provided through the classes `FilteredImageSource` and `Image-Filter` in the `java.awt.image` package. Conceptually, the Filtered-ImageSource sits between the ImageProducer and the ImageConsumer. The FilteredImageSource obtains image data from the ImageProducer, passes it through an ImageFilter object, and then delivers the filtered images to the ImageConsumer. Figure 3.13 shows the filtering model with an image filter that performs a simple image inversion.

Filtered image sources can be used anywhere that an image producer can be used. Given an existing image object `img`, a filtered image can be obtained through method calls similar to the following:

```
ImageFilter invertFilter = new ImageInvertFilter();
Image newImg =createImage(new FilteredImageSource(img.getSource(),
                          invertFilter));
```

A full example of filtered image source utilization will be deferred to Chap. 4, where an image filter is used in conjunction with an image button widget.

SUMMARY

The Java image delivery model was designed to provide downloading of images over potentially low bandwidth connections. To prevent applica-

---

* On the CD-ROM that accompanies this book there is an extension of the Image-Canvas class called ImageRotator that allows for rotating the image in the canvas. The ImageRotator class is a fairly simple extension of the ImageCanvas class that adds a `rotate()` method. The actual rotation is performed by the RawImageRotator class discussed earlier in this chapter. To save space, no formal discussion of the ImageRotator is included in this book. However, the class itself was deemed useful enough to warrant its inclusion on the CD-ROM.

Figure 3.13
The Java image filter-
ing model.

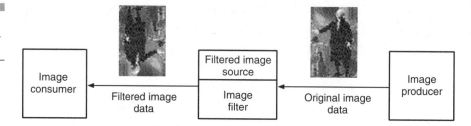

tions from hanging while waiting for images to be downloaded, an asynchronous producer/consumer model was developed. In this model there are three roles: ImageProducer, ImageConsumer, and ImageObserver. ImageProducers generate the raw image data and provide it to Image-Consumers through a series of asynchronous calls to Consumer's `set-Pixels()` method. Each call to `setPixels()` delivers another block of image data. ImageObservers can also receive notification of the delivery of image data by registering with the producer of an image.

In essence, the model is as follows:

- An ImageProducer is created and given a reference to an Image-Consumer object.

- The ImageProducer's `startProduction()` method is called to begin the production of the image data.

- The ImageProducer calls the ImageConsumer's `setPixels()` method to deliver the image data.

- Any ImageObservers are notified that data has been delivered through the `imageUpdate()` method.

The `MediaTracker` class in the `java.awt` package is an ImageObserver that can be used by programmers to either block on or check the status of image loading without having to learn the details of the image delivery model. In this chapter, two alternate image tracking classes, ImageFetcher and ImageGrabber, are presented, both to illustrate how image loading works and to provide functionality not present in the MediaTracker. Specifically, both the ImageFetcher and ImageGrabber classes provide a callback mechanism that extends the AWT and Java-Beans event delegation model. The callback scheme is used to notify an object when an image is downloaded. In addition, the ImageGrabber also provides a reference to a RawImage object that can be used to gain access to the raw pixel data from which the image was constructed. Having access to the raw pixel data is useful whenever specialized image manipulation is required. The RawImageRotator class uses the raw image data to provide a mechanism for rotating images. The ImageGrabber class is also used in conjunction with a double-buffered image canvas class called ImageCanvas. This canvas provides automatic double buffering, image scaling, and canvas resizing, making the task of double buffering images significantly easier.

CHAPTER 4

Extending the Abstract Windowing Toolkit

Introduction

One of the most compelling reasons for using Java is its platform independence. To those who have struggled through developing and maintaining applications targeted at multiple hardware platforms, Java's ubiquity brings relief. A particular challenge of creating software for different operating environments is developing graphical user interfaces (GUIs) that are consistent across platforms. Through the Abstract Windowing Toolkit (AWT) developers can create portable user interfaces that run on multiple windowing systems from a single source code base. The AWT provides a single, consistent programmatic interface that spans windowing systems in a way that is completely transparent to the developer.

The drawback to a toolkit designed for multiple windowing systems is that the toolkit must be restricted to the least common denominator to be as portable as possible. Not every windowing toolkit supports the same graphical elements, or *widgets*. For example, tab widgets, commonly used in the Windows environments, are not available in the Motif toolkit available on most UNIX platforms. If the widget set provided through the AWT does not include a favorite user interface object, you must either do without it or create it yourself. This chapter is for those who don't want to do without. To illustrate how to extend AWT, this chapter focuses on three areas:

1. The connection between AWT and native toolkits
2. The AWT event delivery models
3. Extending AWT by creating custom widgets and Layout Managers

This chapter is not intended to present a comprehensive AWT extension package. Rather, it is hoped that by explaining how AWT works and showing examples and techniques of how it can be extended, you will be better able to extend AWT in ways that are most valuable to you. Furthermore, this chapter does not touch on what is probably the most important part of user interface programming: designing for usability. Regardless of what widgets you use or create, it is combining user interface elements in ways that produce easy-to-use applications that is the true art of user interface programming.

This chapter concentrates on using AWT as a foundation on which to build user interface elements that can contribute to good user interface programming. However, before attempting to extend AWT it is important to have a thorough understanding of the two parts of the toolkit that have the most impact on the extensions: the connection between AWT and the native toolkit, and the AWT event model.

AWT Peers

The design of the AWT provides an elegant solution to a rather difficult problem: How can a windowing toolkit be developed that works on as many windowing systems as possible, yet is itself as portable as possible? The AWT solves this problem by providing an abstract layer between the application code and the native toolkit. To improve portability, much of the abstract layer is written in Java, leaving as small a part of the AWT as possible to be implemented in native methods. Figure 4.1 shows a block diagram that illustrates the layers of AWT. The top layer represents the public APIs to the AWT. This layer includes all the classes in the java.awt package. Objects in the public layer of AWT have associated with them a peer object containing native methods that connect to the native windowing toolkit. The AWT peer layer is comprised of objects in the `java.awt.peer` package. The native methods called by the AWT peers comprise the native peer layer shown in Fig. 4.1. When a method of an

Figure 4.1
The layers of the Abstract Windowing Toolkit.

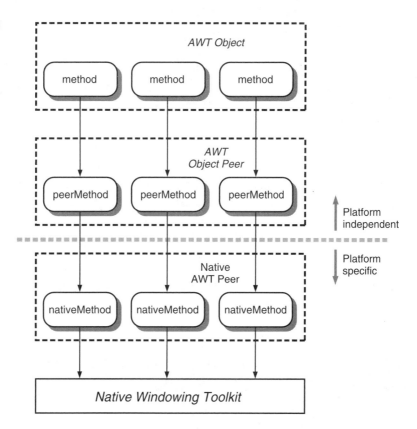

AWT object is called, a related method in the object's peer is called. The peer's method will eventually call a native method which, in turn, makes a call to a function in the native toolkit.

The connection between the AWT object and its counterpart in the native toolkit is not made when the object is instantiated. Until the connection is made, none of the platform-specific resources associated with the AWT object, including default font information and images, can be accessed. The problem this can cause is exemplified by the following code:

```
public class Fail extends Applet {
    int stringWidth;
    String str = "Hello There";
    public Fail() {
        FontMetrics fm = getFontMetrics(getFont());
        stringWidth = fm.getWidth(str);
        ...
    }
    ...
}
```

The intention of the code is to determine the length of the string `str` before the applet is displayed, perhaps to draw it into an off-screen image for double buffering. The call to `getFont()` returns the default font associated with the applet. The `FontMetrics` object `fm` associated with the default font is used to compute the string's length. The applet compiles without error. However, when the applet is run a *NullPointerException* is thrown from the call to `getFontMetrics()`. What went wrong?

When the applet's constructor is called, no connection exists between the Component (the applet) and the native toolkit; the Component peer has not been created. With no connection to the native toolkit, the call to `getFont()` returns *null*, and a NullPointerException is generated when a null font is referenced from within `getFontMetrics()`.

There are two ways to circumvent this problem. The first way is to wait until the connection to the native toolkit has been made before accessing any resources that come from the toolkit. The second way is to get a direct connection to the toolkit.

Peers and the Native Toolkit

Each AWT Component object stores a handle to its peer object in an instance variable called `peer`, which is of type ComponentPeer. *ComponentPeer* is an interface that defines the API supported by the peers of all Component objects. The methods specified in the ComponentPeer interface closely mirror those in the Component class: `hide()`, `show()`, `enable()`, `handleEvent()`, and so on. Just as all AWT widgets (Buttons, Panels, and so on) extend the Component class, all the widget's peers extend the ComponentPeer interface and are thus interfaces, rather than classes. By making all the AWT peers interfaces, the AWT designers have allowed themselves more flexibility in porting the AWT to various platforms. For example, the native implementation of the peers on the Windows platforms could be based on completely different objects than on the Solaris platform. All that matters is that the peers implement the appropriate interface.

Peers are created when a Component gets added to a Container through the Container's `add()` method. The `add()` method calls the Component object's `addNotify()` method which, in turn, creates the Component's peer and saves it in the `peer` instance variable. The actual on-screen object is created by the native peer and native toolkit layers. From a programmer's perspective, this implies that the connection to the native toolkit can be assumed only after `addNotify()` has been called. By overriding `addNotify()`, the resources that require a connection to the native toolkit can be accessed once the peer has been created:

```
public class Succeed extends Applet {
    int stringWidth;
    String str = "Hello There!";
    ...
    public void addNotify() {
        super.addNotify(); //Create the peer!
        FontMetrics fm = getFontMetrics(getFont());
        stringWidth = fm.stringWidth(str);
    }
    ...
}
```

Note that since `addNotify()` is being overridden, `super.addNotify()` must be called first to establish the connection to the peer layer. After the call to `super.addNotify()` the peer and the connection to the native toolkit are in place.

There are times, however, when toolkit resources are needed before a component has been added to a container. In these situations, a handle to the native toolkit can be obtained through the static method `getDefaultToolkit()` of the `Toolkit` class:

```
Toolkit t = Toolkit.getDefaultToolkit();
```

The Toolkit class provides methods for accessing fonts, colors, images, screen dimensions, and screen resolutions. For example, the Succeed applet shown previously could be rewritten to get the default font directly from the default toolkit:

```
String fonts[] = Toolkit.getDefaultToolkit().getFontList();
// font[0] is the default font
Font font = new Font(fonts[0], Font.PLAIN, 12);
FontMetrics fm = new FontMetrics(font)
int length = fm.stringWidth(str);
```

It should be noted that the `getDefaultToolkit()` method is the only way to get a Toolkit object. `Toolkit` is defined as an abstract class and therefore cannot be instantiated. When `getDefaultToolkit()` is called, the object returned is actually an instance of a Toolkit subclass that is platform specific. For example, on the Solaris platform the object returned is an instance of the `sun.awt.motif.MToolkit` class.

The appropriate method for getting to native toolkit resources depends on the situation. Whether `getDefaultToolkit()` is used or resources are obtained from the Component object depends largely on whether it is possible to wait until the peer is created.

The Graphics Class

The *Graphics* class is the workhorse of the AWT. It is through Graphics that all drawing and rendering is done. Like Toolkit objects, there is no way to instantiate graphics objects; their references must be obtained either from existing AWT objects or directly from the Java runtime environment. To get a Graphics reference directly from a Component, the `getGraphics()` method is used. Graphics references are obtained from the runtime when it calls such methods as `paint()`.

Graphics objects are closely tied to the native toolkit. When overriding a method like `paint()` or `update()` that is passed a reference to a Graphics object from the runtime, it is important to keep in mind that the runtime "owns" the Graphics object it passes. The significance of the ownership of the Graphics object can be illustrated by a common mistake new Java programmers often make.

Without utilizing double buffering, programmers can only get a Graphics object and, thus, can only draw in the `paint()` or `update()` methods overriden from Component. Unfortunately, they will often need to draw outside of `paint()`. For example, in an application that draws lines based on mouse movement, the `processMouseMotion-Event()` method is probably appropriate. One approach often taken to facilitate drawing in methods other than `paint()` is to store the Graphics object passed to `paint()` and use it elsewhere:

```
public void paint(Graphics g) {
    if (myG == null) {
        myG = g;
    }
    ...
}

public boolean mouseDrag(Event e, int x, int y) {
    myG.drawLine(0, 0, x, y);   //Behavior undefined!
}
```

Unfortunately, the behavior of the applet resulting from the call to `drawLine()` in the preceding example is undefined. The Graphics object passed to `paint()` is valid only until `paint()` returns. Once `paint()` returns, the runtime is free to modify any or all of the graphics object it passed to `paint()`. For example, if part of the native underpinnings of the Graphics object are deallocated when the `paint()` method returns, references to the methods of such an object will likely generate a NullPointerException.

Double buffering (as described in Chap. 3) is one way around this problem. Doing all drawing with a Graphics object associated with an off-screen buffer owned by the applet or application eliminates the problem of the runtime altering the Graphics object. Another way around the problem is to use the `getGraphics()` method on the Component object that is to be drawn into. Once a Component's peer is created, `getGraphics()` will return the graphics object used to draw in that Component.

AWT Events

Understanding how and when peers are created is the first step in preparing to create AWT extensions. The second step is understanding how events are delivered to and handled by components. There are two event models supported by the JDK 1.1. The first is the original inheritance-based event model introduced by the JDK 1.0. The second is the delegation model that was introduced in the 1.1 release of the JDK.

While the new delegation event model obsoletes the old inheritance model, the old model is still supported, provided that programmers don't mix the two models in the same component. While the focus of this chapter is on the new model, there are enough existing Java programs that use the inheritance model to make it worth discussing the old model.

The Inheritance Event Model

In the inheritance model of processing events, GUI elements inherit methods from the AWT Component class and override them to intercept events corresponding to user interaction with the GUI. For example, an applet designed to track mouse events might override the mouseUp(), mouseDown(), and mouseDrag() methods inherited from Component. In an applet there are typically two ways events are processed. In the first approach, the appropriate methods inherited through the Applet or Panel classes are overridden to intercept an event object. The intercepting method checks the event and processes it based on what GUI element the event was targeted at:

```
public class MyApplet extends Applet {
    ...
    public void action(Event e, Object o) {
        if (e.target instanceof Button) {
            // A Button was pressed...
            ...
        }
        else if (e.target instanceof Choice) {
            // A Choice box checked...
            ...
        }
    }
}
```

The second technique for processing events is to override the callback in a subclass of the user interface object itself:

```
class QuitButton extends Button {
    public void action(Event e, Object o) {
        // A QuitButton was pressed...
        ...
    }
}
```

From a programmer's perspective there are pros and cons to the inheritance model. To its credit, the inheritance model makes it fairly simple to learn event-based programming—for most simple user interfaces, there are few methods to override and, typically, little programming involved. Unfortunately, for more complex user interfaces, the inheritance model has several drawbacks. For designs that utilize many widgets, overriding the action() method in the applet can make for conditional blocks that are both lengthy and potentially hard to understand. In addition, since events are delivered only to classes that derive from the AWT Component and Container classes, there is no way for classes with different lineage to participate directly in the event model. For example, a DataFile object that inherits from the `java.io.File` class cannot be directly notified to write changes to disk when a user presses the *Save* button on a user interface. The *Save* button or its parent container must intercept the event and directly or indirectly manipulate the DataFile object. Finally, the underlying event delivery model is rather complex. It is not difficult for an object interposing on the delivery of events to unintentionally disturb the flow of the events. To understand how event delivery can be disturbed, it is helpful to begin with an example that describes the event delivery path.

When a user presses a mouse button while the pointer is within an area of the sceen occupied by an applet or Java application, several things happen. First, the user's action is translated into a `java.awt.Event` object. The Event object is passed to the Container object whose rectangle encloses the *x* and *y* coordinates at which the event occurred. If the container holds any components that also encompass the coordinates of the event, the event is handed off to the appropriate component by the container. Since Containers are themselves Components, the Event may get passed through several layers of containers until it arrives at the final object in the delivery chain.

Figure 4.2 illustrates a typical example. Button B in the user interface is pressed by a user. Button B is contained by Panel A, which is, in turn, contained by the Frame. Since the Frame is the bottommost container, the Frame initially gets the Event. The Frame determines that the event occurred within the bounds of Panel A, so the Event is passed to Panel A. Panel A determines that the event happened inside the bounds of Button

Figure 4.2

Event delivery to a button on a panel.

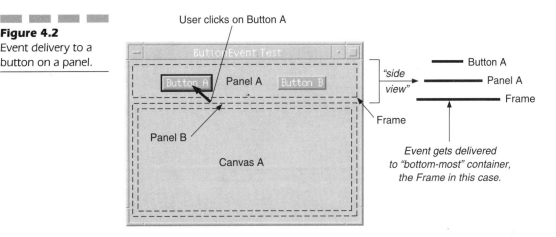

A, so the event is then passed to Button A. If Button A handles the Event (for example, in its `action()` method), the Event delivery would effectively stop at the Button. If, however, the Button ignores the event or returns *false* from its event handler, the Event will be passed back to Panel A. Panel A can then handle the event or pass it back to the Frame. The Frame can then handle or ignore the Event. The Frame is both the first and last object in the delivery chain. Conceptually, events travel up from the bottom of the user interface; then, if not handled at the upper layers, they get passed back down through the layers of objects.

More formally, an Event arrives at a Container through the Container's `deliverEvent()` method. The purpose of the `deliverEvent()` method is to ensure that events are delivered to the appropriate Components. When an Event is passed to a Container's `deliverEvent()` method, the method checks all the Components inside the Container for one at the coordinates of the event. If a Component is found, the event is passed to the Compo-

Figure 4.3
Event delivery to a
container.

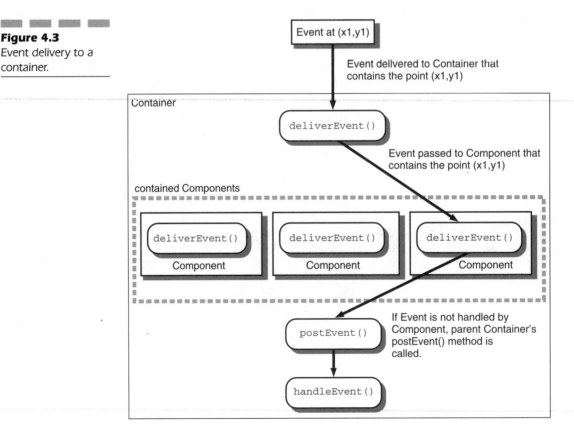

nent's `deliverEvent()` method (see Fig. 4.5). If the Component does not handle the event, it calls the Container's `postEvent()` method as depicted in Fig. 4.3.

If the Container's `deliverEvent()` method does not find any Components at the coordinates of the event, `deliverEvent()` calls `postEvent()` directly, as shown in Fig. 4.4.

The `postEvent()` posts the event within the object. *Posting the event, in essence, means temporarily claiming it for the purpose of allowing event handlers within the object to be called.* The `postEvent()` method calls `handleEvent()`, which is the master event handler for the object. The purpose of `handleEvent()` is to examine the event and call the appropriate handler method based on the type of event seen. The event type is stored in the Event's `id` instance variable. So, if `event.id` is equal to the integer `Event.MOUSE_DOWN`, the `mouseDown()` method is called. The value returned by the handler methods will be propagated by `handleEvent()`. If `handleEvent()` returns *false,* the parent Con-

Figure 4.4
Event delivery when
no objects occupy
the coordinates of
the event.

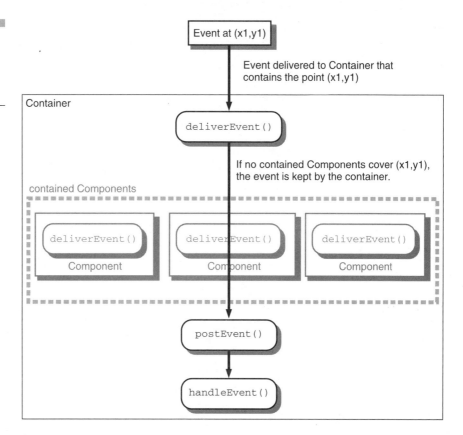

tainer's `postEvent()` method is called (see Fig. 4.5), starting the Event on its journey back down through the layers of Containers to the base Container. If the event has been passed all the way to the top of the user interface stack, and then passed all the way back down without being claimed, the lowest level Container will call its peer's `handleEvent()` method, which will allow the native windowing system to dispose of the event appropriately.

Since interposition is allowed at any point in the event delivery chain, care must be taken to propagate events that are not handled in the overriding methods. Furthermore, the programmer must keep track of where the overridden method is in the event delivery chain and of whether the event should be passed up or down the chain.

Figure 4.5
Event delivery to the
Component.

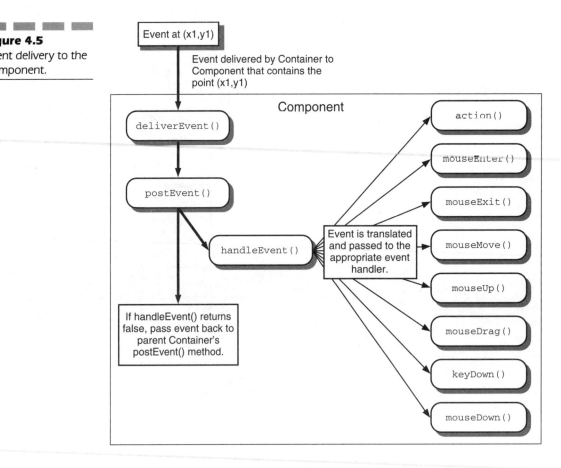

Beyond the complexity of the inheritance-based event model is the problem that the model is heavyweight. Even if events are not of interest, they are propagated through the event delivery chain. For example, an abundance of mouse movement events will be passed through the event delivery chain, regardless of whether or not the events are even of interest. For user interfaces that have several layers of components, there can be a significant amount of event processing happening for no real reason. The many shortcomings of the event model were motivating factors in Java-Soft's redesign of the AWT event model for the JDK 1.1.

The Delegation Event Model

The foundation of the delegation event model is the notion of sources of events and listeners for the generated events. *Event sources* are typically user interface objects that create an event object in response to some user action, then dispatch the event to listeners. In the delegation event model all event classes are defined as subclasses of java.util.Event. *Event listeners* are objects that support a defined *event listener interface* that includes methods to be called when an event is triggered. All event listener interfaces should be subclasses of the java.util.EventListener interface. When an event listener is registered with the event source, it is passed as an instance of the event listener interface. The source will then call the appropriate method of the event listener, passing a reference to the event object.

In the delegation model any object can be notified of events generated by event sources, provided they implement the appropriate interface. For example, assume that a DataFile object should be notified when the *Save* button on a dialog window is pressed. AWT Button objects generate ActionEvent objects when pressed. If the DataFile class implements the java.awt.event.ActionListener interface and defines the `actionPer-formed()` method, it can be registered with the *Save* button. The registration process consists of passing a reference to the DataFile object to the button's `addActionListener()` method (see Fig. 4.6). When the *Save* button is pressed, an ActionEvent object is created and is passed to all registered ActionListeners through their `actionPerformed()` method.

While the basic model is straightforward, event delivery can get more complicated. Specifically, for any object that inherits from java.awt.Component, there is a way to participate in event delivery without implementing the various listener interfaces. Subclasses of Component can enable themselves for specific classes of events and override the event pro-

Figure 4.6
The event delegation
model for a simple
ActionListener.

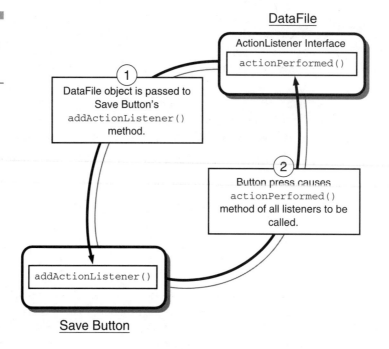

cessing methods inherited from Component, effectively interposing on the event delivery chain. This technique is often useful when creating widgets that will convert low-level events, like mouse movement, to semantic events, such as an event indicating that a dial has been adjusted. Examples of both event-handling techniques are illustrated later in this chapter.

EVENT TYPES. The event delegation model can be easily extended to incorporate other event types. For example, in Chap. 3 the ImageDeliveryEvent class is introduced, which encapsulates information about the delivery of an image object: a handle to the delivered image, and a flag indicating whether the image being delivered is a standard AWT Image object or a RawImage object (see Fig. 3.2 for the ImageDeliveryEvent class definition).

Once the new event class is defined, an appropriate listener interface must be set up. In the case of the ImageDeliveryEvent, the corresponding event listener interface is the ImageDeliveryListener shown in Fig. 3.3. The listener interface must define the methods that can be called based on the characteristics of the event. For example, since the java.awt.Mouse Event can take on several characteristics corresponding to clicks, presses, releases, entering, and exiting of the mouse, there are several callbacks defined in the MouseListener interface: `mousePressed()`, `mouseReleased()`, `mouseEntered()`, and so on. If there are several methods specified by the listener interface, it is helpful to define an adaptor class which defines empty implementations of all the listener methods. Adaptor classes are a convenience when creating listener objects that may only be interested in a specific flavor of an event. Programmers can create a subclass of the adaptor and override the method corresponding to the specific event that is of interest. For instance, the class:

```
public class MyMouseListener extends MouseAdaptor {
    public void mouseEntered(MouseEvent e) {
        // handle just the mouse-enter events.
        ...
    }
}
```

would not have to define the methods `mousePressed()`, `mouseReleased()`, `mouseClicked()`, and `mouseExited()`, since empty versions of these methods are already defined in the MouseAdaptor class.

There are two types of events: unicast and multicast. *Unicast events* are events that can be sent to one and only one recipient. *Multicast events* can have multiple recipients. It is the responsibility of the event source objects to define the types of events that are supported and to dispatch those events appropriately.

EVENT DISPATCHING. As long as existing event source objects, such as standard AWT components, are used, there is no need to worry about the mechanics of event dispatching. However, any class that is to be the source of nonstandard event objects, or which needs to send events other than those generated by a parent class, must handle the registration of event listeners and the dispatch of events to those listeners.

Fundamentally, the event source must simply store the event listeners in some container object such as a hash table, array, or linked list, then iterate through the listeners when events are delivered. In the case of multicast events, adding and removing the listeners are done through methods that have the signatures:

```
public void addListenerName(ListenerName 1)
public void removeListenerName(ListenerName 1)
```

where *ListenerName* is replaced with the name of the EventListener for this event source (for example, `addActionListener()`, `addAdjustmentListener()`, and so on). The body of the `addListenerName()` method should store a reference to the listener object in an appropriate container, and the removeListenerName() method must find the reference to the object in the container and remove it. The classes in the AWT that support multicast event delivery store references to the listeners using a class called the *AWTEventMulticaster.* The AWTEventMulticaster will serve as the basis for event dispatching in the examples that follow in this chapter.

THE AWTEventMulticaster. The AWTEventMulticaster class is a simple container class that contains two EventListener objects: a and b. These two variables are used to create chains of EventListeners that can be traversed to invoke their event callback methods. The AWTEventMulticaster class implements all the EventListener interfaces defined in the java.awt.event package. Thus, instances of the class can be cast to any of the EventListener interfaces as appropriate. There are two static methods defined in the AWTEventMulticaster class, add() and remove(), that are called from the addListenerName() and removeListenerName() methods of the event source. The add() and remove() methods are overloaded to take as arguments each of the EventListener subclasses used by the AWT. For example the MouseListener and ActionListener variants of the add() method have the following signatures:

```
public static MouseListener add(MouseListener a, MouseListener b)
public static ActionListener add(ActionListener a, ActionListener b)
```

When the add() method is called, it is passed a reference to a new event listener and a reference to the listener returned the last time add was called. For example, in any AWT class that is a source of ActionEvents, the following code is typically found:

```
ActionListener al;
public void addActionListener(ActionListner l) {
    al = AWTEventMulticaster.add(al, l);
}
```

If the first argument to the add() method is null, a reference to the second argument is returned. Thus, the first time the addActionListener() method previously shown is called, the instance variable al is set to the ActionListener passed to addActionListener(). The next call to addActionListener() will cause two listeners to be passed to the add() method. In this case, the add() method causes a new AWTEventMulticaster object to be instantiated and returned with the two listeners stored as instance variables. At this point, the instance variable al now points to an AWTEventMulticaster object that contains the two listeners. The third and subsequent times that addActionListener() is called, al is passed as the first argument to AWTEventMulti-caster.add() and the new listener is passed as the second argument, causing a new link in the chain of AWTEventMulticasters to be created and returned. Figure 4.7 depicts how the chain of event listeners maintained internally by an ActionEvent source is built up as three Action-Listeners are registered.

When an event is generated by the event source, the chain of event listeners is traversed by invoking the callback method of the first object in

Figure 4.7
Constructing a chain
of action listeners.

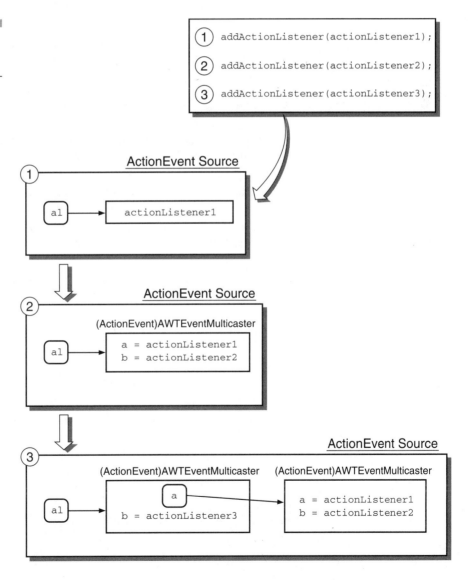

the event listener chain. Again, in a typical AWT component that is a source of ActionEvents, the following code might be found:

```
ActionListener al;
public void processActionEvent(ActionEvent e) {
    if (al != null) {
        al.actionPerformed(e);
    }
}
```

If the ActionListener variable `al` points to one of the registered Action-Listeners, the `actionPerformed()` method is called and the event notification is complete. If `al` points to an AWTEventMulticaster object, the `actionPerformed()` method in that class recursively traverses the chain of listeners, calling `actionPerformed()` on each one in the chain.

Extending the AWT

The remainder of this chapter focuses on creating custom user interface classes by building on existing AWT classes. The classes presented here include custom widget and layout manager. There are two basic categories of widgets that can be created: widgets that derive their look from existing AWT objects and widgets that have a look distinct from anything in AWT. Three examples of each category of widget are presented in the following sections. Each widget illustrates different issues encountered when extending the AWT. The motivation behind the examples is twofold: to show the techniques used in extending AWT and to create extensions that are generally useful.

When you set out to create new user interface objects, an initial design decision must be made: Does the new widget need to have a significantly different look than existing AWT widgets, or can it be created by simply combining existing objects in a new way? The answer to this question will determine what course the implementation takes. If the widget is to look like nothing already in AWT (e.g., a rotary dial) then the new widget must be drawn from scratch, and all events must be managed by methods within the new widget class. If, however, the new widget is a combination of existing AWT objects (e.g., a combination of a scrollbar and a text field to make a numeric slider), then much of the new widget's event management will already be taken care of by the constituent objects. Objects with a unique look and feel are typically derived from the *Canvas* or *Component* classes while objects with an existing look and feel are usually created as a subclass of *Panel* or *Container.*

Lightweight Components

Creating custom widgets that are based on the Panel or Canvas classes has one significant drawback. Associated with the Panel and Canvas classes is a native peer object—an opaque window. The native window makes the creation of widgets with transparent regions impossible. For example, circular widgets that are subclassed from Canvas will always be drawn into a rectangular background that will appear in the on-screen representation. In addition, the supporting native window is fairly heavyweight, so there are performance issues with creating a user interface that uses too many Canvas- or Panel-based widgets.

The JDK 1.1 introduces a new model for creating custom user interface objects. Rather than subclassing from Canvas or Panel, in the Lightweight Component model new widgets are created as direct subclasses of Component or Container. Converting existing Canvas- and Panel-based widgets to the new model primarily involves changing the class from which the UI object inherits. In most cases, changing Canvas to Component or Panel to Container is all that is needed. For example:

```
public class MyWidget extends Canvas {
```

changes to

```
public class MyWidget extends Component {
```

One issue with lightweight components is that they take longer to draw than their counterparts with a native peer. The manifestation of this is that lightweight components will typically *flicker* when they are redrawn on the screen. To eliminate the flickering, it is best to double buffer the drawing of lightweight components that require frequent repainting, through techniques like those described in Chap. 3. Figure 4.8 presents a double-buffered panel class to which lightweight components can be added. The BufferedPanel class is very similar to the BufferedCanvas class presented in Chap. 3. The notable difference between the classes is in the `paint()` method of the BufferedPanel class. The `paint()` method of the Container class ensures that the `paint()` methods of all contained lightweight components get called. Since the BufferedPanel overrides the paint method to do the double buffering, it is critical that the buffered canvas call `super.paint()`—otherwise, no lightweight components will be drawn.

It should be noted that lightweight and nonlightweight components can be freely intermixed in containers. There are no issues with putting standard AWT components or components based on the Canvas or Panel

```
package ajp.awt;

import java.awt.*;
import java.awt.event.*;

/**
 * A double buffered panel that can be used to display lightweight
 * components.
 *
 * @version 2.3
 **/
public class BufferedPanel extends Panel implements ComponentListener {
    static final long serialVersionUID = 4551895494340564224L;
    private Image offImage;
    private boolean debug = false;

    /**
     * Create the buffered panel.
     **/
    public BufferedPanel(){
        this(false);
    }

    // Create the panel with the appropriate debugging flag set.
    public BufferedPanel(boolean debug){
        super();
        this.debug = debug;
        addComponentListener(this);
    }

    /**
     * Retrieves a reference to the off-screen image.
     */
    public Image getOffScreenImage(){
        return offImage;
    }

    /**
     * Create a new off screen image at the current size of the panel.
     */
    protected void createBuffer() {
        offImage = createImage(getSize().width, getSize().height);
    }

    /**
     * overriden to eliminate flicker.
     */
    public void update(Graphics g) {
        paint(g);
    }
```

Figure 4.8
The BufferedPanel
class.

```
    /**
     * Paint the panel. Must call super.paint() from any subclass that
     * wished to override this to ensure any contained lightweight components
     * get repainted.
     */
    public void paint(Graphics g) {
        // create and off-screen image if needed.
        if(offImage == null) {
            createBuffer();
        }
        // Get a Graphics object to draw with.
        Graphics offG = offImage.getGraphics();
        // set clipping to current size.
        offG.setClip(0, 0, getSize().width, getSize().height);
        clearGraphics(offG);
        // Let the parent panel repaint the components inside.
        super.paint(offG);
        // draw the off-screen image to the sreen.
        g.drawImage(offImage, 0, 0, null);

        //crean up the local graphics reference.
        offG.dispose();
    }

    /**
     * Clear the Applet using the specified color.
     **/
    private void clearGraphics(Graphics offG) {
        Color c = offG.getColor();
        offG.setColor(getBackground());
        offG.fillRect(0, 0, getSize().width, getSize().height);
        offG.setColor(c);
    }

    /**
     * Get the parameter string for this Panel.
     **/
    protected String paramString() {
        return super.paramString() + ",width=" + getSize().width
                                   + ",height=" + getSize().height;
    }

    // Required component listener methods...

    /*
     * The panel has been resized.  Create a new off-screen buffer.
     */
    public void componentResized(ComponentEvent e) {
        createBuffer();
        repaint();
    }
```

Figure 4.8

(Continued).

```
    public void componentMoved(ComponentEvent e) {
    }

    public void componentShown(ComponentEvent e) {
    }

    public void componentHidden(ComponentEvent e) {
    }

}
```

Figure 4.8
(*Continued*).

classes inside the same BufferedCanvas. Most the user interface classes developed in this chapter have been created as lightweight components. It is best to use them in conjunction with the BufferedPanel class, or with an alternate double-buffered container of your own.

Inheriting from Container

Creating a new widget that is a combination of existing AWT objects is typically accomplished by creating a subclass of Container. An AWT Container object and its associated LayoutManager will manage the placement and spatial relationship of the combined objects and will allow them to be placed as a group into another container. Because this method employs existing AWT objects, the event management and response to user input is largely provided by the constituent AWT objects. All that might be required to give the object its final look and feel is to provide some interaction between the pieces. For example, in a numeric slider widget you might have the event handlers in a scrollbar change the number in a text field as the user moves the scrollbar's tab.

The drawback to creating a Container-based widget is that the methods it inherits from Container are typically not the ones that give the class an appropriate API. In fact, the API should probably end up looking more like the API for one or more of the objects it contains. For instance, a labeled text field widget, which combines a *Label* and a *Textfield,* should probably have an API just like the standard AWT Textfield class. This will make the new widget easier to use, as it will present a familiar API. There are two possible ways to keep the familiar APIs of the objects in the Container. First, *wrapper* methods can be provided that simply call the like-named methods in the contained objects:

```
class FancyTextField extends Container {
    private TextField t;
    ...
    public String getText() {
        return t.getText();
    }
}
```

Second, the implementation can provide accessor methods that return the standard user interface objects themselves:

```
class AnotherFancyTextField extends Container {
    private TextField t;
    ...
    TextField getTextField() {
        return t;
    }
}
```

The object returned by the accessor can then be used directly via the familiar methods in its API.

There are problems with both of these approaches. When wrappers are created for each of the significant methods of the contained objects, there may be name-space conflicts between the objects. For example, both Label objects and TextField objects support a `getText()` method. A Container-based widget that combines a Label and a TextField can only have its `getText()` method wrap the `getText()` method of one of the two contained objets.

If a Container-based widget provides accessor methods that return handles to the contained widgets there is an assumption that users of the widget won't change the contained object in unexpected ways. For example, suppose you create a widget that contains a button labeled *Reset*, and that you have an `action()` method in the panel that looks for the button based on the string *Reset*. If you provide a handle to the button as part of the API, you risk having the programmer change the button's label, potentially breaking the widget. In general, returning a handle to the internal objects in a widget allows too much risk. In the examples that follow, wrapper methods are preferred.

LabeledTextField

One drawback to the AWT TextField class is that it does not provide an integrated label. When a TextField is used in a user interface, it typically has a label describing the contents of the field associated with it. A TextField for entering a password, for instance, will usually have a label nearby with the string *Password:* or *Enter Password:* in it. Due to its simplicity and utility, a labeled text field class is a reasonable place to begin extending the AWT. Figure 4.9 shows a typical login screen that utilizes two LabeledTextField objects.

The LabeledTextField class has an API that is similar to the TextField, TextComponent, and Label classes. There are four variants of the Labeled-TextField constructor:

1. `public LabeledTextField(String labelString, int width, String initString, boolean readOnly)`

2. `public LabeledTextField(String labelString, int width, String initString)`

3. `public LabeledTextField(String labelString, int width, boolean readOnly)`

4. `public LabeledTextField(String labelString, int width)`

All four constructors take as arguments the string to use for the label, `labelString`, and the number of columns in the text area, `width`. The variants come from the two optional arguments: the string `init-String`, which is used to initialize the text area, and the `readOnly` flag, which indicates whether or not the text area can be used for input.

LabeledTextField contains wrappers for most of the useful methods in TextField and Label. The most significant methods are:

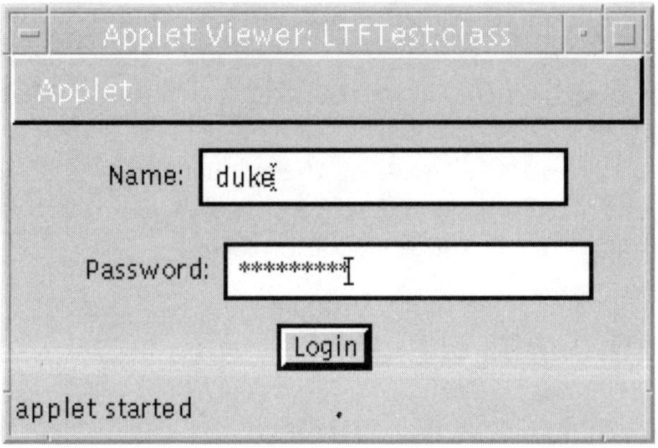

Figure 4.9
A simple applet using LabeledTextField.

```
public void setText(String s)
public String getText()
public void setEchoCharacter(char c)
public void setLabelText(String s)
```

The `setText()`, `getText()`, and `setEchoCharacter()` methods all are wrappers around the methods of the same name in the TextField class. To avoid a name-space conflict, the `setText()` method in the Label class is wrapped by the `setLabelText()` method. The applet shown in Fig. 4.9 uses the LabeledTextField class in a very typical way. The user interface is created in the applet's `init()` method:

```
public void init() {
    nameField = new LabeledTextField("Name: ", 20);
    passwdField = new LabeledTextField("Password: ", 20);
    passwdField.setEchoCharacter('*');
    add(nameField);
    add(passwdField);
    add(new Button("Login"));
}
```

Values in the text areas can be extracted with such code as:

```
System.out.println("Name = " + nameField.getText() + ", "
                 + "Password = " + passwdField.getText());
```

LabeledTextField IMPLEMENTATION. The full LabeledTextField class implementation is shown in Fig. 4.10. One detail of the implementation is worth singling out. Panels and their subclasses have a FlowLayout by default. Yet the implementation of the LabeledTextField reset the layout manager to another FlowLayout. This is done to allow explicit setting of the horizontal gap size between components added to the panel. The gap size in a panel managed by a FlowLayout can only be set in the FlowLayout's constructor. By setting the horizontal gap size to some small value (here it is set to 1), the label and the text field are kept closer together. Other than the constructors, all methods of LabeledTextField simply call methods by the same name in the TextField, TextComponent, or Label class.

The LabeledTextField is a very simple panel-based widget. It merely combines two existing AWT objects in a panel and provides hooks into their existing methods. The next level of complexity is to add some unique functionality to the elements combined in the panel. The ObjectList is a good example.

```
package ajp.awt;

import java.awt.*;
import java.awt.event.*;

/**
 * A labeled TextField.  This class extends Panel to create a panel
 * with a labeled text item on it.  The labeled TextField is centered
 * on the panel.
 *
 * @version    2.3
 **/
public class LabeledTextField extends Panel {
    static final long serialVersionUID = -3575718107530389099L;

    // The TextField.
    protected TextField textField;

    // The label
    protected Label label;

    /**
     * Create the LabeledTextField.
     **/
    public LabeledTextField(String labelString, int width,
                            String initString, boolean readOnly) {
        super();
        setLayout(new FlowLayout(FlowLayout.CENTER, 1, 5));

        label = new Label(labelString, Label.RIGHT);
        label.setAlignment(Label.RIGHT);
        if (initString != null) {
            textField = new TextField(initString, width);
        }
        else {
            textField = new TextField(width);
        }
        if (readOnly) {
            textField.setEditable(false);
        }
        add(label);
        add(textField);
    }

    /**
     * Create the LabeledTextField.
     **/
    public LabeledTextField(String labelString, int width,
                                    boolean readOnly) {
        this(labelString, width, null, readOnly);
    }
```

Figure 4.10
The LabeledTextField
class.

```
/**
 * Create the LabeledTextField.
 **/
public LabeledTextField(String labelString, int width,
                                      String initString) {
    this(labelString, width, initString, false);
}

/**
 * Create the LabeledTextField.
 **/
public LabeledTextField(String labelString, int width) {
    this(labelString, width, null, false);
}

//////////// The Standard TextField methods.. ///////////

/**
 * Returns the character to be used for echoing.
 **/
public char getEchoChar() {
    return textField.getEchoChar();
}

/**
 * Returns true if this TextField has a character set for
 * echoing.
 **/
public boolean echoCharIsSet() {
    return textField.echoCharIsSet();
}

/**
 * Returns the number of columns in this LabeledTextField.
 **/
public int getColumns() {
    return textField.getColumns();
}

/**
 * Sets the echo character for this LabeledTextField. This is useful
 * for fields where the user input shouldn't be echoed to the screen,
 * as in the case of a LabeledTextField that represents a password.
 **/
public void setEchoChar(char c) {
    textField.setEchoChar(c);
}

//////////// The Standard TextComponent methods...///////////

/**
 * Sets the text of this TextComponent to the specified text.
```

Figure 4.10
(Continued).

```
    **/
    public void setText(String t) {
        textField.setText(t);
    }

/**
 * Returns the text contained in this TextComponent.
 **/
 public String getText() {
     return textField.getText();
 }

/**
 * Returns the selected text contained in this TextComponent.
 **/
public String getSelectedText() {
    return textField.getSelectedText();
}

/**
 * Returns the boolean indicating whether this TextComponent is
 * editable or not.
 **/
public boolean isEditable() {
    return textField.isEditable();
}

/**
 * Sets the specified boolean to indicate whether or not this
 * TextComponent should be editable.
 **/
public void setEditable(boolean t) {
    textField.setEditable(t);
}

/**
 * Returns the selected text's start position.
 **/
public int getSelectionStart() {
    return textField.getSelectionStart();
}

/**
 * Returns the selected text's end position.
 **/
public int getSelectionEnd() {
    return textField.getSelectionEnd();
}

/**
 * Selects the text found between the specified start and end locations.
 **/
public void select(int selStart, int selEnd) {
    textField.select(selStart, selEnd);
}
```

Figure 4.10
(*Continued*).

```
    /**
     * Selects all the text in the TextComponent.
     **/
    public void selectAll() {
        textField.selectAll();
    }

    ///////////// Standard Label methods... /////////////////////////

    /**
     * Gets the text of the label.
     **/
    public String getLabelText() {
        return label.getText();
    }

    /**
     * Sets the text for the label to the specified text.
     **/
    public void setLabelText(String l) {
        label.setText(l);
    }

    /**
     * Returns the String of parameters for this LabeledTextField.
     **/
    protected String paramString() {
        return "Label:" + getLabelText() + ",Text:" + getText();
    }

    /**
     * Adds the specified action listener to receive action events
     * from this LabeledTextField.
     **/
    public void addActionListener(ActionListener l) {
        textField.addActionListener(l);
    }

    /**
     * Removes the specified action listener so it no longer receives
     * action events from this LabeledTextField.
     **/
    public void removeActionListener(ActionListener l) {
        textField.removeActionListener(l);
    }
}
```

Figure 4.10

(*Continued*).

ObjectList

The motivation behind the ObjectList class is to create a variant of the AWT List that can associate arbitrary objects with the strings on the List. For example, rather than a List holding just the names of employees in a database, an ObjectList can attach an instance of an Employee class to each entry in the list. When the employee's name is selected, the ObjectList can be set up so that the Employee object is passed to a handler. The handler can then, for instance, display the employee object in a separate frame.

The ObjectList is composed of two AWT components: a *List* and an optional *Label*. A simple applet using an ObjectList is shown in Fig. 4.11. In addition to the List and the Label, the ObjectList contains a nonvisual element, a *Hashtable*, in which the objects added to the list are stored. When the user selects an item on the list by double clicking the mouse, the object associated with the selected item is retrieved from the hash table and passed to an event handler.

Figure 4.11
An applet using an
ObjectList.

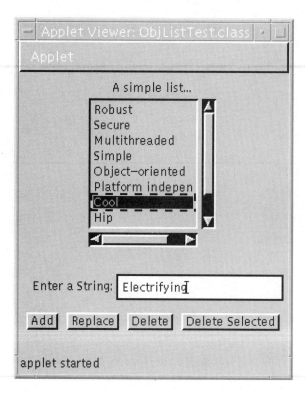

The constructor for the ObjectList class allows the programmer to optionally specify how many lines of the list are visible. Since an optional label can also be set by the constructor, there are a total of four constructors for the class:

1. `public ObjectList()`

2. `public ObjectList(int nLines)`

3. `public ObjectList(String label)`

4. `public ObjectList(int nLines, String label)`

In the forms that don't specify `nLines`, the number of lines displayed defaults to a private constant value. Where no label is specified, no Label object is created. The applet shown in Fig. 4.11 creates the ObjectList it contains in its `init()` method using the last form of the constructor (see Fig. 4.12 for the source code to the applet).

```java
import ajp.awt.*;
import java.awt.*;
import java.awt.event.*;
import java.applet.*;

/**
 * A simple demonstration Object to store on an ObjectList.
 **/
class ListItem {
    String s;
    ListItem(String string) {
        s = string;
    }

    public String toString() {
        return s;
    }
}

/**
 * Adapter to handle presses of the "Add" button.
 **/
class AddAdaptor implements ActionListener {
    ObjectList ol;
    LabeledTextField ltf;
```

Figure 4.12
Sample applet source that uses the ObjectList class.

```
        public AddAdaptor(ObjectList ol, LabeledTextField ltf) {
            this.ol = ol;
            this.ltf = ltf;
        }

        public void actionPerformed(ActionEvent e) {
            String str = ltf.getText();
            ListItem li = new ListItem("String = " + str);
            ol.addItem(str, li);
            ltf.setText("");
        }
}

/**
 * Adapter to handle presses of the "Replace" button.
 **/
class ReplaceAdaptor implements ActionListener {
    ObjectList ol;
    LabeledTextField ltf;

    public ReplaceAdaptor(ObjectList ol, LabeledTextField ltf) {
        this.ol = ol;
        this.ltf = ltf;
    }

    public void actionPerformed(ActionEvent e) {
        String str = ltf.getText();
        ListItem li = new ListItem("String = " + str);
        // Replace object associated with "str" with new ListItem.
        ol.replaceSelectedItem(str, li);
    }
}

/**
 * Adapter to handle presses of the "Delete" button.
 **/
class DeleteAdaptor implements ActionListener {
    ObjectList ol;
    LabeledTextField ltf;

    public DeleteAdaptor(ObjectList ol, LabeledTextField ltf) {
        this.ol = ol;
        this.ltf = ltf;
    }

    public void actionPerformed(ActionEvent e) {
        String str = ltf.getText();
        // Search and delete
        ol.delItem(str);
    }
}
```

Figure 4.12
(*Continued*).

```
/**
 * Adapter to handle presses of the "Delete Selected" button.
 **/
class DeleteSelectedAdaptor implements ActionListener {
     ObjectList ol;
     LabeledTextField ltf;

     public DeleteSelectedAdaptor(ObjectList ol, LabeledTextField ltf) {
          this.ol = ol;
          this.ltf = ltf;
     }

     public void actionPerformed(ActionEvent e) {
          ol.delSelectedItem();
     }
}

/**
 * A simple applet to demonstrate the ObjectList class.
 **/
public class ObjListTest extends Applet implements ItemListener,
                                                    ActionListener {
     LabeledTextField ltf;
     ObjectList objList;

     public void init() {
          // Create the GUI.
          Panel south = new Panel();
          south.setLayout(new GridLayout(2, 1));
          setLayout(new BorderLayout());
          objList = new ObjectList(10, "A simple list...", true);
          // Set the applet as listener to events from ObjectList.
          objList.addItemListener(this);
          objList.addActionListener(this);
          add("Center", objList);

          south.add(ltf = new LabeledTextField("Enter a String:", 20));

          Panel p = new Panel();
          // Create the buttons and add the adaptors as listeners.
          Button b;
          p.add(b = new Button("Add"));
          // the add adaptor will handle events from the button as well
          // as from the labeled text field.
          AddAdaptor aa;
          b.addActionListener(aa = new AddAdaptor(objList, ltf));
          ltf.addActionListener(aa);
          p.add(b = new Button("Replace"));
          b.addActionListener(new ReplaceAdaptor(objList, ltf));
          p.add(b = new Button("Delete"));
          b.addActionListener(new DeleteAdaptor(objList, ltf));
          p.add(b = new Button("Delete Selected"));
          b.addActionListener(new DeleteSelectedAdaptor(objList, ltf));
```

Figure 4.12
(Continued).

```
          south.add(p);
          add("South", south);
          resize(285, 330);
      }

      /**
       * Got a selection on the List (double-click on an item)
       **/
      public void actionPerformed(ActionEvent evt) {
          System.out.println("Got an ActionEvent: " + evt);
          String selected = evt.getActionCommand();
          ListItem l = (ListItem)objList.getItem(selected);
          System.out.println("Object was selected: " + selected);
      }

      /**
       * Item was selected/deselected.
       **/
      public void itemStateChanged(ItemEvent evt) {
          System.out.println("Got a ItemEvent: " + evt);

      }
}
```

Figure 4.12
(*Continued*).

In general, the API for the ObjectList class is very similar to the AWT List class. There are the standard methods for adding to, deleting from, and selecting on the list, which have the same signatures as the corollary methods in the List class. The methods in the List class typically take an integer index into the list as an argument. The ObjectList's methods have forms that take an index into the list and a form that takes a string that is matched against the strings displayed in the list. The public methods of ObjectList are described in Table 4.1.

Prior to dissecting the implementation of the ObjectList, it is worth looking at an example of how the class is used. The applet shown in Fig. 4.11, called *ObjListTest,* is a simple example. The source code for the applet is shown in Fig. 4.12. When an ObjListTest applet is created, the ObjectList it contains is initially empty. When the user types a string into the LabeledTextField and presses the *Add* button, the string is added to the list; an object, a *ListItem,* is created and associated with the entry on the list. The *Replace* button causes the selected list item and its associated object to be replaced with the string in the text field and another ListItem. The *Delete* button searches the list for a string that matches the one currently in the text field and deletes the matching item on the list. After an item is selected, the *Delete Selected* button can be used to remove it.

TABLE 4.1

Public Methods of
the ObjectList Class

Method signature	Description
`void select(int index)`	Selects the item at the specified index
`void select(String key)`	Selects the item that matches the specified String
`void deselect(int index)`	Deselects the item at the specified index
`void deselect(String key)`	Deselects the item that matches the specified String
`void addItem(String key, Object value)`	Adds the String to the list and associates the specified Object with it
`void addItem(String key, Object value, int index)`	Adds the String at the specified index in the list and associates the specified Object with it
`void delItem(int index)`	Deletes the item at the specified index
`void delItem(String key)`	Deletes the item that matches the specified String
`void replaceItem(String newKey, Object newObject, int index)`	Replaces the String and associates Object at `index` with the new String and Object provided
`void replaceItem(String newKey, Object newObject, String key)`	Finds the item that matches `key` and replaces it with the new String and Object
`void clear()`	Clears the list of all items
`int getItemCount()`	Returns the number of items on the list
`boolean isSelected(int index)`	Returns *true* if the item at the specified index is currently selected
`boolean isSelected(String key)`	Returns *true* if the item that matches the specified String is selected
`int getIndex(String key)`	Returns the index of the item that matches the specified string
`Object getItem(String key)`	Returns the Object associated with the specified String
`Object getItem(int index)`	Returns the Object stored at the given index into the list
`Object getSelectedObject()`	Returns the Object associated with the currently selected item
`int selected()`	Returns the index of the currently selected item
`void addActionListener(ActionListener l)`	Adds the specified ActionListener to the chain to be notified when an item on the list is selected
`void removeActionListener(ActionListener l)`	Removes the specified ActionListener from the action notification chain
`void addItemListener(ItemListener l)`	Adds the specified ItemListener to the chain to be notified when an item on the list changes state
`void removeItemListener(ItemListener l)`	Removes the specified ItemListener from the item state change notification chain

The ObjListApplet uses four supporting classes to handle the button press events. These four adaptor classes implement the ActionListener interface and provide the required `actionPerformed()` method. A reference to the ObjectList and to the LabeledTextField is passed to the constructor of each adaptor so that it can interact with the applet. The name of each adaptor class corresponds to the label of the Button in the applet that the adaptor listens to. For example, the AddAdaptor is a listener for ActionEvents generated by the *Add* button. A fifth class supporting the applet is the ListItem class, which is a simple class containing one String instance variable. Instances of the ListItems class are what is placed on the applet's ObjectList.

The AddAdaptor class extracts a string from the LabeledTextField, creates a ListItem from that string, and then adds it to the ObjectList. The ReplaceAdaptor calls the ObjectList's `replaceSelectedItem()` method, passing it the current contents of the LabeledTextField. The DeleteSelectedAdaptor causes the first selected item on the list to be deleted, and the DeleteAdaptor deletes any string in the list that matches the current contents of the text field. Each adaptor is instantiated in the applet's `init()` method and is added to the corresponding button using the button's `addActionListener()` method.

ObjectList IMPLEMENTATION. Figure 4.13 shows the full implementation of the ObjectList class. Within the class is a private instance variable `hasher`, which is on the hash table used to store the objects associated with each item on the list. The strings that appear in the list are the keys used to index into the hash table to store and retrieve objects. For example, if an employee's name is "John Doe" and there is an Employee object `emp` that is to be put on an ObjectList, the list would eventually store the data in the hash table using the equivalent of:

```
hasher.add("John Doe", emp);
```

The Employee object associated with the name "John Doe" on the list could later be retrieved using:

```
emp = (Employee)hasher.get("John Doe");
```

Recall that since HashTables store and return Objects, the result of a `get()` must be cast to the appropriate class.

Since all objects in the hash table are stored via keys that are the strings displayed on the list, care must be taken to avoid adding duplicate strings to the ObjectList. The challenge is in devising a scheme that ensures that

```
package ajp.awt;

import java.awt.*;
import java.awt.event.*;
import java.io.*;
import java.util.*;

/**
 * A list that associates Objects with entries on a scrolling list.
 * Note the list is indexed starting at 0.
 *
 * @version 2.1
 **/
public class ObjectList extends Panel implements ActionListener,
                                                 ItemListener,
                                                 ItemSelectable {

    static final long serialVersionUID = -8427153301585661445L;
    static final String actionListenerK = "actionL";
    protected transient ActionListener actionListener;
    static final String itemListenerK = "itemL";
    protected transient ItemListener itemListener;

    // Stores the items on the list keyed by the strings that
    // appear on the List.
    protected Hashtable hasher;

    // The AWT list
    private List list;

    private static final int DEFAULT_NLINES = 4;

    private boolean debug = false;

    /**
     * Create the ObjectList with the default number of lines.
     **/
    public ObjectList() {
        this(false);
    }

    public ObjectList(boolean debug) {
        this(DEFAULT_NLINES, (String)null, debug);
    }

    /**
     * Create the ObjectList with the specified number of lines.
     **/
    public ObjectList(int nLines) {
        this(nLines, false);
    }
```

Figure 4.13
The ObjectList class.

```
    public ObjectList(int nLines, boolean debug) {
        this(nLines, (String)null, debug);
    }

    /**
     * Create the ObjectList with the default number of lines and
     * specified label.
     **/
    public ObjectList(String label) {
        this(label, false);
    }

    public ObjectList(String label, boolean debug) {
        this(DEFAULT_NLINES, label, debug);
    }

    /**
     * Create the ObjectList with the specified number of lines and label.
     **/
    public ObjectList(int nLines, String label) {
        this(nLines, label, false);
    }

    public ObjectList(int nLines, String label, boolean debug) {
        super();
        this.debug = debug;
        setLayout(new BorderLayout());
        hasher = new Hashtable();
        list = new List(nLines, false);
        list.addItemListener(this);
        list.addActionListener(this);
        add("Center", list);
        if (label != null) {
            add("North", new Label(label, Label.CENTER));
        }
    }

    /**
     * Determine the number of entries in the list.
     **/
    public int getItemCount() {
        return countItems();
    }

    /**
     * Determine the number of entries in the list.
     **/
    public int countItems() {
        return hasher.size();
    }

    /**
     * Is the specified item selected?
```

Figure 4.13

(Continued).

```
    **/
   public synchronized boolean isSelected(int index) {
        return list.isIndexSelected(index);
   }

   /**
    * Is the specified item selected?
    **/
   public synchronized boolean isSelected(String key) {
        int size = list.getItemCount();
        boolean ret = false;

        for (int i=0; i < size; i++) {
            if (key.equals(list.getItem(i))) {
                ret = list.isIndexSelected(i);
                break;
            }
        }
        return ret;
   }

   /**
    * Selects the specified item.
    **/
   public synchronized void select(int index) {
        list.select(index);
   }

   /**
    * Selects the specified item.
    **/
   public synchronized void select(String key) {
        int size = list.getItemCount();

        for (int i=0; i < size; i++) {
            if (key.equals(list.getItem(i))) {
                list.select(i);
                break;
            }
        }
   }

   /**
    * Deselects the specified item.
    **/
   public synchronized void deselect(int index) {
        list.deselect(index);
   }

   /**
    * Deselects the specified item.
    **/
   public synchronized void deselect(String key) {
        int size = list.getItemCount();
```

Figure 4.13

(Continued).

```
        for (int i=0; i < size; i++) {
            if (key.equals(list.getItem(i))) {
                list.deselect(i);
                break;
            }
        }
    }

    /**
     * Returns the index of the specified string on the list.
     *        not found.
     **/
    public synchronized int getIndex(String key) {
        int size = list.getItemCount();
        int ret = -1;

        for (int i=0; i < size; i++) {
            if (key.equals(list.getItem(i))) {
                ret = i;
                break;
            }
        }
        return ret;
    }

    /**
     * Returns the object associated with the specified string.
     **/
    public synchronized Object getItem(String key) {
        return hasher.get(key);
    }

    /**
     * Returns the object stored at the specified index on the list.
     **/
    public synchronized Object getItem(int index) {
        String key = list.getItem(index);
        return hasher.get(key);
    }

    /**
     * A simple method to make a string unique before storing it on the
     * list.  Simply appends an asterix '*' to the string.
     **/
    protected String makeUnique(String key) {
        // If string is not unique, append an asterix
        while (hasher.containsKey(key)) {
            key = key + "*";
        }
        return key;
    }
```

Figure 4.13
(Continued).

```
/**
 * Add an Object to the list and associates it with the given string.
 **/
public synchronized void addItem(String key, Object value) {
    key = makeUnique(key);
    list.addItem(key);
    hasher.put(key, value);
    validate();
}

/**
 * Add an Object to the list at the specified index and
 * associates it with the given string.
 **/
public synchronized void addItem(String key, Object value, int index) {
    key = makeUnique(key);
    list.addItem(key, index);
    hasher.put(key, value);
    validate();
}

/**
 * Deletes the item at the specified index.
 **/
public synchronized void delItem(int index) {
    String key = list.getItem(index);

    if (key != null) {
        list.delItem(index);
        hasher.remove(key);
    }
}

/**
 * Deletes the item associated with the given string.
 * Warning - this can be slow for long lists.
 **/
public synchronized void delItem(String key) {
    int size = list.getItemCount();
    String str;

    for (int i=0; i < size; i++) {
        if (key.equals(list.getItem(i))) {
            list.delItem(i);
            hasher.remove(key);
            break;
        }
    }
}

/**
 * Delete the selected item on the list.
 **/
```

Figure 4.13
(*Continued*).

```
public synchronized void delSelectedItem() {
    int index = selected();

    if (index >= 0) {
        delItem(index);
    }
}

/**
 * Replace the item at the given index with the new one provided.
 **/
public synchronized void replaceItem(String newKey, Object newObject,
                                     int index) {
    delItem(index);
    addItem(newKey, newObject, index);
}

/**
 * Replace the item associated with the given string with the new
 * one provided.
 **/
public synchronized void replaceItem(String newKey, Object newObject,
                                     String key) {
    int index = getIndex(key);
    if (index >= 0) {
        delItem(index);
        addItem(newKey, newObject, index);
    }
}

/**
 * Replace the selected item with with the new
 * one provided.
 **/
public synchronized void replaceSelectedItem(String newKey,
                                             Object newObject) {
    int index = selected();

    if (index >= 0) {
        replaceItem(newKey, newObject, index);
    }
}

/**
 * Clear the list.
 **/
public synchronized void clear() {
    hasher.clear();
    list.removeAll();
}

/**
 * Get a reference to the object associated with the selected string.
```

Figure 4.13

(*Continued*).

```
  **/
public synchronized Object getSelectedObject() {
    return hasher.get(list.getSelectedItem());
}

/**
 * Get the index of the first selected item.
 **/
public synchronized int selected() {
    int size = list.getItemCount();
    int ret = -1;

    for (int i=0; i < size; i++) {
        if (list.isIndexSelected(i)) {
            ret = i;
            break;
        }
    }
    return ret;
}

// The local debug method
void dbg(String str) {
    if (debug) {
        System.out.println(this.getClass().getName() + ": " + str);
        System.out.flush();
    }
}

/**
 * Method called when an item is selected on the list.  Just
 * Passes the item along to any listeners.
 **/
public void actionPerformed(ActionEvent evt) {
    dbg("Got an ActionEvent: " + evt);
    processActionEvent(evt);
}

/**
 * Called when an item on the list changes state.  Passes the
 * event along to listeners.
 **/
public void itemStateChanged(ItemEvent evt) {
    dbg("Got a ItemEvent: " + evt);
    int index = ((Integer)evt.getItem()).intValue();
    processItemEvent(evt);
}

/**
 * Returns the selected items or null if no items are selected.
 **/
public Object[] getSelectedObjects() {
    return null;
}
```

Figure 4.13
(Continued).

```
/**
 * Add a listener to recieve item events when the state of
 * an item changes.
 **/
 public void addItemListener(ItemListener l) {
        itemListener = AJPEventMulticaster.add(itemListener, l);
 }

/**
 * Removes an item listener.
 **/
public void removeItemListener(ItemListener l) {
     itemListener = AJPEventMulticaster.remove(itemListener, l);
}

/**
 * Processes item events occurring on this list by
 * dispatching them to any registered ItemListener objects.
 **/
protected void processItemEvent(ItemEvent e) {
     if (itemListener != null) {
          itemListener.itemStateChanged(e);
     }
}

/**
 * Adds the specified action listener to receive action events
 * from this button.
 **/
public void addActionListener(ActionListener l) {
     actionListener = AJPEventMulticaster.add(actionListener, l);
}

/**
 * Removes the specified action listener so it no longer receives
 * action events from this button.
 **/
public void removeActionListener(ActionListener l) {
     actionListener = AJPEventMulticaster.remove(actionListener, l);
}

/**
 * Processes action events occurring on this button by
 * dispatching them to any registered ActionListener objects.
 **/
protected void processActionEvent(ActionEvent ev) {
     if (actionListener != null) {
          actionListener.actionPerformed(ev);
     }
}

//////// Serialization support. ///////
private int objectListSerializedDataVersion = 1;
```

Figure 4.13

(Continued).

```
/**
 * Write the button to the Output stream.  Must save the
 * Listener references independently.
 **/
private void writeObject(ObjectOutputStream s) throws IOException {
    s.defaultWriteObject();
    AJPEventMulticaster.write(s, actionListenerK, actionListener);
    AJPEventMulticaster.write(s, itemListenerK, itemListener);
    s.writeObject(null);
}

/**
 * Read the ImageButton from the given stream.
 **/
private void readObject(ObjectInputStream s)
                    throws ClassNotFoundException, IOException {
    s.defaultReadObject();

    Object keyOrNull;
    while(null != (keyOrNull = s.readObject())) {
        String key = ((String)keyOrNull).intern();

        if (actionListenerK == key)
            addActionListener((ActionListener)(s.readObject()));
        else if (itemListenerK == key)
            addItemListener((ItemListener)(s.readObject()));
        else // skip value for unrecognized key
            s.readObject();
    }
}
}
```

Figure 4.13
(*Continued*).

the strings being used are unique. One approach to this challenge (and the one taken here) is to append a character to a string if it is already in use. The ObjectList class contains a method, makeUnique(), which is passed a string and which returns a version of the passed string that is not currently in use as a key on the hash table. If the string is already in use, makeUnique() appends an asterisk to the string and checks it again, iterating until a unique string is found. Both the makeUnique() method and the hasher instance variable are declared protected, so that subclasses of ObjectList can implement their own mechanisms for creating unique keys by overriding makeUnique().

EVENT HANDLING IN THE ObjectList. The ObjectList class implements three interfaces: *ActionListener, ItemListener,* and *ItemSelectable.* By implementing the ActionListener and ItemListener interfaces, the ObjectList is able to register as a listener to events that are generated from its internal List object. The ItemSelectable interface requires methods to be implemented that support selections, specifically, `addItemListener()`, `removeItemListener()`, and `getSelectedObjects()`.

In the ObjectList's constructor, the ObjectList adds itself as a listener for Action- and ItemEvents generated by its internal List. If an Action-Event is generated, the ObjectList's `actionPerformed()` method is called, which simply passes the event on to the `processActionEvent()` method. In the `processActionEvent()` method, the event is passed to the ActionListeners installed on the AWTEventMulticaster chain.

Similarly, ItemEvents are passed through `itemStateChanged()` where the index of the selected item is saved before the event is passed to `processItemEvent()`. As was the case for ActionEvents, the ItemEvents are passed to an AWTEventMulticaster chain which dispatches the events to all the listeners.

SERIALIZING THE ObjectList. In order to enable serialization of the ObjectList,* it is necessary to ensure that all contained objects are serializable, or, if not, override the `writeObject()` and `readObject()` methods to explicitly write the objects to the serialization stream. The ObjectList stores references to its ActionListeners and ItemListeners in an event multicaster chain that is not serializable. To enable serialization, the AWTEventMulticaster class provides a static `save()` method that is used by various AWT classes to traverse the chain of multicaster objects. The `save()` method is passed the head of the multicaster chain and a string that identifies the type of listeners being saved. For each AWTEventMulticaster in the chain, `save()` calls the multicaster's `saveInternal()` method, which, in turn, calls the `writeObject()` methods of the listeners the multicaster stores.

As of the final JDK 1.1 release, the `save()` method in the AWTEventMulticaster class is accessible only to members of the java.awt package, even though `saveInternal()` is accessible to subclasses. Therefore, AWT objects can serialize their event multicaster chains, but classes outside the java.awt package cannot. So, currently, to serialize chains created with the

---

* It should be noted that serialization is an important consideration if you intend to create Java Beans. All Beans must support serialization.

AWTEventMulticaster class from outside the java.awt package, a local alternative to the save() method must be created. For this reason, and to handle non-java.awt EventsObjects, the AJPEventMulticaster class shown in Fig. 4.14 was created.

```java
package ajp.awt;

import java.util.EventListener;
import java.io.Serializable;
import java.io.ObjectOutputStream;
import java.io.IOException;
import java.awt.AWTEventMulticaster;
import ajp.awt.event.*;

/**
 * A class to multicast events used by the ajp.awt package.  Chains the
 * listeners together in a linked list.  See the documentation of the
 * parent class for a code example.
 *
 * @version 2.3
 **/
public class AJPEventMulticaster extends AWTEventMulticaster
                                implements ImageDeliveryListener,
                                           FileSelectionListener {
    /**
     * Create the event multicaster.
     **/
    protected AJPEventMulticaster(EventListener a, EventListener b) {
        super(a, b);
    }

    /**
     * Add the specified listener to the chain.
     **/
    public static ImageDeliveryListener add(ImageDeliveryListener a,
                                            ImageDeliveryListener b) {
        return (ImageDeliveryListener)addInternal(a, b);
    }

    /**
     * Remove the specified listener from the chain.
     **/
    public static ImageDeliveryListener remove(ImageDeliveryListener l,
                                               ImageDeliveryListener oldl) {
        return (ImageDeliveryListener) removeInternal(l, oldl);
    }

    /**
     * The method called when an ImageDeliveryEvent occurs.
     **/
```

Figure 4.14
The AJPEventMulti-
caster class.

```
    public void imageReady(ImageDeliveryEvent e) {
        ((ImageDeliveryListener)a).imageReady(e);
        ((ImageDeliveryListener)b).imageReady(e);
    }

    /**
     * Add the specified listener to the chain.
     **/
    public static FileSelectionListener add(FileSelectionListener a,
                                            FileSelectionListener b) {
        return (FileSelectionListener)addInternal(a, b);
    }

    /**
     * Remove the specified listener from the chain.
     **/
    public static FileSelectionListener remove(FileSelectionListener l,
                                               FileSelectionListener oldl) {
        return (FileSelectionListener) removeInternal(l, oldl);
    }

    /**
     * The method called when an FileSelectionEvent occurs.
     **/
    public void fileSelected(FileSelectionEvent e) {
        ((FileSelectionListener)a).fileSelected(e);
        ((FileSelectionListener)b).fileSelected(e);
    }

    /**
     * The method called when an FileSelectionEvent occurs.
     **/
    public void selectionCanceled() {
        ((FileSelectionListener)a).selectionCanceled();
        ((FileSelectionListener)b).selectionCanceled();
    }

    /**
     * Writes the chain of event listeners to the output stream.
     * Note that this is a necessary duplication of the save() method
     * in the parent class.
     **/
    static void write(ObjectOutputStream s, String k,
                      EventListener l) throws IOException {
        if (l == null) {
            return;
        }
        else if (l instanceof AJPEventMulticaster) {
            ((AJPEventMulticaster)l).saveInternal(s, k);
        }
        else if (l instanceof Serializable) {
            s.writeObject(k);
            s.writeObject(l);
        }
    }
}
```

Figure 4.14
(Continued).

The AJPEventMulticaster class extends the AWTEventMulticaster class, and as such is able to create chains of all the standard AWT EventListener subclasses. In addition, the AJPEventMulticaster is capable of handling the ImageDeliveryListeners presented in Chap. 3, as well as FileSelection-Listeners that are introduced in Chap. 7. There are methods for adding and removing both ImageDeliveryListeners and FileSelectionListeners in the class, along with the methods required by those interfaces. The most interesting part of the class is the `write()` method, which is used to serialize the listener chain. The `write()` method essentially duplicates the AWTEventMulticaster's `save()` method. If the `write()` method is passed an AWTEventMulticaster object, it calls the object's `saveInternal()` method. If the object passed to `write()` is any other Serializable object, it is simply written out, prefixed by a keyword string passed to the multicaster that identifies the type of the listener.

The ObjectList supports initialization from a serialized stream through its `readObject()` method. The `readObject()` method simply reads Objects from the stream and adds them to the chain of registered listeners. Each item is read by first reading a string and comparing it to the keyword strings used when writing out ItemListeners and ActionListeners. Based on the value of the keyword string, the object read from the data stream is added to the appropriate listener chain.

LIST LOCKING AND SYNCHRONIZATION. One final note about the implementation: all of the methods that modify the ObjectList are declared synchronized to prevent concurrent updates by multiple threads. This alone is not enough to prevent corruption of the list, however. For instance, there are two ways one might delete the selected item on the list. One way is to get the index of the selected item, then delete it:

```
index = objList.selected();
objList.delItem(index);
```

While both the `selected()` and `delItem()` methods are synchronized, the monitor is released between invocations. Thus, there is a small window of opportunity between getting the index and actually deleting the item when another thread could, for example, delete a different item from the list. Deleting an item would change the indexing of the list, and the item deleted by the preceding code might, in fact, be a different one than intended. Getting the index of the item to be deleted and actually removing it from the list must be atomic with respect to the list's monitor. For this reason, the methods `replaceSelectedItem()` and `deleteSelectedItem()` have been provided. Each method gets the index of the selected item, then modifies the list without releasing the monitor.

Inheriting from Component

Creating custom widgets based on an AWT Container provides new and interesting ways to combine existing AWT Components. While these new widgets may have functionality that is not provided by AWT alone, their appearance is limited to that of existing components. If the functionality of a scroll bar is needed, but the appearance of an analog dial is preferred, existing AWT user interface objects provide no solution. This is where Component-based widgets come in. With Component-based widgets, in addition to the core functionality and event handling of the widget, the programmer must also provide the visual appearance of the object. The widget is literally drawn programmatically. If some user interaction with the widget requires a change in the widget's appearance, the interaction must be tracked, the visual change must be drawn, and appropriate events must be generated by the implementation.

To illustrate the process of creating Component-based widgets, three examples are presented here. The first is a *dial*, analogous to the volume knobs on a stereo. The second is an *LED display* that can be used for both input and output. The third is a *picture button* that allows pictures to be put on a widget that is, in all other respects, analogous to an AWT Button. As with the Container-based widgets, each Component-based widget illustrates a different facet of creating AWT extensions.

Dials

In the real world, people are used to interacting with dials. Dials are everywhere in our daily lives: on stereos, car radios, stoves, computer monitors, and so on. This section presents an AWT extension widget based on a typical analog dial. The Dial class demonstrates most of the fundamental steps in creating a Component-based widget. First of all, the graphical representation of the dial is drawn from scratch, using simple AWT graphics primitives. When the dial is turned, the rotation is animated programmatically—again using the AWT Graphics class. Second, the dial intercepts the user's actions by tracking mouse events and animates the dial accordingly. Finally, the dial generates events that encapsulate the current value of the dial and passes these events on to registered listeners. A simple example of the Dial class is shown in Fig. 4.15. Each dial can be rotated independently, and as they are rotated the current value is displayed in the center of the dial (a feature that will be referred to as *pre-*

viewing). The two buttons labeled + and − below the dials will increment and decrement the far left dial. The darker color of the dials and the panel they are on is intentional. Dial objects get their color from the parent container, which in this case is set to a darker gray than the default used by the AWT.

Like the NumericSlider class, Dials have a very simple API. There are three constructors and, essentially, four public methods. The three forms of the constructor are:

1. `public Dial(String label, int min, int max, int val, int radius)`

2. `public Dial(String label, int min, int max, int val)`

3. `public Dial(String label, int min, int max)`

Dial objects must be created with a label and a minimum and maximum value. The label is printed under the Dial; the minimum and max-

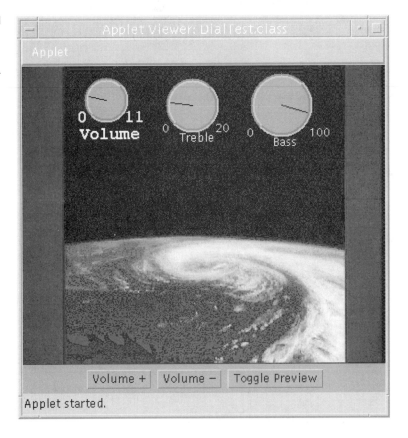

Figure 4.15
An applet using Dials on an ImagePanel.

imum values are printed at 45 degrees below the horizontal center line of the button on each side. The two optional parameters are the initial value and the radius of the Dial in pixels; both assume default values if not specified.

The four public methods in the Dial API are summarized in Table 4.2. There are methods for setting and getting the dial's current value and methods for setting and getting its current preview state. If the preview state is set to *true,* a value will be displayed in the center of the dial as the dial is rotated. Not included in the table are the methods required by the Adjustable interface which have empty implementations in the Dial class.

The code that generates the simple example shown in Fig. 4.15 is presented as Fig. 4.16.

The Dial demonstration applet makes use of a derivative of the BufferedPanel class discussed earlier in this chapter. The ImagePanel class

TABLE 4.2 Public Methods of the Dial Class	**Method signature**	**Description**
	`Dimension getMinimumSize()`	Gets the smallest dimension supported by the Dial
	`Dimension getPreferredSize()`	Gets the Dial's preferred size
	`void setMinMaxColor(Color c)`	Sets the color used by the min and max labels
	`void setValueColor(Color c)`	Sets the color used by the value label
	`void setLabelColor(Color c)`	Sets the color used by the Dial's main label
	`void setNeedleColor(Color c)`	Sets the color used to draw the needle on the Dial
	`void setPreview(boolean preview)`	If `preview` is *true,* enables the display of the value label while the mouse is pressed
	`boolean getPreview()`	Returns the current value of the `preview` flag
	`void setvalue(int val)`	Sets the value displayed on the Dial
	`int getValue()`	Gets the current value of the Dial
	`void addAdjustmentListener (AdjustmentListener 1)`	Adds the specified AdjustmentListener to the chain to be notified when an item on the list is selected
	`void removeAdjustmentListener (AdjustmentListener 1)`	Removes the specified AdjustmentListener from the action notification chain

```
import java.applet.*;
import java.awt.*;
import java.awt.event.*;
import ajp.awt.*;

/**
 * Unlike the ObjListTest applet, the Dial Test uses a
 * monolithic action listener to handle all its buttons.
 **/
class DialTestButtonListener implements ActionListener {
    static final int INCREMENT = 0;
    static final int DECREMENT = 1;
    static final int TOGGLE_PREVIEW = 2;

    int tag;
    Dial dial;
    Dial dials[];

    // Constructor for the "+" and "-" buttons.
    public DialTestButtonListener(int tag, Dial d) {
        dial = d;
        this.tag = tag;
    }

    // Constructor used to listen for the "Preview" button.
    public DialTestButtonListener(int tag, Dial d[]) {
        dials = d;
        this.tag = tag;
    }

    public void actionPerformed(ActionEvent e) {
        switch(tag) {
        case INCREMENT:
            dial.setValue(dial.getValue()+1);
            break;
        case DECREMENT:
            dial.setValue(dial.getValue()-1);
            break;
        case TOGGLE_PREVIEW:
            if (dials != null) {
                for (int i=0; i<dials.length; i++) {
                    dials[i].setPreview(!dials[i].getPreview());
                }
            }
            break;
        }
    }
}

public class DialTest extends Applet {

    public void init() {
        // The Dials...
```

Figure 4.16
The source code of
the DialTest applet.

```
         Dial volume, treble, bass;
         Dial dials[] = new Dial[3];

         Button b;
         DialTestButtonListener dtbl;

         setBackground(Color.gray);
         setLayout(new BorderLayout());
         // Put a image behind the buttons
         ImagePanel ip = new ImagePanel(true, getImage(getCodeBase(),
                                          "images/backdrop.jpg"));
         // Create and add the dials
         dials[0] = volume = new Dial("Volume", 0, 11, 0, 20);
         volume.setFont(new Font("Courier", Font.BOLD, 10));
         ip.add(volume);
         ip.add(dials[1] = treble = new Dial("Treble", 0, 20, 10, 25));
         ip.add(dials[2] = bass = new Dial("Bass", 0, 100, 75, 30));

         // Set some colors on the dials
         volume.setLabelColor(Color.white);
         volume.setMinMaxColor(Color.yellow);
         volume.setValueColor(Color.red);
         treble.setLabelColor(Color.white);
         treble.setMinMaxColor(Color.yellow);
         treble.setValueColor(Color.red);
         bass.setLabelColor(Color.white);
         bass.setMinMaxColor(Color.yellow);
         bass.setValueColor(Color.red);
         // Add the image panel
         add("Center", ip);

         Panel p = new Panel();
         p.add(b = new Button("Volume +"));
         dtbl = new DialTestButtonListener(DialTestButtonListener.INCREMENT,
                                          volume);
         b.addActionListener(dtbl);
         p.add(b = new Button("Volume -"));
         dtbl = new DialTestButtonListener(DialTestButtonListener.DECREMENT,
                                          volume);
         b.addActionListener(dtbl);
         p.add(b = new Button("Toggle Preview"));
         dtbl =
             new DialTestButtonListener(DialTestButtonListener.TOGGLE_PREVIEW,
                                        dials);
         b.addActionListener(dtbl);
         add("South", p);
         resize(400, 350);
     }
 }
```

Figure 4.16
(*Continued*).

allows an Image object to be specified as the background for the panel. When combined with lightweight components, such as the Dial, the visual effect can be striking. Sources for the ImagePanel can be found on the CD-ROM that accompanies this book.

Dial IMPLEMENTATION. While an example that illustrates the entire API for the Dial class is straightforward, the implementation of the Dial itself is not. This is unfortunately typical for Component-based widgets. When creating the visual appearance of the widget, as well as handling the events generated through user interaction, there simply is a lot of code to write. The full implementation can be examined in Figs. 4.19 through 4.25. Before diving immediately into the code, it is helpful to understand the overall layout of the widget.

The Dial class is comprised of several objects, as illustrated in Fig. 4.17. The Dial itself is a subclass of Component. As lightweight components, Dials should be used in conjunction with double-buffered containers to eliminate flickering when the Dial is rotated. The circular knob in the center of the widget is drawn by a *Knob* object. The *min, max,* and *main* labels on the Dial are drawn into the canvas by *DialLabel* objects. Finally, the preview label is drawn by a *ValueLabel* object. All objects that draw into the canvas are created and managed by the Dial class.

The size of the area the Dial is drawn into is based on the size of its constituent pieces. The contributions the objects in the Dial make to its overall size are shown in Fig. 4.18. The width of the Dial is the sum of the diameter of the knob, the width of the minimum and maximum labels, and a small padding factor added to each side of the Dial. The height is comprised of the knob's diameter, the main label height, and a top and

Figure 4.17
The constituent
pieces of a Dial.

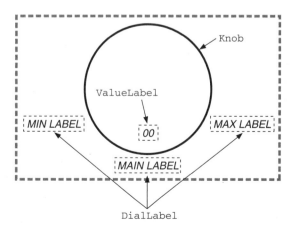

bottom padding factor. If the overall width of the main label is wider than the combination of the dial's diameter and the other two labels, the overall width of the Dial is increased to accommodate the long label.

The knob in the center of the widget has a line, or needle, that points to the current value of the Dial. The position of the needle can be adjusted by dragging or selecting the knob with the mouse. Clicking the mouse will cause the needle to be immediately repositioned, pointing in the direction of the event. Dragging the mouse pointer causes the needle to track the drag events, in effect animating the dial. The "throw" of the knob, the arc over which the needle can travel, is restricted to –45 degrees from horizontal on either side of the knob. At the far left the needle points to the *minimum* label; at the far right it points to the *maximum* label.

The vast majority of the code in the Dial class is dedicated to creating and managing the visual representation of the widget. The actual programmatic interface to the Dial, as was mentioned earlier, is restricted to just a few methods. The implementation of the Dial class is shown in Fig. 4.19. The code is broken down and discussed according to three areas: *initialization, drawing*, and *event handling.*

INITIALIZATION. The initialization of the Dial's geometry is done in the constructor and `addNotify()` methods. The constructor saves the operational parameters—minimum, maximum, radius, and so on—into instance variables. The `addNotify()` method uses the values stored in the instance variables to create the Dial's labels and calculate the Dial's

Figure 4.18
The anatomy of the
Dial class.

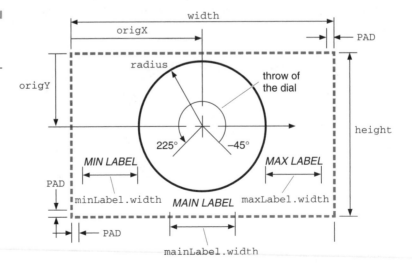

```java
package ajp.awt;

import java.awt.*;
import java.awt.event.*;
import java.util.EventListener;
import java.io.ObjectOutputStream;
import java.io.ObjectInputStream;
import java.io.IOException;
import java.io.Serializable;

/**
 * A Dial class.  Allows you to select values from a range on
 * an analog volume-style knob.
 *
 * @version 2.5
 **/
public class Dial extends Component implements Adjustable {
    static final long serialVersionUID = -1844091465289897863L;
    final static String adjustmentListenerK = "adjustmentL";

    boolean drawValue = false;
    String actionCommand;
    protected transient AdjustmentListener adjustmentListener;

    // Angle conversions
    static final double DEG_RAD = 180.0/Math.PI;

    // Throw of the knob
    static final int MIN_ANGLE = -45;
    static final int MAX_ANGLE = 225;

    // The min and max values
    private int minValue;
    private int maxValue;

    // The current value
    private int value;

    // Dimensions of the Dial
    private int radius;

    // The dial's labels
    private String label;
    private DialLabel mainLabel;
    private DialLabel minLabel;
    private DialLabel maxLabel;
    private ValueLabel valueLabel;
    private Color minMaxColor = Color.black;
    private Color labelColor = Color.black;
    private Color valueColor = Color.black;
    private Color needleColor = Color.black;
    private Font font;
```

Figure 4.19
The Dial class.

```java
        // the knob - based on Circle3D class
        Knob theKnob;

        // Padding in pixels on all sides
        protected int padXY = 3;

        // Current angle of the Dial's needle
        protected int angle = MAX_ANGLE;

        // Range of the knob in degrees
        protected int range = MAX_ANGLE - MIN_ANGLE;

        // Should the Dial display the current value as it is turned.
        protected boolean preview = true;

        protected int width;
        protected int height;

        /**
         * Constructs a Dial widget.
         **/
        public Dial(String label, int min, int max, int val, int radius, int pad) {
            this.label = label;
            minValue = min;
            maxValue = max;
            value = val;
            this.radius = radius;
            padXY = pad;
            if (value != minValue)
                angle = calculateAngle(value);
            enableEvents(AWTEvent.MOUSE_EVENT_MASK |
                        AWTEvent.MOUSE_MOTION_EVENT_MASK);
        }

        /**
         * Constructs a Dial widget.
         **/
        public Dial(String label, int min, int max, int val, int radius) {
            this(label, min, max, val, radius, 7);
        }

        /**
         * Constructs a 20 pixel radius Dial widget.
         **/
        public Dial(String label, int min, int max, int val) {
            this(label, min, max, val, 20);
        }

        /**
         * Constructs a 20 pixel radius Dial widget with initial
         * value of 0.
         **/
        public Dial(String label, int min, int max) {
```

Figure 4.19
(*Continued*).

```
            this(label, min, max, min);
    }

    /**
     * Get the minimum size of this Dial.
     **/
    public Dimension getMinimumSize() {
        return (new Dimension(width, height));
    }

    /**
     * Get the size this Dial would like to be.
     **/
    public Dimension getPreferredSize() {
        Dimension min = getMinimumSize();
        Dimension current = getSize();

        return(new Dimension((min.width < current.width)?
                                current.width : min.width,
                            (min.height < current.height)?
                                current.height : min.height));
    }

    synchronized boolean drawValue() {
        return drawValue;
    }

    synchronized void setDrawValue(boolean val) {
        drawValue = val;
    }

    public void setMinMaxColor(Color c) {
        minMaxColor = c;
        if (minLabel != null) {
            minLabel.setColor(c);
        }
        if (maxLabel != null) {
            maxLabel.setColor(c);
        }
    }

    public void setLabelColor(Color c) {
        labelColor = c;
        if (mainLabel != null) {
            mainLabel.setColor(c);
        }
    }

    public void setValueColor(Color c) {
        valueColor = c;
        if (valueLabel != null) {
            valueLabel.setColor(c);
        }
    }
```

Figure 4.19
(*Continued*).

```
    public void setNeedleColor(Color c) {
        needleColor = c;
        if (theKnob != null) {
            theKnob.setNeedleColor(c);
        }
    }

    /**
     * Copy the off-screen image to the screen.  Do not override.
     **/
    public void paint(Graphics g) {
        // draw the knob
        theKnob.draw(g, angle);

        // draw the min/max labels
        minLabel.draw(g);
        maxLabel.draw(g);
        mainLabel.draw(g);
        if (drawValue()) {
            valueLabel.setValue(value);
            valueLabel.draw(g);
        }
    }

    /**
     * Call paint() directly to avoid flicker.
     **/
    public void update(Graphics g) {
        paint(g);
    }

    /**
     * Set the flag that controls the display of the current value of
     * the Dial.  This label is displayed while the value is changing.
     **/
    public void setPreview(boolean prev) {
        preview = prev;
    }

    public boolean getPreview() {
        return preview;
    }

    protected void processMouseMotionEvent(MouseEvent e) {

        switch(e.getID()) {
        case MouseEvent.MOUSE_DRAGGED:
            value = calculateValue(setAngle(e.getX(), e.getY()));
            drawDial(preview);
            processAdjustmentEvent(new AdjustmentEvent(this, 0,
                                              AdjustmentEvent.TRACK,
                                              value));
```

Figure 4.19
(Continued).

```
                    break;
          }
    }

    protected void processMouseEvent(MouseEvent e) {
         switch(e.getID()) {
         case MouseEvent.MOUSE_RELEASED:
              value = calculateValue(setAngle(e.getX(), e.getY()));
              drawDial();
              processAdjustmentEvent(new AdjustmentEvent(this, 0,
                                 AdjustmentEvent.ADJUSTMENT_VALUE_CHANGED,
                                                     value));
              break;
          }
    }

/**
 * Adds the specified adjustment listener to recieve adjustment events
 * from this dial.
 **/
public void addAdjustmentListener(AdjustmentListener l) {
     adjustmentListener = AJPEventMulticaster.add(adjustmentListener, l);
}

/**
 * Removes the specified adjustment listener so that it no longer
 * receives adjustment events from this scrollbar..
 **/
public void removeAdjustmentListener(AdjustmentListener l) {
     adjustmentListener = AJPEventMulticaster.remove(adjustmentListener, l);
}

/**
 * Processes adjustment events occurring on this dial by
 * dispatching them to any registered AdustmentListener objects.
 **/
protected void processAdjustmentEvent(AdjustmentEvent ev) {
     if (adjustmentListener != null) {
         adjustmentListener.adjustmentValueChanged(ev);
     }
}

 /**
  * Sets the angle based on the current x, y coordinates.
  **/
 private int setAngle(int x, int y) {
      double deltaY = (double)(y - theKnob.centerY);
      double deltaX = (double)(x - theKnob.centerX);

      try {
          angle = -(int)(Math.atan(deltaY/deltaX)*DEG_RAD);
          if (deltaX < 0.0)
```

Figure 4.19
(Continued).

```
                        angle += 180.0;
            }
            catch (RuntimeException ex) {
                angle = 90;
            }
            angle = (angle <= MIN_ANGLE) ? MIN_ANGLE : angle;
            angle = (angle >= MAX_ANGLE) ? MAX_ANGLE : angle;
            return angle;
    }

    /**
     * Set the angle to the one passed as an argument.
     **/
    private int setAngle(int angle) {
        return this.angle = angle;
    }

    /**
     * Create the peer and get font information.
     **/
    public void addNotify() {
        super.addNotify();
        int origY = radius + padXY;
        int origX = radius + padXY;
        Font f = getFont();
        FontMetrics fm = getFontMetrics(f);
        Dimension d;

        minLabel = new DialLabel(String.valueOf(minValue), fm, minMaxColor);
        maxLabel = new DialLabel(String.valueOf(maxValue), fm, minMaxColor);
        mainLabel = new DialLabel(label, fm, labelColor);
        valueLabel = new ValueLabel(fm, valueColor);

        // How big is the whole widget?

        // the base size of the Dial
        int len = 2*(radius + padXY);
        width = len;
        height = len;

        // Add on sides for min and max labels
        d = minLabel.getSize();
        width += d.width;
        origX += d.width;

        d = maxLabel.getSize();
        width += d.width;

        // Add at the bottom for the main label.
        if (label != null) {
            d = mainLabel.getSize();
            height += (d.height + mainLabel.getDescent());
            if (d.width > width) {
```

Figure 4.19
(Continued).

```
                          width = d.width + 2*padXY;
                          origX = width/2;
                  }
                  mainLabel.moveTo(origX - d.width/2 + 4,
                                   origY + radius + d.height);
          }

          maxLabel.moveTo(origX + radius, origY + radius + 4);
          minLabel.moveTo(padXY, origY + radius + 4);
          valueLabel.moveTo(origX, origY + radius);

          Color c = getParent().getBackground();
          // make the 3D-circle for the dial
          theKnob = new Knob(origX, origY, radius, c, needleColor);

          drawDial();
      }

      /**
       * Draw the Dial with no preview.
       **/
      private void drawDial() {
          drawDial(false);
      }

      /**
       * Draw the Dial and show the current value if drawVaue is
       * true.
       **/
      private void drawDial(boolean drawValue) {

          setDrawValue(drawValue);
          repaint();
      }

      /**
       * Calculate the angle to draw the needle at based on a given value.
       **/
      private int calculateAngle(int val) {
          return ((int)((maxValue-val)*range/(double)(maxValue-minValue))-45);
      }

      /**
       * Calculate the value based on a given needle angle.
       **/
      private int calculateValue(int ang) {
          return((int)(maxValue-((ang+45)*(maxValue-minValue)/(double)range)));
      }

      protected String paramString() {
          return super.paramString() + ",min=" + minValue + ",max=" + maxValue
                  + ",value=" + value;
      }
```

Figure 4.19

(*Continued*).

```
/**
 * Gets the orientation of the adjustable object.
 * Not particularly meaningful for a dial.
 **/
public int getOrientation() {
    return Adjustable.HORIZONTAL;
}

/**
 * Not supported for a Dial.
 **/
public void setMinimum(int min) {
}

/**
 * Gets the minimum value of the adjustable object.
 **/
public int getMinimum() {
    return minValue;
}

/**
 * Not Supported for a dial.
 **/
public void setMaximum(int max) {
}

/**
 * Gets the maximum value of the adjustable object.
 **/
public int getMaximum() {
    return maxValue;
}

/**
 * Sets the unit value increment for the adjustable object.
 **/
public void setUnitIncrement(int u) {
}

/**
 * Gets the unit value increment for the adjustable object.
 **/
public int getUnitIncrement() {
    return -1;
}

/**
 * Sets the block value increment for the adjustable object.
 **/
public void setBlockIncrement(int b) {
}
```

Figure 4.19
(*Continued*).

```java
/**
 * Not supported.
 **/
public int getBlockIncrement() {
    return -1;
}

/**
 * Not supported.
 **/
public void setVisibleAmount(int v) {
}

/**
 * Not supported
 **/
public int getVisibleAmount() {
    return -1;
}

/**
 * Set the value of the Dial.
 **/
public void setValue(int val) {
    value = val;
    if (value < minValue)
        value = minValue;
    if (value > maxValue)
        value = maxValue;
    angle = calculateAngle(value);
    drawDial();
}

/**
 * Get the current value of the Dial.
 **/
public int getValue() {
    return(value);
}

//////////// Serialization support. /////////////////////

private int dialSerializedDataVersion = 1;

private void writeObject(ObjectOutputStream s) throws IOException {
    s.defaultWriteObject();

    AJPEventMulticaster.write(s, adjustmentListenerK,
                        (EventListener)adjustmentListener);
    s.writeObject(null);
}

private void readObject(ObjectInputStream s) throws ClassNotFoundException,
                                        IOException {
```

Figure 4.19

(*Continued*).

```
            s.defaultReadObject();

        Object keyOrNull;
        while(null != (keyOrNull = s.readObject())) {
            String key = ((String)keyOrNull).intern();

            if (adjustmentListenerK == key)
                addAdjustmentListener((AdjustmentListener)(s.readObject()));

            else // skip value for unrecognized key
                s.readObject();
        }
    }
}
```

Figure 4.19
(*Continued*).

size. A good deal of the computation needed to position and draw the visual elements of the Dial is done in addNotify() as well. The computation is done once, in addNotify(), to keep the computation out of the actual rendering of the Dial, which happens frequently.

All labels on the Dial are created in addNotify(). Since a FontMetrics object is needed to compute the widths, the labels are not created until the canvas's peer has been created. The *DialLabel* and *ValueLabel* classes (see Figs. 4.20 and 4.21, respectively) are used to encapsulate the labels so that the positions and widths of the labels can be calculated once, at the time the labels are created. The ValueLabel class is a subclass of DialLabel that adds the setValue() method, allowing the label's contents to be reset and its width to be recalculated dynamically.

The circular knob in the center of the widget is created by a Knob object. Knobs are a subclass of the *Circle3D* class, which draws circles with a three-dimensional look. The Knob class adds a needle to the circle drawn by the Circle3D class, giving the Knob the appearance of an analog dial. The constructor for the Knob class takes the x and y coordinates of the Knob's center, the radius, and the background color as arguments. From these parameters, everything necessary to draw the knob is calculated and stored in instance variables in the parent Circle3D class. The Circle3D class is shown in Fig. 4.22. The Knob class is presented in Fig. 4.23.

DRAWING. The rendering of the Dial is driven by the method draw-Dial(). Since changes to the Dial's image are driven by user interaction,

Figure 4.20
The DialLabel class.

```
package ajp.awt;

class DialLabel implements Serializable {
    static final long serialVersionUID = 1877768792740437152L;

    // The String to display.
    String string;
    // The position of the label
    int x = 0;
    int y = 0;
    // The width and height of the label
    int width;
    int height;
    // The descent of the label
    int descent;
    // Color to draw the label with.
    Color color;
    // Font and Fontmetrics for the label
    Font f;
    FontMetrics fm;

    /*
     * Create the label with the specified string, font and color
     */
    DialLabel(String s, FontMetrics fm, Color c) {
        string = s;
        this.fm = fm;
        width = fm.stringWidth(string);
        height = fm.getHeight();
        descent = fm.getMaxDescent();
        color = c;
    }

    /*
     * Set the color of the label of the font.
     */
    void setColor(Color c) {
        color = c;
    }

    /*
     * translate the coordinates of the label.
     */
    void moveTo(int x, int y) {
        this.x = x;
        this.y = y;
    }

    /*
     * Draw the label.
     */
    void draw(Graphics g) {
        Font f = g.getFont();
        Color temp = g.getColor();
        g.setColor(color);
        g.setFont(fm.getFont());
        g.drawString(string, x, y);
```

Figure 4.20
(*Continued*).

```
                  g.setColor(temp);
                  g.setFont(f);
        }

        /*
         * Returns the size of the label
         */
        Dimension getSize() {
              return new Dimension(width, height);
        }

        /*
         * Returns the descent of the label.
         */
        int getDescent() {
              return descent;
        }
}
```

Figure 4.21
The ValueLabel class.

```
package ajp.awt;

/*
 * A class for attaching numeric labels to a Dial.
 */
class ValueLabel extends DialLabel {
      static final long serialVersionUID = -8777115349488736997L;

      /*
       * Create the label.
       */
      ValueLabel(FontMetrics fm, Color c) {
            super("", fm, c);
      }

      /*
       * Set/change the value displayed in the label.
       */
      void setValue(int v) {
            string = String.valueOf(v);
            width = fm.stringWidth(string);
      }

      /*
       * Draw the label.
       */
      void draw(Graphics g) {
            Color temp = g.getColor();
            g.setColor(color);
            g.drawString(string, x - width/2, y - fm.getMaxDescent());
            g.setColor(temp);
      }
}
```

Figure 4.22

The Circle3D class.

```java
package ajp.awt;

import java.awt.*;
import java.io.Serializable;

/**
 * A class for drawing circles with a 3D look
 *
 * @version 2.2
 **/
public class Circle3D implements Serializable {
    static final long serialVersionUID = 8898051159449893690L;
    // The center coordinates of the circle
    int centerX;
    int centerY;

    // The upper left of the circle's bounding box
    int x;
    int y;

    // The radius of the circle
    int radius;

    // The circle's diameter
    int diameter;

    // The colors needed to get the 3D look.
    Color bgColor;
    Color brighter;
    Color darker;

    /**
     * Create the 3D circle
     **/
    public Circle3D(int centerX, int centerY, int radius, Color c)
    {
        this.centerX = centerX;
        this.centerY = centerY;
        this.radius = radius;
        diameter = 2*radius;
        bgColor = c;
        brighter = c.brighter();
        darker = c.darker();
        x = centerX - radius;
        y = centerY - radius;
    }

    /**
     * Draw the circle.
     **/
    void draw(Graphics g) {
        // Note: using fillArc to get thicker highlights

        // Draw the outer ring of the highlight
        g.setColor(darker);
        g.fillArc(x-4, y-4, diameter+8, diameter+8, 45, 180);
        g.setColor(brighter);
        g.fillArc(x-4, y-4, diameter+8, diameter+8, 225, 180);
```

Figure 4.22
(*Continued*).

```
                   // Draw the inner ring of the highlight
                   g.setColor(darker);
                   g.fillArc(x-2, y-2, diameter+4, diameter+4, 225, 180);
                   g.setColor(brighter);
                   g.fillArc(x-2, y-2, diameter+4, diameter+4, 45, 180);

                   // fill the center
                   g.setColor(bgColor);
                   g.fillArc(x, y, diameter, diameter, 0, 360);
         }

         public void clear(Graphics g) {
                   // fill the center
                   g.setColor(bgColor);
                   g.fillArc(x, y, diameter, diameter, 0, 360);
         }

}
```

Figure 4.23
The Knob class.

```
package ajp.awt;

import java.awt.*;
import java.awt.event.*;
import java.util.EventListener;
import java.io.ObjectOutputStream;
import java.io.ObjectInputStream;
import java.io.IOException;
import java.io.Serializable;

/**
 * A class for creating analog knobs as part of the Dial class.
 *
 * @version 2.5
 **/
class Knob extends Circle3D {
     static final long serialVersionUID = -8422621076113321609L;

     // Color of the needle.
     Color needleColor = Color.black;

     // Angle conversion
     static final double RAD_DEG = Math.PI/180.0;

     /**
      * Create a Knob
      **/
     Knob(int centerX, int centerY, int radius, Color c, Color nc) {
          super(centerX, centerY, radius, c);
          needleColor = nc;
     }
```

Figure 4.23
(*Continued*).

```
/**
 * Create a Knob
 **/
Knob(int centerX, int centerY, int radius, Color c) {
    super(centerX, centerY, radius, c);
}

/**
 * Create a Knob using the desktop control color as background.
 **/
Knob(int centerX, int centerY, int radius) {
    super(centerX, centerY, radius, SystemColor.control);
}

void setNeedleColor(Color c) {
    needleColor = c;
}

/**
 * Draw the knob with the needle pointing at the given angle.
 **/
void draw(Graphics g, int angle) {
    super.draw(g);
    double rad = angle*RAD_DEG;

    // Draw the needle
    Color temp = g.getColor();
    g.setColor(needleColor);
    g.drawLine(centerX, centerY,
            centerX + (int)(radius * Math.cos(rad)),
            centerY - (int)(radius * Math.sin(rad)));
    g.setColor(temp);
}
}
```

most of the calls to drawDial() will happen in the context of event handling. The drawDial() method has two signatures, one that takes a boolean as an argument and one that takes no arguments. The latter form of the method calls just the former, passing false as an argument. When drawDial() is called, it simply passes its boolean argument to the set-DrawValue() method, then calls repaint. The actual drawing of the dial happens in the paint() method.

All of the visual components of Dial are separate objects: three Dial-Labels, a Knob, and a ValueLabel. The Dial's paint() method simply calls the draw() methods of each of these objects, passing a reference to the Graphics object that paint() was called with. The draw() methods of the Dial's subobjects are all fairly simple, with the possible exception of the Circle3D class from which a Knob inherits (see Fig. 4.22).

To draw an object that will have a three-dimensional look, highlights created from lighter and darker shades of a base color are typically drawn as if a light source were present above and to the left of the object. For a circle, this can be implemented by drawing a dark semicircle counterclockwise from 45 degrees above the horizontal and placing a light semicircle just inside it. Similarly, a light semicircle just outside a dark semicircle is drawn counterclockwise from 225 degrees. The catch is that if the arcs are drawn, rather than filled, gaps will appear between the two curves since true curves are impossible on pixel-based displays. So, when a Circle3D object renders itself it starts from the outside, first filling the outer highlight arcs, then the inner highlights, and finally filling the face of the circle in the background color.

EVENT HANDLING.   Event Handling in the Component-based widgets breaks down into two parts:

1. Tracking registering for and handling events that correspond to user interaction with the widget.

2. Generating and dispatching appropriate events to registered event listeners.

The Dial class must track mouse motion and mouse-click events. The first step in processing these events is either to register as a listener for such events, or to enable these events directly. In the Dial constructor, the mouse events of interest are enabled directly:

```
enableEvents(AWTEvent.MOUSE_EVENT_MASK |
             AWTEvent.MOUSE_MOTION_EVENT_MASK);
```

By calling `enableEvents()`, the Dial becomes the recipient of any mouse events. The events are passed to the Dial's `processMouseMotionEvent()` and `processMouseEvent()` methods, which will (1) calculate a new value for the Dial based on the x and y coordinates of the event, (2) call `drawDial()`, and then (3) create an AdjustmentEvent object and dispatch it to all the AdjustmentListeners that have registered with the Dial. The AdjustmentEvents are created with a flag that indicates that the event corresponds to the Dial being rotated (`AdjustmentEvent.TRACK`) or that the value of the Dial has changed (`AdjustmentEvent.ADJUSTMENT_VALUE_CHANGED`).[*]

---

[*] The DialTest applet in Fig. 4.16 does not need to use the values of the Dials immediately as they change, and as such does not register as a listener for the AdjustmentEvents the Dials produce. There is an example applet called *DialLED* on the CD-ROM that illustrates the handling of AdjustmentEvents generated from a Dial.

ImageButton

While an ImageButton looks and behaves just like an AWT Button, it is not directly related to the Button class at all. The idea behind the Image-Button class is to provide a simple mechanism for creating buttons with a three-dimensional look that have GIF or JPEG images, rather than simple text, on their faces. Figure 4.24*a* shows an Applet with two ImageButtons, one with an image of Abraham Lincoln and one with an image of George Washington. As the buttons are pressed by the user (Fig. 4.24*b*), the image on the button is darkened and the border highlights invert, giving the visual impression that the surface of the button has been pushed into the screen.

From the programmer's perspective, the behavior of the buttons is identical to that of AWT buttons. When the button is pressed, an ActionEvent is generated and passed through the normal event-delivery chain to registered ActionListeners. The programmatic interface to the ImageButton class is actually simpler than that of the AWT Button class. Other than event-handling methods, ImageButton adds only one new public method to Component, getName(), which retrieves the name assigned to the button on instantiation. The code that creates the simple example pictured in Fig. 4.24 illustrates the simplicity of the API (see Fig. 4.25).

Figure 4.24
(a) An applet with two ImageButtons in the *up* position. (b) The same applet with the right ImageButton pressed.

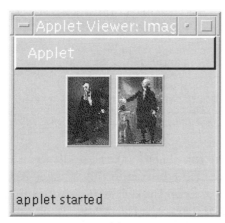
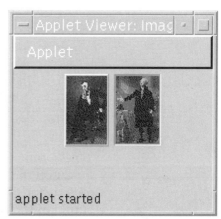

(a)   (b)

```
import java.applet.*;
import java.awt.*;
import java.awt.event.*;
import ajp.awt.ImageButton;
import ajp.awt.BufferedApplet;

public class ImageButtonTest extends BufferedApplet
                             implements ActionListener {
    ImageButton ib;

    Image im;
    public void init() {
        im = getImage(getCodeBase(), "images/presidents/al16.gif");
        ib = new ImageButton(im, "Lincoln");
        ib.addActionListener(this);
        add(ib);
        im = getImage(getCodeBase(), "images/presidents/gw1.gif");
        ib = new ImageButton(im, "Washington");
        ib.addActionListener(this);
        add(ib);

    }
    public void actionPerformed(ActionEvent e) {
        System.out.println("My name is " + e.getActionCommand());
    }
}
```

Figure 4.25
A sample applet class
that uses Image-
Buttons.

The constructor for the ImageButton class has several forms:

```
public ImageButton(Image upImage, Image downImage,
                   String name, boolean shadeDownImage)
public ImageButton(Image upImage, Image downImage,
                   String name)
public ImageButton(Image upImage, Image downImage)
public ImageButton(Image upImage, String name)
public ImageButton(Image upImage)
```

All forms of the constructor take a handle to an Image object that will appear on the face of the button in the *up* state—the *up-image*. Where the constructor takes a second image, that image is used on the face of the button in the *down* state—the *down-image*. If no down-image is specified, a darkened version of the up-image is used. When a down-image is specified, it too is darkened unless *false* is passed as the last argument to the first form of the constructor shown previously. Where the constructors take a string argument, the string is used by the button as the button's name. By default, the name of the ImageButton is passed as part of the ActionEvent sent to listeners when the button is pressed. The forms of the constructor that take no name parameter use the string `ImageButton` to identify the ImageButton.*

IMPLEMENTATION. Much of the basic implementation of the ImageButton class parallels that of the Dial class. The implementation is responsible for rendering the button, changing its image when an appropriate event occurs, and generating events that can be passed through the event chain. Probably the two most significant differences between the ImageButton and Dial implementations are that the ImageButton creates its visual representation from images rather than from drawing primitives and that the ImageButton must handle user interaction differently than the Dial.

The Dial class was created entirely from drawing methods of the Graphics class. The implementation of the ImageButton class employs a combination of drawing primitives and image manipulation. For example, the edges of the button that generate the three-dimensional effect can be created with methods in the Graphics class. However, in order to display the image on the face of the button and the darkened image that is shown when the button is pressed, the ImageButton must directly manage and manipulate AWT Image objects.

Whereas the Dial is a new user interface object with no close parallel in the AWT package, the ImageButton is modeled after the AWT Button. Users have a priori expectations of how the ImageButton should react to certain patterns of interaction. For instance, when a button is pressed, if the user drags the pointer off the button prior to releasing the button, nothing happens; no event is generated. The ImageButton class must behave exactly like an AWT Button to be acceptable to users.

---

* The buttons created by the ImageButton class are the same size as the image passed to the constructor. On the CD-ROM accompanying this book is a *ScaledImageButton* class that subclasses ImageButton. The ScaledImageButton class will scale the image to fit a specified width and height.

The source code for the ImageButton class is shown in Fig. 4.26. Like the Dial, the ImageButton's implementation falls into code associated with initialization, drawing, and event handling. As before, each of these categories of the implementation are discussed separately.

```java
package ajp.awt;

import java.io.*;
import java.awt.*;
import java.awt.image.*;
import java.awt.event.*;
import java.util.*;

/**
 * A button that allows the look of the button to be defined by an
 * Image object passed to the constructor.  The behavior of the
 * ImageButton is otherwise similar to the AWT Button class.
 *
 * @version 2.6
 **/
public class ImageButton extends Component {
    static final long serialVersionUID = 1852071232547249930L;
    static final String actionListenerK = "actionL";

    static int nButtons = 0;

    protected transient ActionListener actionListener;

    protected String actionCommand;

    // the up (lighter)  and down (darker) images for the button's face
    protected Image upImage;
    protected Image downImage;

    // double-buffer for the widget
    private Image offImage;

    // dimensions of the button
    protected int height = 0;
    protected int width = 0;
    // Is the button currently pressed
    protected boolean buttonUp;
    // Name of the Button
    private String name;
    // If true, the "down" image is derived by filtering the "up" image.
    private boolean shadeDownImage = true;
    // The container for the button.
    private Container parent;
```

Figure 4.26
The ImageButton
class.

```
/**
 * Create the ImageButton using the Image  passed on the face of the
 * button.
 **/
public ImageButton(Image upImage, Image downImage,
                   String name, boolean shadeDownImage) {
    this.upImage = upImage;
    this.downImage = downImage;
    this.name = new String(name);
    this.shadeDownImage = shadeDownImage;
    enableEvents(AWTEvent.MOUSE_EVENT_MASK);
}

/**
 * Create the ImageButton using the Image  passed on the face of the
 * button.
 **/
public ImageButton(Image upImage, Image downImage, String name) {
    this(upImage, downImage, name, true);
}

/**
 * Create the ImageButton using the Image  passed on the face of the
 * button.
 **/
public ImageButton(Image upImage, Image downImage) {
    this(upImage, downImage, "Image Button" + ++nButtons);
}

/**
 * Create the ImageButton using the Image  passed on the face of the
 * button.
 **/
public ImageButton(Image img, String name) {
    this(img, (Image)null, name);
}

/**
 * Create the ImageButton using the Image  passed on the face of the
 * button.
 **/
public ImageButton(Image img) {
    this(img, (Image)null);
}

/**
 * Available for sub-classes that wish to auto-scale images.
 * Call this method before the button is added to the container.
 **/
protected void setButtonSize(int width, int height) {
    this.width = width;
    this.height = height;
}
```

Figure 4.26

(*Continued*).

```
/**
 * Get the name of the button.
 **/
public String getName() {
    return new String(name);
}

/**
 * Set up the button. Load the images and wait for them.
 **/
public void addNotify() {
    Image downSource;
    super.addNotify();

    parent = getParent();

    // Use a MediaTracer to download the images.
    MediaTracker tracker = new MediaTracker(this);

    // Where do we get the down image from?
    downSource = (downImage == null) ? upImage : downImage;

    if (shadeDownImage) {
        FilteredImageSource f =
            new FilteredImageSource(downSource.getSource(),
                                    new PressFilter(25));
        downImage = createImage(f);
    }

    tracker.addImage(upImage, 0);
    tracker.addImage(downImage, 0);
    try {
        tracker.waitForAll();
    }
    catch (InterruptedException e) {
        System.out.println("Error waiting for button's up & down images.");
    }
    if (tracker.isErrorID(0)) {
        System.out.println("Media Tracker Error. Check image location.");
    }

    if (height == 0) {
        height = upImage.getHeight(this);
    }
    if (width == 0) {
        width = upImage.getWidth(this);
    }
    //Add some padding to the image to accomodate the 3D border.
    height += 4;
    width += 4;
    offImage = createImage(width, height);
    buttonUp = true;
    drawButton();
}
```

Figure 4.26

(Continued).

```
    // Overridden to avoid flicker
    public void update(Graphics g) {
        paint(g);
    }

    /**
     * Draw the button.
     **/
    public void paint(Graphics g) {
        g.drawImage(offImage, 0, 0, this);
    }

    /**
     * The actual drawing of the button is done here.
     **/
    private void drawButton() {
        Color c = parent.getBackground();
        Graphics dg;

        dg = offImage.getGraphics();
        // Draw the 3D rect for the button.
        dg.setColor(c);
        dg.fill3DRect(0, 0, width, height, buttonUp);
        // Now paint the image in the center of the button
        if (buttonUp) {
            dg.drawImage(upImage, 2, 2, width-4, height-4, this);
        }
        else {
            dg.drawImage(downImage, 2, 2, width-4, height-4, this);
        }
        dg.dispose();
    }

    /**
     * What is the smallest size supported?  Needed by Layout Managers.
     **/
    public Dimension getMinimumSize() {
        return (new Dimension(width, height));
    }

    /**
     * What is the desired size of the button?  Needed by Layout Managers.
     **/
    public Dimension getPreferredSize() {
        return getMinimumSize();
    }

    /**
     * Handle events
     **/
    protected void processMouseEvent(MouseEvent e) {
        boolean redraw = false;
        switch(e.getID()) {
```

Figure 4.26
(Continued).

```
            case MouseEvent.MOUSE_PRESSED:
                  buttonUp = false;
                  redraw = true;
                  break;
            case MouseEvent.MOUSE_RELEASED:
                  int x = e.getX();
                  int y = e.getY();
                  // if the mouse up happens outside the button,
                  // or if the mouse down initiated elsewhere, ignore.
                  if (! buttonUp && (x <= width && x >= 0) &&
                      (y <= height && y >= 0)) {
                        processActionEvent(new ActionEvent(this, 0,
                                                     getActionCommand()));
                  }
                  buttonUp = true;
                  redraw = true;
                  break;
        }
        if (redraw) {
              drawButton();
              repaint();
        }
  }

  /**
   * Adds the specified action listener to receive action events
   * from this button.
   **/
  public void addActionListener(ActionListener l) {
      actionListener = AJPEventMulticaster.add(actionListener, l);
  }

  /**
   * Removes the specified action listener so it no longer receives
   * action events from this button.
   **/
  public void removeActionListener(ActionListener l) {
      actionListener = AJPEventMulticaster.remove(actionListener, l);
  }

  /**
   * Sets the command name of the action event fired by this button.
   * By default this will be set to the label of the button.
   **/
  public void setActionCommand(String command) {
      actionCommand = command;
  }

  /**
   * Returns the command name of the action event fired by this button.
   **/
  public String getActionCommand() {
```

Figure 4.26
(*Continued*).

```
          return (actionCommand == null? name : actionCommand);
    }

    /**
     * Processes action events occurring on this button by
     * dispatching them to any registered ActionListener objects.
     **/
    protected void processActionEvent(ActionEvent ev) {
        if (actionListener != null) {
            actionListener.actionPerformed(ev);
        }
    }

    /**
     * Returns the parameter String of this button.
     **/
    protected String paramString() {
        return super.paramString() + ",name=" + name;
    }

    /////////////// Serialization support. //////////////////////
    private int imageButtonSerializedDataVersion = 1;

    /**
     * Write the button to the Output stream.  Must save the
     ^ Listener references independently.
     **/
    private void writeObject(ObjectOutputStream s) throws IOException {
        s.defaultWriteObject();
        AJPEventMulticaster.write(s, actionListenerK, actionListener);
        s.writeObject(null);
    }

    /**
     * Read the ImageButton from the given stream.
     **/
    private void readObject(ObjectInputStream s)
                        throws ClassNotFoundException, IOException {
        s.defaultReadObject();

        Object keyOrNull;
        while(null != (keyOrNull = s.readObject())) {
            String key = ((String)keyOrNull).intern();

            if (actionListenerK == key)
                addActionListener((ActionListener)(s.readObject()));
            else // skip value for unrecognized key
                s.readObject();
        }
    }
}
```

Figure 4.26
(Continued).

INITIALIZATION. Most of the initialization of the ImageButton class happens in the `addNotify()` method. The connection to the native toolkit is needed to support the creation of the images used by the ImageButton. Within the `addNotify()` method is a *MediaTracker* object that is used to force the downloading of images from their source when the ImageButton is added to a container. Since there are two ways that the down-image for the button can be provided—either explicitly by the programmer or implicitly by deriving it from the up-image—there is some logic in `addNotify()` to set up the down-image before downloading it. First, the source of the down-image must be determined:

```
downSource = (downImage == null) ? upImage : downImage;
```

If no down-image was passed to the constructor, `downImage` will be null and the `upImage` is used as the source for the down-image. Once the source for the ImageButton's down-image has been determined, the down-image may need to be filtered. In this case, filtering the image means passing the pixels of the image through a method that darkens them by 25 percent as the image is downloaded. This filtering is done through an *RGBImageFilter* subclass called `PressFilter` (see `java.awt` `.image.RGBImageFilter`). The PressFilter class (see Fig. 4.27) overrides the method `filterRGB()` from RGBImageFilter. The `filterRGB()` method is passed each pixel of the image as it is downloaded. The integer pixel is decomposed into red, green, and blue components. The RGB values are multiplied by a percentage, throttled to the range 0 to 255, and then recomposed into an integer pixel value that is returned to the caller.

To get the pixels of the source image passed through the PressFilter, a *FilteredImageSource* object is used (see `java.awt.image.FilteredImage-` `Source`). The FilteredImageSource's constructor is passed an *ImageProducer* object and an *ImageFilter* object. The ImageProducer is extracted from the source image using the method `getSource()`. The ImageFilter object is an instance of the PressFilter class just described. Once the FilteredImage-Source is created, it can be passed to the `Component.createImage()` method, which will then use the filter when the image is downloaded.

Thus, when the `shadeDownImage` boolean is set to *true* the shading will be performed on the down-image:

```
if (shadeDownImage) {
    FilteredImageSource f =
        new FilteredImageSource(downSource.getSource(),
                                new PressFilter(25));
    downImage = createImage(f);
}
```

```
package ajp.awt;

package ajp.awt;

/**
 * A class to filter the button's "down" image.  Simply darkens the
 * RGB values of all pixels.
 */
class PressFilter extends RGBImageFilter {
    private int percent;
    private boolean brighter;
    private int factor;

    /**
     * Create the Filter
     **/
    public PressFilter(int percent) {
        this.percent = percent;
        canFilterIndexColorModel = true;
        factor = (100 - percent);
    }

    /**
     * Filter the pixels.
     **/
    public int filterRGB(int x, int y, int rgb) {
        // Strip out the R, G, B bits
        int r = (rgb >> 16) & 0xff;
        int g = (rgb >> 8) & 0xff;
        int b = (rgb >> 0) & 0xff;

        // scale the RGB values
        r = (r * factor / 100);
        g = (g * factor / 100);
        b = (b * factor / 100);

        // Throttle the values to the acceptable range
        if (r < 0) r = 0;
        if (g < 0) g = 0;
        if (b < 0) b = 0;
        if (r > 255) r = 255;
        if (g > 255) g = 255;
        if (b > 255) b = 255;
        // recombine and return
        return (rgb & 0xff000000) | (r << 16) | (g << 8) | (b << 0);
    }

}
```

Figure 4.27
The PressFilter class.

The last part of the ImageButton initialization is the creation of `buffer`, an off-screen image used for double buffering the drawing of the button. The off-screen image is created at 4 pixels larger in each dimension than the up-image. This is done to accommodate the highlights used on the border that create the three-dimensional look of the button.

DRAWING. The ImageButton is drawn using fairly standard double-buffering techniques. The images and highlights are rendered into the off-screen image in the `drawButton()` method using the `fill3DRect()` and `drawImage()` methods. Note that `fill3DRect()` was intentionally selected over `draw3DRect()` to clear the off-screen image prior to drawing the up-image or down-image into it. This allows transparent GIFs to be used on the face of the button without the images overlaying each other. First a filled three-dimensional rectangle is drawn using the default background color of the parent container; then either the up-image or the down-image is drawn, depending on the state of the ImageButton as indicated by the boolean `buttonUp`.

The off-screen buffer is copied into the parent container's Graphics object in the `paint()` method. As with the Dial class, repainting of the widget is triggered by events. Here, the ImageButton enables mouse events in its constructor much as the Dial class does. The events are delivered to the ImageButton through the `processMouseEvent()` method, which eventually triggers a redraw by calling the `drawButton()` method.

EVENT HANDLING. To give the Image button the same feel to the user as standard AWT buttons, the following behavior is implemented in the `processMouseEvent()` method:

- When a MOUSE_PRESSED event is detected, the down-image is displayed and the boolean `buttonUp` is set to *false*.

- When a MOUSE_RELEASED event is detected, the up-image is displayed and an ActionEvent is generated only if `buttonUp` is *false*.

- If a MOUSE_RELEASED is detected but its coordinates fall outside the bounds of the ImageButton, the up-image is displayed but no ActionEvent is generated.

The second case prevents events from being generated when the user presses the mouse button outside the ImageButton, drags the mouse pointer onto the ImageButton, and releases the button while the pointer is inside the bounds of the ImageButton. The third case allows the user to cancel the button press by dragging the mouse off the ImageButton before releasing the mouse button. The ImageButton generates events only when a MOUSE_RELEASED event is seen. The ImageButton creates an ActionEvent object and passes the event to all registered listeners.

From both the programmer's and the user's perspectives, the Image-Button is just like the AWT Button. Both buttons provide visual feedback to the user and use an identical method for providing feedback to the programmer through events.

LEDPanel

The final Component-based widget example is probably the most complex of the three. It is a numeric display and input widget called an *LED-Panel*. The LEDPanel is a Component subclass that represents a collection of seven-segment LEDs, like those used in digital clocks, for example. Like the Dial and ImageButton classes, the LEDPanel must construct its visual representation from scratch, drawing it into a canvas. Unlike the Dial or ImageButton, when the LEDPanel is used as an input area it must interact with the keyboard and deal with input focus.

Constructing LEDs programmatically can be a good exercise in object-oriented programming. LEDs lend themselves very nicely to decomposition into separate objects. In this implementation, the LEDPanel is composed of *SevenSegmentLED* objects which are themselves composed of *LEDSegments*. The LEDSegments are the lowest-level objects in the LED-Panel. Each LEDSegment is an individual six-sided object that can render itself in either of two colors, one for *on* and one for *off*. The SevenSeg-mentLED class is a subclass of the LED class, containing seven LEDSeg-ments, arranged four vertically and three horizontally as shown in Fig. 4.28. The SevenSegmentLED class can display numbers from 0 to 9 and the letters *E, r,* and *o.* The LED class is an abstract class that is used as a starting point for creating specific types of LED objects. For instance, LEDs for displaying more than just numeric values can be created by subclasses with more than seven LEDSegments.

To keep the discussion manageable, the focus of this section is on the LEDPanel implementation itself rather than on the lower-level classes, LEDSegment, LED, and SevenSegmentLED. The full sources for all the classes can be found on the CD-ROM that accompanies this book and in App. A.

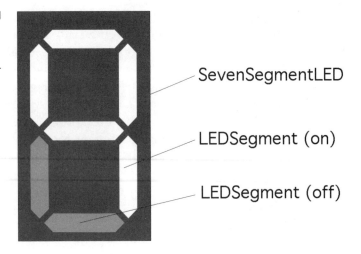

Figure 4.28
A SevenSegmentLED
object.

SevenSegmentLED

LEDSegment (on)

LEDSegment (off)

The LEDPanel class supports several variations of the object based on parameters passed to the constructors. There are five forms of the constructor:

1. `public LEDPanel(int nDigits)`

2. `public LEDPanel(int nDigits, boolean readOnly)`

3. `public LEDPanel(int nDigits, boolean readOnly, boolean neg)`

4. `public LEDPanel(int nDigits, boolean readOnly, boolean neg,`
   `            boolean wrap)`

5. `public LEDPanel(int nDigits, boolean readOnly, boolean neg,`
   `            boolean wrap, int width, int thick)`

The parameters passed to the constructors determine:

- The number of LED digits in the panel
- Whether the panel is read-only
- Whether the panel supports negative numbers
- Whether the counter goes to 0 on overflow or displays an error message
- The size of the individual LEDs in the panel

When an LEDPanel is created that supports negative numbers, the far-left digit is reserved for the minus sign.

The API supported by the class consists of the methods described briefly in Table 4.3. The API supports setting the values and getting the value of the LEDPanel, querying its state with respect to overflow, resetting it, and displaying an error message on the panel.

A simple demonstration of LEDPanel API is shown in Fig. 4.29. The example applet, LEDTest, consists of two LEDPanels: the one at the top of the applet is read-only and is used as the display for a counter; the one below it is used as an input area. The user can select a digit in the lower LEDPanel, change the value of the digit, then press the *Reset* button at the bottom of the applet to change the current value of the upper LEDPanel to the value displayed in the lower LEDPanel. The two *Checkboxes* at the bottom of the applet allow the direction of the counter to be changed. If the upper LEDPanel overflows, it displays the panel's error message, as shown in Fig. 4.29. The source code for the applet is shown in Fig. 4.30.

The LEDTest applet implements the *Runnable* interface and creates a separate thread, *updateThread,* to execute the applet's `run()` method. The `run()` method begins by calling the clearing `counter`, the upper LED-Panel. The value of `setter`, the lower LEDPanel, is then extracted by calling the `getValue()` method, and is assigned into the upper LED-Panel using the `setValue()` method:

TABLE 4.3	**Method signature**	**Description**
Public Methods of the LEDPanel Class	`void setForeground(Color fg)`	Sets the foreground color of the LEDs in the LEDPanel
	`void setBackground(Color bg)`	Sets the background color of the LEDs in the LEDPanel
	`synchronized int getValue()`	Gets the current value displayed in the LEDPanel
	`synchronized int setValue(int val)`	Sets the value of the LEDPanel
	`void reset()`	Clears the LEDPanel and sets its value to zero
	`boolean hasOverflowed()`	Returns *true* if the LEDPanel has exceeded the maximum it can display
	`void error()`	Sets the value displayed on the LED-Panel to as many letters of the word *Error* as can be displayed

Figure 4.29
An applet using two
LEDPanels.

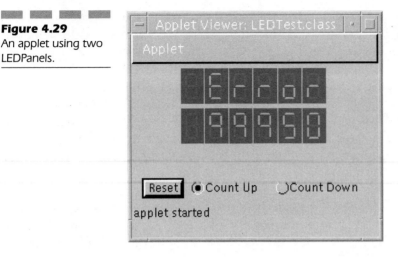

```
import java.applet.*;
import java.awt.*;
import java.awt.event.*;
import ajp.awt.*;

/**
 * A single adaptor for Check boxes and reset button.
 **/
class LEDUIAction implements ActionListener, ItemListener {
    static final int INCREMENT = 0;
    static final int DECREMENT = 1;
    static final int RESET     = 2;

    int tag;
    LEDTest led;

    public LEDUIAction(int tag, LEDTest l) {
        led = l;
        this.tag = tag;
    }

    public void itemStateChanged(ItemEvent e) {
        processEvent();
    }

    public void actionPerformed(ActionEvent e) {
        processEvent();
    }
```

Figure 4.30
The source code for
the LEDPanel test
applet.

```java
      void processEvent() {
          switch(tag) {
          case INCREMENT:
                led.setCountUp(true);
                break;
          case DECREMENT:
                led.setCountUp(false);
                break;
          case RESET:
                led.reset();
                break;
          }
      }
}

/**
 * A test applet that shows the programmatic interface to the
 * LEDPanel class.
 **/
public class LEDTest extends Applet implements Runnable {
      LEDPanel counter;
      LEDPanel setter;
      int count;
      Thread updateThread;
      boolean visible = false;
      boolean countUp = true;

      public synchronized void setCountUp(boolean val) {
          countUp = val;
      }

      public void init() {
          Checkbox cbUp;
          Checkbox cbDown;
          Button reset;
          // Create the upper panel and the two LCDPanels
          ImagePanel lp = new ImagePanel(getImage(getCodeBase(),
                                           "images/backdrop.jpg"));
          lp.add(counter = new LEDPanel(6, true, true)); // make it read-only
          lp.add(setter = new LEDPanel(6, false, true));
          setter.setValue(99750);

          // Create the controls
          Panel bp = new Panel();
          bp.add(reset = new Button("Reset"));
          CheckboxGroup cbg = new CheckboxGroup();
          bp.add(cbUp = new Checkbox("Count Up", cbg, true));
          bp.add(cbDown = new Checkbox("Count Down", cbg, false));

          // Add the listeners
          reset.addActionListener(new LEDUIAction(LEDUIAction.RESET, this));
          cbUp.addItemListener(new LEDUIAction(LEDUIAction.INCREMENT, this));
          cbDown.addItemListener(new LEDUIAction(LEDUIAction.DECREMENT, this));
```

Figure 4.30
(Continued).

```
          setLayout(new BorderLayout());
          add("Center", lp);
          add("South", bp);
          resize(275, 150);

          // Create the thread to run the counter and start it
          updateThread = new Thread(this);
          updateThread.start();
     }

     public void run() {
          counter.reset();
          count = setter.getValue();
          counter.setValue(count);
          while(true) {
               try {
                    Thread.sleep(100);
               }
               catch (InterruptedException e) {}
               if (countUp)
                    count++;
               else
                    count--;
               if (visible)
                    counter.setValue(count);
               if (counter.hasOverflowed())
                    break;
          }
     }

     public void stop() {
          visible = false;
     }

     public void start() {
          visible = true;
     }

     public void reset() {
          if (updateThread.isAlive()) {
               updateThread.stop();
          }
          updateThread = new Thread(this);
          updateThread.start();
     }
}
```

Figure 4.30
(*Continued*).

```
counter.reset();
count = setter.getValue();
counter.setValue(count);
```

The `run()` method then enters an infinite loop that causes update Thread to sleep for 100 milliseconds, either increment or decrement the variable `count`, then update counter with the current value of `count`. The upper LEDPanel is checked for overflow after each update and the loop is exited if an overflow is detected.

The controls at the bottom of the applet interact with the two LED-Panels through the applet's `action()` method. The `action()` method traps all events and filters for those targeted at the *Reset* button or one of the two Checkboxes. If the *Reset* button is pressed, the update thread is killed and a new thread is instantiated and started. The Checkboxes toggle the variable `countUp`, which is used in the `run()` method to determine whether to increment or decrement `count`.

IMPLEMENTATION. The implementation of the LEDPanel follows the basic model of the other two Canvas-based widgets discussed in this chapter. In the case of the LEDPanel, the bulk of the code is involved with creating and drawing the LEDs. Since that aspect of the implementation offers nothing additional to the discussion of Canvas-based widgets, the source code for the LEDSegment, LED, and SevenSegmentLED classes is not presented here. The full source code for these classes is presented on the CD-ROM, and in App. A for those without immediate access to a CD-ROM. The source code for the LEDPanel class is presented in Fig. 4.31.

```
package ajp.awt;

import java.awt.*;
import java.awt.event.*;
import java.util.EventListener;
import java.io.ObjectOutputStream;
import java.io.ObjectInputStream;
import java.io.IOException;

/**
 * A panel of LEDs for displaying positive and negative integer values.
 * If the value is too large for the display, it will overflow, printing
 * "Error" in the display, or, optionally, it will truncate the higher
 * order digits, effectively wrapping to zero.
 *
```

Figure 4.31
The LEDPanel class.

```
 * @version 2.5
 **/
public class LEDPanel extends Component {
     static final long serialVersionUID = 3666503096819247541L;

     // the off-screen graphics object
     private Graphics offG;

     // the off-screen image
     private Image img;

     // array of LEDs
     private SevenSegmentLED led[];

     // current value;
     private int value;

     // x coordinate of panel
     private int x;

     // y coordinate of panel
     private int y;

     // width of the panel
     private int width;

     // height of the panel
     private int height;

     // FG and BG colors
     private Color fgColor = Color.green;
     private Color bgColor = Color.darkGray;

     // Has the underlying canvas peer been created yet?
     private boolean peerCreated = false;

     // Does this panel of LEDs display negative numbers?
     // If so, the far left LED is reserved for the minus sign.
     private boolean canBeNegative = false;

     // Does this panel of LEDs show error on overflow or does it wrap to 0?
     private boolean canWrap = false;

     // Does this panel allow user input
     private boolean readOnly = false;

     // indicates an overflow has occured
     private boolean overflow = false;

     // Has the panel been painted?
     private boolean painted = false;

     private static final int DEFAULT_WIDTH = 25;
     private static final int DEFAULT_THICK = 2;
     private static final int PAD = 2;
```

Figure 4.31
(*Continued*).

```
/**
 * Create a panel of LEDs for displaying integer values.
 **/
public LEDPanel(int nDigits, boolean readOnly, boolean neg, boolean wrap,
                int width, int thick) {
    Dimension d = new Dimension(0,0);
    // Save args...
    this.x = 0;
    this.y = 0;
    this.width = 0;
    this.height = 0;
    this.readOnly = readOnly;
    canBeNegative = neg;
    canWrap = wrap;

    // create the panel of LEDs
    led = new SevenSegmentLED[nDigits];
    // create each LED and position it in the panel
    for(int i = 0; i < nDigits; i++) {
        led[i] = new SevenSegmentLED(x + i*(width + PAD), y, width, thick);
        // accumulate the width of the whole panel of LEDs
        d = led[i].size();
        this.width += (d.width + PAD);
    }
    this.height = d.height;
    enableEvents(AWTEvent.MOUSE_EVENT_MASK | AWTEvent.KEY_EVENT_MASK);
}

/**
 * Create a panel of LEDs for displaying positive integer values.
 * No "wrapping" performed.  Overflows will display error message.
 **/
public LEDPanel(int nDigits) {
    this(nDigits, false, false, false, DEFAULT_WIDTH, DEFAULT_THICK);
}

/**
 * Create a panel of LEDs for displaying positive integer values.
 * No "wrapping" performed.  Overflows will display error message.
 **/
public LEDPanel(int nDigits, boolean readOnly) {
    this(nDigits, readOnly, false, false, DEFAULT_WIDTH, DEFAULT_THICK);
}

/**
 * Create a panel of LEDs for displaying positive or negative integer
 * values.  No "wrapping" performed.  Overflows will display error
 * message.
 **/
public LEDPanel(int nDigits, boolean readOnly, boolean neg) {
    this(nDigits, readOnly, neg, false, DEFAULT_WIDTH, DEFAULT_THICK);
}
```

Figure 4.31
(*Continued*).

```
    /**
     * Create a panel of LEDs for displaying positive or negative integer
     * values.
     **/
    public LEDPanel(int nDigits, boolean readOnly,
                    boolean neg, boolean wrap) {
        this(nDigits, readOnly, neg, wrap, DEFAULT_WIDTH, DEFAULT_THICK);
    }

    /**
     * Set the foreground color of the LED panel. This corresponds to the
     * "on" color of the individual LED's segments.
     **/
    public void setForeground(Color fg) {
        fgColor = fg;

        for(int i = 0; i < led.length; i++) {
            led[i].setForeground(fg);
        }
    }

    /**
     * Sets the background color of the LED panel.  The segments will get a
     * slightly lighter version of this for a realistic effect.
     **/
    public void setBackground(Color bg) {
        bgColor = bg;

        for(int i = 0; i < led.length; i++) {
            led[i].setBackground(bg);
        }
    }

    /**
     * Get the value of the LED panel.
     **/
    public synchronized int getValue() {
        return value;
    }

    /**
     * Set the value of the LED panel.
     **/
    public synchronized void setValue(int val) {
        value = val;
        int stop = 0;

        if (overflow)
            return;

        // set the LEDs
        if (canBeNegative) {
            if (val < 0) {
                led[0].setValue(SevenSegmentLED.MINUS);
            }
```

Figure 4.31
(Continued).

```
        else {
            led[0].setValue(SevenSegmentLED.OFF);
        }
        stop = 1;
    }

    // set the digits right to left
    val = Math.abs(val);
    for (int i = led.length - 1; i >= stop; i--) {
        if (val > 0) {
            led[i].setValue(val%10);
            val = val / 10;
        }
        else {
            if (i == led.length - 1) {
                led[i].setValue(0);
            }
            else {
                led[i].setValue(SevenSegmentLED.OFF);
            }
        }
    }
    // check for overflow and display "Error" if allowed.
    if (!canWrap && val > 0) {
        overflow = true;
        error();
    }
    if (peerCreated) {
        drawPanel();
        repaint();
    }
}

/**
 * Reset the value of the LED panel based on user input.
 **/
private synchronized void resetValue() {
    int val = 0;
    int tmp;
    int stop = 0;
    int mul = 1;

    // set the LEDs
    if (canBeNegative) {
        tmp = led[0].getValue();
        if (tmp == SevenSegmentLED.MINUS) {
            mul = -1;
        }
        stop = 1;
        }

        // get the digits right to left
        for (int i = led.length - 1; i >= stop; i--) {
            tmp = led[i].getValue();
```

Figure 4.31
(Continued).

```
                        if (tmp >= 0) {
                             val +=  tmp * mul;
                        }
                        mul *= 10;
                }
                setValue(val);
        }

        /**
         * Reset the LED panel.  Clears overflow flag and any value or error
         * displayed.
         **/
        public void reset() {
            clear();
            overflow = false;
            value = 0;
        }

        /**
         * Check for overflow condition.
         **/
        public boolean hasOverflowed() {
            return overflow;
        }

        /**
         * Make display show the word "Error", "Err" or "E" depending
         * on the number of digits in the display.
         **/
        public void error() {
            clear();
            if (led.length >= 5) {
                   led[led.length-1].setValue(SevenSegmentLED.LETTER_r);
                   led[led.length-2].setValue(SevenSegmentLED.LETTER_o);
                   led[led.length-3].setValue(SevenSegmentLED.LETTER_r);
                   led[led.length-4].setValue(SevenSegmentLED.LETTER_r);
                   led[led.length-5].setValue(SevenSegmentLED.LETTER_E);
            }
            else if (led.length >= 3) {
                   led[led.length-1].setValue(SevenSegmentLED.LETTER_r);
                   led[led.length-2].setValue(SevenSegmentLED.LETTER_r);
                   led[led.length-3].setValue(SevenSegmentLED.LETTER_E);
            }
            else {
                   led[led.length-1].setValue(SevenSegmentLED.LETTER_E);
            }
        }

        /**
         * Clear the LED panel.
         **/
        void clear() {
            for(int i = 0; i < led.length; i++) {
```

Figure 4.31
(Continued).

```
                    led[i].setValue(SevenSegmentLED.OFF);
        }
    }

    /**
     * How big is the LED panel.
     **/
    public Dimension getMinimumSize() {
        return new Dimension(width, height);
    }

    public Dimension getPreferredSize() {
        return getMinimumSize();
    }

    /**
     * draw the panel into its off screen image.
     **/
    void drawPanel() {
        if (!painted) {
            offG.setColor(getParent().getBackground());
            offG.fillRect(0, 0, width, height);
            painted = true;
        }
        for(int i = 0; i < led.length; i++) {
            led[i].draw(offG);
        }
    }

    /**
     * Post-peer creation initializations.
     **/
    public void addNotify() {
        super.addNotify();
        img = createImage(width, height);
        offG = img.getGraphics();
        setForeground(fgColor);
        setBackground(bgColor);
        drawPanel();
        peerCreated = true;
    }

    /**
     * copy the off-screen image to the screen.
     **/
    public void paint(Graphics g) {
        g.drawImage(img, 0, 0, this);
    }

    /**
     * Eliminate flicker in the Canvas
     **/
    public void update(Graphics g) {
        paint(g);
    }
```

Figure 4.31

(Continued).

```
/**
 * Handle mouse events.
 **/
protected void processMouseEvent(MouseEvent e) {
    boolean changed = false;

    switch(e.getID()) {
    case MouseEvent.MOUSE_RELEASED:
        if (!readOnly) {
            // Get the input focus for future keystrokes.
            requestFocus();

            // Step across the LEDs
            for(int i = 0; i < led.length; i++) {
                if (led[i].inside(e.getX(), e.getY())) {
                    // if event is on a LED, select or deselect
                    if (led[i].isSelected()) {
                        led[i].deselect();
                    }
                    else {
                        led[i].select();
                    }
                    changed = true;
                }
                else if (led[i].isSelected()) {
                    // if event is not on LED and it is selected,
                    // deselect it.
                    led[i].deselect();
                    changed = true;
                }
            }
            if (changed) {
                // If any LED was changed, redraw and repaint.
                drawPanel();
                repaint();
            }
        }
        break;
    }
}

/**
 * Handle key press events.
 **/
protected void processKeyEvent(KeyEvent e) {
    char key = e.getKeyChar();

    switch(e.getID()) {
    case KeyEvent.KEY_PRESSED:
        if (!readOnly) {
            if ((key == '-' || key == ' ' || key == '+') &&
                led[0].isSelected() && canBeNegative) {
```

Figure 4.31
(Continued).

```
                      // Process +/- for LEDPanels that can go negative
                      if (key == '-') {
                          led[0].setValue(SevenSegmentLED.MINUS);
                      }
                      else {
                          led[0].setValue(SevenSegmentLED.OFF);
                      }
                      resetValue();
                      return;
                  }

              if (key >= '0' && key <= '9') {
                  // If keystroke is a number, step across the LEDs
                  for(int i = 0; i < led.length; i++) {
                      if (led[i].isSelected()) {
                          // if current LED is selected change value
                          led[i].setValue(key - '0');
                          resetValue();
                      }
                      break;
                  }
              }
          }
        break;
      }
    }
}
```

Figure 4.31
(*Continued*).

The key difference between the LEDPanel implementation and that of either Dial or ImageButton is in the event handling. With one exception, the general initialization and drawing of the LEDPanel is very similar to that of the other two widgets. The exception is in the initialization. Whenever the setValue() method is called, the value it is passed should be drawn into the LEDPanel immediately. However, setValue() can be called any time after an LEDPanel is created, and the canvas and image for double buffering into the canvas are not fully initialized until after addNotify() is called. To avoid having code like

```
LEDPanel led = new LEDPanel(6);
led.setValue(42);
```

generate exceptions, a flag, peerCreated, is checked in the setValue() method before the LEDPanel is redrawn. In addNotify(), once the canvas and double-buffering image have been created, the peerCreated flag is set to *true*.

EVENT HANDLING. The purpose of the event handling in the LED-Panel is to enable its use as an input widget. The LEDPanel does not generate any events itself. The user interaction that is allowed in the widget is selecting one of the LEDs in the panel and typing either numbers, a space, or the plus or minus key.* To facilitate this interaction the LEDPanel uses the `processMouseEvent()` and `processKeyEvent()` methods.

In the `processMouseEvent()` method, three scenarios are possible:

1. The user selects an unselected LED, in which case any currently selected LED must be deselected.

2. The user selects an already selected LED, in which case that LED must be deselected.

3. The user presses the mouse button while pointing to an area not covered by an LED (e.g., between two LEDs).

Regardless of the scenario, when an event is delivered to `process-MouseEvent()` the LEDPanel requests the input focus by calling `requestFocus()`. Presumably, a user selects a LED to change the number it displays. By getting the input focus, subsequent keyboard events will be delivered to the LEDPanel. After requesting the input focus, the array of LEDs that comprises the panel is stepped across, and each LED is examined to see if the coordinates of the event fall within it. Any selected LED that is not the target of the event is deselected. Once the LED that is the target of the event is determined, its state (selected or deselected) will be toggled. Finally, if any LED was changed in the process of delivering the event, the panel is redrawn to reflect that change.

Keystrokes are processed in the `processKeyEvent()` method. When a keyboard event is delivered, the type of the LEDPanel is first checked. The panel must not be read-only to accept input. Next, if the panel is allowed to display negative numbers the keystroke is checked to see if it is *plus, minus,* or *space.* If it is one of those three keys, the far-left LED is checked and, if found to be currently selected, the state of the LED is changed. When numeric keystrokes are delivered, the LEDs are checked. If an LED is selected, it is changed to display the number that was typed, and the value associated with the LEDPanel as a whole is reset.

---

* A selected LED is indicated visually by highlighting its perimeter with a line of contrasting color, red by default. The selection of LEDs is actually implemented in the LED class. The LEDPanel just calls the LED's `select()` method.

Custom Component Summary

There are fundamentally two ways of creating platform-independent custom widgets with AWT: subclassing from Container or Panel or subclassing from Component or Canvas. Container-based widgets are limited to combinations of existing widgets, typically those provided by AWT, and are usually the easiest to implement. The widget based on a Panel usually needs to provide event handling, event generation, and interaction between its constituent Components. Component-based widgets are typically more complex and more flexible. Since the widget is usually drawn from scratch using a combination of graphics primitives and images, there are virtually no limits to the widget's appearance. Like Container-based widgets, implementing Component-based widgets usually involves both handling and generating events.

Creating custom widgets adds a new dimension to programming with the Java AWT. Another readily customizable part of the AWT is the layout managers, which control how objects are placed in containers. By creating custom layout managers, you can not only have custom widgets, you can also organize them in new and interesting ways on the screen.

LayoutManager

When Components are added to Containers, they are merely added to an array maintained by the Container. The Container, in and of itself, does nothing to manage the placement of the objects it contains. That task is delegated to an *AWT LayoutManager.* There is a layout manager associated with all the standard AWT Container objects by default. Panels have a FlowLayout by default; Windows and Frames have a BorderLayout by default. If a container has no layout manager, it is the responsibility of the programmer to explicitly position all objects in the Container.* Furthermore, without a layout manager, the programmer must reposition the objects any time the container gets resized, if the relative positions of the contained objects are to be maintained.

---

* Since all the standard containers have layout managers by default, the only way to get a standard container with no layout manager is to explicitly set its layout manager to *null*. For example: `panel.setLayout(null)`.

By separating the method of laying out objects in a Container from the implementation of the container, the designers of the AWT have greatly enhanced the flexibility of the toolkit. Programmers are not limited to BorderLayouts, FlowLayouts, CardLayouts, and so on, but are free to implement their own layout mangers that enforce their own policies for arranging objects. If there is a drawback to this model it is that the added flexibility adds to complexity for the programmer. When designing a complex user interface, it can take a while to determine what combination of layout managers will give the interface just the right look.

The LayoutManager Model

The AWT LayoutManager is actually an interface, rather than a class. This gives programmers the most flexibility, for subclasses of other objects that act as layout managers can be created. For example, an applet can be created that is itself a layout manager. Programmers developing layout managers must simply create a class that implements the following five methods:

1. `void addLayoutComponent(String name, Component comp)`

2. `void removeLayoutComponent(Component comp)`

3. `Dimension preferredLayoutSize(Container parent)`

4. `Dimension minimumLayoutSize(Container parent)`

5. `void layoutContainer(Container parent)`

The first two methods in the interface, `addLayoutComponent()` and `removeLayoutComponent()`, are called from the Container class's `add()` and `remove()` methods. The `addLayoutComponent()` method is used to explicitly register a Component with the layout manager. Components that have been registered with the layout manager are removed with `removeLayoutComponent()`. Recall that the `add()` method of the Container class has three forms:

1. `void add(Component c)`

2. `void add(Component c, int pos)`

3. `void add(String s, Component c)`

The actual work of adding the Component is done in the second form of the `add()` method shown here. When a Component is added to a Container, a reference to the Component is saved in an array within the

Container. The `pos` argument passed to `add()` specifies the location in the array where the Component is to be added. The Container's array of Components is used by layout managers to determine what has been added to a Container. The Container provides accessor methods that can be used to get at the contents of the array:

```
int n = container.countComponents();

for (int i = 0 ; i < nmembers ; i++) {
    Component m = container.getComponent(i);
    // move the Component to the appropriate location
    ...
}
```

As it turns out, both of the other forms of the `add()` method eventually call the form that specifies the offset into the Component array. However, the last form of the `add()` method shown previously also calls the layout manager's `addLayoutComponent()`. This gives the layout manager an alternate method of determining what needs to be laid out in the Container. Consider the BorderLayout class. Components are added to a Panel or Frame that uses a BorderLayout, with calls to the `add()` method that look like:

```
add("North", label);
add("Center", canvas);
add("South", buttonPanel);
```

This form of the `add()` method will call the `addLayoutComponent()` method of the BorderLayout, passing it the Components and the strings that describe where the Components are to be placed. The BorderLayout will save a handle to up to five components, one for each of the positions: *north, south, east, west,* and *center.* When the BorderLayout lays out the Container, it doesn't walk across the Container's array of Components; instead, it looks only at the objects passed to it through `addLayoutComponent()`:

```
Component north, south, east, west, center;

public void layoutContainer(Container target) {
    ...
    if ((north != null) && north.visible) {
        // position the Component in the North
        ...
    }
    if ((south != null) && south.visible) {
        // position the Component in the South
        ...
```

```
        }
   if ((east != null) && east.visible) {
        // position the Component in the East
        ...
   }
   if ((west != null) && west.visible) {
        // position the Component in the West
        ...
   }
   if ((center != null) && center.visible) {
        // position the Component in the Center
        ...
   }
 }
```

So, layout managers that need to manage the references to contained objects directly must implement the addLayoutComponent() and removeLayoutComponent() methods. If the layout manager can rely on the array in the container to supply references to all the contained objects, both addLayoutComponent() and removeLayoutComponent() can be implemented as empty methods. For many classes of layout managers you need only write full implementations of three of the methods in the interface.

In order to be resized and positioned inside other containers correctly, a container must be able to calculate its size based on what it contains. The space needed to display the objects in a container is directly related to how the layout manager has arranged the contents, thus the need for the LayoutManager methods preferredLayoutSize() and minimumLayoutSize(). Both of these methods examine the contents of the container, either by traversing the container's component array or by looking at the objects the layout manager is tracking directly, and return a Dimension object that describes the total space that these objects require or prefer. An interesting note about these methods is that they are usually almost identical. Typically, the only difference is that as the components are being examined, preferredLayoutSize() calls each component's preferredSize() method, while minimumLayoutSize() calls each component's minimumSize() method. This similarity between the methods is exploited in the layout manager implementation that follows.

The final method in the LayoutManager API is layoutContainer(). The layoutContainer() method does the actual work of arranging the container's contents and resizing them as needed to accommodate the layout. The sequence of events that lead to calling layoutContainer() is illustrated in Fig. 4.32. Each Component has a flag, valid, that indicates whether or not it needs to be laid out. The valid flag is set to *false* when a component is added to a container or is reshaped (moved and/or resized). When a container is resized, the peer of the Frame or Window initiates a call to `validate()`, which eventually calls `layoutContainer()`. The `validate()` method of Container works recursively, so that any Panel inside another container will be validated and eventually laid out as well.

Example: A SortedLayout Manager

To illustrate how LayoutManagers are implemented, a variant of the FlowLayout is presented in the following sections. This new layout manager, the SortedLayout, arranges objects in a container in sorted order. Each object is added to a container using the form of the `add()` method that takes a string and a component as arguments:

```
Panel p = new Panel();
p.setLayout(new SortedLayout());
p.add("A", new Button("Letter A"));
```

Figure 4.32
Methods that trigger the laying out of a Container.

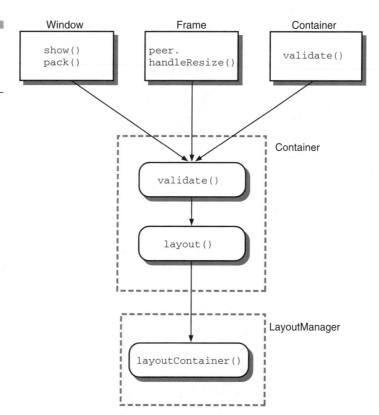

The string passed to add() is used by the SortedLayout manager to sort the objects alphabetically. The sorted objects are then arranged using a policy identical to java.awt.FlowLayout. Figure 4.33 shows an applet that uses a SortedLayout manager to arrange ImageButtons in alphabetical order in a pop-up frame. Each ImageButton contains a picture of a U.S. president. The buttons are added to the frame with the president's last name as the sorting key, using code equivalent to the following:

```
frame.setLayout(new SortedLayout());
String name = "Lincoln";
Image im = createImage(getCodeBase(), "images/" + name
                                      + ".gif");
frame.add(name, new ImageButton(im));
```

The actual code for this example is presented in Chap. 9. A discussion of the full implementation of the example is not germane to understanding layout mangers. The only interaction the example program has with the SortedLayout manager is calling its constructor and, through the Frame's add() method, calling its addLayoutComponent() method.

Figure 4.33
An applet that uses a SortedLayout manager to sort ImageButtons.

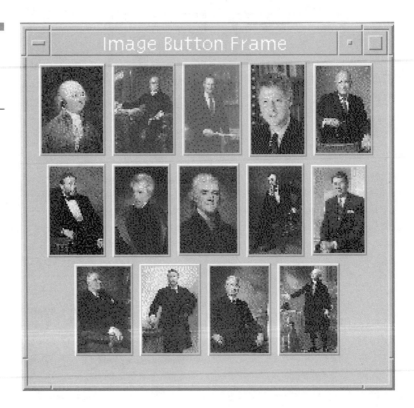

IMPLEMENTATION.   Under the hood of the SortedLayout manager is a BinaryTree, whose implementation is discussed in Chap. 2. Since the objects stored on a SortedList must implement the Comparable interface, a wrapper class, *SortedComponent*, allows the Components to be added to the SortedLayout. The SortedComponent class (see Fig. 4.34) consists of a Component, a String that stores the name associated with the Component, and the three methods required by the Comparable interface:

1. `boolean isLessThan(Comparable compObj);`

2. `boolean isGreaterThan(Comparable compObj) ;`

3. `boolean isEqualTo(Comparable compObj) ;`

When a Component is passed to the SortedLayout manager, it is placed in a SortedComponent wrapper and then added to the BinaryTree.

```
package ajp.awt;

import java.awt.*;
import java.util.Enumeration;
import ajp.util.*;

/**
 * A class to store components for sorting.
 *
 * @version 2.1
 **/
class SortedComponent implements Comparable, java.io.Serializable {
    // The name of the component, the sorting key
    private String name;
    // The component itself
    private Component comp;

    /**
     * Create a sorted component with the given name.
     **/
    SortedComponent(String name, Component c) {
        this.name = new String(name);
        comp = c;
    }

    /**
     * Get the component associated with this sorted component.
     **/
```

Figure 4.34
The SortedCompo-
nent class.

```
Component getComponent() {
     return comp;
}

/**
 * Get the name associated with this sorted component.  The name
 * is the key on which the components are sorted.
 **/
String getName() {
     return name;
}

/**
 * Is the current SortedComponent less than another.
 * Used to insert items on the list.
 **/
public boolean isLessThan(Comparable c) {
     return (name.compareTo(((SortedComponent)c).getName()) < 0);
}

/**
 * Is the current SortedComponent greater than another.
 **/
public boolean isGreaterThan(Comparable c) {
     boolean ret = false;
     if (c instanceof SortedComponent) {
          ret =  (name.compareTo(((SortedComponent)c).getName()) > 0);
     }
     return ret;
}

/**
 * Is the current SortedComponent equal to another.
 * Used to remove from the SortedLayout.
 **/
public boolean isEqualTo(Comparable c) {
     boolean ret = false;
     if (c instanceof SortedComponent) {
       ret =  (comp == (((SortedComponent)c).getComponent()));
     }
     return ret;
}
}
```

Figure 4.34
(Continued).

One interesting implementation detail of the SortedComponent class is that when the isEqualTo() method is called it compares Components rather than names when checking for equality to the object passed. Since multiple Components can be given the same name, comparing the actual objects is the only way to really know if two SortedComponents are equal.

A SortedLayout manager can be created using one of the following forms of its constructors:

```
public SortedLayout(int align, int hGap, int vGap)
public SortedLayout(int align)
public SortedLayout()
```

The first form of the constructor provides the most control. The `align` variable is analogous to the alignment parameter used by the AWT FlowLayout manager and can take on any of the following three values: *CENTER, LEFT,* or *RIGHT.* The alignment refers to the alignment of components across a particular row. The `hGap` and `vGap` parameters specify the number of pixels between components in a row and between adjacent rows in the parent container. By default, the alignment is CENTER and the horizontal and vertical gap sizes are 5 pixels. This mirrors the defaults in the FlowLayout class.

The full implementation of the layout manager is presented in Fig. 4.35. The SortedLayout is most easily discussed by breaking it down into three areas: adding and removing Components, calculating the size needed, and laying out the Components in the Container.

ADDING AND REMOVING COMPONENTS. The simplest part of the implementation is adding Components to and removing Components from the layout. As Components are added to the layout, they are first placed in a SortedComponent object which is placed on the BinaryTree, `components`. The Components are sorted by the name passed to `addLayout-`

```
package ajp.awt;

import java.awt.*;
import java.util.Enumeration;
import ajp.util.*;

/**
 * A sorted layout manager that places components in a container
 * according to lexical order.  This layout manager uses the string passed
 * to add() to determine ordering.  The SortedLayout is modeled
 * closely on the FlowLayout manager.
 *
 * @version    2.1
```

Figure 4.35
The SortedLayout
class.

```
  **/
public class SortedLayout implements LayoutManager, java.io.Serializable {
    static final long serialVersionUID = -835720468290953620L;

    /**
     * The left alignment variable.
     **/
    public static final int LEFT    = FlowLayout.LEFT;

    /**
     * The center alignment variable.
     **/
    public static final int CENTER  = FlowLayout.CENTER;

    /**
     * The right alignment variable.
     **/
    public static final int RIGHT   = FlowLayout.RIGHT;

    // The alignment of components in the container.
    private int align;

    // Number of pixels between items in each row.
    private int hGap;

    // Number of pixels between each row.
    private int vGap;

    // The sorted list of components
    private BinaryTree components;

    /**
     * Create a new Sorted Layout.
     **/
    public SortedLayout() {
        this(CENTER, 5, 5);
    }

    /**
     * Create a new Sorted Layout with the specified alignment.
     **/
    public SortedLayout(int align) {
        this(align, 5, 5);
    }

    /**
     * Create a new Sorted Layout with the specified alignment and
     * gap sizes.
     **/
    public SortedLayout(int align, int hGap, int vGap) {
        this.align = align;
        this.hGap = hGap;
        this.vGap = vGap;
```

Figure 4.35
(Continued).

```
                components = new BinaryTree();
    }

    /**
     * Add a component to the sorted layout. The item is sorted
     * according to the name passed in via >add().
     * Note that only components added with a string tag:
     *
     *      add("ButtonX", buttonX);  // This gets added
     *      add(someButton);          // This does not!
     *
     * will be displayed or figured into laying out the container..
     **/
    public void addLayoutComponent(String name, Component comp) {
        components.addItem(new SortedComponent(name, comp));
    }

    /**
     * Removes the specified component from the layout.
     *
     **/
    public void removeLayoutComponent(Component comp) {
        components.removeItem(new SortedComponent("Unknown", comp));
    }

    /**
     * Calculate the preferred or minimum dimensions of the objects
     * in the container.
     **/
    private Dimension getDimension(Container target, boolean preferred) {
        // The returned object.
        Dimension dim = new Dimension(0, 0);
        SortedComponent sComp;  // the sorted componets in the list.
        Component comp;         // the actual component to be examined
        boolean first = true;   // the first item on the list?

        /*
         * The insets of the container passed in.  These must be
         * added in to the overall dimensions.
         **/
        Insets insets = target.getInsets();

        /*
         * Step across the sorted linked list and check each visible
         * item's preferred or minimum dimensions.  Add the widths
         * togther and save the maximum height.  The loop exits when an
         * OffListException is thrown indicating we have stepped of the
         * end of the list.
         **/
        Enumeration e = components.elements();
        while(e.hasMoreElements()) {
            sComp = (SortedComponent)e.nextElement();
            comp = sComp.getComponent();
```

Figure 4.35

(Continued).

```
            if (comp.isVisible()) {
                // get preferred or minimum size based on "mode"
                Dimension d;
                if (preferred) {
                    d = comp.getPreferredSize();
                }
                else {
                    d = comp.getMinimumSize();
                }
                dim.height = Math.max(dim.height, d.height);
                if (!first) {
                    dim.width += hGap;
                }
                first = false;
                dim.width += d.width;
            }
        }
        // Add in the insets plus the gaps on all sides.
        dim.width += insets.left + insets.right + hGap*2;
        dim.height += insets.top + insets.bottom + vGap*2;

        return dim;
    }

    /**
     * Returns the preferred dimensions for this layout given the components
     * in the specified target container.
     **/
    public Dimension preferredLayoutSize(Container target) {
        return getDimension(target, true);
    }

    /**
     * Returns the minumum dimensions for this layout given the components
     * in the specified target container.
     **/
    public Dimension minimumLayoutSize(Container target) {
        return getDimension(target, false);
    }

    /**
     * Justifies the components in the row represented by the given
     * array, if there is any slack.
     **/
    private void justifyRow(Component comp[], int x, int y, int slack,
                            int height, int nComps) {
        switch (align) {
        case LEFT:
            break;
        case CENTER:
            x += slack / 2;
            break;
        case RIGHT:
```

Figure 4.35

(Continued).

```
              x += slack;
            break;
      }

      // Step across array, moving
      for (int i = 0 ; i < nComps ; i++) {
          Dimension d = comp[i].getSize();
          comp[i].setLocation(x, y + (height - d.height) / 2);
          x += hGap + d.width;
      }
}

/**
 * Lays out the container.  Components in the container are layed out
 * as they are in a standard FlowLayout manager,
 * except that they are sorted according to the tag used to add them.
 **/
public void layoutContainer(Container target) {
      // The insets of the container
      Insets insets = target.getInsets();

      // How wide can we go?
      int maxwidth = target.getSize().width -
                    (insets.left + insets.right + hGap*2);

      // This array is created larger than typically needed , but will
      // always be large enough.
      Component compArr[] = new Component[target.getComponentCount()];

      // Starting coordinates
      int x = 0;
      int y = insets.top + vGap;

      // height of the current row.
      int rowh = 0;
      // number of components in this row.
      int nComps = 0;

      SortedComponent sComp;  // the sorted componets in the list.
      Component comp;         // the actual component to be examined
      boolean first = true;   // the first item on the list?

      /*
       * Step across the sorted linked list and check each visible
       * item's preferred size.  Add the each component to the compArr
       * until we have as many as will fit in a row.  Then call
       * justifyRow() to justify the components.
       * The loop exits when an OffListException is thrown,
       * indicating we have stepped of the end of the list.
       **/
      Enumeration e = components.elements();
      while(e.hasMoreElements()) {
            // get the component off the sorted list
```

Figure 4.35
(Continued).

```
                    sComp = (SortedComponent)e.nextElement();
                    comp = sComp.getComponent();
                    if (comp.isVisible()) {
                        // get the components preferred size and resize it.
                        Dimension d = comp.getPreferredSize();
                        comp.setSize(d.width, d.height);

                        // If this component would not go beyond the
                        // max extent of the row...
                        if ((x == 0) || ((x + d.width) <= maxwidth)) {
                            if (x > 0) {
                                x += hGap;
                            }
                            x += d.width;
                            //...check it's height...
                            rowh = Math.max(rowh, d.height);
                            //...and add it to the array for this row.
                            compArr[nComps] = comp;
                            nComps++;
                        }
                        else {  // beyond the end of the row...
                            // justify the components in this row.
                            justifyRow(compArr, insets.left + hGap, y,
                                        maxwidth - x, rowh, nComps);

                            // reset x and y coordinates for next row.
                            x = d.width;
                            y += vGap + rowh;
                            rowh = d.height;
                            // reset the component array
                            compArr[0] = comp;
                            nComps = 1;
                        }
                    }
                }
            justifyRow(compArr, insets.left + hGap, y,
                        maxwidth - x, rowh, nComps);
    }

    /**
     * Returns the String representation of this FlowLayout's values.
     **/
    public String toString() {
        String str = "";
        switch (align) {
          case LEFT:   str = ",align=left"; break;
          case CENTER: str = ",align=center"; break;
          case RIGHT:  str = ",align=right"; break;
        }
        return getClass().getName() + "[hGap=" + hGap + ",vGap=" +
                                        vGap + str + "]";
    }

}
```

Figure 4.35
(*Continued*).

Component(), which is the same string used by the programmer as an argument to the parent container's add() method.

Removal of Components from the layout simply removes the objects from the BinaryTree. While the removeLayoutComponent() method will eliminate the Component from the tree, it will not cause the container to be laid out again. If the container is to be laid out after a Component is removed, call the validate() method of the Container:

```
panel.remove(unwantedButton);
panel.validate();
```

To remove an object from the BinaryTree, the SortedLayout must construct a temporary SortedComponent:

```
components.removeItem(new SortedComponent("Unknown", comp));
```

The BinaryTree's remove() method uses the SortedComponent's isEqualTo() method to find the object to remove from the list. Since isEqualTo() compares Components, rather than the strings used to name them, the string passed to the constructor of the SortedComponent is unimportant when removing objects from the layout.

CALCULATING SIZE.   The two methods for calculating the size required by the layout, preferredLayoutSize() and minimumLayoutSize(), are very similar, as was mentioned earlier. So similar, in fact, that both methods have been written as shells that immediately call another method:

```
private Dimension getDimension(Container target,
                        boolean preferred)
```

The target variable is the container that is to be laid out. If the boolean preferred is *true*, it indicates that the preferred layout size is to be calculated; if preferred is *false*, the minimum layout size is needed. The preferred size for a layout is typically the larger of its current size or its minimum size.

The getDimension() method is fairly straightforward. It iterates across the BinaryTree of Components, keeping a running total of the widths of the objects plus the gaps between them, and it tracks the maximum height of all the objects in the container. When determining the size of the Components in the list, either their preferredSize() or minimumSize() methods will be called, depending on which of the two LayoutManager methods called getDimension(). After all Components in the list have been checked the *insets* of the parent container are added in. Insets are distances between the sides of the container and anything inside it.

LAYING OUT THE CONTAINER. The bulk of the work done by the layout manager is in the `layoutContainer()` method. The general procedure the SortedLayout manager follows when laying out the container is as follows:

- Determine how wide the parent container is.
- Allocate an array to store a row's worth of components.
- Begin at the upper left corner of the containers.
- Iterate across the sorted list of components, laying Components out a row at a time.

As the manager iterates across the BinaryTree it accumulates Components into the array it created. Once the total width of all the Components in the array is such that adding one more Component would push the total greater than the width of the container, the array is passed to the method `justifyRow()`. `justifyRow()` positions the Components horizontally in the Container based on an alignment that was specified when the SortedLayout manager was created (that is, CENTER, LEFT, or RIGHT). The justification of the Components in a row will be shifted either right, left, or centered in the row. After a row of Components has been positioned by `justifyRow()`, the array of components is reset and the next row is processed.

SUMMARY

The AWT provides a flexible toolkit for creating platform-independent graphical user interfaces. To keep the AWT portable across as many windowing systems as possible, compromises between features and funtionality had to be made. The result of these design decisions is that several widgets not available across all native toolkits are not provided by the AWT. Fortunately, however, the event model and class structure is flexible enough to allow programmers to extend the AWT by creating custom user interface classes.

The two basic catagories of AWT extension classes are discussed in this chapter: those that extend the Panel or Container classes and those that extend Canvas or Component classes. Container-based widgets are useful for combining existing AWT user interface objects in new ways. While the Container class provides the layout and drawing needed by a new widget, the programmer may need to supply some event handling. Widgets that extend the Component class must be created whenever the look and feel of the widget is unlike anything in the AWT. Component-based widgets must provide event-handling and event generation and must also handle painting themselves in response to user interaction.

The AWT layout manager model provides a flexible way of organizing user interface objects in containers. Although several layout managers are provided in the AWT, there may be times when a custom layout manager is needed. Custom classes implementing the LayoutManager interface can be created to accommodate special needs in applications, as the SortedLayout class in this chapter demonstrates.

Interapplet Communication

Introduction

The Java object model allows applets to be reused through inheritance. By creating applets in an object-oriented way, future applets can be built on existing ones, significantly reducing development time. Of course, it is not necessary to extend an applet to reuse it. Applets as building blocks for Web pages can be reused without extension or modification; one need only reference the applet in the page's HTML. From a Java programmer's perspective, there is another aspect of reusing applets that is important: how to combine the behavior or functionality of existing applets with minimal modification.

To illustrate the reuse of applets, consider the following scenario. Suppose you have developed an applet that displays temperature data from cities around the world. The data is sent over a network connection from a remote host and is displayed in a scrolling ticker tape panel. Later you decide to create an applet that needs to access temperature information for a particular city in order to dynamically display that city's time and temperature. The functionality for obtaining the temperature information from the remote host already exists in the ticker tape applet. Assuming you decide to reuse rather than reimplement, several options exist for incorporating the temperature information into the new time-and-temperature applet.

First, if the ticker tape applet has been designed appropriately, perhaps by delegating the network communication and data collection to separate classes, you might be able to reuse only those classes necessary to open a connection to the remote server and extract the data points of interest from the stream of data the server is sending. Unfortunately, if the design of the Web page on which the applet is to be placed includes the original ticker tape applet as well, the browser would now have two connections open to the remote temperature server.

If both applets are to be used on the same page, a second approach would be to combine the entire functionality of the ticker tape applet into the new time-and-temperature applet. The new applet could place the ticker tape in a separate panel or frame and query it for only the temperature information of interest. Now only one connection would exist between the client and server; however, to achieve this goal, the original ticker tape applet would have to be cannibalized to create the new applet. With two versions of at least some of the ticker tape's sources, there is the opportunity for bugs to appear or to be fixed in one version but not the other. Furthermore, by incorporating the ticker tape directly into the time-and-temperature applet, the Web-page designer has less flexibility in how the ticker tape and time-and-temperature display are to be presented—they are physically colocated in the same applet.

A third solution to reusing the ticker tape applet is to design the new applet to communicate with the existing ticker tape through some form of interapplet communication. This option is the best choice for designing the new time-and-temperature applet.

The Java platform provides several means of interapplet communication: one is an API provided in the java.applet package, a second is a side effect of the design of the language, and a third is a server application to act as a relay for messages between applets. The JDK's java.applet package defines the AppletContext interface that is implemented by all Java-compatible browsers. Applets are able to communicate directly by obtaining references to each other through the AppletContext API. Armed with a direct handle to an applet, any public method can be called and any public instance variable can be accessed. Through static methods and class variables, applets can communicate not only with applets on the same page, but with any applets downloaded from the same host, even across HTML pages. Finally, by using a server process as a relay, information can be exchanged between applets regardless of page, or even browser boundaries. This chapter presents examples of these three forms of interapplet communication and uses the Remote Method Invocation (RMI) API to illustrate the server-relay technique. The advantages and disadvantages of each communication form are discussed.

The AppletContext Class

The AppletContext interface is an abstraction of the environment in which an applet is running: a Web browser or the JDK's appletviewer. There are two groups of methods in the applet context of particular interest—one group that allows for manipulation of the browser and one group that can be used to access other applets running on the same page in the browser. The methods for manipulating the browser are discussed in Chap. 9. We focus our efforts here on methods that provide access to other applets.

A reference to the AppletContext object associated with an applet can be retrieved using the applet's `getAppletContext()` method. From the AppletContext, references to all other applets on the same page can be obtained using the following methods:

```
Applet getApplet(String name)
Enumeration getApplets()
```

The `getApplet()` method is passed a String that contains the name of an applet as specified in the HTML APPLET tag. For example, an applet embedded in an HTML document with the tag

```
<applet src=MyApplet.class name="simple">
</applet>
```

can be referenced from within another applet embedded in the same HTML page by calling `getApplet()` as follows:

```
MyApplet ma = (MyApplet)getAppletContext().getApplet("simple");
```

Once the handle is returned from `getApplet()`, any of the public methods and instance variables in the MyApplet object can be referenced.

An alternate way an applet can obtain references to other applets on the same page is to use the `getApplets()` method, which returns an Enumeration of all the applets on the current page. The disadvantage to using the `getApplets()` method to obtain a reference to a particular applet on a page is that the Enumeration must be traversed to find the applet. For example, to scan the enumeration of all applets on a page and locate the instance of the *MyApplet* applet, the following code could be used:

```
Enumeration e = getAppletContext().getApplets();
while(e.hasMoreElements()) {
    Applet a = (Applet)e.nextElement();
    if (a instanceof MyApplet) {
        ma = (MyApplet)a;
        break;
    }
}
```

If there are multiple occurrences of the same applet on a page, the technique illustrated in the preceding example is of limited use. Since there is no method in the Applet class for accessing the name given to the applet in its APPLET HTML tag, it can be difficult to distinguish which instance of an applet is the one being sought.

Limitations

There are some important limitations to using the AppletContext as a mechanism for interapplet communication. First and foremost is that the AppletContext provides references only to applets on the same HTML page. Applets on previous pages, or even on the same page but in different frames, cannot access one another through the AppletContext interface.

Another limitation is that the order in which applets are loaded is under the control of the browser. You will not know the order in which applets are loaded, or be guaranteed that the order will be the same each time a page is visited. It should also be pointed out that applets are not available through the `getApplet()` method until after their `init()` method has completed. The `getApplet()` method will return a null reference for any named applet that is either not present or has not completed its `init()` method. Thus, the references to applets obtained through `getApplet()` should always be checked before they are dereferenced so that unexpected *NullPointerExceptions* can be avoided.

Simple Examples

Figure 5.1 shows three applets that use the AppletContext to communicate, running in the HotJava Browser. The applet at the top of the browser is called a *CounterApplet;* the two applets below it are called *WatcherApplets.* The CounterApplet displays a number in an LEDPanel and provides two buttons that increment and decrement the number. Each WatcherApplet also contains an LEDPanel that is updated by the CounterApplet such that all three applets display the same value.

The CounterApplet's implementation, shown in Fig. 5.2, is very simple in most respects. The applet's `init()` method creates the user interface elements and its `actionPerformed()` method traps the events generated by the two buttons. Once the WatcherApplets obtain a handle to the CounterApplet, they will then access the Counter's LEDPanel directly through the reference returned by the `getLED()` method.

The LEDPanel used by the CounterApplet is a subclass called *LEDEventPanel,* shown in Fig. 5.3. The purpose of the LEDEventPanel class is to provide event notification whenever the value displayed in the LED changes. Much of the code in the LEDEventPanel is dedicated to providing the ActionListener infrastructure (for example, support for adding and removing listeners, and for serializing the event multicaster chain) that is seen in several of the classes in Chap. 4. The overridden `setValue()` method triggers the notification of registered ActionListeners which, when notified, can call the LEDEventPanel's `getValue()` method to obtain the new value.

Figure 5.1
The CounterApplet
and WatcherApplets
running in the Hot-
Java browser.

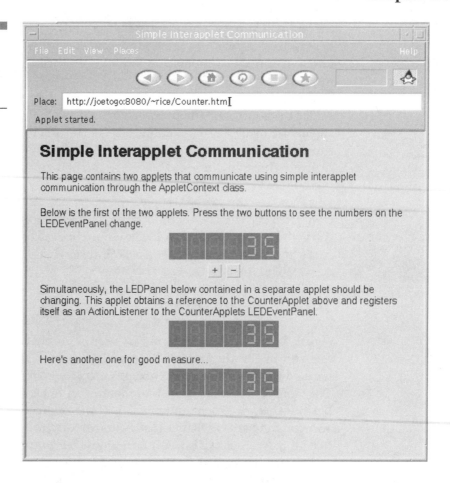

When the WatcherApplets are displayed, they access the AppletContext from the browser in which they are running and request a reference to the CounterApplet. To ensure the CounterApplet has completed its `init()` method, the call to `getApplet()` is placed in a loop that will reattempt to obtain the reference to the applet if `getApplet()` returns *null*. Once the reference has been returned, the WatcherApplets register themselves as ActionListeners of the CounterApplet's LEDEventPanel. Once registered, any time the value in the CounterApplet is updated, the watcher's `actionPerformed()` method is called, which sets a new value in the watcher's LEDPanel. The WatcherApplet class is shown in Fig. 5.4.

The same basic example of counter and watchers can be rewritten to use the `getApplets()` method, since no distinction must be made between the individual WatcherApplets. The modification is straightforward. The *NewCounterApplet* class calls `getApplets()` from its `start` method, then

```
import java.applet.*;
import java.awt.*;
import java.awt.event.*;
import java.util.*;
import ajp.awt.LEDEventPanel;
import ajp.awt.BufferedApplet;

/**
 * A simple counter class that provides an increment and decrement
 * button.  The class is utilizes an ObservableValue object to notify
 * WatcherApplets of changes in the LEDPanel's value.
 *
 * @version 2.1
 **/
public class CounterApplet extends BufferedApplet implements ActionListener {
     LEDEventPanel valueLED;
     Button upButton;
     Button downButton;

     public void init() {
         setLayout(new BorderLayout());
         Panel p = new Panel();
         p.add(valueLED = new LEDEventPanel(6, true, true));
         add("Center", p);
         p = new Panel();
         p.add(upButton = new Button("+"));
         p.add(downButton = new Button("-"));
         upButton.addActionListener(this);
         downButton.addActionListener(this);
         add("South", p);

         setSize(new Dimension(275, 75));

     }

     public void actionPerformed(ActionEvent e) {
         if (e.getSource().equals(upButton)) {
                 valueLED.setValue(valueLED.getValue() + 1);
         }
         else {
           valueLED.setValue(valueLED.getValue() - 1);
         }
     }

     public LEDEventPanel getLED() {
         return valueLED;
     }

}
```

Figure 5.2
The CounterApplet
class.

```
package ajp.awt;

import java.awt.*;
import java.awt.event.*;
import java.util.EventListener;
import java.io.ObjectOutputStream;
import java.io.ObjectInputStream;
import java.io.IOException;

/**
 * An LEDPanel that generates events when its value changes.
 *
 * @version 1.2
 **/
public class LEDEventPanel extends LEDPanel {
    static final long serialVersionUID = 8849777754047273282L;
    final static String actionListenerK = "actionL";
    protected String actionCommand;
    protected transient ActionListener actionListener;

    /**
     * Create a panel of LEDs for displaying integer values.
     **/
    public LEDEventPanel(int nDigits, boolean readOnly, boolean neg,
                         boolean wrap, int width, int thick) {
        super(nDigits, readOnly, neg, wrap, width, thick);

    }

    /**
     * Create a panel of LEDs for displaying positive integer values.
     * No "wrapping" performed.  Overflows will display error message.
     **/
    public LEDEventPanel(int nDigits) {
        super(nDigits);
    }

    /**
     * Create a panel of LEDs for displaying positive integer values.
     * No "wrapping" performed.  Overflows will display error message.
     **/
    public LEDEventPanel(int nDigits, boolean readOnly) {
        super(nDigits, readOnly);
    }

    /**
     * Create a panel of LEDs for displaying positive or negative integer
     * values.  No "wrapping" performed.  Overflows will display error
     * message.
     **/
    public LEDEventPanel(int nDigits, boolean readOnly, boolean neg) {
        super(nDigits, readOnly, neg);
    }
```

Figure 5.3
The LEDEventPanel
class.

```
/**
 * Create a panel of LEDs for displaying positive or negative integer
 * values.
 **/
public LEDEventPanel(int nDigits, boolean readOnly,
              boolean neg, boolean wrap) {
    super(nDigits, readOnly, neg, wrap);
}

/**
 * Set the value of the LED panel.
 **/
public synchronized void setValue(int val) {
    super.setValue(val);
    processActionEvent(new ActionEvent(this, 0, "" + getValue()));
}

/**
 * Adds the specified action listener to receive action events
 * from this LEDEventPanel.
 **/
public void addActionListener(ActionListener l) {
    actionListener = AJPEventMulticaster.add(actionListener, l);
}

/**
 * Removes the specified action listener so it no longer receives
 * action events from this LEDEventPanel.
 **/
public void removeActionListener(ActionListener l) {
    actionListener = AJPEventMulticaster.remove(actionListener, l);
}

/**
 * Sets the command name of the action event fired by this LEDEventPanel.
 * By default this will be set to the label of the LEDEventPanel.
 **/
public void setActionCommand(String command) {
    actionCommand = command;
}

/**
 * Returns the command name of the action event fired by this
 * LEDEventPanel.
 **/
public String getActionCommand() {
    return (actionCommand == null? "" + getValue(): actionCommand);
}

/**
 * Processes action events occurring on this LEDEventPanel by
 * dispatching them to any registered ActionListener objects.
 **/
protected void processActionEvent(ActionEvent ev) {
```

Figure 5.3
(Continued).

```
        if (actionListener != null) {
            actionListener.actionPerformed(ev);
        }
    }

    protected String paramString() {
        return super.paramString() + ",value=" + getValue();
    }

    /////////////// Serialization support. /////////////////////////

    private int LEDEventPanelSerializedDataVersion = 1;

    /**
     * Write the listeners to the output stream.
     **/
    private void writeObject(ObjectOutputStream s) throws IOException {
        s.defaultWriteObject();
        AJPEventMulticaster.write(s, actionListenerK, actionListener);
        s.writeObject(null);
    }

    /**
     * Reinstantiate listeners from stream.
     **/
    private void readObject(ObjectInputStream s) throws ClassNotFoundException,
                                                        IOException {
        s.defaultReadObject();

        Object keyOrNull;
        while(null != (keyOrNull = s.readObject())) {
            String key = ((String)keyOrNull).intern();

            if (actionListenerK == key) {
                addActionListener((ActionListener)(s.readObject()));
            }
            else {
                s.readObject();
            }
        }
    }
}
```

Figure 5.3
(Continued).

iterates through the Enumeration, adding each NewWatcherApplet as an ActionListener to its LEDEventPanel. The NewWatcherApplet class is greatly simplified since all it needs to do is create the user interface and handle notifications from the LEDEventPanel. The modified classes are shown in Figs. 5.5 and 5.6.

```
import java.applet.*;
import java.awt.*;
import java.awt.event.*;
import ajp.awt.LEDEventPanel;
import ajp.awt.LEDPanel;
import ajp.awt.BufferedApplet;

/**
 * A class to watch a CounterApplet class.  Registers as a Observer
 * and is later notified when the CounterApplet's LEDPanel changes.
 *
 * @version 2.1
 **/

public class WatcherApplet extends BufferedApplet implements ActionListener {
    LEDPanel valueLED;
    CounterApplet counter;
    String counterName;

    public void init() {
        add(valueLED = new LEDPanel(6, true, true));
        setSize(new Dimension(225, 50));

        counterName = getParameter("counterName");

        if (counterName == null || counterName.equals(""))
            counterName = "CounterApplet";

        Applet a = getAppletContext().getApplet(counterName);
        while( a == null ) {
            System.out.println("Unable to find " + counterName);
            try {
                Thread.sleep(2000);
            }
            catch (Exception e) {}

            a = getAppletContext().getApplet("CounterApplet");
        }
        System.out.println("Found: " + a.toString());
        counter = (CounterApplet)a;
        (counter.getLED()).addActionListener(this);
    }

    /*
     * Get the notification of the CounterApplet's change.
     */
    public void actionPerformed(ActionEvent e) {
        valueLED.setValue(((LEDEventPanel)e.getSource()).getValue());
    }

}
```

Figure 5.4
The WatcherApplet
class.

```
import java.applet.*;
import java.awt.*;
import java.awt.event.*;
import java.util.*;
import ajp.awt.LEDEventPanel;
import ajp.awt.BufferedApplet;

/**
 * A simple counter class that provides an increment and decrement
 * button.  The class is utilizes an ObservableValue object to notify
 * WatcherApplets of changes in the LEDPanel's value.
 *
 * @version 2.1
 **/
public class NewCounterApplet extends BufferedApplet implements ActionListener {
    LEDEventPanel valueLED;
    Button upButton;
    Button downButton;
    boolean foundWatchers = false;

    public void init() {
        setLayout(new BorderLayout());
        Panel p = new Panel();
        p.add(valueLED = new LEDEventPanel(6, true, true));
        add("Center", p);
        p = new Panel();
        p.add(upButton = new Button("+"));
        p.add(downButton = new Button("-"));
        upButton.addActionListener(this);
        downButton.addActionListener(this);
        add("South", p);

        setSize(new Dimension(275, 75));

    }

    public void start() {
        if (! foundWatchers) {
            try {
                Thread.sleep(2000);
            }
            catch (Exception ex) {}

            Enumeration e = getAppletContext().getApplets();
            while(e.hasMoreElements()) {
                Applet a = (Applet)e.nextElement();
                System.out.println("Found: " + a.toString());
                if (a instanceof NewWatcherApplet) {
                    valueLED.addActionListener((NewWatcherApplet)a);
                    foundWatchers = true;
                }
```

Figure 5.5
The NewCounter-
Applet class.

```
                }
            }
        }

    public void actionPerformed(ActionEvent e) {
        if (e.getSource().equals(upButton)) {
                valueLED.setValue(valueLED.getValue() + 1);
        }
        else {
          valueLED.setValue(valueLED.getValue() - 1);
        }
    }
}
```

Figure 5.5
(Continued).

```
import java.applet.*;
import java.awt.*;
import java.awt.event.*;
import java.util.*;
import ajp.awt.LEDPanel;
import ajp.awt.BufferedApplet;

/**
 * A class to watch a NewCounterApplet class.
 *
 * @version 2.1
 **/
public class NewWatcherApplet extends BufferedApplet implements ActionListener {
     LEDPanel valueLED;
     CounterApplet counter;
     String counterName;

     public void init() {
         add(valueLED = new LEDPanel(6, true, true));
         setSize(new Dimension(225, 50));
     }

     /*
      * Get the notification of the NewCounterApplet's change.
      */
     public void actionPerformed(ActionEvent e) {
         valueLED.setValue(((LEDPanel)e.getSource()).getValue());
     }
}
```

Figure 5.6
The NewWatcher-
Applet class.

Static Methods and Variables

A second technique for interapplet communication exploits a feature of the language that comes from static methods and variables. Any method or variable declared as *static* in a class definition exists once for all instances of that class. When applets are downloaded to a browser, they are placed into a name space that is prefixed by the name of the host from which they were downloaded. This means that any public static method is visible to all other classes downloaded from the same host—even across HTML page boundaries. The upshot of this scenario is that by creating static methods and variables, a way is created for any applets downloaded from a particular host to communicate.

A class containing a static hash table, for example, can be created that provides methods to add and retrieve objects from the table. Figure 5.7 shows a straightforward instance of such a class, called *CommonData*. Applets can access the `CommonData.put()` and `CommonData.get()` methods to exchange objects. Since *Hashtables* can store any object, the applets can even store references to themselves on the table. Furthermore, since the static methods in the CommonData class are visible across HTML page boundaries, applet references can be passed across pages or frames.

Limitations

As with the AppletContext, there are limitations to using static methods and variables for communication between applets. First, there are name space problems. Suppose two people have homepages on the same server and that both include applets that use the CommonData hash table shown in Fig. 5.7. Since static objects are common across applets downloaded from the same host, both applets will refer to the same Common-Data class methods. If applets from both homepages store different objects on the hash table using the same key, the results are unpredictable. In one scenario, exceptions will be thrown when applets attempt to use objects pulled from the hash table that turn out to be of an unexpected class. In another scenario, the object pulled from the table is of the correct class, but it is a reference to an object put in the hash table by a different object. Only by dynamically generating unique keys in each applet can this problem be avoided.

Another name-space problem occurs if two applets downloaded from the same host use different classes of the same name with static methods and variables. The second applet to reference the class name will be given a reference to the class that is already loaded, causing exceptions to be

Figure 5.7
The CommonData
class.

```java
import java.util.Hashtable;

/**
 * A class for storing shared objects in a hash table.
 *
 * @version 2.1
 **/
public class CommonData {
    // The objects stored in CommonData and their associted names
    protected static Hashtable hash = new Hashtable();

    /**
     * Put an object in the hash table.
     **/
    public static void put(String key, Object obj){
        hash.put(key, obj);
    }

    /**
     * Retrieve and object from the hash table.
     **/
    public static Object get(String key){
        return hash.get(key);
    }
}
```

thrown. One technique that will help avoid these name-space collisions is to place classes in packages and give them descriptive, unique names. Since Objects are qualified in the name space by package name, `ajp .util.misc.MySpecialStaticHashtable` is not as likely to collide with more common names such as `StaticHashtable`.

The way browsers deal with applets can also affect the usability of static methods and variables. Defining the disposition of applets not currently displayed is a design decision made by the browser developer. While the interface to the applets—when the `init()`, `start()`, and `stop()` methods are called—is well defined, how long nonvisible applets must be retained by the browser is not. For instance, a browser might decide to dispose of objects that are several pages removed from the visible page and reload or restore them later as needed. Experience has shown that while static methods and variables provide interesting solutions to specific problems, like having applets communicate across frames, they should be used cautiously; there are just too many ways the browser can cause them to be unreliable.

A Simple Example

As was mentioned, a problem that cannot be solved with the AppletContext but can be solved with static methods and variables is communication across HTML frames. As an extension to HTML, frames present an interesting challenge to applet programmers. Although frames allow the presentation of multiple HTML pages in a single browser window, the HTML page barrier that keeps applets from communicating across pages also exists across frames. Web-site developers who want to integrate applets into a multiframe page design may find their designs hampered by their inability to have applets communicate across frames.

Let's consider the time-and-temperature applet that was discussed in the beginning of the chapter, since it could be integrated nicely into a two-frame page design. One frame could display the scrolling ticker tape of cities and temperatures; the other frame could display the selected city's time-and-temperature applet along with some information about that city. Each time a new city is displayed, only the latter frame would need to be changed; the frame with the ticker tape applet could always remain visible. Static methods can be utilized to enable the applets in the two frames to communicate.

Figure 5.8 shows the counter and watcher applets running in separate frames inside Sun's HotJava Browser. The two applets work in much the same way as they did in their original versions shown in Figs. 5.2 and 5.4. The difference in the versions designed to work with frames is that the watcher obtains a handle to the counter from a CommonData hash table rather than through the AppletContext.

The modified counter class, renamed *CommonCounter,* is shown in Fig. 5.9. Just before the CommonCounter applet's `init()` method completes, it calls the static `put()` method of the CommonData class, placing a reference to itself in the hash table stored under the string `counterName`, which can be initialized via the APPLET HTML tag. The HTML tag for the applet might appear as follows:

```
<applet code=CommonCounter.class
        CODEBASE="http://www.somehost.com:8888/~rice/classes"
        width=250 height=75>
<param name=counterName value=CommonCounter>
</applet>
```

The modified watcher applet, *CommonWatcher,* is shown in Fig. 5.10. Again, the difference between the version designed to work with the CommonData hash table and the original version is minor. The applet's `init()` method is changed slightly to use the CommonData `get()` method, but it still attempts to obtain the reference to the Common-Counter inside a while-loop—there is no way to know when the CommonCounter will be initialized and placed into the hash table.

Figure 5.8
The CommonCounter and Common-Watcher applets communicating across frames in the HotJava browser.

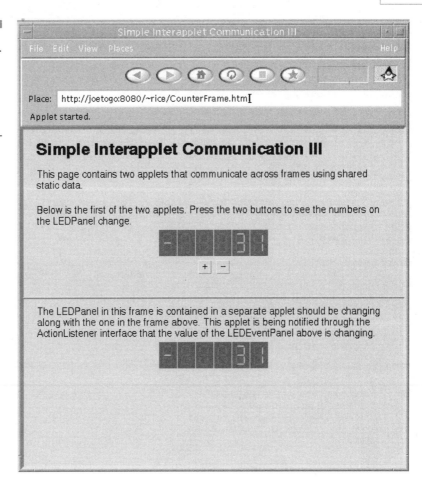

Interapplet Communication with RMI

The third mechanism for interapplet communication is through a *server relay.* The server relay is a process that receives messages from one applet and relays the message to other applets as appropriate. With the networking support in the JDK, there are many ways such a message-passing scheme can be constructed. One way would be to create a message protocol that applets could exchange with the server using the socket classes of the java.net package. Another way to facilitate interapplet communication is through the *Remote Method Invocation* (RMI) API.

```
import java.applet.*;
import java.awt.*;
import java.awt.event.*;
import java.util.*;
import ajp.awt.LEDEventPanel;
import ajp.awt.BufferedApplet;

/**
 * A simple counter class that provides an increment and decrement
 * button.  The class is utilizes an ObservableValue object to notify
 * WatcherApplets of changes in the LEDPanel's value.
 *
 * @version 2.1
 **/
public class CommonCounter extends BufferedApplet implements ActionListener {
    LEDEventPanel valueLED;
    Button upButton;
    Button downButton;

    public void init() {
        String counterName = getParameter("counterName");

        if (counterName == null || counterName.equals(""))
            counterName = "CommonCounter";

        setLayout(new BorderLayout());
        Panel p = new Panel();
        p.add(valueLED = new LEDEventPanel(6, true, true));
        add("Center", p);
        p = new Panel();
        p.add(upButton = new Button("+"));
        p.add(downButton = new Button("-"));
        upButton.addActionListener(this);
        downButton.addActionListener(this);
        add("South", p);

        setSize(new Dimension(275, 75));

        // Put it on the static hashtable
        CommonData.put(counterName, this);
    }

    public void actionPerformed(ActionEvent e) {
        if (e.getSource().equals(upButton)) {
                valueLED.setValue(valueLED.getValue() + 1);
        }
        else {
          valueLED.setValue(valueLED.getValue() - 1);
        }
    }
```

Figure 5.9
The CommonCounter
class.

```
        public LEDEventPanel getLED() {
            return valueLED;
        }

    }
```

▆▆ ▆▆ ▆▆ ▆▆
Figure 5.9
(*Continued*).

Interapplet communication with RMI is programmatically similar to the AppletContext interface. RMI provides references to objects running on remote hosts that can be treated as local object references. Invoking a method of the RMI-provided object reference causes the method to be executed on the remote machine. Arguments and return values are passed back and forth across the network without requiring the programmer to create protocols, sockets, or other traditional network programming objects.*

Limitations

Perhaps the biggest argument against using RMI as a vehicle for interapplet communication is that for many situations it is overkill. For applications requiring communication only between applets on the same page, for example, it is simpler and faster to obtain a direct reference to another applet through the AppletContext interface. RMI also introduces added dependencies on network connectivity and bandwidth that are usually unnecessary if both applets are running in the same browser. Furthermore, any objects passed as arguments to remote methods or returned from remote methods must be packaged, transmitted, and unpacked. The packaging and unpacking of data adds a reasonable amount of overhead that may introduce an unacceptable performance impact on the application. For some applications, better performance may be obtained by devising a custom client/server communication protocol and using the

---

* It should be pointed out at the onset that it is beyond the scope of this book to act as a definitive guide to programming with RMI. The intent of this section is to merely act as an overview of the technology and to provide a useful example that shows an application of RMI to applet programming.

```
import java.applet.*;
import java.awt.*;
import java.awt.event.*;
import ajp.awt.LEDEventPanel;
import ajp.awt.LEDPanel;
import ajp.awt.BufferedApplet;

/**
 * A class to watch a CounterApplet class.  Registers as a Observer
 * and is later notified when the CounterApplet's LEDPanel changes.
 *
 * @version 2.1
 **/

public class CommonWatcher extends BufferedApplet implements ActionListener {
    LEDPanel valueLED;
    CommonCounter counter;

    public void init() {
        String counterName;
        add(valueLED = new LEDPanel(6, true, true));
        setSize(new Dimension(225, 50));

        counterName = getParameter("counterName");

        if (counterName == null || counterName.equals(""))
            counterName = "CommonCounter";

        counter = (CommonCounter)CommonData.get(counterName);
        while (counter == null) {
            System.out.println("Unable to find " + counterName);
            try {
                Thread.sleep(2000);
            }
            catch (Exception e) {}

            counter = (CommonCounter)CommonData.get(counterName);
        }
        System.out.println("Found: " + counter.toString());
        (counter.getLED()).addActionListener(this);
    }

    /*
     * Get the notification of the CounterCounter's change.
     */
    public void actionPerformed(ActionEvent e) {
        valueLED.setValue(((LEDEventPanel)e.getSource()).getValue());
    }
}
```

Figure 5.10
The CommonWatcher
class.

custom protocol over a socket connection. For others, the flexibility and ease of use of RMI will often outweigh any shortcomings.

A Multiuser Chat Service

One thing that RMI provides that none of the other forms of interapplet communication discussed thus far provide is a means for applets to communicate between browsers. To illustrate, this section describes a simple multiuser chat service. The chat service consists of two pieces: a chat server that resides on the web server, and chat clients that are downloaded and run as Java applets. The chat service allows users on different hosts to interactively broadcast messages to other users participating in the chat session. When users download the chat client, they are asked to provide a name that they wish to be known by in the chat session. This *public name* will be attached to each message they submit to the chat session and will prefix the messages as they are displayed in the chat client user interface. Figure 5.11 shows the chat client applet displaying messages sent from three users on different hosts.

THE CHATSERVER. Central to the chat service is the ChatServer interface shown in Fig. 5.12. The chat server provides the `register()` method through which clients can sign on to the service. The clients obtain a reference to the chat server through RMI and then call `register()`, passing a reference to themselves and the name they wish to appear next to the messages they submit to the server. The `register()` method returns a unique identification string to each client as they register. This identification string is used by the server to authenticate messages submitted by clients. The `unregister()` method is used by the clients to remove themselves from the chat session. When clients wish to submit a message to the chat server, they do so using the `sendMessage()` method, which relays the message to all registered clients participating in the chat session. Each method in the ChatServer interface is declared to throw *RemoteException* objects. This is required for any method that will be invoked through RMI. RemoteExceptions are thrown when RMI cannot successfully complete the method call.

The actual chat server is defined in the class *ChatServerImplementation*. The chat server maintains a hash table of ChatClient objects, whose class definition is shown in Fig. 5.13. The ChatClient class is a simple container that holds the public name of the clients in the chat session and a reference to the client applets that is used by the server to deliver messages.

Figure 5.11
The chat applet.

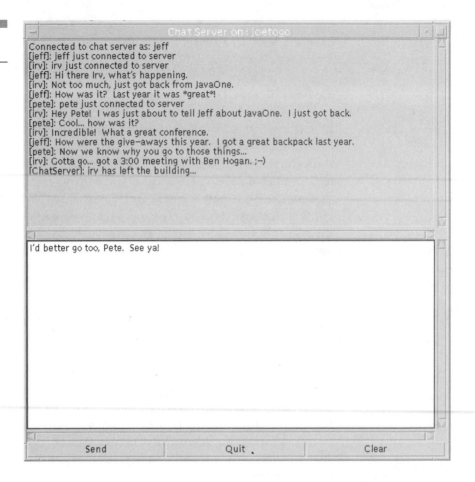

Chat Server on : joetogo

Connected to chat server as: jeff
[jeff]: jeff just connected to server
[irv]: irv just connected to server
[jeff]: Hi there Irv, what's happening.
[irv]: Not too much, just got back from JavaOne.
[jeff]: How was it? Last year it was *great*!
[pete]: pete just connected to server
[irv]: Hey Pete! I was just about to tell Jeff about JavaOne. I just got back.
[pete]: Cool... how was it?
[irv]: Incredible! What a great conference.
[jeff]: How were the give-aways this year. I got a great backpack last year.
[pete]: Now we know why you go to those things...
[irv]: Gotta go... got a 3:00 meeting with Ben Hogan. ;-)
[ChatServer]: irv has left the building...

I'd better go too, Pete. See ya!

| Send | Quit | Clear |

Each chat session is limited to a fixed number of participants that is specified in the ChatServerImplementation constructor. The `increment-Connections()` and `decrementConnections()` methods are used to keep the number of connections at or below the maximum allowed. When a client registers by calling the `register()` method, it passes a reference to itself and the string that the user specified when signing in to the chat session. The server creates a ChatClient object from these two objects and places the client on a hash table. The hash code of the newly created ChatClient object is converted to a string and used as the key into the hash table that is later used to access the ChatClient object. The hash code string is also returned to the client as the *registration string,* which

```
package ajp.rmi;

import java.rmi.*;
import java.io.*;

/**
 * An interface defining the role of a Chat server.
 *
 * @version 2.2
 **/
public interface ChatServer extends Remote {

    /**
     * Register with the ChatServer, with a String that publicly identifies
     * the chat client.  A String that acts as a "magic cookie" is returned
     * and is sent by the client on future remote method calls as a way of
     * authenticating the client request.
     **/
    public String register(ChatCallback object,
                           String publicName) throws RemoteException;

    /**
     * Remove the client associated with the specified registration string.
     **/
    public void unregister(String registeredString) throws RemoteException;

    /**
     * The client is sending new data to the server.
     **/
    public void sendMessage(String registeredString, String message)
                                               throws RemoteException;

}
```

Figure 5.12
The ChatServer
interface.

the server uses to associate requests with a particular client.* When clients
call unregister() they pass the registration string to the server. The
server removes the corresponding ChatClient object from the hash table
and informs the remaining chat clients that a participant has withdrawn
from the session. Messages are sent to the chat server through the
sendMessage() method. The string passed to the server is relayed to all
registered clients by iterating through the hash table as an enumeration.

---

* Since the hash values of all objects are unique, they make good choices as keys into a
hash table. First, the uniqueness assures that two clients won't accidentally get stored at the
same location in the hash table. Second, since the hash codes are typically very large integer numbers, it is hard for a modified client to guess another client's registration string.

```
/**
 * A class that bundles the ChatCallback reference with a public name used
 * by the client.
 **/
class ChatClient {
    private ChatCallback callback;
    private String publicName;

    ChatClient(ChatCallback cbk, String name) {
        callback = cbk;
        publicName = name;
    }

    // returns the name.
    String getName() {
        return publicName;
    }

    // returns a reference to the callback object.
    ChatCallback getCallback() {
        return callback;
    }
}
```

Figure 5.13
The ChatClient class.

The ChatServerImplementation class is shown in Fig. 5.14. The server process is started through the main() method by passing it the name of the host the server will be running on. Prior to starting the ChatServer, the RMI name registry must be started on the server. The RMI registry is part of the JDK distribution (versions 1.1 and higher). The call to the Naming.rebind() method in main() essentially informs the RMI registry that the chat server is now running and can be made available to remote clients.

On Windows 95 and Windows NT, the RMI registry* is started with the command:

```
start rmiregistry
```

On Solaris and other UNIX platforms the command is:

```
rmiregistry &
```

Once the registry is started the chat server can be started. However, first the server's implementation must be compiled with the RMI com-

---

*For more information on the RMI registry and the options it supports, see the online documentation that accompanies the JDK.

```
package ajp.rmi;

import java.rmi.*;
import java.util.*;
import java.rmi.server.*;
import java.io.*;

/**
 * A ChatServer implementation.
 *
 * @version 2.3
 **/
public class ChatServerImplementation extends UnicastRemoteObject
implements ChatServer {

    // The table of clients connected to the server.
    Hashtable clients;
    // The number of current connections to the server.
    private int currentConnections;
    // The maximum number of connections to the server.
    private int maxConnections;

    // The output stream to write messages to.
    PrintWriter writer;

    /**
     * Create a ChatServer.
     **/
    public ChatServerImplementation(int maxConnections) throws RemoteException {
        clients = new Hashtable(maxConnections);
        this.maxConnections = maxConnections;
    }

    /**
     * Increment the counter keeping track of the number of connections.
     **/
    synchronized boolean incrementConnections() {
        boolean ret = false;
        if (currentConnections < maxConnections) {
            currentConnections++;
            ret = true;
        }
        return ret;
    }

    /**
     * Decrement the counter keeping track of the number of connections.
     **/
    synchronized void decrementConnections() {
        if (currentConnections > 0) {
            currentConnections--;
```

Figure 5.14
The ChatServerImple-
mentation class.

```
            }
        }

        /**
         * Register with the ChatServer, with a String that publicly identifies
         * the chat client.  A String that acts as a "magic cookie" is returned
         * and is sent by the client on future remote method calls as a way of
         * authenticating the client request.
         **/
        public synchronized String register(ChatCallback object, String publicString)
                                            throws RemoteException {
            String assignedName = null;

            if (incrementConnections()) {
                ChatClient client = new ChatClient(object, publicString);
                assignedName = "" + client.hashCode();
                clients.put(assignedName, client);
                //out("Added callback for: " + client.getName());
            }

            return assignedName;
        }

        /**
         * Remove the client associated with the specified registration string.
         **/
        public synchronized void unregister(String registeredString)
                                            throws RemoteException {
            ChatCallback cbk;
            ChatClient sender;
            if (clients.containsKey(registeredString)) {
                ChatClient c = (ChatClient)clients.remove(registeredString);
                decrementConnections();
                //out("Removed callback for: " + c.getName());
                for (Enumeration e = clients.elements(); e.hasMoreElements(); ) {
                    cbk = ((ChatClient)e.nextElement()).getCallback();
                    cbk.addMessage("ChatServer",
                                    c.getName() + " has left the building...");
                }
            }
            else {
                out("Illegal attempt at removing callback (" + registeredString + ")");
            }
        }

        /**
         * Sets the logging stream.
         **/
        protected void setLogStream(Writer out) throws RemoteException {
            writer = new PrintWriter(out);
        }

        /**
         * The client is sending new message to the server.
```

Figure 5.14

(Continued).

```
    **/
public synchronized void sendMessage(String registeredString, String message)
                                throws RemoteException {
    ChatCallback cbk;
    ChatClient sender;
    try {
        //out("Recieved from " + registeredString);
        //out("Message: " + message);
        if (clients.containsKey(registeredString)) {
            sender = (ChatClient)clients.get(registeredString);
            for (Enumeration e = clients.elements(); e.hasMoreElements(); ) {
                cbk = ((ChatClient)e.nextElement()).getCallback();
                cbk.addMessage(sender.getName(), message);
            }
        }
        else {
            out("Client " + registeredString+ " not registered");
        }
    }
    catch(Exception ex){
```

Figure 5.14
(Continued).

piler, rmic. The RMI compiler generates class files used by RMI to facilitate access to the server by remote clients. The command to generate the RMI support classes takes the form:

```
rmic -d path_to_classes ajp.rmi.ChatServerImplementation
```

The path_to_classes specifies the destination directory into which the support classes are to be placed. The current class path is searched for the class to be compiled, ajp.rmi.ChatServerImplementation in this case.

The command to start the registry will look something like:

```
java -Djava.rmi.server.codebase=http: //hostname/path_to_classes
     ajp.rmi.ChatServerImplentation
```

where the java.rmi.server.codebase parameter specifies the URL where the remote clients can obtain the server's RMI support classes that are generated by rmic.

THE ChatClient. The chat client applets are themselves remotely accessible objects. In addition to obtaining a reference to the server and calling methods on the server, the applets must pass a reference to themselves back to the server so that the server can relay messages from other clients to the applets. This remote callback to the clients is facilitated through the *ChatCallback* interface shown in Fig. 5.15.

The ChatCallback interface specifies a single method, `addMessage()`, to which the server passes the public name of the client that sent the message and the message itself. A RemoteException is thrown to the server if RMI is unable to complete the remote method call.

The *ChatApplet* class, shown in Fig. 5.16, implements the ChatCallback interface. In the applet's `addMessage()` method, the message from the server is formatted and displayed in the text area of the applet's GUI. The only other unique aspect to the implementation comes toward the end of the `init()` method.

After the user interface is created, the applet makes itself available to the chat server as a remote object. This is done with the `UnicastRemote-Object.exportObject()` method. The `exportObject()` method allows the ChatApplet to pass references to itself back to the server. The applet passes itself as a ChatCallback object to the server's `register()`, `unregis-ter()`, and `sendMessage()` methods.

```
package ajp.rmi;

import java.rmi.*;

/**
 * The ChatCallback class is used by clients wishing to connect to a ChatServer.
 * Whenever new data comes in, the name of the client who added the String and
 * the String itself will be sent to this callback.  When the server goes down,
 * the callback will be notified.  The clients unique registration ID is sent to
 * the client on shutdown to "authenticate" the message.
 *
 * @version 2.2
 **/
public interface ChatCallback extends Remote {

    /**
     * The server has a new message for the client from one of the chat
     * participants.
     **/
    public void addMessage(String publicName,
                           String message) throws RemoteException;

}
```

Figure 5.15
The ChatCallback
interface.

```
import java.rmi.*;
import java.applet.*;
import java.awt.event.*;
import java.awt.*;
import java.io.*;
import java.rmi.server.*;
import ajp.rmi.*;

/**
 * A Chat session client applet.  Connects to a chat server via RMI
 * and recieves broadcast messages from the server that originate from
 * all participants in the chat session.
 *
 * @version 1.2
 **/
public class ChatApplet extends Applet implements ActionListener, ChatCallback {
    // The buttons
    Button sendButton;
    Button quitButton;
    Button startButton;
    Button clearButton;

    // The Text fields
    TextField nameField;
    TextArea displayArea;
    TextArea typeArea;;

    // The dialog for entering your name
    Dialog nameDialog;

    // The name the server knows us as
    String privateName;
    // The name we want to be known as in the chat session
    String publicName;
    // The remote chats erver
    ChatServer chatServer;

    // The main Chat window and its panels
    Frame mainFrame;
    Panel center;
    Panel south;

    public void init() {

        // Create the main Chat frame.
        mainFrame = new Frame("Chat Server on : " +
                              getCodeBase().getHost());
        mainFrame.setSize(new Dimension(600, 600));
        displayArea = new TextArea();
        displayArea.setEditable(false);
        typeArea = new TextArea();
        sendButton = new Button("Send");
        quitButton = new Button("Quit");
```

Figure 5.16
The ChatApplet class.

```
        clearButton = new Button("Clear");
        // Add the applet as a listener to the button events.
        clearButton.addActionListener(this);
        sendButton.addActionListener(this);
        quitButton.addActionListener(this);
        center = new Panel();
        center.setLayout(new GridLayout(2, 1));
        center.add(displayArea);
        center.add(typeArea);
        south = new Panel();
        south.setLayout(new GridLayout(1, 3));
        south.add(sendButton);
        south.add(quitButton);
        south.add(clearButton);
        mainFrame.add("Center", center);
        mainFrame.add("South", south);
        center.setEnabled(false);
        south.setEnabled(false);
        mainFrame.show();

        // Create the login dialog.
        nameDialog = new Dialog(mainFrame, "Enter Name to Logon: ");
        startButton = new Button("Logon");
        startButton.addActionListener(this);
        nameField = new TextField();
        nameDialog.add("Center", nameField);
        nameDialog.add("South", startButton);

        try {
            // Export ourselves as a ChatCallback to the server.
            UnicastRemoteObject.exportObject(this);
            // Get the remote handle to the server.
            chatServer = (ChatServer)Naming.lookup("//" + getCodeBase().getHost() +
                                                    "/ChatServer");
        }
        catch(Exception e) {
            e.printStackTrace();
        }
        nameDialog.setSize(new Dimension(200, 200));
        nameDialog.show();
    }

    /**
     * Handle the button events.
     **/
    public void actionPerformed(ActionEvent e) {
        if (e.getSource().equals(startButton)) {
            try {
                nameDialog.setVisible(false);;
                publicName = nameField.getText();
                privateName = chatServer.register(this, publicName);
```

Figure 5.16
(*Continued*).

```
                    center.setEnabled(true);
                    south.setEnabled(true);
                    displayArea.setText("Connected to chat server as: " +
                                        publicName);
                    chatServer.sendMessage(privateName, publicName +
                                        " just connected to server");
                }
                catch(Exception ex) {
                    ex.printStackTrace();
                }
            }
        else if (e.getSource().equals(quitButton)) {
            try {
                    displayArea.setText("");
                    typeArea.setText("");
                    center.setEnabled(false);
                    south.setEnabled(false);
                    chatServer.unregister(privateName);
                    nameDialog.show();
                }
                catch(Exception ex) {
                    ex.printStackTrace();
                }
            }
        else if (e.getSource().equals(sendButton)) {
            try{
                    chatServer.sendMessage(privateName, typeArea.getText());
                    typeArea.setText("");
                }
                catch(Exception ex) {
                    ex.printStackTrace();
                }
            }
        else if (e.getSource().equals(clearButton)) {
            displayArea.setText("");
            }

    }

    public void addMessage(String publicName,
                        String message) throws RemoteException {
        displayArea.append("\n" + "[" + publicName + "]: " + message);
    }

    public void destroy() {
        try {
            super.destroy();
            mainFrame.setVisible(false);;
            mainFrame.dispose();
            chatServer.unregister(privateName);
        }
```

Figure 5.16
(*Continued*).

```
         catch(Exception e) {
             e.printStackTrace();
         }
     }
}
```

Figure 5.16
(*Continued*).

The applet requests a reference to the remote server with the `Naming` `.lookup()` method. The reference returned by the `lookup()` method is a local reference, through which the applet can cause the server, running on another computer, to execute code.

SUMMARY

There are three common techniques for interapplet communication: using an AppletContext object obtained from the browser or appletviewer, using static methods and variables accessible by any applets downloaded from the same host, and using a server process as a message relay between applets. Each technique has advantages and disadvantages.

Using the AppletContext provides a well-defined interface to obtain references to applets on a common HTML page. However, only applets downloaded into the same context (i.e., the same page) can communicate, excluding communication between applets on different pages or in different frames. Care must also be taken when using the applet context so that null references are returned for any applet that has completed its init() method.

Static methods and variables provide an interesting alternative to the AppletContext interface in that any static method or variable in a class is accessible to any applet downloaded from the same host. By using a static object like the hash table shown in this chapter, containers can be created that may be used by applets on different HTML pages and or in separate frames. The hazard in using static methods is that the programmer is somewhat at the mercy of the browser as to how and when classes are loaded and unloaded.

RMI provides a solution to a problem neither the AppletContext nor static variables and methods can solve: how to get applets to communicate between browsers. RMI can be used as a way to easily access a server application that can, in turn, directly interact with applets running in other browsers. While other approaches to network communication, such as sockets, can be used to solve this problem, the RMI model is directly based on the Java object model. The remote object reference returned by RMI is used to access public methods as if the object were local.

As supported interfaces, RMI and the AppletContext are recommended over static methods and objects as an approach to interapplet communication. For the scenarios that require communication not supported by RMI or the AppletContext, static objects provide an alternative, but they should be used with caution since management of classes and applets not associated with a visible page may vary from one browser to the next.

CHAPTER **6**

Multithreaded Programming

Introduction

Fundamentally, there are two parts to multithreaded programming in Java: *thread life cycle* and *thread synchronization*. The programmatic interface to the life cycle of a thread—creating, running, and terminating threads of execution—is generally the easier part of the programming model to grasp. Managing thread synchronization—keeping threads from deadlock or starvation, preventing data corruption, and implementing schemes to allow threads to share resources—can prove challenging, to say the least. This chapter focuses on understanding the details behind the thread life cycle and using that knowledge to better manage thread synchronization. Several aspects of the life cycle of a thread are addressed:

- The two mechanisms for creating new threads of execution within an application
- The thread state model
- How threads transition between states

The latter sections of this chapter present implementations of three common locking models: *multiple reader/single writer locks, semaphores,* and *barrier locks.* These examples illustrate how, armed with an understanding of the Java thread model, you can extend the model to accommodate more sophisticated locking schemes.

The Java Multithreaded Programming Model: A Review

Java's runtime environment supports multiple threads of execution that vie for time on the virtual machine. Within the runtime is a scheduler that controls access to the virtual machine by threads based on their priority, with higher priority threads given preference to lower priority threads.

When the virtual machine executes code, it does so in the context of a *Thread object.* Some threads of execution are created explicitly by the programmer; many are generated implicitly by the runtime. There are typically two Java objects associated with the execution of any code: the object that provides the code to execute and the Thread object that provides the execution context.[*] For example, a Car class is created with a method called turn():

```
public class Car {
    ...
    public void turn() {
        ...
    }
}
```

When a Car object is instantiated and its turn() method is called, the Java runtime interacts with both the Car object, whose methods and instance variables are accessed, and with a Thread object, created by the runtime, that determines the context of execution (see Fig. 6.1). The execution context includes such attributes as priority, thread name, state, thread group, and so on. In the preceding example, the thread associated with the execution of turn() is created implicitly by the runtime. Even though this thread was not created explicitly, it can nonetheless be accessed explicitly by calling the currentThread() method in the Thread class:

```
public void turn() {
    Thread t = Thread.currentThread();
    ...
    System.out.println("Thread " + t + " is in Car.turn() "
                            + this);
}
```

---

[*] The only time there is just one object associated with code running is when a Thread object has been explicitly created by the programmer, as is described in the next section.

Figure 6.1
The content and context of execution for car.turn().

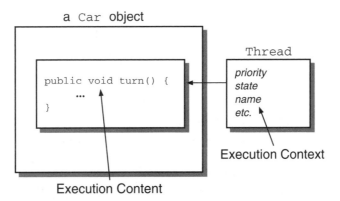

Once a handle to the current thread is obtained, the thread can be manipulated using any of the standard methods in the Thread class: `stop()`, `suspend()`, `resume()`, and so on. While accessing implicitly created threads can be useful, it is more often explicitly created threads that need to be manipulated and managed directly.

Creating Threads

There are two ways to explicitly create new threads of execution, both of which involve instantiating from the Thread class or a subclass thereof. When a subclass of Thread is created, it provides both the execution context, through its instance variables, and execution content through its `run()` method. Since the `run()` method in the base Thread class doesn't do anything (unless you pass the Thread's constructor a *Runnable object*, as will be seen in the next few paragraphs), any subclass of Thread should override the `run()` method to provide the subclass with some useful task to perform. Once a subclass of Thread is defined, a new thread of execution can be obtained by instantiating, and calling the new thread's `start()` method:

```
MyThread t = new MyThread();
t.start();
```

The `start()` method, which is inherited from Thread, is typically implemented as a native method that creates the runtime's internal representation of the thread, sets its priority, and calls the `run()` method.

Threads can also be created by passing an object that implements the Runnable interface to the Thread constructor:

```
class BornToRun implements Runnable {
    public void run() {
        ...
    }
}
...
    BornToRun btr = new BornToRun();
    Thread t = new Thread(btr);
    t.start();
```

When a Thread is created with a Runnable object, a reference to the Runnable object is saved in an instance variable in the Thread. When the `run()` method of the thread is called, if the reference to the Runnable object is non-null, the `run()` method of the runnable object is called. The Thread object provides the context; the Runnable object provides the content.

Regardless of how threads are created, once started, all threads must be managed and all threads are managed in the same way.

Thread States

Thread management consists mainly of controlling the priority with which threads execute and transitioning the threads appropriately between thread states. Threads are transitioned between states programmatically by invoking their methods `start()`, `stop()`, `sleep()`, `suspend()`, and `resume()`, as described in the Java API documentation. The basic thread states and the methods that effect transitions between the states are shown in Fig. 6.2. When threads are created they are initially placed in the SUS-PENDED state. However, once their `run()` method is called, the runtime transitions them to the RUNNABLE state via an internal equivalent of `Thread.resume()`. Threads move between the RUNNABLE and SUS-PENDED states through the `suspend()` and `resume()` methods. When `sleep()` is called, a thread is moved to the SLEEPING state and will transition back to RUNNABLE after its sleep interval expires. The transition from RUNNABLE to TERMINATED happens when the thread's `stop()` method is called. There are some subtleties to thread termination that warrant further explanation.

Thread termination is usually caused by some asynchronous event—a user pressing a *quit* button or a browser removing an applet when it is no longer accessible. Hence, it is difficult to know exactly what code will be executing when another object somewhere calls a thread's `stop()` method. When a thread's `stop()` method is called, the Java runtime generates a *ThreadDeath object* and throws it at the thread. This thrown object will normally cause the thread to terminate. Once a thread has terminated, it cannot be restarted.

ThreadDeath is a subclass of *Error*, which is a subclass of *Throwable*. When programmers trap for exceptions, they typically catch Exception or

Figure 6.2
Basic thread states
and state transitions.

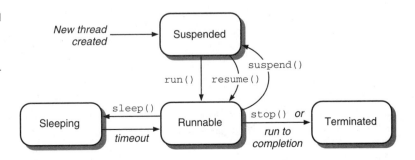

Exception subclass objects. When ThreadDeath is thrown at an object, even one that has exception handling, usually ThreadDeath will not be caught. This is not to say that ThreadDeath cannot be caught, however. In fact, catching ThreadDeath does provide an interesting hook that can be used to perform any last minute cleanup prior to a thread exiting. For example, the main thread in a word processor may wish to save any data to disk prior to exiting:

```
public void run() {
    try {
        ...
        editor main loop
        ...
    }
    catch (ThreadDeath d) {
        save files, etc.
    }
}
```

While catching ThreadDeath is a useful way to clean up after a thread, catching ThreadDeath as a means of keeping a thread alive may cause problems in the context of a Web browser. Consider the following example:

```
public void run() {
    while (true) {
        try {
            ...
            run forever
            ...
        }
        catch (ThreadDeath d) {}
    }
}
```

If the stop() method of a thread with the preceding run() method is called, the ThreadDeath thrown to kill the thread will be caught and ignored. The thread will continue to run. However, within the context of a Web browser, threads are not always under the direct control of the applet with which they are associated. Browsers must manage the threads directly and, for example, kill all threads associated with an applet if the applet is no longer accessible. Within some browsers, if a thread does not exit when the browser throws it a ThreadDeath object, the browser will throw another ThreadDeath object. And another. And another. Ad infinitum, until the Thread actually terminates, which it will steadfastly refuse to do. So, to eliminate the risk of your application and your favorite browser entering into a contest of wills, make certain that threads in applets exit after catching ThreadDeath or otherwise rethrow it.

Thread Priorities and *yield()*

Another important part of managing threads is setting their priorities. Thread priorities range from `Thread.MIN_PRIORITY` to `Thread.MAX_PRIORITY` (1 to 10). When a new thread is created it is assigned a default priority of `Thread.NORM_PRIORITY` (5). Threads can be created with or assigned different priorities, making them more or less likely to be scheduled for execution by the scheduler. Since the virtual machine typically runs on a single CPU, all threads will compete for the same CPU.* Furthermore, while the scheduling of threads on the VM is preemptive (i.e., higher-priority threads will preempt lower-priority threads running on the VM), scheduling within a given priority level is essentially run-to-completion. This situation places some burden on the programmer to either select different priorities for threads or force threads to release the virtual CPU by calling `yield()`, `sleep()`, or `wait()`, or by blocking on I/O. For example, consider the simple multithreaded application shown in Fig. 6.3.

Since no priorities were explicitly given to the threads, they all default to 5, `Thread.NORM_PRIORITY`. When the program is run, the threads will execute in order of creation, with each thread running to completion before another thread is placed into execution. Since all threads have the same priority, the running thread will not be preempted by any of the

---

* On some platforms—Sun's Solaris operating system, for example—Java virtual machines are available that support native multithreading.

Figure 6.3
A simple multi-threaded program.

```
public class RTC extends Thread {

    public void run() {
        for (int i=0; i<100; i++) {
            System.out.println("Thread " + getName()
                                      + " running.");
        }
        System.out.println("Thread " + getName() + " done.");
    }

    public static void main(String args[]) {
        RTC t;

        for (int i = 0; i<20; i++) {
            t = new RTC();
            t.start();
        }
    }
}
```

other threads that are created. A sample of the output generated by the program is shown in Fig. 6.4.

By modifying the program slightly—adding a call to `yield()` in each iteration of the loop—the virtual machine can be shared in a much more equitable fashion. The modified run method:

```java
public void run() {
    for (int i=0; i<100; i++) {
        System.out.println("Thread " + getName()
                        + " running.");
        yield(); // Allow other threads to run.
    }
    System.out.println("Thread " + getName() + " done.");
}
```

produces the following results:

```
% java RTC
Thread Thread-4 running.
Thread Thread-5 running.
Thread Thread-6 running.
     . . .
Thread Thread-21 running.
Thread Thread-22 running.
Thread Thread-23 running.
Thread Thread-4 running.
Thread Thread-5 running.
Thread Thread-6 running.
     etc.
%
```

Figure 6.4
Output from the simple multithreaded program.

```
% java RTC
Thread Thread-4 running.
Thread Thread-4 running.
Thread Thread-4 running.
     . . .
Thread Thread-4 done.
Thread Thread-5 running.
Thread Thread-5 running.
Thread Thread-5 running.
     . . .
Thread Thread-5 done.
Thread Thread-6 running.
Thread Thread-6 running.
Thread Thread-6 running.
     . . .
Thread Thread-6 done.
     etc.
Thread Thread-23 running.
Thread Thread-23 running.
Thread Thread-23 running.
     . . .
Thread Thread-23 done.
%
```

An unexpected side effect of not yielding to other threads is that, by failing to yield, object monitors appear to take on some unusual runtime behavior. For example, suppose an application creates several threads with the same priority and that none of the threads voluntarily gives up the virtual CPU. If one thread enters a synchronized method, it will seem that the monitor has locked the entire object, even parts not protected by the monitor. Since the thread has essentially locked the virtual machine, no other thread will run and, thus, no other part of the object will be accessed.

The interaction of threads and monitors in Java, while simple in principle, can be very confusing in practice, particularly when situations arise like the one previously described. To effectively use threads, it is critical to understand these interactions. Toward that end, it is worth taking a short detour to review some fundamental characteristics of *locks* and *threads.*

Locks and Thread States

The locking of objects in Java is based on the concepts of monitors and condition variables. *Monitors* are a form of lock associated with each class and each object in Java. The locking model in Java supports mandatory locking; that is, when one thread acquires an object's monitor, no other thread can obtain the monitor. Other threads attempting to enter synchronized blocks or methods associated with a locked object are placed in a wait state called MONITOR_WAIT. Objects in the MONITOR_WAIT state are placed in a first-in-first-out priority queue.* While the locking is mandatory, only the methods and blocks prefixed with the synchronized keyword are protected. Nonsynchronized methods and blocks can be accessed by other threads.

Associated with each monitor is a *condition variable.* Threads utilize the condition variable by calling the wait() or notify() method of the object associated with the monitor. When a thread owns a monitor it may call wait() to release the monitor and be placed in a wait state called CONDVAR_WAIT. This wait state is also implemented as a first-in-first-out priority queue. Another thread that subsequently acquires the monitor can call notify() before it releases the monitor. The notify() method causes the first thread to be taken out of the CONDVAR_WAIT queue and placed in

---

* The priority queue used by the runtime is a Java-internal priority queue, and should not be confused with the PriorityQueue class described in Chap. 2.

the MONITOR_WAIT queue. When the monitor is released, the first thread
in the MONITOR_WAIT queue is granted the lock and allowed to continue.

A common example of the use of condition variables is a multithreaded print queue. One thread pulls data off a queue and prints it
while multiple other threads generate and place data to be printed in the
queue. Both the thread that pulls the data off the queue (the *consumer*)
and the threads that place data on the queue (the *producers*) need exclusive
access to the print queue. A problem arises in that the consumer must
lock the queue to check it for entries. Rather than releasing the queue's
monitor if there are no entries, the consumer typically calls wait() after
checking the queue's status:

```
synchronized (queue) {
    while(queue.isEmpty()) {
        queue.wait();
    }
    // process items on the queue...
}
```

The producer threads will notify the consumer of new entries after
they place them in the queue:

```
synchronized (queue) {
    // put data in the queue...
    ...
    queue.notify();
}
```

The interaction between two threads using a condition variable is
shown in Fig. 6.5. Initially, thread *A* owns the monitor associated with the
object obj. While thread *A* is running, thread *B* attempts to enter a block
that requires obj's monitor. At this stage, thread *B* is queued in a wait state.
Eventually, thread *A* calls obj.wait(). The monitor is released to thread
B and thread *A* is placed in a wait state, awaiting notification via a call to
obj.notify(). Eventually, *B* calls obj.notify() and *A* is taken out of
the wait state associated with the condition variable and placed into the
wait state queue associated with obj's monitor. When thread *B* exits the
synchronized block, obj's monitor is released; thread *A* reacquires it and
resumes execution.

Figure 6.6 is a more complete version of the Java thread state diagram
originally presented in Fig. 6.2.

It is important to point out that a thread that has called wait() will
not be awakened immediately after another thread calls notify(). The
call to notify() transitions only the waiting thread from the COND-
VAR_WAIT state to the MONITOR_WAIT state. Only when the monitor is

Figure 6.5
The interaction
between two threads
using a condition
variable.

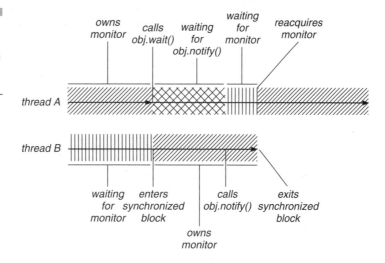

released and reacquired will the waiting thread get to run again. Furthermore, if there are other threads waiting on the same monitor, there is no guarantee that the waiting thread will be the first thread to get the monitor when it is released. For example, if multiple threads, all using the same monitor, have called wait() and another thread calls notify-All(), all the waiting threads will be moved from the CONDVAR_WAIT state to the MONITOR_WAIT state. But only one thread at a time will ever own the monitor. The others have to wait their turn.

Figure 6.6
The Java thread state
diagram.

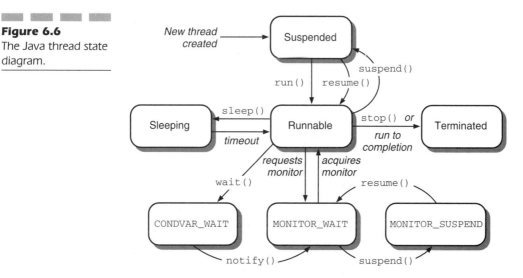

Implementing Locking Schemes

In a multithreaded environment, you will often be faced with situations that require locking schemes more sophisticated than simple monitors and condition variables. While the simplicity of the Java object-locking model might, at first, seem an impediment to more advanced multi-threaded programming, most common locking schemes can be implemented with Java monitors and condition variables. The remainder of this chapter examines three common locking models employed in multi-threaded programming environments: *reader-writer locks, semaphores,* and *barrier locks.* Each locking scheme is presented as an example of how to extend the basic Java multithreaded programming model. All three locking schemes are implemented in the package `ajp.threads`. Since it is not the intention of this book to be a definitive reference on multithreaded programming in general, the discussion of the various locking schemes will be limited to a brief description of the locking scheme, its implementation in Java, and an example of how to use each type of lock.[*]

One characteristic common to all three locking schemes presented here is that they are all implemented as *thread managers.* That is, they all actively manage the threads that utilize the lock. So, for instance, when a reader/writer lock is used by a thread, the reader/writer object will actively control when the thread is allowed to access the object that the lock protects. The task of managing threads that utilize simple Java monitors falls to the Java runtime. Locking schemes implemented above the runtime layer must take on the management role.

Reader/Writer Locks

It is often the case that applications allow both read and write access to data. To prevent data corruption, the reading and writing must be serialized in some fashion. In single-threaded environments this is not a problem and is seldom given more than a passing thought. Where there is only one thread of execution, all reads and writes are implicitly serialized. In

---

[*] For a more complete discussion of MT programming, see Bil Lewis and Daniel J. Berg, *Threads Primer—A Guide to Multithreaded Programming* (Englewood Cliffs, N.J.: SunSoft Press/Prentice-Hall, 1996, ISBN 0-13-443698-9). Even though the focus of their book is POSIX and Solaris threads and they use the C programming language, Lewis and Berg present concepts and approaches to multithreaded programming that are applicable in other languages and environments.

multithreaded environments, the programmer must serialize the access to the data. For most cases, simple monitors and condition variables will provide sufficient control. There are, however, scenarios where using simple locks will significantly impact performance. For example, when the data that must be protected is large, and the time it takes to read it increases accordingly, enforcing strict serial access to the data by each reading thread can severely slow execution. When there are many reading threads, it makes more sense to allow multiple readers to access the data concurrently and serialize only the access by writers. This is the idea behind multiple-reader/single-writer locks, or reader/writer locks, for short.

Reader/writer locks grant multiple threads read access to a protected object, but when any thread needs to modify the object, an exclusive lock on the object is obtained and all other threads (including other writers) are blocked from accessing the object. Reader/writer locks are typically implemented by creating two priority-ordered queues, one for threads waiting to read the object and one for threads waiting to write to it.

When a thread requests read access to an object, there are two possible scenarios. First, if there are no writer threads waiting to obtain a lock on the object, the reader thread is given access immediately. There may already be other threads reading, but that does not prevent a new reader from accessing the data. Second, if there are any threads writing, or waiting to obtain the lock for writing, the incoming reader thread will be placed on the queue of pending readers until all writers queued for access have completed their writing. Once all writers have completed and the writer queue is empty, all readers are released and allowed to begin reading.

When a writer thread requests access to the lock, it will be allowed immediate access if no other threads own the lock. If there are any threads currently reading or writing, and thus owning the lock, the incoming writer thread will be queued and must wait for access. The way reader/writer locks queue waiting threads gives preference to writers, regardless of the priority of waiting readers. While the merits of favoring writers at the expense of higher-priority readers can be debated, most reader/writer locks, including the one described here, are implemented this way.

A READER/WRITER LOCK IMPLEMENTATION. The reader/writer lock presented here is not a lock in the traditional sense. That is, it is not directly associated with a specific object or specific data that other objects are trying to read and write. Instead, this reader/writer class provides a mechanism by which reading and writing can be done by multiple threads in a multiple-reader/single-writer fashion. In the implementation of the reader/writer lock described here, objects implementing either a *Reader* or *Writer* interface are passed to a *RWLock object*. The RWLock object then manages the objects and creates threads as needed to do the reading and writing.

The Reader and Writer interfaces are simple: they merely specify a `read()` or a `write()` method as is seen in Figs. 6.7 and 6.8. Objects which wish to use a RWLock must implement the methods in the interfaces to do the actual work of reading and writing. Although the RWLock will manage the calling of the `read()` and `write()` methods, it does not prevent you from creating a `read()` method that actually writes rather than reads. The burden is placed on the programmer to ensure that the reads and writes are doing the right things.

The RWLock itself is a subclass of Thread and runs as a separate thread of execution. RWLocks have three public methods of primary interest:

1. `public synchronized void addReader(Reader reader, int priority)`

2. `public synchronized void addWriter(Writer writer, int priority)`

3. `public void run()`

The `addReader()` and `addWriter()` methods add objects to the RWLock that implement the Reader and Writer interfaces. These objects get placed on priority-sorted queues that are managed by the lock. The priority argument to `addReader()` and `addWriter()` is the thread priority and is used to determine position on the queues. Typical use of a RWLock consists of creating it, starting it, and then adding Reader and Writer objects to it:

Figure 6.7
The Reader interface.

```
package ajp.threads;

/**
 * An interface for reading.
 *
 * @version 1.3
 */
public interface Reader {
    /**
     * Read the data shared with other Readers (and/or Writers)
     */
    public void read();
}
```

Figure 6.8

The Writer interface.

```
package ajp.threads;

/**
 * An interface for writing.
 *
 * @version 1.3
 */
public interface Writer {
    /**
     * Write the data shared with other Readers (and/or Writers)
     */
    public void write();
}
```

Figure 6.8
The Writer interface.

```
int priority;
RWLock rwLock = new RWLock();
...
rwLock.start();
...
rwLock.addReader(aReader, priority);
...
rwLock.addWriter(aWriter, priority);
...
```

Readers and writers can be added to the RWLock at any time after the lock is created. Once the RWLock is started it begins checking the priority queues, pulling objects off the queues and calling their read() or write() methods. The implementation of the RWLock class is shown in Fig. 6.9.

The RWLock contains two PriorityQueue objects declared at the beginning of the class definition:

1. `private PriorityQueue readers;`

2. `private PriorityQueue writers;`

These PriorityQueues are queues that store the Reader and Writer objects. The queues are continually checked by calling checkQueues() in an infinite loop in the RWLock's synchronized run() method. If no readers or writers are queued, the RWLock releases its monitor by calling wait():

```
while (true) {
    try {
        while ((queueStatus = checkQueues()) == EMPTY) {
            dbg("Queues are empty...");
            wait();
        }
    }
    catch (InterruptedException e) {
        break;
    }
    do the reading or writing
}
```

```
package ajp.threads;

import java.io.IOException;
import java.util.Observer;
import java.util.Observable;
import ajp.util.*;

class PriorityObject {
    Object obj;
    int priority;

    public PriorityObject(Object o, int priority) {
        obj = o;
        this.priority = priority;
    }

    public String toString() {
        return new String("[pri=" + priority + ", obj=" + obj + "]");
    }
}

/**
 * A class for creating multiple reader / single writer (MR/SW) locks.
 *
 * @version 1.6
 **/
public class RWLock extends Thread implements Observer {
    static final int EMPTY   = 0;
    static final int READERS = 2;
    static final int WRITERS = 4;

    private int nReaders;
    private PriorityQueue readers;
    private PriorityQueue writers;
    private boolean debug;

    /**
     * Create a Reader/Writer lock.
     **/
    public RWLock() {
        this(false);
    }

    public RWLock(boolean debug) {
        readers = new PriorityQueue();
        writers = new PriorityQueue();
        this.debug = debug;
    }

    /**
     * Decrement the nReaders variable.
     **/
    private synchronized void decrReaders() {
```

Figure 6.9
The RWLock class.

```
            nReaders--;
    }

    /**
     * Add a Reader to the RWLock at <tt>Thread.NORM_PRIORITY</tt>
     **/
    public synchronized void addReader(Reader r) {
        addReader(r, Thread.NORM_PRIORITY);
    }

    /**
     * Add a Reader to the RWLock at a specified priority.  The priority
     * is throttled to between Thread.MIN_PRIORITY and
     * Thread.MAX_PRIORITY
     **/
    public synchronized void addReader(Reader r, int priority) {
        dbg("Adding READER");
        if (priority < Thread.MIN_PRIORITY) {
            priority = Thread.MIN_PRIORITY;
        }
        else if (priority > Thread.MAX_PRIORITY) {
            priority = Thread.MAX_PRIORITY;
        }
        readers.insert(new PriorityObject(r, priority), priority);
        notify();
    }

    private void dbg(String str) {
        if (debug) {
            System.out.println(str);
            System.out.flush();
        }
    }

    /**
     * Add a Writer to the RWLock at Thread.NORM_PRIORITY
     **/
    public synchronized void addWriter(Writer w) {
        addWriter(w, Thread.NORM_PRIORITY);
    }

    /**
     * Add a Writer to the RWLock at a specified priority.  The priority
     * is throttled to between Thread.MIN_PRIORITY and
     * Thread.MAX_PRIORITY
     **/
    public synchronized void addWriter(Writer w, int priority) {
        dbg("Adding WRITER");
        if (priority < Thread.MIN_PRIORITY) {
            priority = Thread.MIN_PRIORITY;
        }
        else if (priority > Thread.MAX_PRIORITY) {
            priority = Thread.MAX_PRIORITY;
```

Figure 6.9
(Continued).

```
        }
        writers.insert(new PriorityObject(w, priority), priority);
        notify();
    }

    /**
     * Notify the RWLock that a Reader has finished.  Should not
     * be overridden.
     **/
    public final void update(Observable o, Object arg) {
        decrReaders();
    }

    /**
     * This is where the work is done...  The RWLock runs as a
     * separate thread that does the management ot the two priority queues.
     **/
    public synchronized void run() {
        int queueStatus;

        dbg("Starting Lock RWLock.");
        while (true) {
            try {
                while ((queueStatus = checkQueues()) == EMPTY) {
                    dbg("Queues are empty...");
                    wait();
                }
            }
            catch (InterruptedException e) {
                break;
            }
            switch (queueStatus) {
            case READERS:
                releaseReaders();
                break;
            case WRITERS:
                releaseNextWriter();
                break;
            }
        }
    }

    /**
     * Allow all the readers in the priority queue to read...
     **/
    private void releaseReaders() {
        int queueLength = readers.numItems();
        ReaderObject r;
        PriorityObject p;
        Thread t;

        if (debug) {
            try {
```

Figure 6.9
(Continued).

```
                    readers.dumpTo(System.out);
            }
            catch (IOException e) {}
    }
    for (int i = 0; i < queueLength; i++) {
            // Spawn new threads for all readers on queue
            p = (PriorityObject)readers.popHead();
            if (p != null) {
                r = new ReaderObject((Reader)p.obj);
                r.addObserver(this);
                t = new Thread(r);
                t.setPriority(p.priority);
                nReaders++;
                t.start();
            }
    }
    /* Each reader must decrement the count when completed
     * This is done through the update method, called asynchronously
     * from the ReadObject's notifyObeservers() method.
     **/
}

/**
 * Allow the next Writer in the queue to write.
 **/
private void releaseNextWriter() {
    PriorityObject p;

    // wait for any readers to complete
    try {
        while (nReaders > 0) {
            // call wait() because we need to release the
            // Monitor to allow readers to decrement the count
            dbg("releaseNextWriter waiting for " + nReaders + " readers");
            wait(250L);

            dbg("releaseNextWriter awake");
        }
    }
    catch (InterruptedException e) {
        return;
    }
    // Get next writer from queue and wait for its write to complete
    p = (PriorityObject)writers.popHead();
    if (p != null) {
        ((Writer)p.obj).write();
    }
}

/**
 * Check to see if anything is waiting in either queue.
 **/
private int checkQueues() {
```

Figure 6.9
(Continued).

```
        int ret;
        int n;

        // Check the Writers first
        if ((n = writers.numItems()) > 0) {
            dbg(n + " items in Writer queue.");
            ret = WRITERS;
        }
        else if ((n = readers.numItems()) > 0) {
            dbg(n + " items in Reader queue.");
            ret = READERS;
        }
        else {
            ret = EMPTY;
        }

        return ret;
    }
}
```

Figure 6.9
(*Continued*).

Calling wait() releases the monitor, allowing readers and writers to be added via the addReader() and addWriter() methods, both of which are synchronized. If the reader or writer queues are nonempty, run() will call releaseReaders() or releaseNextWriter() to dequeue all waiting readers or a single writer. Since the two release methods are called from within run(), their execution is likewise protected by the RWLocks monitor. Thus, calls to addReader() or addWriter() will block until the release methods return and run() calls wait() again. This effectively serializes access to the priority queues, preventing them from corruption.

Multiple readers are allowed to read concurrently. Since there is no way to know ahead of time how much data each reader will read and, therefore, how long the reads will take, the readers will complete asynchronously. Thus, the RWLock must keep track of how many readers are active at any given time, which it does through the instance variable nReaders:

```
    private int nReaders;
```

As each reader begins reading, nReaders is incremented. Since the readers complete asynchronously, they must notify the RWLock when they have completed reading so that nReaders can be decremented. Asynchronous notification is accomplished through the Observer interface and the Observable class found in the `java.util` package as is explained following.

The `releaseReaders()` method traverses the reader's priority queue, popping the head item off the queue as it goes. For each item removed from the priority queue, an observable ReaderObject is created, the RWLock is added as an Observer of the ReaderObject, the ReaderObject is added to a new thread, and the new thread is started:

```
for (int i = 0; i < queueLength; i++) {
    // Spawn new threads for all readers on queue
    p = (PriorityObject)readers.popHead();
    if (p != null) {
        r = new ReaderObject((Reader)p.obj);
        r.addObserver(this);
        t = new Thread(r);
        t.setPriority(p.priority);
        nReaders++;
        t.start();
    }
}
```

The ReaderObject class gets the `addObserver()` method from its parent class *Observable*. The ReaderObject also implements the Runnable interface allowing it to be passed to the Thread constructor. The implementation of ReaderObject is shown in Fig. 6.10.

When the thread associated with a ReaderObject is started, the Reader-Object's `run()` method will be called. The `run()` method calls `read()` on the object extracted from the reader queue. Once the `read()` method completes, the ReaderObject calls `setChanged()` and `notifyObservers()`, notifying the RWLock that the read has completed. The notification comes in the form of an asynchronous call to the `update()`

Figure 6.10
The ReaderObject class.

```
import java.util.Observer;
import java.util.Observable;

// Observable class that is created for each Reader in the queue.
class ReaderObject extends Observable implements Runnable {
    Reader reader;

    public ReaderObject(Reader r) {
        reader = r;
    }

    public void run() {
        reader.read();
        setChanged();
        notifyObservers();
    }
}
```

method of all registered observers. In the RWLock class, the `update()` method simply decrements the `nReaders` counter, indicating that a reader is done.

If the RWLock finds that the writer queue is nonempty, it calls `releaseNextWriter()`, which must first check for any readers still in progress. This is done in the loop:

```
try {
    while (nReaders > 0) {
        dbg("releaseNextWriter waiting for " + nReaders
            + " readers");
        wait(250L);
        dbg("releaseNextWriter awake");
    }
}
catch (InterruptedException e) {
    return;
}
```

Note that if there are any reads in progress, the writer must sleep until they are done. Rather than calling `sleep()`, it calls `wait()` with a time-out interval to avoid a deadlock that will occur when the reader completes and `update()` is called. The deadlock scenario plays out as follows: The `update()` method calls `decrReaders()`, which is synchronized and which will block as long as `releaseNextWriter()` owns the monitor. If `nReaders` is never decremented, `releaseNextWriter()` will never return. So, unless the monitor is relinquished within `releaseNextWriter()`, a deadlock is possible.

Once all readers have completed their reads, the writer's `write()` method is called directly by the RWLock, rather than spawning a new thread as was done for each reader. Since only a single writer can be active at a time, there is little merit in creating a new thread to do the write. The main thread of the RWLock would simply have to wait for the write to complete anyway.

A READER/WRITER LOCK EXAMPLE. Figure 6.11 shows a Java application that demonstrates the use of the RWLock class. The application has a user interface consisting of four ObjectLists (the ObjectList class is discussed in Chap. 4). The two left lists show the names of threads waiting to read or write. On the right are lists that contain the names of any threads currently reading or writing. The application randomly creates reader and writer objects at a ratio of roughly four readers to each writer and adds them to a RWLock. The names of the Reader and Writer objects appear in the appropriate lists as the objects are transitioned from

Figure 6.11
A graphical demonstration of a reader/
writer lock.

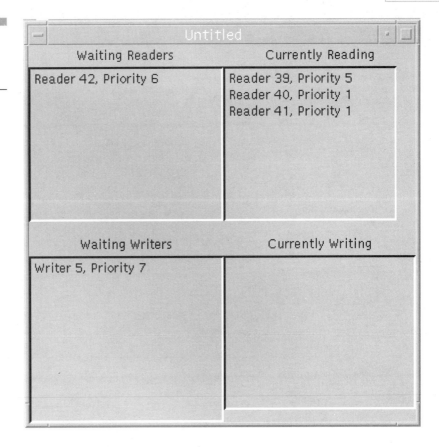

Figure 6.11
A graphical demonstration of a reader/
writer lock.

waiting to running. When the threads created by the RWLock complete, the names of the associated readers and writers are removed from the lists in the user interface.

There are three classes involved in the application shown in Fig. 6.11. First are two classes that implement the Reader and Writer interfaces, *SimpleReader* and *SimpleWriter*. The other class, *RWTest*, creates the user interface and a RWLock, then randomly generates SimpleReader and SimpleWriter objects to be managed by the RWLock.

Figure 6.12 shows the implementation of the SimpleReader class. Of primary interest in SimpleReader is the read() method. The read() method removes the object from the waiting ObjectList, places it in the running ObjectList and sleeps, simulating a delay that a thread might incur while actually reading something. Once the SimpleReader wakes up, it removes itself from the running ObjectList and returns. The SimpleWriter is almost identical to the SimpleReader and is shown in Fig. 6.13.

```
class SimpleReader implements Reader {
    int priority;
    int id;

    public SimpleReader(int p, int id) {
        priority = p;
        this.id = id;
    }

    public int getID() {
        return id;
    }

    public void read() {
        RWTest.delReader(this);
        RWTest.Reading(this);
        try {
            Thread.sleep(5000);
        }
        catch (InterruptedException e) {}
        RWTest.doneReading(this);
    }

    public String toString() {
        return new String("Reader " + id + ", Priority " + priority);
    }
}
```

Figure 6.12
The SimpleReader
class.

The RWTest class is shown in Fig. 6.14. As a stand-alone Java application, the core of RWTest is in the method `main()`. When `main()` is called, the application creates several SimpleReaders via the `addSimpleReader()` method. It then creates a single SimpleWriter by calling `addSimple-Writer()`. Next, the user interface is created and the RWLock is started. Finally, an infinite loop is entered in which readers and writers are randomly created. It should be noted that the bulk of the code associated with the RWTest application is associated with creating and manipulating the user interface. The actual interaction with the RWLock is restricted to instantiating the lock and adding the readers and writers to it.

Semaphores

A second common form of lock in multithreaded programming environments is the *semaphore*. Semaphores are used to manage access to a pool

```
class SimpleWriter implements Writer {
    int priority;
    int id;

    public SimpleWriter(int p, int id) {
        priority = p;
        this.id = id;
    }

    public int getID() {
        return id;
    }

    public void write() {
        RWTest.delWriter(this);
        RWTest.Writing(this);
        try {
            Thread.sleep(1000);
        }
        catch (InterruptedException e) {}
        RWTest.doneWriting(this);

    }

    public String toString() {
        return new String("Writer " + id + ", Priority " + priority);
    }
}
```

Figure 6.13
The SimpleWriter
class.

of limited resources. When a thread needs access to a resource from the pool, it must first acquire a semaphore. The number of semaphores available equals the number of unallocated resources in the pool. Once a thread owns the semaphore, it is free to access a resource in the pool. When the thread is done with the resource, it returns the semaphore to the pool. The model is analogous to a parking garage with a fixed number of parking spaces available. As cars arrive, they take a ticket and are allowed to enter the garage. Once the garage is full, no more cars can enter until one leaves. For each car that leaves, another ticket is made available for arriving cars.

Semaphores are ideal for use in situations where it is necessary to limit the concurrent threads accessing an object. For example, semaphores could be used to limit the number of client connections to a Java-based network game server, keeping the number of players in the game below some limit. Once one player leaves the game, a new connection could be allowed.

```
import ajp.threads.RWLock;
import ajp.threads.Reader;
import ajp.threads.Writer;
import ajp.awt.ObjectList;
import java.awt.*;
import java.util.Random;

public class RWTest {
    static Random rand = new Random();
    static RWLock rw = new RWLock();
    static ObjectList readers = new ObjectList("Waiting Readers");
    static ObjectList writers = new ObjectList("Waiting Writers");
    static ObjectList reading = new ObjectList("Currently Reading");
    static ObjectList writing = new ObjectList("Currently Writing");
    static int nReaders = 1;
    static int nWriters = 1;

    public static void main(String args[]) {
        int priority;

        for (int i = 0; i < 5; i++) {
            addSimpleReader();
        }
        addSimpleWriter();

        Frame f = new Frame( );
        f.setLayout(new GridLayout(2, 2));
        f.resize( 400, 400 );
        f.add(readers);
        f.add(reading);
        f.add(writers);
        f.add(writing);
        f.show();

        rw.start();
        while(true) {
            if (rand.nextInt()%5 == 0) {
                addSimpleWriter();
            }
            else {
                addSimpleReader();
            }
            try {
                Thread.sleep(1000);
            }
            catch (InterruptedException e) {}
        }
    }

    static void addSimpleReader() {
        int priority = newPriority();
        SimpleReader r = new SimpleReader(priority, nReaders);
        rw.addReader(r, priority);
```

Figure 6.14
The RWTest class.

```
        readers.addItem(r.toString(), r);
        nReaders++;
    }

    static void addSimpleWriter() {
        int priority = newPriority();
        SimpleWriter w = new SimpleWriter(priority, nWriters);
        rw.addWriter(w, priority);
        writers.addItem(w.toString(), w);
        nWriters++;
    }

    static void delReader(SimpleReader r) {
        readers.delItem(r.toString());
    }

    static void delWriter(SimpleWriter w) {
        writers.delItem(w.toString());
    }

    static void Reading(SimpleReader r) {
        reading.addItem(r.toString(), r);
    }

    static void Writing(SimpleWriter w) {
        writing.addItem(w.toString(), w);
    }

    static void doneReading(SimpleReader r) {
        reading.delItem(r.toString());
    }

    static void doneWriting(SimpleWriter w) {
        writing.delItem(w.toString());
    }

    static int newPriority() {
        return (Math.abs(rand.nextInt()) % Thread.MAX_PRIORITY);
    }
}
```

Figure 6.14
(*Continued*).

The API to typical semaphore implementations includes two core methods: *wait* and *post*. The traditional semaphore wait method stalls the calling thread until a resource is available. When the wait method returns, the resource is allocated, and the thread is free to access it. After the thread is done with the resource, the post method is called, returning the semaphore to the pool.

A SEMAPHORE IMPLEMENTATION. Like the reader/writer lock implementation, the semaphore described here is actually a thread manager. The Semaphore class keeps a counter of the number of threads that are allowed to run concurrently, presumably accessing a limited resource. The Semaphore forces threads to sleep if a resource they are waiting for is not available. As soon as a resource is returned to the pool, the semaphore wakes up one of the sleeping threads. Typical use of the Semaphore class would be to create an instance as a static class variable. For example, consider the class shown in Fig. 6.15.

Every instance of the *MyThread* class shown in Fig. 6.14 will have to acquire one of the five available semaphores to get past the `semaWait()` call. Once the work is done, the static semaphore's `semaPost()` method is called, freeing the resource. Figure 6.16 shows the implementation of the Semaphore class.

There are two significant instance variables in the Semaphore class: `ht`, a hash table, and `nResources`, an integer. The `nResources` counter is initialized by the constructor to indicate how many resources the semaphore is managing. Each time a resource is allocated, `nResources` is decremented. The hash table `ht` is used to store references to the threads to which the resources have been allocated.

The two synchronized methods in the implementation are `sema-Wait()` and `semaPost()`. The `semaWait()` method will call `wait()` if

Figure 6.15

A program illustrating the Semaphore class's API.

```java
class MyThread extends Thread {
    static Semaphore mySema = new Semaphore(5);
        ...

    public void run() {
        // wait until a semaphore is available...
        try {
            mySema.semaWait();
        }
        catch (InterruptedException e) {
            ...
        }
        ...

        // Do some work
        ...
        try {
            mySema.semaPost();
        }
        catch (ThreadNotRegisterredException e) {
            ...
        }
    }
}
```

```
package ajp.threads;
import java.util.Hashtable;

/**
 * A class for creating semaphores.  Threads that attempt to acquire a
 * a sempahore will run if one is available, or block it one is not.
 * Threads should release the semaphore when they are done so that other
 * threads can run.
 *
 * @version 1.5
 */
public class Semaphore {

    protected Hashtable ht;
    protected int nResources;
    protected boolean debug;

    public Semaphore (int n, boolean debug) {
        nResources = n;
        ht = new Hashtable(n);
        this.debug = debug;
    }

    /**
     * Create a semaphore with <tt>n</tt> resources.
     **/
    public Semaphore (int n) {
        this(n, false);
    }

    private void dbg(String s) {
        if (debug) {
            System.out.println(s);
            System.out.flush();
        }
    }

    /**
     * Wait for a resource to become available.
     **/
    public synchronized void semaWait() throws InterruptedException {
        Thread t = Thread.currentThread();

        while (nResources == 0) {
            wait();
        }
        nResources--;
        ht.put(t, t);
        dbg("Thread " + ((Thread)ht.get(t)).getName() + " got a resource: " +
            nResources + " remaining.");
    }
```

Figure 6.16
The Semaphore class.

```
/**
 * Return a resource to the pool.
 **/
public synchronized void semaPost() throws ThreadNotRegisteredException {
    Thread t = Thread.currentThread();

    if (t == ht.get(t)) {
        ht.remove(t);
        nResources ++;
        dbg("Thread " + t.getName() + " released resource: " +
            nResources + " remaining.");
        notify();
    }
    else
        throw new ThreadNotRegisteredException();
    }
}
```

Figure 6.16
(*Continued*).

nResources is 0, indicating all resources are allocated. When the thread is awakened by a call to notify() in the semaPost() method, nResources is decremented, the thread is placed in the hash table of registered threads, and semaWait() returns.

In semaPost(), the calling thread is first checked to make sure it is on the hash table. If not, a ThreadNotRegisteredException is thrown. Provided the thread is found on the hash table, it is removed, nResources is incremented, and notify() is called.

A SEMAPHORE EXAMPLE. To illustrate the use of semaphores, an example much like the example reader/writer lock program has been created. The example, shown in Fig. 6.17, is a Java application with three Object lists in the user interface. The three lists are used to hold threads that are waiting at semaWait(), threads that are running after semaWait() has

Figure 6.17
A graphical demonstration of the semaphore.

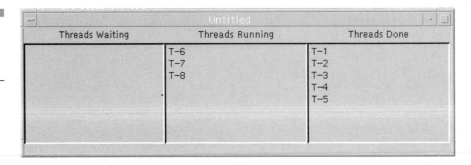

returned, and threads that have returned the semaphore to the pool by calling `semaPost()`. As the application runs, the names of threads will begin to appear in the *waiting* and *running* lists. When threads release the semaphore, their names will move from the *running* list to the *done* list. At no time will there be more than five threads (the number passed to the semaphore's constructor) identified in the *running* list.

Source code for the *SemaphoreTest* class is shown in Fig. 6.18. There are four static variables in the SemaphoreTest class: the Semaphore and the three Object Lists. These variables will be manipulated directly by the `main()` and so are static to allow for convenient access. The `run()` method fulfills the Runnable interface that SemaphoreTest implements. The `run()` method contains most of the actual interaction with the semaphore. First a semaphore is acquired. Next the thread is transitioned from the *waiting* to the *running* list by deleting its entry on the former, then adding it to the latter. The actual work of the thread is simulated by a five-second sleep. Once `sleep()` returns, the thread is removed from the *running* list and placed on the *done* list and `semaPost()` is called.

The three other methods of importance in the SemaphoreTest class are the `add()`, `del()`, and `main()`. The `add()` and `del()` methods add or remove the current thread from the ObjectList that is passed as an argument. It is worth noting that while the `add()` and `del()` methods are not synchronized, they do contain synchronized blocks that use the monitor associated with the list that was passed as an argument. This synchronization prevents one thread from deleting items on the list while another thread is adding to it.

As in the reader/writer lock example, `main()` constructs the user interface then spawns several threads that will use the lock. Here the threads are created by passing a new SemaphoreTest object to the thread's constructor. By passing a new instance of the SemaphoreTest class to each thread, potential data corruption that might occur through concurrent access to methods is avoided. Once all the threads are created, they are started and the threads begin to appear in the lists of the user interface.

Barriers

A barrier lock provides a way for multiple threads of execution to rendezvous at a particular point. When a barrier lock is created, it is told how many threads will be using it. As the threads are created, they must register with the barrier lock. When a thread gets to the rendezvous point, it

```
import ajp.threads.*;
import ajp.awt.*;
import java.awt.*;

class SemaphoreTest implements Runnable {
    static Semaphore semaphore;
    static ObjectList waiting = new ObjectList("Threads Waiting");
    static ObjectList running = new ObjectList("Threads Running");
    static ObjectList finished = new ObjectList("Threads Done");

    public void run() {
        try {
            add(waiting);
            semaphore.semaWait();
        }
        catch (InterruptedException e) {}

        del(waiting);
        add(running);
        sleep(5000);
        try {
            semaphore.semaPost();
            del(running);
            add(finished);
        }
        catch (ThreadNotRegisteredException e) {
            System.out.println("Thread " +
                                Thread.currentThread().getName() +
                                " not registered.");
        }

    }

    void add(ObjectList l) {
        Thread t = Thread.currentThread();
        String name = t.getName();
        synchronized(l) {
            l.addItem(name, t);
        }
    }

    void del(ObjectList l) {
        synchronized(l) {
            l.delItem(Thread.currentThread().getName());
        }
    }

    static void sleep(int ms) {
        try {
            Thread.sleep(ms);
        }
```

Figure 6.18
The SemaphoreTest
class.

```
            catch (InterruptedException e) {}
    }

    public static void main(String args[]) {
        int number;
        semaphore = new Semaphore(5, true);
        Thread t[];

        try {
            number = Integer.parseInt(args[0]);
        }
        catch (Exception e) {
            number = 8;
        }
        t = new Thread[number];

        Frame f = new Frame();
        f.setLayout(new GridLayout(1, 3));
        f.setSize(newDimension(600, 200));
        f.add(waiting);
        f.add(running);
        f.add(finished);
        f.show();

        for(int i=0; i<t.length; i++) {
            t[i] = new Thread(new SemaphoreTest(), "T-" + (i + 1));
        }
        for(int i=0; i<t.length; i++) {
            t[i].start();
        }
    }
}
```

Figure 6.18
(*Continued*).

calls the barrier's stall() method. The barrier will hold all stalled threads captive until the last registered thread has arrived at the barrier. Once the last thread has arrived, all the captive threads are released and allowed to run again.

One application of a barrier lock might be to stall multiple threads in an applet until all threads have initialized. Another application might be to create a barrier shared by multiple applets that holds the applets until all have competed their init() methods.

A BARRIER IMPLEMENTATION. There are two types of barrier locks available from the following implementation. One works as described previously: the barrier is created with a known number of threads that it will manage. The other is created without specifying the number of threads to be managed. The type of barrier is determined by the constructor used to create it:

1. `public Barrier()`

2. `public Barrier(int nThreads)`

The first form of the constructor just shown allows threads to register until the first thread arrives at the barrier. Once one thread has arrived, no more threads will be allowed to register. The second form creates a barrier that will allow exactly `nThreads` to register.

Threads can be registered with the barrier using one of two methods provided:

1. `public boolean registerExpectedThread(Thread t)`

2. `public boolean registerThread(Thread t)`

Both registration methods will return *true* if the thread was able to register, or *false* if the thread was not registered. Threads will always be registered unless the first thread has arrived at the barrier. The first form of registration, `registerExpectedThread()`, is used when the barrier is created with a known number of threads. The `registerThread()` method can be used for either variety of barrier lock. In the case of a barrier with a specified number of threads arriving, `registerThread()` actually calls `registerExpectedThread()` to do the registration.

The final method in the public API is:

```
public synchronized void stall() throws InterruptedException,
                                ThreadNotRegisteredException
```

The `stall()` method keeps the calling thread captive until all the registered threads have arrived at the barrier. The source for the *Barrier* class is shown in Fig. 6.19.

The Barrier class has four significant instance variables:

1. `protected Hashtable ht;`

2. `protected int nWaiters;`

3. `protected int nExpected;`

4. `protected int nRegistered;`

When threads are registered, a reference is stored in the hash table, `ht`. Later, when threads arrive at the barrier, the `stall()` method looks up the calling thread on the hash table and generates an exception if the thread is not found. The other three variables, `nWaiters`, `nExpected`,

```
package ajp.threads;

import java.util.Hashtable;

/**
 * A Barrier synchronization object.  Multiple threads can register with a
 * Barrier object.
 *
 * @version 1.4
 */
public class Barrier {
        // The Hashtable that stores the waiting threads.
     protected Hashtable ht;

        // The number of waiting threads.
     protected int nWaiters;

        // The number of threads expected at the Barrier.
     protected int nExpected;

        // The number of threads that have actually registered.
     protected int nRegistered;

     // The debug flag.
     private boolean debug;

     public Barrier(int nThreads, boolean debug) {
          nExpected = nThreads;
          this.debug = debug;
          ht = new Hashtable(nThreads);
     }

     public Barrier(boolean debug) {
          this.debug = debug;
          ht = new Hashtable();
          nExpected = 0;
     }

     /**
      * Create a Barrier without specifing the number of threads to register.
      **/
     public Barrier() {
          this(false);
     }

     /**
      * Create a Barrier with a specified number of threads to register.
      **/
     public Barrier(int nThreads) {
          this(nThreads, false);
     }
```

Figure 6.19
The Barrier class.

```
/*
 * A method to allow for selective printing of debug messages.
 **/
private void dbg(String s) {
    if (debug) {
        System.out.println(s);
    }
}

/**
 * Register a thread with the Barrier
 **/
public synchronized boolean registerThread(Thread t) {
    boolean ret;

    if (nExpected > 0) {
        return registerExpectedThread(t);
    }
    if (nWaiters == 0) {
        nRegistered++;
        ht.put(t, t);
        dbg("Registering thread " + ((Thread)ht.get(t)).getName());
        ret = true;
    }
    else {
        ret = false;
    }
    return ret;
}

/**
 * Register an expected thread with the Barrier
 **/
public synchronized boolean registerExpectedThread(Thread t) {
    boolean ret;

    if (nExpected > 0 && nRegistered < nExpected) {
        nRegistered++;
        ht.put(t, t);
        dbg("Registering expected thread "
            + ((Thread)ht.get(t)).getName());
        ret = true;
    }
    else {
        ret = false;
    }

    return ret;
}

/**
 * Wait at the barrier until all registered threads have arrived.
 **/
```

Figure 6.19
(*Continued*).

```
    public synchronized void stall() throws InterruptedException,
                                             ThreadNotRegisteredException {
        Thread th = Thread.currentThread();
        int waitingFor = (nExpected > 0) ? nExpected - 1
                                         : nRegistered - 1;

        if (ht.get(th) == null) {
            throw (new ThreadNotRegisteredException());
        }

        if (nWaiters == waitingFor) {
            nWaiters = 0;
            dbg("Waking all waiters...");
            notifyAll();
        }
        else {
            nWaiters++;
            dbg("Thread " + th.getName() + " stopped at barrier.");
            wait();
        }
        ht.remove(th);
        dbg("Thread " + th.getName() + " past barrier.");
    }
}
```

Figure 6.19
(Continued).

and nRegistered, are used by the barrier to track the number of threads that are currently waiting at the barrier, the number that are expected at the barrier, and the number that have registered by calling one of the registration methods. The hash table and nExpected are initialized in the constructors, while the other instance variables are set in the registration and stall methods.

The primary function of the two registration methods is to add the thread passed as the argument in the hash table, and to increment the nRegistered counter. In registerThread(), the only addition to this functionality is that if nExpected was set in the constructor, register-ExpectedThread() is called to do the registration:

```
if (nExpected > 0) {
    return registerExpectedThread(t);
}
```

If nExpected is equal to 0 and no threads are already waiting, the thread is put on the hash table using the thread itself as the key, and nRegistered is incremented.

When registerExpectedThread() is called, the logic is actually a bit simpler. As long as the number of threads expected is greater than zero and greater than the number of threads already registered, the thread will be registered. Notice that `registerExpectedThread()` makes no check against already waiting threads. This is intended to allow the expected number of threads to register under all circumstances, even if one thread has already reached the barrier. Otherwise, a deadlock would occur with stalled threads waiting for threads to arrive that would never get there, since they were prevented from registering.

The `stall()` method causes threads to stop calling `wait()`. When the last registered thread calls `stall()` all threads are awakened through the `notifyAll()` method. Both the `wait()` and `notifyAll()` calls happen within `stall()`, which uses the barrier's monitor for synchronization. If a calling thread does not register with the barrier, a `ThreadNotRegisteredException` will be thrown. If an interrupt occurs while a thread is in the `wait()` call, the `InterruptedException` is propagated to the calling thread.

Each time a registered thread calls `stall()`, the `nWaiters` instance variable is incremented and `wait()` is called. When `stall()` is called by the last registered thread, `nWaiters` will be one less than either `nExpected`, or one less than `nRegistered`, a value stored in the local variable `waitingFor`:

```
int waitingFor = (nExpected > 0) ? nExpected - 1
                                  : nRegistered - 1;
```

Once `nWaiters` equals `waitingFor`, all threads are released by the barrier:

```
if (nWaiters == waitingFor) {
    nWaiters = 0;
    dbg("Waking all waiters...");
    notifyAll();
}
```

Upon notification, the awakened threads remove themselves from the hash table and return from the call to `stall()`. Keep in mind that `notifyAll()` will wake the sleeping threads one at a time as scheduling, access to the monitor, and priorities permit.

BARRIER DEMO. The first illustration of the use of a barrier lock is a simple application that will create eight threads, each of which will count from zero to a specified number with a random delay inserted between steps. When each thread gets to the halfway point in its counting it will stall at the barrier, waiting for all the other threads to catch up. Once the last thread has arrived, all threads will continue counting.

To make the demonstration easier to visualize, each thread is represented by a vertical scrollbar in a Frame. The tab on the scrollbar will move from top to bottom as the thread counts. The scrollbars associated with threads having a short delay will proceed rapidly to the barrier, while those with longer delays will advance more slowly to the halfway point. When the last thread reaches the barrier, all threads will be released and the scrollbar's tabs will proceed to the bottom. Figure 6.20 shows the first Barrier demo running. The source to the barrier demonstration class, *BarrierUITest*, is presented in Fig. 6.21.

The demonstration class, BarrierUITest, consists of three methods: a constructor, main(), and run(), which overrides the run() method from the parent Thread class. The constructor for the BarrierUITest class has the signature:

```
public BarrierUITest(int countTo, int sleepTime,
                     String name, Barrier b)
```

Figure 6.20
A graphical demonstration of the barrier lock.

```
import java.awt.*;
import java.applet.*;
import java.util.Random;
import ajp.threads.*;

public class BarrierUITest extends Thread {
     private int howFar;
     private int halfWay;
     private int sleep;
     private String myName;
     Barrier barrier;
     Scrollbar s;
     Frame f;

     static int WHEREX;
     static int WIDTH = 50;
     static int HEIGHT = 600;

     public BarrierUITest(int countTo, int sleepTime,
                          String name, Barrier b){
         WHEREX += WIDTH + 30;
         howFar = countTo;
         halfWay = howFar/2;
         sleep = sleepTime;
         myName = name;
         barrier = b;
         f = new Frame();
         f.setSize(new Dimension(WIDTH, HEIGHT));
         f.setLocation( WHEREX, 50 );
         s = new Scrollbar( Scrollbar.VERTICAL, 0, 10, 0, countTo );
         f.add( "Center", s );
         f.show();
     }

     public void run(){
         int i=0;

         while(i <= howFar){
             // System.out.println( myName + ": " + i );
             s.setValue(++i);

             if (i == halfWay) {
                 try {
                     barrier.stall();
                 }
                 catch(ThreadNotRegisteredException e) {}
                 catch(InterruptedException e) {}
             }

             try{
                 sleep(sleep);
```

Figure 6.21
The BarrierUITest
class.

```
                    } catch(InterruptedException e){
                        System.out.println(e);
                    }
            }
        }

        public void cleanUp() {
            WHEREX = 0;
            f.setVisible(false);
            f.dispose();
            f = null;
            stop();
        }

        public static void main( String args[] ){
            // How high do we count to...
            int count;
            try {
                count = Integer.parseInt( args[0] );
            }
            catch (Exception e) {
                count = 50;
            }
            Random r = new Random();
            Barrier barrier = new Barrier(8);
            BarrierUITest b[] = new BarrierUITest[8];
            count = Math.max( count, 1 );

            for(int i = 0; i < 8; i++) {
                b[i] = new BarrierUITest(count, (int)(r.nextDouble()*1000),
                                    "Thread" + i, barrier);
                barrier.registerThread(b[i]);
            }

            for(int i = 0; i < 8; i++) {
                b[i].start();
            }
        }
    }
}
```

Figure 6.21
(Continued).

The variable countTo is the integer value that an instance of the class will count up to. Between each increment from 0 to value of countTo the thread will sleep for sleepTime milliseconds. The String name is passed to the parent Thread class constructor to name the thread, and b is the barrier the thread will synchronize to. The constructor saves the arguments into instance variables, then creates a new frame and vertical scrollbar to display the current count. Each frame is placed to the right of the previous frame by setting its *x*-coordinate equal to an offset from the static variable WHEREX:

```
static int WHEREX;
...
```
in the constructor…
```
    WHEREX += WIDTH + 30;
    ...
    f.move( WHEREX, 50 );
```

In the `run()` method of each BarrierUITest object, there is a while loop that runs from 0 to the targeted value, `howFar`. If the count variable *i* is not equal to one-half the value of `howFar`, it is incremented and the thread is allowed to sleep for the interval specified in the constructor. If the current count is one-half the targeted value, the thread will call the barrier's `stall()` method and will wait for all the other threads to catch up. Once the thread reaches the targeted count, it exits the `run()` method and terminates.

The application is driven by the `main()` method, in which eight Barrier-UITest objects are instantiated along with the single shared barrier object. Each thread will count to the value specified on the command line. If none is specified, an exception is thrown by `parseInt()` and the default target is set to 50. The shared barrier is initialized to accept eight threads, all of which are created and register within `main()`. Once the Barrier-UITest threads are created and have registered, they are started, initiating the demonstration.

The BarrierUITest demonstrates how multiple threads within a single application or applet can synchronize at a barrier. Possibly more compelling is using the barrier to synchronize threads from different applets, downloaded from a common host.

SHARING A BARRIER AMONG MULTIPLE APPLETS. A commonly asked question among Java applet programmers is "How can I get multiple applets to synchronize with each other?" One example would be to have all animation applets on a Web page delay displaying their animations until all applets have downloaded their images. Another example might be to have an audio player applet and a separate animation applet periodically synchronize to keep a soundtrack coordinated with a visual display. Both these examples can be accomplished with a barrier lock, shared among multiple applets.

One way to share a barrier among multiple applets of the same class is to make the barrier a static member of the class. This will expose the barrier to all applets of that class downloaded from the same host, as is described in Chap. 5. To share a barrier among applets of different classes, the barrier can be placed in a separate applet and accessed via the applet context. The interapplet barrier presented here will synchronize multiple applets of the same class. The applets that share the barrier will be instances of a subclass of the *Animator* demonstration applet distributed with the JDK. The subclass, called *SyncAnimator,* will cause all applets in the class to stall until all the applets have downloaded their images.

The SyncAnimator applet uses the form of the Barrier that is initialized with the number of expected threads. Thus, the first SyncAnimator applet downloaded must specify how many animations on the page will be sharing the barrier. This is done through the applet HTML tag, which must specify the number of animations on the page via the nAnimations parameter. A typical applet tag is shown in the example HTML file given as Fig. 6.22. Once the applets are downloaded and start running, there is no difference from standard Animator applets.

The first applet to be initialized will create a shared barrier that will register the number of threads passed in the nAnimations parameter. Since you have little control over the speed or order in which applets are downloaded in the Web environment, it is wise to put the nAnimations parameter in each applet tag.

Figure 6.22
HTML file illustrating the use of the Sync-Animator applet.

```
<title>The Animator Applet</title>
<hr>

<applet code=SyncAnimator.class width=75 height=75>
   <param name=imagesource value="images/Duke1">
   <param name=endimage value=10>
   <param name=pause value=200>
   <param name=nAnimations value=4>
</applet>

<applet code=SyncAnimator.class width=75 height=75>
   <param name=imagesource value="images/Duke2">
   <param name=endimage value=10>
   <param name=pause value=200>
   <param name=nAnimations value=4>
</applet>

<applet code=SyncAnimator.class width=75 height=75>
   <param name=imagesource value="images/Duke3">
   <param name=endimage value=10>
   <param name=pause value=200>
   <param name=nAnimations value=4>
</applet>

<applet code=SyncAnimator.class width=75 height=75>
   <param name=imagesource value="images/Duke4">
   <param name=endimage value=20>
   <param name=pause value=200>
   <param name=nAnimations value=4>
</applet>
<hr>
```

The SyncAnimator class itself is fairly simple, since it derives most of its functionality from the parent class Animator. Sources for the applet are shown in Fig. 6.23.

There are three significant methods in the class: init(), initBarrier(), and fetchImages(). The init() method simply gets the nAnimations parameter specified in the HTML, calls initBarrier() with the number of animations on the page, and then calls the init() method in the parent class. The initBarrier() method creates the shared Barrier object for all the SyncAnimator. Since it is static and synchronized, only one object in the class will be in the method at a time. The if statement

```
if (barrier == null) {
    barrier = new Barrier(nThreads);
}
```

ensures that only one Barrier object gets created.

The fetchImages() method is overridden from the Animator class. The signature of the method is:

```
protected URL fetchImages(Vector images)
```

Images are downloaded from a server and stored in the vector passed as an argument. The functionality that SyncAnimator needs to add to this method is registering with the barrier before the images are downloaded and stalling after the download has completed. Eliminating debugging messages and exception handling distills the overridden method to:

```
protected URL fetchImages(Vector images) {
    URL url;
    barrier.registerThread(Thread.currentThread()) ;
    URL url = super.fetchImages(images);
    barrier.stall();
    return url;
}
```

It is worth pointing out that little is needed to be known about the URL object that Animator.fetchImages() returns. Likewise, the purpose and contents of the images vector do not have to be known to implement the method. The images vector is simply passed through to the parent method and the returned URL object is passed, untouched, back to the caller.

```
import java.applet.*;
import java.awt.*;
import java.net.URL;
import java.util.Vector;
import ajp.threads.*;

/**
 * A class to demonstrate the use of multiple applets sharing a
 * Barrier lock to synchronize.  This Applet uses a shared (static)
 * Barrier to enable Animator applets to wait until all images have been
 * downloaded to begin.  The static Barrier object provides a simple means
 * of interapplet synchronization.
 */
public class SyncAnimator extends Animator {

    static Barrier barrier;

    public void init() {
        int nThreads;

        // init the barrier on the number of SyncAnimation objects
        // being used.
        try {
            nThreads = Integer.parseInt(getParameter("nAnimations"));
        }
        catch (Exception e) {
            nThreads = 1;
        }
        try {
            debug = Boolean.valueOf(getParameter("debug")).booleanValue();
        }
        catch (Exception e) {
            debug = false;
        }
        initBarrier(nThreads);

        super.init();
    }

    static synchronized void initBarrier(int nThreads) {
        if (barrier == null) {
            barrier = new Barrier(nThreads);
        }
    }

    /**
     * Overrride the Animator's fetchImages method.  It registers
     * the thread that is doing the fetching with the barrier.  Then,
     * it calls the Animator's fetchImages() method.  When all the images
     * have been fetched, it stalls at the barrier until all registered
```

Figure 6.23
The SyncAnimator
class.

```
     * Applets have downloaded their images.
     */
    protected URL fetchImages(Vector images) {
        URL url;
        if (barrier.registerThread(Thread.currentThread()) == false) {
            return null;
        }
        url = super.fetchImages(images);
        try {
            dbg("Stalling...");
            barrier.stall();
            dbg("Running...");
        }
        catch (InterruptedException e) {
            dbg("Interrupted...");
        }
        catch (ThreadNotRegisteredException e) {
            dbg("Not Registered...");
        }
        return url;
    }
}
```

Figure 6.23
(*Continued*).

SUMMARY

Java provides a very simple, powerful, and elegant model for multithreaded programming through monitors and condition variables. While much can be done directly with monitors and condition variables, part of the power and elegance of the model is that it can be extended to allow for more complicated locking and thread-management schemes. This chapter presents three such schemes implemented on top of the monitors and condition variables provided by Java: multiple-reader/single-writer locks, semaphores, and barrier locks.

Files and File I/O

Introduction

The topics of accessing files and performing file I/O may not initially seem appropriate for an advanced programming book. Nonetheless, there are several reasons why they have been included here. First, since much of the attention focused on Java has centered on creating applets, and since most browsers have not allowed applets that are downloaded from the Net to access files directly, many Java programmers are still unfamiliar with the classes in the `java.io` package. Second, restrictions placed by browsers on applets will not remain as policy indefinitely. Now that authentication of downloaded applets has been incorporated into the JDK, applet programmers can fully utilize the `java.io` package. Trusted applets can read and write files to a local disk—opening up a new range of possibilities for applet programmers. Third, as more applet programmers move toward using Java as a general-purpose programming language, and start to create Java applications that are free from any restrictions imposed by browsers, familiarity with Java's I/O model and the `java.io` package will become essential. And finally, whereas the Java I/O package is an elegant and easy-to-use package, it may be unfamiliar to programmers who have not come from a C++ background where the I/O model is very similar to Java. The Java I/O model allows for nesting or chaining I/O objects to obtain behavioral characteristics of the combined I/O objects. For these reasons, the Java File and File I/O models are the central themes of this chapter.

There are two parts to this chapter. The first part covers the Java *File* class and how it can be extended. Included in the discussion of the File class is an extension called *DirectoryEntry* that provides a mechanism for scanning and traversing directories. The DirectoryEntry class provides the foundation for a platform-independent file dialog extension to the AWT that is presented at the conclusion of the Java File section. The second part of this chapter deals with the I/O model implemented by the classes in the `java.io` package. Two classes are presented that illustrate how the `java.io` package can be easily extended to accommodate special I/O requirements. The two classes, `EncryptedOutputStream` and `DecryptedInputStream`, provide for simple encryption and decryption of data streams.

Throughout the discussion of the `java.io` package we refer to using the classes in the context of Java applications. This is not to say that the classes and discussion do not apply to applets. Even applets running in the context of restrictive Web browsers can use the I/O classes to read from and write to sockets. The discussion in the latter part of the chapter is equally applicable to Java applets and serves as background material for Chap. 8, "Network Programming."

The File Class

The File class in the `java.io` package provides basic methods for accessing files and for determining their states. The *state* of a file consists of such attributes as size, permissions, and date of last modification. The methods in the File class are, for the most part, wrappers around native methods that provide the actual access to and manipulation of the file. Before calling the native methods, a File object first checks the default security manager for permission to perform the requested operation. The native method will be called, provided that the security manager approves the access.* The `exists()` method of the File class is a typical example:

```
private native boolean exists0();
...
/**
 * Returns a boolean indicating whether or not a file exists.
 */
public boolean exists() {
    SecurityManager security = System.getSecurityManager();
    if (security != null) {
        security.checkRead(path);
    }
    return exists0();
}
```

If the security manager disallows reading of local files, it will throw a SecurityException from within the `checkRead()` method. If no exception is thrown, or if no SecurityManager is in use, the native method, `exist0()`, will be called. Note that no exception handling is done in the `exists()` method and that the method itself is not declared to throw any exceptions. Because the SecurityException thrown by `checkRead()` is a subclass of RuntimeException, it can be thrown without prior declaration in the method signature.

---

* For the details of how security managers work, see Chap. 10.

Extending the File Class: DirectoryEntry

Java File objects are used to represent both files and directories. The API to the File class is fairly intuitive and provides all the methods that might be expected to be supported across a variety of operating systems. Provided by the class are methods for determining the size of and permissions on files, contents of directories, and so on. Rather than showing a trivial example that illustrates all the methods in the class, this section presents an extension to the File class that will be used in the custom file dialog class later (see the section titled "Constructing a File Dialog" later in this chapter). The extension, called *DirectoryEntry,* is a class that is designed to represent directory objects only, rather than files and directories as the base File class does. The functionality that the DirectoryEntry class adds to File is a method for scanning the contents of the directory. This method places the files into a sorted Vector of File objects and the directories into a sorted Vector of DirectoryEntry objects. The two vectors can be sorted either on the basis of file names or modification dates of the files. Both ascending- and descending-ordered sorting is provided. The DirectoryEntry class also contains methods for retrieving the names of the files or directories as arrays of Strings.

The DirectoryEntry class provides two constructors:

1. `public DirectoryEntry(String path)`
2. `public DirectoryEntry (String path, FilenameFilter filter)`

Each constructor requires a path to the actual directory on disk. The latter form also takes a FilenameFilter object that is used by a DirectoryEntry object when scanning the directory. Through the FilenameFilter interface, the DirectoryEntry object is able to do pattern matching on file names and directory names. As the directory is scanned, the filter is applied to the names of the files. Only those files with names that are matched by the filter are stored by the DirectoryEntry object. The details of the Filename-Filter will be discussed in the section covering the implementation of the DirectoryEntry class. There are nine methods in the public API to the Directory entry class (see Table 7.1). The details of these methods will be discussed along with the other aspects of the implementation.

IMPLEMENTATION. The implementation of the DirectoryEntry class is shown in Fig. 7.1. Each DirectoryEntry object corresponds to a directory on disk. The `scanFiles()` method determines the contents of

TABLE 7.1

Public Methods in
the DirectoryEntry
Class

Method signature	Description
void setFoldCase(boolean fc)	If *true* is passed in, file names are all converted to lowercase prior to sorting.
void setFilter(FilenameFilter aFilter)	Sets the FilenameFilter to the one passed as an argument.
void setNoFilter()	Clears the FilenameFilter for subsequent scans.
void scanFiles(int sortBy)	Scans the directory for files.
boolean errorOccurred()	Returns *true* if the last scan produced an error.
Vector getDirectories()	Returns the vector of DirectoryEntry objects corresponding to the directories found during the last scan.
Vector getFiles()	Returns the vector of File objects corresponding to the files found during the last scan.
String[] getFileNames()	Returns an array of absolute pathnames for each file found during the last scan.
String[] getDirectoryNames()	Returns an array of absolute pathnames for each directory found during the last scan.

the directory and divides the contents into a Vector of files and a Vector of directories. References to the two vectors can be obtained through the methods getFiles() and getDirectories(). The work of determining the contents of the directory is done by the list() method that DirectoryEntry inherits from its parent class, File. The File class's list() method returns an array of Strings, each string containing the name of a file in the directory.

The list() method has two forms:

1. public String[] list()

2. public String[] list(FilenameFilter filter)

The first form of list() returns the names of all files in the directory. The latter form applies the pattern matching implemented in the FilenameFilter to each file and adds to the array only those filenames that match the filter.

The FilenameFilter interface specifies one method:

boolean accept(File dir, String name)

```
package ajp.io;

import java.io.*;
import java.util.*;

/**
 * An extension of the File class specifically targeted at
 * directories.  In addition to the standard File methods, it also
 * provides methods for scanning the directory, which creates a vector
 * of the files and a vector of the files contained.
 **/
public class DirectoryEntry extends File {
      public static final int NO_SORT                 = 0;
      public static final int SORT_BY_NAME_ASCENDING  = 1;
      public static final int SORT_BY_NAME_DESCENDING = 2;
      public static final int SORT_BY_DATE_ASCENDING  = 3;
      public static final int SORT_BY_DATE_DESCENDING = 4;
      public static final int SORT_BY_SIZE_ASCENDING  = 5;
      public static final int SORT_BY_SIZE_DESCENDING = 6;

      private boolean debug = false;

      // The files and Directories I contain
      private Vector files;
      private Vector directories;

      // The filter to use when scanning if any at all
      private FilenameFilter filter;

      // Did an error occur on the last action taken
      private boolean anError = false;

      // should name sorting be case sensitive
      private boolean foldCase = false;

      /**
       * Creates a DirectoryEntry object with the given path
       * to start from.  errorOccurred could be called which
       * would be true if the path does not exist.
       **/
      public DirectoryEntry(String directoryPath) {
          this(directoryPath, (FilenameFilter)null, false);
      }

      /**
       * Creates A DirectoryEntry object with the specified path to start and
       * a specified FilenameFilter to use when scanning the directories
       **/
      public DirectoryEntry (String directoryPath, FilenameFilter aFilter) {
          this(directoryPath, aFilter, false);
      }
```

Figure 7.1
The DirectoryEntry
class.

```
    public DirectoryEntry (String directoryPath, FilenameFilter aFilter, boolean debug) {
        super(directoryPath);
        this.debug = debug;
        if (!exists())
            anError = true;
        filter = aFilter;
    }

void dbg(String str) {
    if (debug) {
        System.out.println(this.getClass().getName() + ": " + str);
        System.out.flush();
    }
}

public void setFoldCase(boolean fc) {
    foldCase = fc;
}

/**
 * Sets the FilenameFilter to use when scanning the directory
 **/
public void setFilter(FilenameFilter aFilter) {
    filter = aFilter;
}

/**
 * Scans the directory referenced by this object and breaks up
 * the contents into files and directories.  These can be
 * accessed by getFiles() and getDirectories() Will use the
 * FilenameFilter set by setFilenameFilter if it is not null
 **/
public void scanFiles(int sortBy) {
    String[] fileList;

    try{

        if(filter != null) {
            fileList = list(filter);
        }
        else {
            fileList = list();
        }

        files = new Vector(fileList.length);
        directories = new Vector(fileList.length);

        for(int x=0; x<fileList.length; x++) {

            String path = getAbsolutePath();
            File aFile;
```

Figure 7.1
(Continued).

```
                  if(path.endsWith(separator)) {
                      aFile = new File(getAbsolutePath() + fileList[ x ]);
                  }
                  else {
                      aFile = new File(getAbsolutePath() + separator + fileList[ x
]);
                  }

                  if(aFile.isDirectory()) {
                      addToVector(directories,
                              new DirectoryEntry(aFile.getAbsolutePath()),
                              sortBy);
                  }
                  else {
                      addToVector(files, aFile, sortBy);
                  }
              }
          }
          catch(Exception e) {
              anError = true;
          }
      }

      /**
       * Did an error occur during the last method called?  Note that
       * the internal error flag is only set in the constructor and in
       * scanFiles().
       **/
      public boolean errorOccurred() {
          return anError;
      }

      /**
       * Return the directories found after the last
       * scanFiles() call.  If scanFiles() has not be
       * done yet, null is returned.  The Objects returned in
       * the vector must be cast to the appopriate class (either File
       * or DirectoryEntry).
       **/
      public Vector getDirectories() {
          return directories;
      }

      /**
       * Return the files found after the last scanFiles()
       * call.  If scanFiles() has not be done yet,
       * null is returned.  The Objects returned in the vector
       * must be cast to the appopriate class (either File or
       * DirectoryEntry).
       **/
      public Vector getFiles() {
          return files;
      }
```

Figure 7.1
(*Continued*).

```
/**
 * Eliminates the current filter used when scanning directories.
 **/
public void setNoFilter() {
    filter = null;
}

/**
 * Return an array of Strings containing names of all the files
 * in the DirectoryEntry object.
 **/
public String[] getFileNames() {
    String[] ret = new String[ files.size() ];
    for (int x=0; x<files.size(); x++) {
        ret[x] = ((File)files.elementAt(x)).getAbsolutePath();
    }
    return ret;
}

/**
 * Return an array of Strings containing names of all the directories
 * in the DirectoryEntry object.
 **/
public String[] getDirectoryNames() {
    String[] ret = new String[directories.size()];
    for (int x=0; x<directories.size(); x++) {
        ret[x] = ((DirectoryEntry)directories.elementAt(x)).getAbsolutePath();
    }
    return ret;
}

private void addToVector(Vector v, File f, int sortBy) {
    String fName;
    String oName;
    int count = v.size();
    boolean inserted = false;
    File o;

    if (count == 0 || sortBy == NO_SORT) {
        v.addElement(f);
        dbg("Added file " + f.getName());
        return;
    }

    for (int i=0; i<count; i++) {
        o = (File)v.elementAt(i);
        switch (sortBy) {
        case SORT_BY_DATE_ASCENDING:
            if (f.lastModified() < o.lastModified()) {
                v.insertElementAt(f, i);
                inserted = true;
            }
            break;
```

Figure 7.1

(Continued).

```
                  case SORT_BY_DATE_DESCENDING:
                      if (f.lastModified() > o.lastModified()) {
                          v.insertElementAt(f, i);
                          inserted = true;
                      }
                      break;
                  case SORT_BY_SIZE_ASCENDING:
                      if (f.length() < o.length()) {
                          v.insertElementAt(f, i);
                          inserted = true;
                      }
                      break;
                  case SORT_BY_SIZE_DESCENDING:
                      if (f.length() > o.length()) {
                          v.insertElementAt(f, i);
                          inserted = true;
                      }
                      break;
                  case SORT_BY_NAME_ASCENDING:
                      fName = f.getName();
                      oName = o.getName();
                      if (foldCase) {
                          oName = oName.toLowerCase();
                          fName = fName.toLowerCase();
                      }
                      if (fName.compareTo(oName) < 0) {
                          v.insertElementAt(f, i);
                          inserted = true;
                      }
                      break;
                  case SORT_BY_NAME_DESCENDING:
                      fName = f.getName();
                      oName = o.getName();
                      if (foldCase) {
                          oName = oName.toLowerCase();
                          fName = fName.toLowerCase();
                      }
                      if (fName.compareTo(oName) > 0) {
                          v.insertElementAt(f, i);
                          inserted = true;
                      }
                      break;
                  }
                  if (inserted) {
                      dbg("Added file " + f.getName());
                      break;
                  }
              }
          if (!inserted)
              v.addElement(f);
      }
}
```

Figure 7.1
(Continued).

As each file in the directory is encountered by the `list()` method, its name is passed to `accept()`, which will return *true* if the name satisfies the pattern-matching algorithm that `accept()` implements. For example, a trivial `accept()` method could be written to always return *true*, in effect implementing a wildcard (e.g., `*` or `*.*`) pattern match.[*]

Once the `list()` method returns its array of file names, the Directory-Entry object must convert the file names into File and DirectoryEntry objects and place the results into separate Vector objects. Without knowing which file names correspond to files and which correspond to directories, it is impossible to allocate two appropriately sized Vectors to contain them. To avoid the overhead of having the Vectors resize during insertion, both are allocated the same size as the array of file names. While this may waste some space, it is a reasonable trade-off to avoid the overhead of reallocating the Vectors and copying objects from an old to a new Vector as it grows. Once the Vectors are allocated, the array of file names is traversed and the names are used to create File objects. Each File is checked to see if it represents a directory and, if so, the File is used to create a Directory-Entry object. The Files and DirectoryEntry objects are inserted into the appropriate Vectors by the method `addToVector()`.

When `addToVector()` is called by `scanFiles()`, it is passed an integer flag, `sortBy`, which can take on one of the seven values specified at the top of the class definition:

1. `NO_SORT`
2. `SORT_BY_NAME_ASCENDING`
3. `SORT_BY_NAME_DESCENDING`
4. `SORT_BY_DATE_ASCENDING`
5. `SORT_BY_DATE_DESCENDING`
6. `SORT_BY_SIZE_ASCENDING`
7. `SORT_BY_SIZE_DESCENDING`

The value of the `sortBy` flag will determine the manner in which Files are inserted into the Vectors. For example, if the flag is set to `SORT_BY_NAME_ASCENDING`, once the `scanFiles()` method returns, the `files` and `directories` Vectors will be filled with File objects sorted alphabetically according to file name. Similarly, files can be sorted

---

[*] The file dialog described in the "Constructing a File Dialog" section of this chapter uses a simple wildcard FilenameFilter that matches the `*` character in combination with alphanumeric characters.

by size and date of last modification. The sorting of File objects by name will by default be case sensitive; if the `setFoldCase()` method has been called, however, and the `foldCase` instance variable is set to *true,* all file names will be converted to lowercase prior to sorting.

The DirectoryEntry class is a useful extension to the File class in that it provides a convenient way to differentiate between files and directories. Once the files are segregated, they can be accessed using any of the file I/O methods in the `java.io` package.

Constructing a File Dialog

The DirectoryEntry class provides most of the functionality needed to traverse directory hierarchies and examine files within directories. This functionality, combined with a graphical user interface, is what is provided by a file dialog widget. The file dialog widget included in the AWT, like all the other AWT widgets, is linked to a peer object that, in turn, is tied to an object in the native windowing toolkit. This linkage unfortunately means that the behavior and appearance of the AWT file dialog cannot be modified by creating a FileDialog subclass. For example, a File-Dialog will block when its `show()` method is called, essentially tying up a thread of execution until its *Save/Load* or *Cancel* button is pressed. This behavior cannot be altered through subclassing. Furthermore, there is no way to have a method called when the buttons are pressed, or to have a string other than *Save* or *Load* appear in the dialog's buttons.

The FileDialogPanel class is an extension to AWT that provides a file dialog that is designed to look and behave like the native file dialog on the Solaris/Motif platforms, but that can be extended through subclassing. In addition, since the FileDialogPanel is created as an extension of the AWT Panel class, it can be used anywhere a Panel can be used and is not restricted to use only in pop-up windows. Figure 7.2 shows a FileDialog-Panel contained in an AWT frame. Subclasses can override the methods associated with the *OK* and *Cancel* buttons, giving the file dialog new behavior. Finally, since the FileDialogPanel class is built upon the DirectoryEntry class, it provides for sorting the files and directories according to name, size, or modification date.

There are three constructors for the FileDialogPanel class:

1. `public FileDialogPanel(String pathToStart)`

2. `public FileDialogPanel(String pathToStart,`
`boolean foldCase)`

Figure 7.2
The FileDialogPanel
displayed in a Frame.

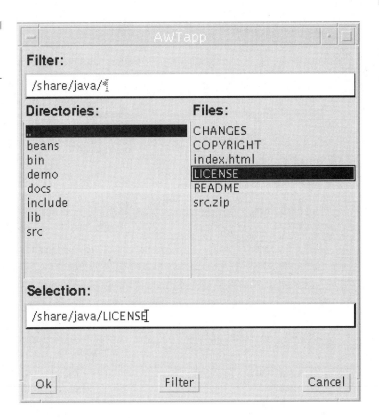

3. public FileDialogPanel(String pathToStart,
   int sorting, boolean foldCase)

Each constructor takes as an argument the name of the initial directory that is to be displayed in the dialog panel. The optional argument fold-Case is a boolean flag that, if set to *true*, will cause case to be ignored when sorting file names. The argument sorting specifies how the Directory-Entry object used by the dialog will sort the files. The values sorting can assume are the same constants outlined previously in the discussion of the DirectoryEntry class, NO_SORT, SORT_BY_NAME_ASCENDING, and so on.

The public methods in the FileDialogPanel's API are summarized in Table 7.2.

The FileDialogPanel follows the AWT delegation event model, and propagates ajp.awt.event.FileSelectionEvent objects when a file is selected. The FileSelectionEvent class, shown in Fig. 7.3, contains an instance variable in which the selected File object is stored. Listeners can use the get-File() accessor method to obtain a reference to the selected file.

TABLE 7.2

Public Methods of
the FileDialogPanel
Class

Method signature	Description
void setFileDialogFilter (FileDialogFilter df)	Sets the filter to be used when directories are scanned.
void setFoldcase(boolean fc)	If the parameter is *true*, case is ignored when sorting the names of files and directories.
void setSorting(int how)	Sets the sorting method (by name, size, date, and so on).
File getSelectedFile()	Returns a reference to the selected file in the panel
void setCancelButtonLabel (String label)	Sets the label on the *Cancel* button to the string provided.
void setOKButtonLabel (String label)	Sets the label on the *OK* button to the string provided.
void gotoDirectory(String path)	Changes the working directory of the dialog panel.
void addFileSelectionListener (FileSelectionListener 1)	Adds the given listener to the chain of objects being notified when a selection or cancellation happens.
void removeFileSelection-Listener(FileSelection-Listener 1)	Removes the given listener to the chain of objects being notified when a selection or cancellation happens.

Objects that must be notified when files are selected in the FileDialog-Panel must implement the FileSelectionListener interface shown in Fig. 7.4. The `fileSelected()` method of the listener is called each time a file is selected, and the `selectionCancelled()` method is called if the *Cancel* button in the dialog panel is pressed.

The event interaction between the FileDialogPanel and an applet is illustrated by the program shown in Fig. 7.5. The TestDialogApplet's `init()` method creates a FileDialogPanel, registers as an event listener, and places the dialog in a Frame. The applet's `fileSelected()` method simply prints the name of the file selected, and the `cancelSelection()` method hides the popup frame. The applet also provides a button that will redisplay the frame after it has been dismissed.

Since the FileDialogPanel accesses local files, the applet must be authenticated prior to running in a browser. The steps to authenticate the applet are described later in this chapter.

IMPLEMENTATION. The source code for the FileDialogPanel is shown in Fig. 7.6. While most of the interaction with Java File objects is

```
package ajp.awt.event;

import java.io.File;
import java.util.EventObject;
import ajp.awt.RawImage;

/**
 * A class representing events generated by a file dialog panel.
 *
 * @version 2.2
 **/
public class FileSelectionEvent extends EventObject {
    static final long serialVersionUID = -3631109216524508423L;

    // The file.
    protected File file;

    /**
     * Created an event object from representing cancelling of
     * the selection in the file dialog panel.
     **/
    public FileSelectionEvent() {
        super(new Object());
        file = null;
    }

    /**
     * Created an event object from representing selection of a file
     * in the file dialog panel.
     **/
    public FileSelectionEvent(File f) {
        super(f);
        file = f;
    }

    /**
     * Returns a handle to the File object selected.
     **/
    public File getFile() {
        return(file);
    }

}
```

Figure 7.3
The FileSelection-
Event class.

handled by the DirectoryEntry class discussed previously, there are several aspects of the implementation worth pointing out.

The purpose of the FileDialogPanel's constructor is primarily to set up the GUI through the setUpComponents() method. The listener class shown in Fig. 7.7, FileDialogActionListener, is used to handle all events generated by the user interface elements of the FileDialogPanel. Separate

Figure 7.4

The FileSelection-
Listener interface.

```
package ajp.awt.event;

import java.util.EventListener;

/**
 * An interface supported by Objects wishing to receive notification
 * of the selection of a file in a file dialog panel.
 *
 * @version 2.1
 **/
public interface FileSelectionListener extends EventListener {
    /**
     * Called when a file was selected in the dialog.
     **/
    void selectionCanceled();

    /**
     * Called when a file was selected in the dialog.
     **/
    void fileSelected(FileSelectionEvent evt);
}
```

instances of the listener class are created and added as a listener to each of the three buttons and two lists in the panel. The two lists display the contents of the current directory, with subdirectories on the left, and files on the right. The three buttons allow the user to apply the current pattern-matching filter, select a file, or cancel the current selection.

A significant part of the initialization is performed in the add-Notify() method rather than in the constructor. The reason all initialization is not done in the constructor is that part of the initialization process involves scanning the initial directory and populating the lists with the file and directory names. The scanning process involves applying a filter to the names as the directory is scanned. Programmers wishing to use a more sophisticated pattern-matching filter than the default filter provided can do so by passing their own filters to the setFileDialogFilter() method. By delaying the scanning of the initial directory until addNotify(), a new filter can be passed to the panel any time between the creation of the panel and when the panel is added to a container.

The FileDialogPanel can also be customized by changing the names on the *OK* and *Cancel* buttons using the setOkButtonLabel() and setCancelButtonLabel() methods. These methods should be called prior to adding the panel to a component to ensure that buttons are sized appropriately for the labels.

Events propagation in the panel begins in the FileDialogActionListener class. When the *OK* or *Cancel* buttons are pressed, the FileDialog-

```
import java.applet.*;
import java.awt.*;
import java.io.File;
import java.util.*;
import ajp.awt.*;
import ajp.awt.event.*;

/**
 * A FileDialogApplet.
 * @version 1.1
 **/
public class TestDialogApplet extends Applet implements FileSelectionListener {
    FileDialogPanel dialog;

    public void init() {
        String filename = getParameter("fileName");
        dialog = new FileDialogPanel(filename);
        dialog.setDebug(true);
        dialog.addFileSelectionListener(this);
        add(dialog);
    }

    public void fileSelected(FileSelectionEvent evt) {
        File f = evt.getFile();

        System.out.println("File = " + f.getAbsolutePath());
    }

    public void selectionCanceled() {
        System.out.println("Cancel selected");
    }
}
```

Figure 7.5
The *TestDialogApplet*
class.

Panel's `okAction()` or `cancelAction()` methods are called. The `cancelAction()` method calls the `processSelection()` method, passing *null* as the argument, which causes the `cancelSelection()` method of each of the panel's event listeners to be called. From the `okAction()` method, `processSelection()` is called with a reference to the selected File object. The File object is used by `processSelection()` to create a FileSelectionEvent which is then passed to the event listener's `fileSelected()` method.

The user interface includes a text field into which a file name matching pattern is entered. When the *Filter* button is pressed, the `filterAction()` method is called, which creates a new DirectoryEntry object. The DirectoryEntry object is used to scan the directory specified in the text field. The results of the scan are used to populate the panel's two lists.

```java
package ajp.awt;

import java.util.*;
import java.awt.*;
import java.awt.event.*;
import java.io.*;

import ajp.io.*;
import ajp.awt.event.*;

/**
 * A non-native, extensible file dialog class.  This class provides a dialog
 * that can be sub-classed to add new functionality as well as a call-back
 * scheme to notify Observer's of a selection in the dialog.
 *
 * @version 2.6
 **/
public class FileDialogPanel extends Panel {
    static final long serialVersionUID = 4066147759423045846L;
    static final String fileSelectionListenerK = "fileSelectionL";

    protected transient FileSelectionListener fileSelectionListener;

    public static final
      int NO_SORT               = DirectoryEntry.NO_SORT;
    public static final
      int SORT_BY_NAME_ASCENDING  = DirectoryEntry.SORT_BY_NAME_ASCENDING;
    public static final
      int SORT_BY_NAME_DESCENDING = DirectoryEntry.SORT_BY_NAME_DESCENDING;
    public static final
      int SORT_BY_DATE_ASCENDING  = DirectoryEntry.SORT_BY_DATE_ASCENDING;
    public static final
      int SORT_BY_DATE_DESCENDING = DirectoryEntry.SORT_BY_DATE_DESCENDING;
    public static final
      int SORT_BY_SIZE_ASCENDING  = DirectoryEntry.SORT_BY_SIZE_ASCENDING;
    public static final
      int SORT_BY_SIZE_DESCENDING = DirectoryEntry.SORT_BY_SIZE_DESCENDING;

    // button states, not really needed now but could be used
    public static final int CANCEL = 0;
    public static final int OK = 1;
    protected int buttonSelected;

    // default labels for the ok and cancel buttons,
    // can be set to be other labels
    protected String okLabel = "Ok";
    protected String cancelLabel = "Cancel";
    protected Button cancelButton;
    protected Button okButton;
    protected Button filterButton;

    // Label for what is put above the directories part of the file dialog
    protected Label directoryLabel;
```

Figure 7.6
The FileDialogPanel
class.

```
        // The starting path of the dialog box
        protected String startingPath;

        // The current things in the windows of the file dialog
        protected Vector currentDirectories;
        protected Vector currentFiles;
        protected String currentSelection;
        protected String currentEntry;

        // Some of the GUI components
        protected List files;
        protected List directories;
        protected TextField entry;
        protected TextField filter;

        // The current DirectoryEntry we are pointing at
        protected DirectoryEntry myEntry;

        // The file object created based on the selection to be returned
        protected File fileSelected;
        protected Font boldFont = new Font ("Helvetica", Font.BOLD, 14);

        protected int sortBy = NO_SORT;

        protected FileDialogFilter fdf;

        protected String wildcard = "*";

        protected boolean foldCase = true;

        private boolean debug = false;

        /**
         * Create the file dialog.
         **/
        public FileDialogPanel(String pathToStart) {
            this(pathToStart, SORT_BY_NAME_ASCENDING, true, false);
        }

        /**
         * Create the file dialog.
         **/
        public FileDialogPanel(String pathToStart, boolean fc) {
            this(pathToStart, SORT_BY_NAME_ASCENDING, fc, false);
        }

        /**
         * Create the file dialog.
         **/
        public FileDialogPanel(String pathToStart, int sorting,
                               boolean fc) {
```

Figure 7.6
(Continued).

```
            this(pathToStart, sorting, fc, false);
    }

    // As above, but with the "hidden" debug flag...
    public FileDialogPanel(String pathToStart, boolean fc,
                           boolean debug) {
        this(pathToStart, SORT_BY_NAME_ASCENDING, fc, debug);
    }

    // As above, but with the "hidden" debug flag...
    public FileDialogPanel(String pathToStart, int sorting,
                           boolean fc, boolean debug) {
        super();
        setSorting(sorting);
        startingPath = pathToStart;
        this.debug = debug;
        foldCase = fc;
        setUpComponents();
    }

    public void setDebug(boolean debug) {
        this.debug = debug;
    }

    public void addNotify() {
        super.addNotify();

        /* The filter is set after add() is called to give the programmer
           a chance to change it prior to having the dialog scan the
           initial directory. **/
        if (fdf == null) {
            fdf = new FileDialogFilter(debug);
        }
        fdf.setFilter(startingPath, wildcard);
        myEntry = new DirectoryEntry(startingPath, fdf, debug);
        myEntry.setFoldCase(foldCase);

        if (!myEntry.errorOccurred()) {
            myEntry.scanFiles(sortBy);
            currentFiles = myEntry.getFiles();
            currentDirectories = myEntry.getDirectories();
        }

        if (!myEntry.errorOccurred()) {
            currentEntry = myEntry.getAbsolutePath();
            updateAll();
        }
    }

    /**
     * This method does the grunt work of setting up the GUI.
     **/
```

Figure 7.6
(Continued).

```
protected void setUpComponents() {
    setLayout(new BorderLayout());
    setSize(700, 450);

    Panel filterPanel = new Panel();
    Panel dirPanel = new Panel();
    Panel filePanel = new Panel();
    Panel middlePanel = new Panel();
    Panel entryPanel = new Panel();
    Panel buttonPanel = new Panel();
    Panel controlPanel = new Panel ();

    add("North", controlPanel);
    add("South", buttonPanel);

    controlPanel.setLayout (new BorderLayout ());
    controlPanel.add("North", filterPanel);
    controlPanel.add("Center",  middlePanel);
    controlPanel.add("South",  entryPanel);
    controlPanel.setSize (700, 425);

    filterPanel.setLayout(new BorderLayout());
    directoryLabel = new Label("Filter: ");
    directoryLabel.setFont (boldFont);
    filterPanel.add("North",   directoryLabel);
    filter = new TextField();
    FileDialogActionListener fdal =
        new FileDialogActionListener(
                    FileDialogActionListener.FILTER_TEXT_ACTION,
                    this);
    filter.addActionListener(fdal);
    filterPanel.add("South",  filter);

    Label dirLabel;
    Label fileLabel;

    middlePanel.setLayout(new GridLayout(1, 2));
    middlePanel.add(dirPanel);
    middlePanel.add(filePanel);
    middlePanel.setSize (600, 400);

    dirPanel.setLayout(new BorderLayout ());
    dirPanel.add("North", dirLabel = new Label("Directories:"));
    dirLabel.setFont (boldFont);
    directories = new List(10, false);
    fdal = new FileDialogActionListener(
                    FileDialogActionListener.DIR_LIST_ACTION, this);
    directories.addActionListener(fdal);
    dirPanel.add("South",  directories);
    dirPanel.setSize (300, 400);

    filePanel.setLayout(new BorderLayout ());
    filePanel.add("North", fileLabel =  new Label("Files:"));
```

Figure 7.6
(*Continued*).

```
          fileLabel.setFont (boldFont);
          files = new List(10, false);
          fdal = new FileDialogActionListener(
                      FileDialogActionListener.FILE_LIST_ACTION, this);
          files.addActionListener(fdal);
          fdal = new FileDialogActionListener(
                      FileDialogActionListener.FILE_SELECT_ACTION, this);
          files.addItemListener(fdal);
          filePanel.add("South",  files);
          filePanel.setSize (300, 400);

          Label selLabel;

          entryPanel.setLayout(new BorderLayout ());
          entryPanel.add("North", selLabel = new Label("Selection:"));
          selLabel.setFont (boldFont);
          entry = new TextField();
          fdal = new FileDialogActionListener(
                      FileDialogActionListener.ENTRY_TEXT_ACTION, this);
          entry.addActionListener(fdal);
          entryPanel.add("South",   entry);

          // Set up button panel
          buttonPanel.setLayout(new BorderLayout());
          Panel tmpPanel = new Panel ();
          tmpPanel.setLayout (new FlowLayout(FlowLayout.LEFT));
          okButton = new Button(okLabel);
          fdal = new FileDialogActionListener(
                      FileDialogActionListener.OK_ACTION, this);
          okButton.addActionListener(fdal);
          tmpPanel.add(okButton);
          buttonPanel.add("West", tmpPanel);

          tmpPanel = new Panel ();
          tmpPanel.setLayout (new FlowLayout(FlowLayout.CENTER));
          filterButton = new Button("Filter");
          fdal = new FileDialogActionListener(
                      FileDialogActionListener.FILTER_ACTION, this);
          filterButton.addActionListener(fdal);
          tmpPanel.add(filterButton);
          buttonPanel.add("Center", tmpPanel);

          tmpPanel = new Panel ();
          tmpPanel.setLayout (new FlowLayout(FlowLayout.RIGHT));
          cancelButton = new Button(cancelLabel);
          fdal = new FileDialogActionListener(
                      FileDialogActionListener.CANCEL_ACTION, this);
          cancelButton.addActionListener(fdal);
          tmpPanel.add(cancelButton);
          buttonPanel.add("East", tmpPanel);

          validate();
     }
```

Figure 7.6
(Continued).

```
/**
 * Set the filter to be used when directories are scanned.
 **/
public void setFileDialogFilter(FileDialogFilter fdf) {
    this.fdf = fdf;
}

// The local debug method
void dbg(String str) {
    if (debug) {
        System.out.println(this.getClass().getName() + ": " + str);
        System.out.flush();
    }
}

/**
 * Set the folding of case on sorting.
 **/
public void setFoldCase(boolean fc) {
    foldCase = fc;
}

/**
 * Set the sortiing style to either SORT_BY_DATE_x,
 * SORT_BY_NAME_x, or SORT_BY_SIZE_x, where x is either ASCENDING
 * or DESENDING.
 **/
public void setSorting(int how) {
    switch(how) {
    case SORT_BY_DATE_ASCENDING:
    case SORT_BY_DATE_DESCENDING:
    case SORT_BY_NAME_ASCENDING:
    case SORT_BY_NAME_DESCENDING:
    case SORT_BY_SIZE_ASCENDING:
    case SORT_BY_SIZE_DESCENDING:
        sortBy = how;
        break;
    case NO_SORT:
    default:
        sortBy = NO_SORT;
        break;
    }
}


public File getFileSelected() {
    return fileSelected;
}

public int getButtonSelected() {
    return buttonSelected;
}
```

Figure 7.6
(*Continued*).

```
public void setOkButtonLabel(String label) {
    okLabel = label;
    okButton.setLabel(label);
}

public void setCancelButtonLabel(String label) {
    cancelLabel = label;
    cancelButton.setLabel(label);
}

protected void updateAll() {
    updateFiles();
    updateDirectories();
    updateFilter();
    updateEntry();
}

protected void updateFiles() {
    files.removeAll();
    if (currentFiles != null) {
        for(int x=0; x<currentFiles.size(); x++) {
            File aFile = (File)currentFiles.elementAt(x);
            files.addItem(aFile.getName());
        }
    }
}

protected void updateDirectories() {

    directories.removeAll();
    if (currentDirectories != null) {
        if (! fdf.getPathString().equals(File.separator))
            directories.addItem("..");
        for(int x=0; x<currentDirectories.size(); x++) {
            DirectoryEntry aDir =
                (DirectoryEntry)currentDirectories.elementAt(x);
            directories.addItem(aDir.getName());
        }
        directories.select(0);
    }
}

protected void updateFilter() {
    String path = fdf.getPathString();
    if (path.equals(File.separator)) {
        filter.setText( path + fdf.getFilterString());
    }
    else {
        filter.setText( path + File.separator + fdf.getFilterString());
    }
}
```

Figure 7.6
(Continued).

```
    protected void updateEntry() {
        String path = myEntry.getAbsolutePath();
        if (!path.equals(File.separator))
            path += File.separator;

        entry.setText(path);
    }

    String extractFilter(String pathPlusFilter) {
        int index = pathPlusFilter.lastIndexOf(File.separatorChar);
        String filterPart = (index < 0) ?
            wildcard : pathPlusFilter.substring(index + 1);

        if (filterPart == null || filterPart.equals(""))
            filterPart = wildcard;
        return filterPart;
    }

    String extractPath(String pathPlusFilter) {
        int index = pathPlusFilter.lastIndexOf(File.separatorChar);
        String pathPart = (index < 0) ?
            File.separator : pathPlusFilter.substring(0, index);

        return pathPart;
    }

    protected void filterAction() {
        String pathPart = fdf.getPathString();
        String filterPart = fdf.getFilterString();

        if (pathPart == null || pathPart.equals("")) {
            pathPart = File.separator;
            fdf.setPathString(pathPart);
        }

        DirectoryEntry dirEnt =
            new DirectoryEntry(pathPart, fdf, debug);
        dirEnt.setFoldCase(foldCase);

        setCursor(Cursor.getPredefinedCursor(Cursor.WAIT_CURSOR));
        dirEnt.scanFiles(sortBy);
        setCursor(Cursor.getDefaultCursor());

        if (!dirEnt.errorOccurred()) {
            currentDirectories = dirEnt.getDirectories();
            currentFiles = dirEnt.getFiles();
            myEntry = dirEnt;
            updateAll();
        }
    }

    protected void fileSelectedAction() {
        String path = fdf.getPathString();
```

Figure 7.6
(Continued).

```
            if (path.equals(File.separator)) {
                entry.setText(path + files.getSelectedItem());
            }
            else {
                entry.setText(path + File.separator + files.getSelectedItem());
            }
        }

    protected void fileDeselectedAction() {
        entry.setText(fdf.getPathString());
    }

    protected void fileListAction() {
        fileSelectedAction();
        okAction();
    }

    protected void dirListAction() {
        String dir = directories.getSelectedItem();
        String path = fdf.getPathString();

        if (dir.equals("..")) {
            int index = path.lastIndexOf(File.separatorChar);
            String tmp = path.substring(0, index);
            if (index < 0) {
                tmp = File.separator;
            }
            dir = tmp;
        }
        else if (path.equals(File.separator)) {
            dir = path + dir;
        }
        else {
            dir = path + File.separator + dir;
        }
        gotoDirectory(dir);
    }

    protected void filterTextAction() {
        String path = filter.getText();
        fdf.setPathString(extractPath(path));
        fdf.setFilterString(extractFilter(path));
        filterAction();
    }

    protected void okAction() {
        String text = entry.getText();
        if (text == null || text.equals("")) {
            text = startingPath;
            entry.setText(text);
        }
        fileSelected = new File(text);
        buttonSelected = OK;
```

Figure 7.6
(*Continued*).

```
            dbg("oKAction: " + text + "File = " + fileSelected);
            processSelection(fileSelected);
    }

    protected void cancelAction() {
        processSelection(null);
    }

    public void gotoDirectory(String dir) {
        fdf.setPathString(dir);
        fdf.setFilterString(extractFilter(filter.getText()));
        updateFilter();
        filterAction();
    }

    /**
     * Adds the specified listener to receive selection events
     * from this file dialog.
     **/
    public void addFileSelectionListener(FileSelectionListener l) {
        fileSelectionListener =
            AJPEventMulticaster.add(fileSelectionListener, l);
    }

    /**
     * Removes the specified listener so it no longer receives
     * selection events from this file dialog.
     **/
    public void removeFileSelectionlListener(FileSelectionListener l) {
        fileSelectionListener =
            AJPEventMulticaster.remove(fileSelectionListener, l);
    }

    /**
     * Processes selection events occurring on this file dialog by
     * dispatching them to any registered SelectionListener objects.
     **/
    protected void processSelection(File f) {
        if (fileSelectionListener != null) {
            if (f == null) {
                fileSelectionListener.selectionCanceled();
            }
            else {
                fileSelectionListener.fileSelected(
                                new FileSelectionEvent(f));
            }
        }
    }

//////////////////// Serialization support. //////////////////////

    private int fileDialogPanelSerializedDataVersion = 1;
```

Figure 7.6
(Continued).

```
    private void writeObject(ObjectOutputStream s) throws IOException {
        s.defaultWriteObject();

        AJPEventMulticaster.write(s, fileSelectionListenerK,
                             (EventListener)fileSelectionListener);
        s.writeObject(null);
    }

    private void readObject(ObjectInputStream s)
                         throws ClassNotFoundException, IOException {
        s.defaultReadObject();

        Object keyOrNull;
        while(null != (keyOrNull = s.readObject())) {
            String key = ((String)keyOrNull).intern();

            if (fileSelectionListenerK == key)
                addFileSelectionListener(
                         (FileSelectionListener)(s.readObject()));

            else // skip value for unrecognized key
                s.readObject();
        }
    }
}
```

▀▀▀ ▀▀▀ ▀▀▀ ▀▀▀
Figure 7.6
(*Continued*).

The file name filtering is done by a subclass of `java.io.Filename-Filter` called FileDialogFilter, shown in Fig. 7.8. The FileDialogFilter class provides simple wildcard matching that uses the asterisk (*) to match any characters in the filename (e.g., `*`, `*.txt`, `File*.java`, and so on). A FileDialog-Filter object is composed of two parts: a *pathname*, which is the absolute path prefixing a pattern to be matched, and a *filter part*, which is the pattern used when applying the filter. The two parts of the FileDialogFilter can be set individually or both at the same time using its methods:

```
public void setPathString(String path)
public void setFilterString(String filter)
public void setFilter(String path, String filter)
```

The FileDialogFilter used by the FileDialogPanel is updated each time a change is made to the panel. The update usually happens immediately prior to the `filterAction()` method being called. For example, in the FileDialogPanel's `filterTextAction()` method, when the filter Text-Field is modified, the filter and path portions of the string in the text area are extracted and passed to the FileDialogFilter just prior to scanning the directory:

```
package ajp.awt;

import java.util.*;
import java.awt.*;
import java.awt.event.*;
import java.io.*;

import ajp.io.*;
import ajp.awt.event.*;

/**
 * A listener for File Dialog button events.
 * @version 2.6
 **/
class FileDialogActionListener implements ActionListener,
                                          Serializable,
                                          ItemListener {
    static final long serialVersionUID = 2060142712042558257L;
    static final int OK_ACTION = 0;
    static final int FILTER_ACTION = 1;
    static final int CANCEL_ACTION = 2;
    static final int FILE_LIST_ACTION = 3;
    static final int DIR_LIST_ACTION = 4;
    static final int FILTER_TEXT_ACTION = 5;
    static final int ENTRY_TEXT_ACTION = 6;
    static final int FILE_SELECT_ACTION = 7;

    private boolean debug;
    int tag;
    FileDialogPanel fileDialog;

    public FileDialogActionListener(int tag, FileDialogPanel fd) {
        this(tag, fd, false);
    }

    public FileDialogActionListener(int tag, FileDialogPanel fd,
                                    boolean debug) {
        fileDialog = fd;
        this.tag = tag;
        this.debug = debug;
    }

    public void itemStateChanged(ItemEvent evt) {
        switch(evt.getStateChange()) {
        case ItemEvent.SELECTED:
            fileDialog.fileSelectedAction();
            break;
        case ItemEvent.DESELECTED:
            fileDialog.fileDeselectedAction();
            break;
        }
    }
```

Figure 7.7
The FileDialogAction-
Listener class.

```
    public void actionPerformed(ActionEvent e) {
        dbg("got an action: " + tag);
        switch(tag) {
        case OK_ACTION:
        case ENTRY_TEXT_ACTION:
            fileDialog.okAction();
            break;
        case FILTER_ACTION:
            fileDialog.filterAction();
            break;
        case CANCEL_ACTION:
            fileDialog.cancelAction();
            break;
        case FILE_LIST_ACTION:
            fileDialog.fileListAction();
            break;
        case DIR_LIST_ACTION:
            fileDialog.dirListAction();
            break;
        case FILTER_TEXT_ACTION:
            fileDialog.filterTextAction();
            break;
        }
    }
    // The local debug method
    void dbg(String str) {
        if (debug) {
            System.out.println(this.getClass().getName() + ": " + str);
            System.out.flush();
        }
    }
}
```

Figure 7.7
(Continued).

```
        ...
        String path = filter.getText();
        fdf.setPathString(extractPath(path));
        fdf.setFilterString(extractFilter(path));
        filterAction();
        ...
```

The actual work of the FileDialogFilter is done in its `accept()` method, as was described in the discussion of the DirectoryEntry class. Again, the file name matching used by the FileDialogFilter is rather limited. By subclassing from the FileDialogFilter and overriding its `accept()` method, however, more sophisticated behavior can be obtained.

```
package ajp.io;

import java.io.*;
import java.util.*;
/**
 * The following class is needed to do the filtering for the filter
 * object It does implement FilenameFilter and will behave
 * appropriately in those cases To use, give it a filter string
 * "*.whatever" and it will accept only files Ending with that string
 * As a beneficial side effect you can also pass it a path then a
 * filter string and it will parse it for you and give you the
 * pathString and the filterString
 *
 **/
public class FileDialogFilter implements FilenameFilter {

    public String filterString;
    public String pathString;
    protected boolean acceptAll = false;
    boolean acceptAfter;
    boolean acceptBefore;
    private boolean debug = false;

    public String tokens[];

    public FileDialogFilter() {
        this(false);
    }

    public FileDialogFilter(boolean debug) {
        this.debug = debug;
        pathString = File.separator;
    }

    void dbg(String str) {
        if (debug) {
            System.out.println(this.getClass().getName() + ": " + str);
            System.out.flush();
        }
    }

    public void setFilter(String path, String filter) {
        setFilterString(filter);
        setPathString(path);
    }

    public String getFilterString() {
        return new String(filterString);
    }
```

Figure 7.8
The FileDialogFilter
class.

```
    public String getPathString() {
        return new String(pathString);
    }

    public void setPathString(String path) {
        pathString = new String(path);
        // expand wildcards for home directory...
    }

    public void setFilterString(String filter) {
        acceptAll = false;
        acceptAfter = false;
        acceptBefore = false;

        if (filter == null) {
            acceptAll = true;
            filterString = "*";
        }
        else {
            filterString = new String(filter);
            if (filterString.startsWith("*")) {
                acceptBefore = true;
            }

            if (filterString.endsWith("*")) {
                acceptAfter = true;
                dbg("AcceptAfter = true");
            }

            StringTokenizer t = new StringTokenizer(filterString, "*",
                                                    false);
            tokens = new String[ t.countTokens() ];
            int x=0;
            while (t.hasMoreTokens()) {
                tokens[ x++ ] = t.nextToken();
                dbg("Token found: " + tokens[ x -1 ]);
            }

            if (x == 0)
                acceptAll = true;
        }

    }

    public boolean accept(File dir, String name) {
        if (acceptAll)
            return true;
        if ((!acceptBefore) && (!name.startsWith(tokens[0]))) {
            return false;
        }
        boolean accepted = true;
        for(int x=0; x<tokens.length; x++) {
            if (name.indexOf(tokens[x]) == -1) {
                return false;
```

Figure 7.8
(Continued).

```
            }
        }
        // if it still is okay then check for acceptAfter

        if (acceptAfter)
            return true;

        if (name.endsWith(tokens[ tokens.length - 1 ])) {
            return true;
        }
        else
            return false;

    }
}
```

Figure 7.8
(*Continued*).

There are a few final implementation details that merit discussion. Although the FileDialogPanel class uses the AWT event delegation model for callbacks, the fileSelected() callback is not the only way selection information can be obtained from the panel. The getFile-Selected() and getButtonSelected() methods can be used to determine what file was selected and which button was pressed. Also, with the addFileSelectionListener() and removeFileSelec-tionListener() methods, any other objects that implement the File-SelectionListener interface can participate in or be removed from the callback process.

By using the gotoDirectory() method, different directories can be programmatically loaded into the panel. This method of changing the directory loaded in the panel is useful when the same FileDialogPanel is to be reused within an application. The panel can be created and displayed, then hidden after a file is selected and redisplayed later on, possibly after calling gotoDirectory().

One final detail: In order to make the FileDialogPanel portable, explicit references to file separator characters (/ or \) have been avoided. The java.io.File class provides the constants File.separator and File.separatorChar, which should *always* be used in favor of explicit references to the actual separator character. Even if you don't think that a particular application will be run on other hardware or OS platforms, it is wise to make this minor implementation decision to help ensure portability.

Extending the FileDialogPanel

One of the big advantages of the FileDialogPanel over the FileDialog in the JDK is that the FileDialogPanel can be extended through subclassing. Figure 7.9 shows a screen snapshot of such a subclass, called AddFileDialog-Panel. The dialog in Fig. 7.9 adds a list of selected files to the FileDialog. As the user traverses directories and selects files, they are added to the list on the right. Selected files can be individually deleted from the list by pressing the *Remove* button. When the *Done* button is pressed, the names of all the selected files are printed. This example could be used as the basis of an archiving or file-transfer application. Files accumulated in the list of selected files can be accumulated from different directories, then processed all at once by changing the functionality behind the *Done* button.

The application shown in Fig. 7.9 is an AWT Frame that contains two panels. One is a subclass of FileDialogPanel called *AddFileDialogPanel*. The other is a Panel subclass called *ListFilesPanel*. The source code for the application is almost trivial but is nonetheless shown in Fig. 7.10. The application creates the two panels and adds them to a grid layout in a frame, then shows the frame.

The ListFilesPanel class is a Panel subclass that implements the FileSelectionListener interface (see Fig. 7.11). Each time a file is selected in the file

Figure 7.9
An extension of the
FileDialogPanel class.

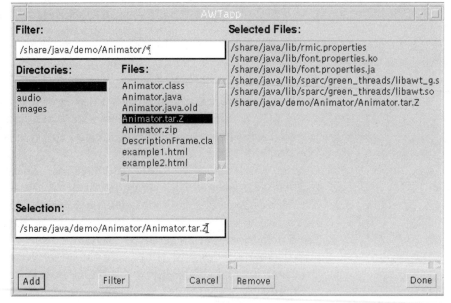

```
class TestAddDialog {

    public static void main(String args[]) {
        ListFilesPanel p = new ListFilesPanel();
        AddFileDialogPanel a = new AddFileDialogPanel(args[0]);
        a.addFileSelectionListener(p);
        Frame f = new Frame();
        f.setLayout(new GridLayout(1, 2));
        f.setSize(new Dimension(600, 400));
        f.add(a);
        f.add(p);
        f.show();
    }

}
```

dialog panel, a reference to the file will be added to the list. The panel's
fileSelected() method will be passed a FileSelectionEvent object from
which the file can be accessed. To keep this reference for later use, the File is
placed on an ObjectList, introduced in Chap. 4. When the *Done* button is
pressed, the method doneHit() is called, processing the files on the list.

The only method in the AddFileDialogPanel class shown in Fig. 7.12 is
a constructor that takes a directory name and a reference to the List-
FilesPanel that is adjacent in the GUI. The only real change to the FileDialogPanel is that the *OK* button's label is changed. All new functionality
is introduced through the ListFilesPanel.

Using FileDialogPanels in Applets

With the introduction of the JDK 1.1, trusted applets can be granted
privileges that were heretofore denied by the applet security manager.
Specifically, browsers disallowed any file access by applets downloaded
from the network. All applets were considered untrusted and were prevented from any privileged operations such as reading and writing files.
This section describes the basics of how to archive and sign the AddFile-
DialogPanel of the previous example so that it can be run as a trusted
applet in a browser.

The distribution of trusted applets is based on a certificate and public
key encryption scheme. As a developer or distributor of applets, you create
a *public key* that you give to anyone who wishes to download trusted applets
from you. Your public key is like your signature on a credit card. Merchants
can compare the signature on a credit receipt to the signature on the back
of your credit card to verify that you are allowed to make a purchase.

```
import java.awt.*;
import java.awt.event.*;
import java.util.*;
import java.io.*;
import ajp.awt.*;
import ajp.awt.event.*;

/**
 * This class works with our redefined file dialog to implement the
 * list and remove features.  Calls our producer object and lets it
 * know when it's buttons are hit.
 **/
class ListFilesPanel extends Panel implements FileSelectionListener,
                                              ActionListener {

    protected Font boldFont = new Font ("Helvetica", Font.BOLD, 14);
    ObjectList listOfFiles = new ObjectList(10);

    ListFilesPanel() {
        super();

        setLayout (new BorderLayout ());

        Button b;
        Panel btnPanel = new Panel ();
        btnPanel.setLayout (new BorderLayout());
        Panel tmpPanel = new Panel ();
        tmpPanel.setLayout (new FlowLayout(FlowLayout.LEFT));
        tmpPanel.add(b = new Button("Remove"));
        b.addActionListener(this);
        btnPanel.add("West", tmpPanel);

        tmpPanel = new Panel ();
        tmpPanel.setLayout (new FlowLayout(FlowLayout.RIGHT));
        tmpPanel.add(b = new Button("Done"));
        b.addActionListener(this);
        btnPanel.add("East", tmpPanel);

        Panel listPanel = new Panel();
        listPanel.setLayout (new GridLayout (1,1));
        listPanel.add(listOfFiles);

        Label label = new Label("Selected Files: ");
        label.setFont(boldFont);

        add("North", label);
        add("Center", listPanel);
        add("South", btnPanel);

    }

    public void addItemToList(String itemToAdd, Object o) {
```

Figure 7.11
The ListFilesPanel
class.

```
            listOfFiles.addItem(itemToAdd, o);
    }

    protected void removeItemFromList() {
        try{
            listOfFiles.delSelectedItem();
        }
        catch(Exception e) {}
    }

    public void actionPerformed(ActionEvent e) {
        System.out.println("ActionEvent: " + e);
        String cmd = e.getActionCommand();

        if(cmd == "Remove") {
            removeItemFromList();
        }
        else if (cmd == "Done") {
            doneHit();
        }

    }

    public void fileSelected(FileSelectionEvent evt) {
        File f = evt.getFile();

        addItemToList(f.getAbsolutePath(), f);
    }

    public void selectionCanceled() {
        System.out.println("Cancel selected");
        System.exit(0);
    }

    public void doneHit() {
        int count = listOfFiles.countItems();
        File f;

        System.out.println("The following files were selected:");
        for(int x=0; x < count; x++) {
            f = (File)listOfFiles.getItem(x);
            System.out.println("\t" + f.getAbsolutePath());
        }
    }

}
```

Figure 7.11
(*Continued*).

```
import ajp.awt.*;

/**
 *      This class is our extension of FileDialogPanel that shows
 *      the reuse we get with that class and also how to and why we
 *      would want to override certain features of that class and set
 *      the different button labels.  This class communicates with our
 *      producer and also with our ListFilePanel item so that it can
 *      add items to the list when it's Add button is hit
 **/
public class AddFileDialogPanel extends FileDialogPanel {

     AddFileDialogPanel(String pathToStart) {
         super(pathToStart);
         setOkButtonLabel("Add");
     }

}
```

Figure 7.12
The AddFileDialog-
Panel class.

Browsers can use your public key to verify that a signed applet was signed by the same person who generated the public key. Users or site administrators can maintain an *identity database* of approved signatures that will be used to authenticate applets. Since the identity database is the source of authentication data, it is important to put only valid keys in the database. Knowing the person who gives you the key is the first step in preserving the integrity of the identity database. While some public keys come directly from the source of the key, to assure users of the validity and integrity of keys, others come from certificate authorities—trusted organizations that distribute public keys with a digitally signed document called a *certificate*.

Once applets have been authenticated, the granularity of privileges granted the applet will vary from browser to browser. For example, Hot-Java will allow the specification of specific readable and writeable directories based on the source of the applet. At present it is up to the browser vendors to define what trusted applets are and are not allowed to do.

Figure 7.13 shows an AddFileDialogPanel in a trusted applet running in the HotJava browser. The downloaded applet is browsing files on the file system of the local host. HotJava has granted the applet the privilege to read these files and directories because it is signed and comes from a known source, or *signer*. The first step in providing signed code is creating a signature for yourself.

Figure 7.13
A trusted applet
using an AddFile-
DialogPanel.

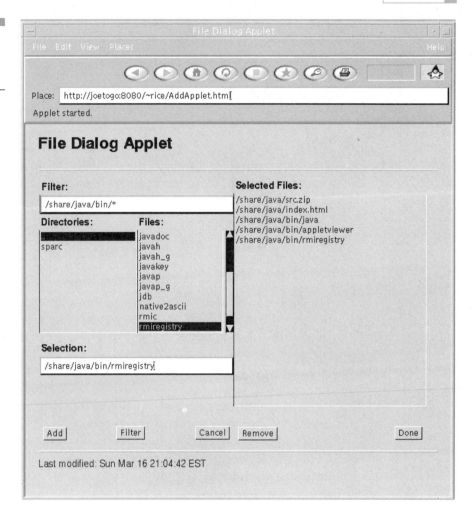

The `javakey` utility is used to create and manage signatures and identity databases.[*] To create a signature, you must first pick a name for yourself. In the example that follows we have chosen the name *ajp*. The name *ajp* is introduced as a signer in the local identity database with the command:

```
javakey -cs ajp true
```

---

[*] Full documentation for javakey is available in the JDK 1.1 documentation. Rather than describing all the options to the javakey command, we will simply show those options needed for our example.

The `true` argument to the command indicates that *ajp* is a trusted signer. Once *ajp* is in the identity database as a signer, a public key can be created that can be distributed to those wishing to run trusted code *ajp* has signed. The public key is generated and put in the file `public.key` with the command:

```
javakey -gk ajp DSA 512 public.key
```

The `DSA` parameter specifies the signature algorithm, and `512` is the number of bits in the generated key. The `public.key` file can be given to others, who can incorporate it into their own identity databases by running the following commands:

```
javakey -c ajp true
javakey -ik ajp public.key
```

The first command creates the trusted name *ajp*, and the second associates the public key with *ajp*. At this point, any remote user whose browser accesses the updated identity database will now be able to download and run trusted code from *ajp*.

To create the trusted applets, they must be archived and signed by *ajp*. The first step is to create a Java Archive (JAR) file containing any of the classes that will perform privileged operations. In many cases, the easiest approach to creating the archive will be to bundle all the class files in the applet. In addition to being signable, the JAR files compress the class files so the overall download time is faster—this provides added incentive to archive the whole applet, rather than just specific pieces that actually require the signature.

The jar utility in the JDK is used to create JAR files. In the case of the AddFileDialogApplet the following command* archives all the needed files and places them in an archive called `addFileApplet.jar`:

```
jar cf addFileApplet.jar AddFileDialogApplet.class
 ListFilesPanel.class
      AddFileDialogPanel.class
      ajp/awt/event/FileSelectionListener.class
      ajp/awt/ObjectList.class ajp/awt/FileDialogPanel.class
      ajp/awt/FileDialogActionListener.class
      ajp/awt/AJPEventMulticaster.class
      ajp/io/DirectoryEntry.class
```

---

* We are showing the jar command using Solaris syntax for path names. On Windows, simply use the backslash as the file separator.

Once the JAR file is created, it must be signed. To sign a JAR file, the javakey utility requires a directive file—a file that contains information about who is signing the JAR file. The JAR file for this example is shown in Fig. 7.14. The comments in the file describe the various parameters the file specifies.

The JAR file is signed with the command:

```
javakey -gs addFileApplet.directive addFileApplet.jar
```

In accordance with the directive file, the signed JAR is left in the file addFileApplet.jar.sig.

The final step is to place the signed JAR file and an appropriate HTML file on a Web server. The JAR file is specified using the archive parameter in the APPLET HTML tag. In this case the HTML tag will look like:

```
<applet code=AddFileDialogApplet
        codebase=classes
        width=600 height=400
        archive="addFileApplet.jar.sig">
<param name=fileName value="/share/java">
</applet>
```

The signed JAR file should be placed in the location specified by the codebase parameter. Here, the JAR file is in the class's subdirectory, below the directory containing the HTML.

```
#
# JAR signing directive file.
#

# The signers name in the identity database.
signer=ajp

# Certificate number to use for this signer.
cert=1

# Not supported.
chain=0

# The name to give to the generated signature file and associated signature
# block. This must be 8 characters or less.
signature.file=AJP

# (Optional) The name to give to the signed JAR file.
out.file=addFileApplet.jar.sig
```

Figure 7.14
A signature directive
file for a Java Archive.

Browsers that encounter the JAR file will attempt to authenticate it against their local identity database. If the *ajp* name is found, the public key is used to verify the JAR file. Once the JAR file is authenticated, it is up to the browser's security manager to define the bounds on what applets signed with the *ajp* signature are permitted to do.

The Java I/O Model

The Java I/O model is based on a stream I/O model wherein each file can be thought of as a stream of sequential data that flows either from the data source to the application or from the application to the data destination. Data sources and destinations can be files, network connections, or platform-specific devices, such as keyboards or displays. The flow of data is analogous to the flow of water through a pipe. Likewise, the various classes in the `java.io` package are like pieces of pipe that can be combined to change the nature of the flow of data. Each new piece of pipe can manipulate or condition the data passing through the pipe, giving the data a different characteristic or behavior as it exits the pipe.

Figure 7.15 shows the structure of the JDK's I/O class hierarchy. At the base of the hierarchy are abstract base I/O classes: the *InputStream, OutputStream, Reader,* and *Writer* classes. These four classes are the foundation of I/O in Java. Below the base classes are fundamental I/O classes. These are nonabstract classes that inherit from the base classes and provide basic reading and writing functionality. Each fundamental I/O class corresponds to a different source or destination for reading or writing: *file, StringBuffer, array,* and so on. Below the fundamental I/O classes are the I/O filter classes. Filter classes derive from the base I/O classes as well, but they are used to wrap around the fundamental classes or other filter classes. Each filter class in some way conditions the data as it passes through the stream. For example, the BufferedInputStream class is a filter class that buffers the data passing through the InputStream it contains.

The interesting thing about the Java I/O model is the way in which the input streams can be combined. For example, a FileInputStream provides only variants of the `read()` method that allow either single bytes or arrays of bytes to be read. By converting the stream to a DataInputStream, data can be read as Java data types rather than bytes:

```
FileInputStream fis = new FileInputStream("SomeFile");
DataInputStream dis = new DataInputStream(fis);
```

Figure 7.15
The structure of the
JDK I/O classes.

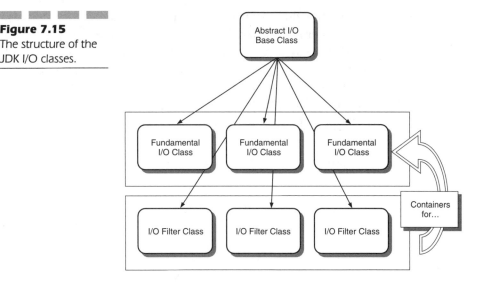

To add buffering to the DataInputStream, one need only add another filter layer:

```
FileInputStream fis = new FileInputStream("SomeFile");
DataInputStream dis = new DataInputStream(new
 BufferedInputStream(fis));
```

A convenient feature of the filter classes is that by closing the outermost filter object, the contained filters will all be closed until, eventually, the base stream will be closed too.

An I/O Extension

The Java I/O stream model can easily be extended by creating your own filter classes. To illustrate, this section presents an encrypted output stream that buffers data as it flows through the output pipe and encrypts it before flushing it to the output target. Similarly, a decrypting input stream is presented that reverses the work done by the output stream encrypter. To keep the example simple, a trivial exclusive-or (XOR) type encryption is used. While this form of encryption provides only minimal data protection and under no circumstances should be considered secure, it does have the benefit of being extremely easy to implement.

Since part of the task of the encryption and decryption filter classes is to buffer the data as it flows through the data stream, the implementations will extend the BufferedInputStream and BufferedOutputStream classes and allow them to buffer the data. The EncryptedOutputStream and DecryptedInputStream classes provide no additional public methods beyond those provided by their parent classes. Internally, they will intercept calls to the read() and write() methods and encrypt or decrypt the internal buffers whenever the buffers are refilled.

The constructors for the new filter stream classes are as follows:

```
public DecryptedInputStream(InputStream in, String key)
public EncryptedOutputStream(OutputStream out, String key)
```

Each constructor takes the appropriate input or output stream and an encryption key as arguments. The newly created stream can be used wherever parent class can be used. For example, Fig. 7.16 shows a simple pro-

```java
import java.io.*;
import ajp.io.*;

public class CryptTest {

    public static void main( String args[] ) throws Exception {
        String key = "qwertyuiop1234567890";

        FileOutputStream out = new FileOutputStream( "test.data" );
        EncryptedOutputStream eos = new EncryptedOutputStream(out, key);
        PrintStream pr = new PrintStream(eos);


        pr.println( "This string should be scrambled." );
        pr.println( "As should this one." );
        pr.flush();
        pr.println( "And this one too." );
        pr.flush();
        DataOutputStream dos = new DataOutputStream(eos);

        double x = 2.0;
        float y = (float)1.5;
        int foo = 42;
        boolean yea = true;

        dos.writeDouble(x);
        dos.writeFloat(y);
        dos.writeInt(foo);
        dos.writeBoolean(yea);
        dos.close();
    }
}
```

Figure 7.16
The CryptTest class.

gram that writes a few strings to a file, followed by a few fundamental Java data types. The output stream used to write the strings is an encrypted PrintStream. The Java data types are written using a DataOutputStream that contains the same encryption filter. Note that the EncryptedOutput-Stream allows buffered data to be flushed, just as the BufferedOutput-Stream class does. It is also important to note that the same encryption filter is used by both the PrintStream and the DataOutputStream. The sharing of the encryption filter is significant because the filter is not stateless. Using a different filter when writing the Java data types would require that two different filters be used in exactly the same sequence when the data is decrypted.

Figure 7.17 shows a program that will read the encrypted data produced by the application in Fig. 7.16 and echo the decrypted text to `System.out`. As was the case with the encryption of the data, no part of the decryption other than the constructor for the DecryptedInputStream is

```
import java.io.*;
import ajp.io.*;

public class DecryptTest {

    public static void main( String args[] ) throws Exception {
        String key = "qwertyuiop1234567890";
        String data;

        FileInputStream in = new FileInputStream( "test.data" );
        DataInputStream di =
                new DataInputStream(new DecryptedInputStream(in, key));

        data = di.readLine();
        System.out.println( data );
        data = di.readLine();
        System.out.println( data );
        data = di.readLine();
        System.out.println( data );
        double x = di.readDouble();
        float y = di.readFloat();
        int foo = di.readInt();
        boolean yea = di.readBoolean();
        System.out.println("x=" + x + ", y=" + y + ", foo=" + foo +",
                            yea=" + yea);
        di.close();
    }
}
```

Figure 7.17
The DecryptTest class.

visible to the programmer. The data is encrypted or decrypted as it passes through the data stream, completely transparently.

IMPLEMENTATION. The EncryptedOutputStream is the simpler side of the encryption/decryption filters. Since all the data is buffered by the parent class, BufferedOutputStream, the child class does not need to encrypt data each time the parent's `write()` method is called, but rather only just before the data is passed down the stream. In the BufferedOutputStream class, the data is flushed down the pipe each time the `flush()` method is called, either by direct invocation by the programmer or internally by the BufferedOutputStream, whenever its internal buffer fills up. Thus, the EncryptedOutputStream class consists only of the constructor and a `flush()` method that overrides its namesake in the parent class. Figure 7.18 shows the full implementation of the EncryptedOutputStream class.

The `flush()` method first calls on the `encrypt()` method, then calls the `flush()` method of the parent BufferedOutputStream class. The `encrypt()` method iterates across the byte array `buf`, XORing each byte with a corresponding byte in the key array. In order to later decrypt the data passed through the encryption filter, it is important to preserve the order in which bytes in the key are referenced. To preserve the order, a separate counter variable `keyPos` is used. Each time the last byte in the key is referenced, `keyPos` is reset to 0, beginning the cycle through the key again.

The decryption filter, DecryptedInputStream, is a bit more complex than the encryption filter, although not because what it does is more complicated than the task performed by the encryption filter. The EncryptedOutputStream overrides `flush()` and encrypts the buffered data each time the buffer is filled. The method corresponding to `flush()` in the BufferedInputStream class is `fill()`, which reads a block of data from the input stream into a byte array. Unfortunately, `fill()` is a private method and cannot be overridden. Thus, interposition on the flow of data through the input stream must occur elsewhere. The only other methods available are the `read()` methods.

A second complication to the DecryptedInputStream class is that the BufferedInputStream class supports marking and resetting the input stream. Marking and resetting the input stream allows programmers to read ahead into an input stream, then reset the stream back to a previous mark. Since the decryption implemented in the DecryptedInputStream relies on sequential reads through the data, the `mark()`, `reset()`, and `skip()` methods are overridden to do nothing. Furthermore, the mark–

Figure 7.18
The Encrypted-
OutputStream class.

```
package ajp.io;

import java.io.*;

/**
 * An encrypted, buffered output stream.
 *
 * @version 2.1
 **/
public class EncryptedOutputStream extends BufferedOutputStream {
    private byte key[];
    private int keyLength;
    private int keyPos = 0;

    /**
     * Creates a new encrypted output stream.
     **/
    public EncryptedOutputStream(OutputStream out, String key) {
        super(out);
        keyLength = key.length();
        this.key = key.getBytes();
    }

    /**
     * Flushes the stream. This will write any buffered
     * output bytes.
     **/
    public synchronized void flush() throws IOException {

        encrypt();
        super.flush();
    }

    protected void encrypt() {
        for(int i=0; i<count; i++) {
            buf[i] = (byte)(buf[i] ^ key[keyPos]);
            keyPos++;
            if (keyPos == keyLength)
                keyPos = 0;
        }
    }
}
```

Supported() method is overridden to return *false*, indicating that the mark and reset are not supported by the EncryptedInputStream class.

Figure 7.19 shows the implementation of the DecryptedInputStream class. Most of the actual work of manipulating the input stream is handled in the two read() methods. In each of the two methods, the variable pos, which indicates the position in the byte array the next data will be read from, is compared to the variable count, which holds the total number of bytes in the internal byte array, buf. If pos is greater than or equal to count, more data must be read from the input stream into buf.

```
package ajp.io;

import java.io.*;

/**
 * A decrypted input stream.
 *
 * @version 2.1
 */
public class DecryptedInputStream extends BufferedInputStream {
    private byte key[];
    private int keyLength;
    private int keyPos = 0;

    /**
     * Creates a new encrypted output stream.
     **/
    public DecryptedInputStream(InputStream in, String key) {
        super(in);
        keyLength = key.length();
        this.key = key.getBytes();
    }

    /**
     * Not supported.
     **/
    public void mark() {}

    /**
     * Not supported.
     **/
    public void reset() {}

    /**
     * Reads a byte of data. This method will block if no input is available.
     **/
    public synchronized int read() throws IOException {
        boolean decryptNeeded = false;
        int ret;

        if (pos >= count) {
            decryptNeeded = true;
        }
        ret = super.read();
        if (decryptNeeded) {
            decrypt();
            if (pos <= 0)
                throw new IOException("Encryption Buffer index error.");
            ret = buf[pos - 1] & 0xff;
        }
        return ret;
    }
```

Figure 7.19
The DecryptedInput-
Stream class.

```
    /**
     * Reads into an array of bytes.
     * Blocks until some input is available.
     *           returned when the end of the stream is reached.
     **/
    public synchronized int read(byte b[], int off, int len)
                                                    throws IOException {
        boolean decryptNeeded = false;
        int ret;

        if (pos >= count) {
            decryptNeeded = true;
        }
        if ((ret = super.read(b, off, len)) >= 0) {
            if (decryptNeeded) {
                decrypt();
                System.arraycopy(buf, pos-ret, b, off, ret);
            }
        }
        return ret;
    }

    protected void decrypt() {
        for(int i=0; i<count; i++) {
            buf[i] = (byte)(buf[i] ^ key[keyPos]);
            keyPos++;
            if (keyPos == keyLength)
                keyPos = 0;
        }
    }

    /**
     * Not supported on encrypted data streams.
     **/
    public synchronized long skip(long n) throws IOException {
        throw new IOException();
    }

    /**
     * Returns a boolean indicating if this stream type supports
     * mark/reset.
     **/
    public boolean markSupported() {
        return false;
    }
}
```

Figure 7.19
(Continued).

Once the data is read into `buf`, it must be decrypted; hence, the flag `decryptNeeded` is set to *true*. Next, the appropriate `read()` method from the superclass is called, filling `buf` with data. The buffer is then decrypted in the `decrypt()` method and the number of bytes read is returned.

While the encryption techniques shown here are trivial, the filter classes could easily be extended to provide more sophisticated encryption simply by subclassing and overriding the `encrypt()` method in the output stream and the `decrypt()` method in the input stream. Again, it should be pointed out that the EncryptedOutputStream and Decrypted-InputStream classes should not be considered in their present forms as a means of creating secure data streams. Rather, they are intended to illustrate the mechanics of extending the Java I/O filter classes. That these filter classes are not completely secure does not imply that the filters are not usable as is. Simple exclusive-or encryption is usually sufficient to prevent anyone from "unintentionally" accessing data which is not meant to be seen.

SUMMARY

The Java File class forms the foundation for all file interaction from Java. The File class is used to represent both files and directories, and can easily be extended for particular needs. In this chapter, an extension to the File class called DirectoryEntry is shown that is used to represent directories and their contents. By creating a subclass of File that is specifically targeted at representing directories, classes that traverse directory hierarchies are more easily constructed.

The DirectoryEntry class is utilized by the FileDialogPanel class as a means for traversing directories and selecting files. The standard AWT FileDialog class provides similar functionality, but it cannot be extended through subclassing, does not provide a mechanism for asynchronous notification of selection, and cannot be created as anything other than a separate pop-up Frame. All of these shortcomings are overcome by the FileDialogPanel. In addition, the FileDialogPanel class is constructed entirely of AWT Components and as such is portable across multiple platforms.

While File access and I/O is restricted to trusted applets and applications, I/O is available even to untrusted applets in restricted forms. Communication between untrusted applets and the hosts they were downloaded from is usually possible through the use of the various socket classes in the `java.net` package, as is discussed in Chap. 8. Data passed through a socket is read and written using the various stream I/O classes in the `java.io` package. This chapter shows two simple I/O filter classes that build on existing classes in the `java.io` package. The EncryptedOutputStream and DecryptedInputStream classes can be used to add simple encryption to existing I/O streams in Java and show how easily the I/O model can be extended. Chapter 8 builds on these encryption filters to demonstrate how they can be applied to socket-based communications.

8

Network
Programming

Introduction

Network programming has long been somewhat of an elite specialization in the computer industry. Some engineers and programmers have dedicated entire careers to burrowing deep into the details of network protocols and transports. Without a doubt, the complexity of creating network-based applications has been one of the hindrances to the growth of client/server computing. One of the great promises of the Java programming environment is that by making the creation of network-based applications accessible to a much wider audience of programmers, it will foster a surge in the growth of client/server applications available on a wide range of hardware platforms.

The foundation on which Java's network programming model is based is the Internet Protocol (IP) and the associated Internet transports— Transmission Control Protocol (TCP) and User Datagram Protocol (UDP). The TCP/IP protocol suite is the lifeblood of the Internet, so it is natural that Java, a platform designed for creating Internet and intranet applications, should use TCP/IP. Fortunately, the details of the protocols themselves are largely hidden from the programmer by the Java network class libraries; you don't have to be a TCP/IP guru to be able to create network-based applications in Java.

This chapter focuses on creating client/server applications with the classes in the JDK. We begin with the socket model supported by Java and how to create simple client/server applications using Java sockets. The bulk of the chapter, however, is targeted at how to use the classes provided in the JDK to enhance the socket model and enrich the client/server programming environment. Specifically, descriptions of how to create multi-threaded socket servers, applying I/O filters to sockets, and creating an interface for passing object state constitute the major topics.

It should be pointed out that this chapter does not attempt to cover TCP/IP programming in general, or the theory behind TCP/IP networks, but rather focuses on network programming as supported by the JDK.* Furthermore, there are several emerging APIs for creating different forms

---

* There are many books available that cover the broad range of network programming topics. An excellent reference on network programming in the UNIX environment is W. Richard Stevens, *UNIX Network Programming* (Englewood Cliffs, N.J.: Prentice-Hall, 1990). Stevens gives an accessible yet thorough overview of network protocols and programming models—the "Network Primer" and "Communication Protocol" chapters alone are worth the price of admission. What is widely regarded as the definitive reference on TCP/IP is the four-volume series by Douglas Comer, *Internetworking with TCP/IP.* The first volume, *Principles, Protocols, and Architecture* (3d Ed., Englewood Cliffs, N.J.: Prentice-Hall, 1995) contains just about everything you might ever want to know about TCP/IP.

of client/server applications. Examples include JavaSoft's Java Remote Method Invocation (Java RMI), as well as several APIs for connecting Java applets and applications to CORBA-compliant object request brokers. While some of these APIs may eventually become integrated into the JDK, this chapter covers only what is supported by the JDK in both the 1.0.x and the 1.1x releases.

Sockets

The Java network programming model is based on *sockets,* a client/server model introduced by the Berkeley-UNIX operating system in the early 1980s. The simplicity and elegance of the socket model has made network programming with sockets one of the most, if not *the* most, popular ways to create client/server applications. The socket model as supported by Java is quite simple: two applications act as endpoints of a two-way communication channel which supports the transfer of data using the Java I/O model discussed in Chap. 7. In the socket model, one application assumes the role of the server and one or more applications take on the role of client. The server monitors a network port and listens for client connection requests.

A network port can be thought of as a logical address on a networked computer. When data is sent to a socket-based server, it is tagged with the network address of the computer the server is running on and the port number the server is listening to. The operating system multiplexes network traffic arriving at its network address to the applications monitoring the various ports. For example, a host called *joetogo* is connected to a TCP/IP network and is given the address 50.100.150.1, as shown in Fig. 8.1. On joetogo are several processes that are monitoring different network ports: process A is monitoring port 21; process B is monitoring port 6001. When network traffic arrives at joetogo's network connection, it is checked for a local port number and delivered to the appropriate process. A packet of data addressed to 50.100.150.1, port 6001, will be delivered to process B, for example.

When a Java server application receives a connection request, it creates a Socket object. On the client side, once the request is accepted by the server the client will receive a Socket object connected to the server's Socket input and output streams. The I/O streams can be used by client and server to establish two-way communications between applications.

There are some restrictions to socket operations supported by the JDK that revolve around the Java security model. For example, unsigned

Figure 8.1
Multiple servers'
processes running
on a networked
machine.

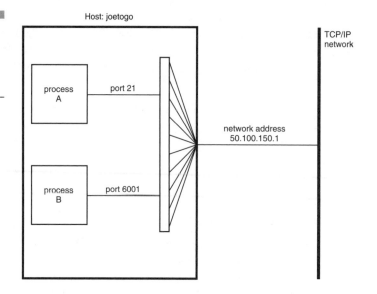

applets running in Web browsers cannot be socket servers. The restrictions placed on a particular applet's or application's use of sockets will depend on the security manager in place. (Refer to the Security FAQ document http://java.sun.com/sfaq for the most recent information on what socket operations are and are not permitted in various browsers.)

Types of Sockets

The JDK supports two types of sockets: TCP and UDP. *TCP* sockets are used for session-oriented, reliable connections. Data sent via a TCP socket is guaranteed to be delivered, which is to say that the data will either be delivered or an exception will be thrown. With TCP sockets, if a packet of data sent is lost, it will be retransmitted. Whenever a client/server connection is needed and every piece of data is important and must be delivered, TCP sockets are appropriate.

UDP, or *Datagram,* sockets are appropriate for situations where the requirements for speed outweigh the need for each piece of data to be reliably delivered. UDP sockets are packet-oriented and are not guaranteed to be delivered. If a packet is lost, the data associated with that packet is gone. Datagram sockets are typically used for applications like process monitoring or transmitting video over a network—applications that have time-critical requirements. If a packet representing an individual frame of a video is dropped, it is usually better to simply skip the frame and go on to the next rather than stall the video while the packet is resent. Similarly, if an applet is displaying data that shows the position of a robot's arm as it moves to pick up an object, it is better to miss a packet of data than to get out of sync with the robot while waiting for a packet to be resent.

For those who have not yet written socket-based Java programs, it will be useful to review how TCP and UDP sockets are created and used. The following two sections show simple examples of TCP and UDP client/ server applications. If you are already comfortable with creating simple socket-based applications in Java, you may wish to skip to the section titled "Multithreaded Communication."

TCP Sockets

The first task in creating the server side of any socket-based client/server application is to decide which port to have the server listen to. Port numbers can assume the range of values supported by an unsigned 16-bit integer. In the TCP/IP domain, port numbers 1 through 5,000 are reserved. Ports 1 through 1,023 are privileged ports reserved for use by well-known or privileged-user-assigned processes. Ports 1,024 through 5,000 are also reserved and are dynamically assigned to privileged processes by the operating system. That leaves ports 5,001 through 65,535 for use by user-defined servers. If an attempt is made to open a socket on a privileged port, an exception is thrown. When creating a socket server, you are at liberty to choose any port number in the 5,001 to 65,535 range that is not already in use.

There are three steps to creating a TCP socket server:

1. Create a `java.net.ServerSocket` object listening to a particular port.
2. Wait for client connections with the ServerSocket's `accept()` method.
3. Use the Socket object returned by `accept()` to communicate with the client.

Figure 8.2 shows a simple Java application that is a TCP socket server. When a client establishes a connection to the server, the server sends a series of integer and floating-point numbers to the client until the client closes the connection. Once the connection is closed, the server returns to listening for new connections.

```java
import java.applet.*;
import java.io.*;
import java.net.*;
import java.util.*;

/**
 * A simple single-threaded TCP socket server.
 * @version 1.1
 **/
class TCPServer {
    static boolean debug = false;

    // The local debug method
    static void dbg(String str) {
        if (debug) {
            System.out.println(str);
            System.out.flush();
        }
    }

    public static void main(String args[]) {
        DataInputStream dis;
        DataOutputStream dos;
        ServerSocket server = null;

        if (args.length == 1) {
            if (args[0].equals("debug"))
                debug = true;
        }

        try {
            server = new ServerSocket(42421);
            dbg("Stared Server: " + server.toString());
        }
        catch (IOException e) {
            e.printStackTrace();
            System.exit(1);
        }

        while (true) {
            Socket socket = null;
            int count = 1;

            try {
                socket = server.accept();
                dbg("Got connection: " + socket.toString());
                dos = new DataOutputStream(socket.getOutputStream());
                while (true) {
                    dos.writeInt(count);
                    dos.writeDouble(count * 2.0 / 3.0);
                    dos.flush();
                    count++;
                }
```

Figure 8.2
The TCPServer class.

```
                }
                catch (IOException e) {
                }
                try {
                    if (socket != null) {
                        socket.close();
                        dbg("Socket closed.");
                    }
                }
                catch (IOException e) {
                }
            }
        }
    }
```

▰▰▰ ▰▰▰ ▰▰▰ ▰▰▰

Figure 8.2
(*Continued*).

When a ServerSocket is created, the port number to be monitored by the server is passed to the constructor. There is a second parameter that the constructor supports which is used to indicate how many client connections will be allowed to wait in line for the server before clients are turned away. (The default value allows 50 clients to wait for connections.) The server in Fig. 8.2 monitors port 42,421 for client connections. After opening the port, the server enters a `while` loop checking for connections using `accept()`, which blocks until a connection is established. The `accept()` method returns a reference to a Socket object that represents one endpoint of the connection to the client application. The Socket object has both an InputStream and an OutputStream object associated with it. In this example, the socket connection is used as a one-way connection only—server to client—so only the socket's OutputStream is used. To facilitate writing Java data types across the socket connection, the OutputStream is filtered by a DataOutputStream in the line:

```
dos = new DataOutputStream(socket.getOutputStream());
```

Data is then written to the socket until the client closes the socket connection, at which point an exception is thrown. In the exception handler, the server closes the socket connection. With the data transfer complete, the server returns to listening for new client connections.

Creating a client application that uses a TCP socket is essentially a one-step operation. The client need only create a Socket object and then use the Socket's InputStream and OutputStream just as the server did. Figure 8.3 shows a TCP Socket client that received the data sent by the server presented

```
import java.applet.*;
import java.io.*;
import java.net.*;
import java.util.*;

/**
 * A simple single-threaded TCP socket client.
 * @version 1.1
 **/
public class TCPClient extends Applet {
    String host;
    int port;
    DataInputStream dis;
    boolean debug;

    // The local debug method
    void dbg(String str) {
        if (debug) {
            System.out.println(str);
            System.out.flush();
        }
    }

    public void init() {
        try {
            debug = Boolean.valueOf(getParameter("debug")).booleanValue();
        }
        catch (Exception e) {
            debug = false;
        }
        host = getCodeBase().getHost();
        if (host == null || host.equals(""))
            host = "localhost";
        dbg("host = " + host);
        try {
            port = Integer.parseInt(getParameter("port"));
        }
        catch (Exception e) {
            port = 42421;
        }

        doSocketStuff();
    }

    public void doSocketStuff() {
        Socket socket = null;
        try {
            socket = new Socket(host, port);

            dis = new DataInputStream(socket.getInputStream());

            for (int i=0; i<10; i++) {
                System.out.println("Read: " + dis.readInt()
```

Figure 8.3
The TCPClient class.

```
                                        +", " + dis.readDouble());
            }
            socket.close();
    }
    catch (IOException e) {
        try {
            if (socket != null)
                socket.close();
        }
        catch (IOException ex) {}
        e.printStackTrace();
    }
```

Figure 8.3
(*Continued*).

in Fig. 8.2. The client must create the Socket object using one of the class's constructors, typically passing it both the host name and port number. The client in Fig. 8.3 creates the Socket object, passing it the name of the host of the downloaded applet as determined from the CODEBASE of the HTML:

```
host = getCodeBase().getHost();
```

The port number is passed to the applet through the APPLET tag in the HTML.

It is important to note that untrusted applets are typically restricted only to opening connections to the host from which they were downloaded. Furthermore, the host name passed to the constructor must exactly match the host name the browser used to download the applet. Thus, it is best to determine the host name of the server dynamically, as shown previously, rather than hard-coding the host name in the applet or even specifying it in the HTML that specified the applet.

With the connection to the server established, the client creates a DataInputStream from the Socket's OutputStream and reads data from the stream using the usual methods. When the client is done reading data, it simply closes the connection.

One limitation of the client/server example previously presented is that the server supports only one client/server connection at a time. Through the use of Java threads, it is simple to create a multithreaded server capable of supporting many concurrent connections. Multithreaded servers are discussed later in this chapter, in the section entitled "Multithreaded Communications." Before embarking on an exploration of multithreaded socket servers, however, the presentation of supported socket types will first be completed by looking at UDP Sockets.

UDP Sockets

UDP sockets employ a slightly different programming model than TCP sockets. To start with, the distinction between the server and the client blurs slightly since datagram sockets are not connection-oriented. With datagram sockets, the roles are perhaps better described as *sender* and *receiver.* A datagram socket sender performs the following tasks:

1. Creates a DatagramSocket object.

2. Constructs a DatagramPacket object.

3. Sends the packet with the DatagramSocket's `send()` method.

The DatagramPacket object constructed in Step 2 encapsulates the data to be sent, as well as the Internet address and port of the recipient of the packet.

A datagram socket receiver performs the following tasks:

1. Creates a DatagramSocket object that monitors a particular port.

2. Constructs a DatagramPacket object containing a buffer large enough to hold the data received.

3. Uses the DatagramSocket's `receive()` method to receive the packet.

Before looking at an example of UDP sockets in use, it is necessary to review how DatagramSockets and DatagramPackets are constructed as well as the methods that the two classes support.

DatagramSocket objects are created with one of the two forms of its constructor:

1. `public DatagramSocket() throws SocketException`

2. `public DatagramSocket(int port) throws SocketException`

The DatagramSocket can be passed a port number to monitor, using the second form of the constructor, or it can be assigned a port number automatically by the runtime, using the first form. Typically, UPD sockets opened with the first form are used for sending packets, while sockets opened with the latter form are used for receiving packets, although sockets opened with either form can be used for both sending and receiving. Once the DatagramSocket has been created, there are four methods of importance, which are summarized in Table 8.1.

DatagramPackets are used by DatagramSockets for both receiving and sending data. DatagramPackets to be used for receiving data are constructed using the following form of the class's constructor:

TABLE 8.1	Method signature	Purpose
Public Methods of the Datagram-Socket Class	`void send(DatagramPacket p)`	Sends the DatagramPacket. The packet encapsulates the data and the target host and port.
	`void receive(DatagramPacket p)`	Receives a DatagramPacket. The packet passed as an argument is filled with data and host information on return.
	`int getLocalPort()`	Returns the port this socket is listening to or sending from.
	`void close()`	Closes the socket.

```
public DatagramPacket(byte ibuf[], int ilength)
```

The byte array passed to the constructor is used to receive `ilength` bytes of data from the port to which the DatagramSocket is listening. Typical use would look something like:

```
DatagramSocket ds = new DatagramSocket (12345);
DatagramPacket dp = new DatagramPacket (new byte[128], 128);
ds.receive(dp);
```

To create a DatagramPacket to be sent via a DatagramSocket, the following form of the constructor is used:

```
public DatagramPacket(byte ibuf[], int ilength,
                      InetAddress iaddr, int iport)
```

When sending a DatagramPacket, the data to be sent must first be placed in a byte array. Next, the Internet address of the destination DatagramSocket must be encapsulated in an InetAddress object and provided along with the destination DatagramSocket's port number. The InetAddress object can be obtained for a particular host name through the InetAddress class method `getByName()`, subject to the approval of the resident security manger. Code for sending a DatagramPacket might look something like:

```
byte buf[] = new byte[256];
…some code to fill buf with data…
DatagramSocket ds = DatagramSocket();
DatagramPacket dp = DatagramPacket(buf, buf.length,
        InetAddress.getByName("www.targethost.com"), 12345);
ds.send(dp);
```

To illustrate the use of UDP sockets, Figs. 8.4 and 8.5 show a simple UDP socket-based client/server application. The Java application shown in Fig. 8.4 is called *UDPServer;* the applet shown in Fig. 8.5 is called *UDPClient.* The interaction between the two programs runs as follows:

1. UDPServer opens a DatagramSocket on port 42,424 and waits for an incoming packet.
2. A UDPClient applet sends a DatagramPacket to UDPServer from a dynamically assigned port number.
3. UDPServer receives the packet and then sends 21 packets containing an integer and a double to the host and port number from which UDPClient's packet came.
4. UDPClient receives packets until it sees a packet containing the pair [–1, –1.0].
5. UDPServer closes the socket and starts again at Step 1.
6. UDPClient closes its socket connection.

Several aspects of the UDPClient/UDPServer application are worth pointing out. Both sides of the application want to send Java data types across the socket, but DatagramPackets are constructed out of arrays of bytes. Therefore, both the UDPClient and UDPServer create ByteArray-InputStreams filtered by DataInputStreams to read from and ByteArrayOutputStreams filtered by DataOutputStreams to write to. The ByteArrayOutputStream was previously used in Chap. 3 as a means of buffering pixel data in an ImageConsumer. Here it is used to buffer data to be sent in a DatagramPacket. The ByteArrayOutputStream is placed in a DataOutputStream, then the Java data types to be sent in a packet are written using the DataOutputStream's `writeInt()` and `writeDouble()` methods. After the data is written to the stream, the byte array, which now contains the integer and the double encoded as an array of bytes, is extracted from the ByteArrayOutputStream using the `toByteArray()` method. The byte array is used to create a DatagramPacket and the packet is sent. After each packet is sent, the ByteArrayOutputStream's `reset()` method is called. This keeps subsequent data written to the array from causing the array to grow.

A second aspect of interest regarding the UDPClient/UDPServer application is the fact that only the UDPServer's DatagramSocket is opened at a specified port. When the UDPClient's DatagramPacket arrives at

```java
import java.applet.*;
import java.io.*;
import java.net.*;
import java.util.*;

/**
 * A simple single-threaded UDP socket server.
 * @version 1.2
 **/
class UDPServer {
    static boolean debug = false;

    // The local debug method
    static void dbg(String str) {
        if (debug) {
            System.out.println(str);
            System.out.flush();
        }
    }

    public static void main(String args[]) {
        ByteArrayInputStream  byteIn;
        ByteArrayOutputStream byteOut;
        DataInputStream dis;
        DataOutputStream dos;
        DatagramPacket sendPkt;
        DatagramPacket recPkt;
        DatagramSocket socket = null;

        if (args.length == 1) {
            if (args[0].equals("debug"))
                debug = true;
        }

        try {
            byte buf[] = new byte[4];
            recPkt = new DatagramPacket(buf, 4);

            byteOut = new ByteArrayOutputStream(128);
            dos = new DataOutputStream(byteOut);

            while (true) {
                socket = new DatagramSocket(42424);
                dbg("Starting server on port: " + socket.getLocalPort());
                socket.receive(recPkt);

                dbg("Received from inet address: "
                    + recPkt.getAddress().toString()
                    + " port number: "
                    + recPkt.getPort());

                byteIn = new ByteArrayInputStream(buf);
                dis = new DataInputStream(byteIn);
```

Figure 8.4
The UDPServer class.

```
              dbg("Remote Port: " + dis.readInt());

              int count = 101010;
              for (int i=0; i<20; i++) {

                   dos.writeInt(count);
                   dos.writeDouble(count / 2.0);
                   dos.flush();
                   count++;

                   dbg("Sending " + byteOut.size() + " bytes.");
                   sendPkt = new DatagramPacket(byteOut.toByteArray(),
                                               byteOut.size(),
                                               recPkt.getAddress(),
                                               recPkt.getPort());
                   socket.send(sendPkt);
                   byteOut.reset();
              }
              dos.writeInt(-1);
              dos.writeDouble(-1.0);
              dos.flush();

              sendPkt = new DatagramPacket(byteOut.toByteArray(),
                                          byteOut.size(),
                                          recPkt.getAddress(),
                                          recPkt.getPort());
              socket.send(sendPkt);
              byteOut.reset();
              socket.close();
              dbg("Socket closed.");
          }
      } catch (Exception e) {
          e.printStackTrace();
      }
   }
}
```

Figure 8.4
(*Continued*).

the server, the return address and port are extracted from the Datagram-Packet. The client creates its DatagramSocket without specifying a port number, allowing the Java runtime to allocate a port dynamically.

As with the TCPServer class, the UDPServer is single-threaded in that it is written to handle only one connection at a time. The following section describes a set of extension classes that provide for the creation of multi-threaded TCP socket servers that can handle multiple client connections concurrently.

```
/*
 * Copyright (c) 1996 Jeffrey C. Rice and Irving Salisbury III
 * Version 1.2
 */

import java.applet.*;
import java.io.*;
import java.net.*;
import java.util.*;

/**
 * A simple single-threaded UDP socket client.
 * @version 1.2
 **/
public class UDPClient extends Applet {
    String host;
    int port;
    DatagramSocket socket = null;

    ByteArrayInputStream  byteIn;
    ByteArrayOutputStream byteOut;
    DataInputStream dis;
    DataOutputStream dos;
    boolean debug;

    // The local debug method
    void dbg(String str) {
        if (debug) {
            System.out.println(str);
            System.out.flush();
        }
    }

    public void init() {

        try {
            debug = Boolean.valueOf(getParameter("debug")).booleanValue();
        }
        catch (Exception e) {
            debug = false;
        }
        host = getCodeBase().getHost();
        if (host == null || host.equals(""))
            host = "localhost";
        dbg("host = " + host);
        try {
            port = Integer.parseInt(getParameter("port"));
        }
        catch (Exception e) {
            port = 42424;
```

Figure 8.5
The UDPClient class.

```
        }
        doSocketStuff();

    }

    public void doSocketStuff() {
        int localPort;
        int n;
        double x;

        try {
            byteOut = new ByteArrayOutputStream(8);
            dos = new DataOutputStream(byteOut);

            InetAddress addr[] = InetAddress.getAllByName(host);
            socket = new DatagramSocket();
            localPort = socket.getLocalPort();

            dbg("Client bound to port:" + localPort);

            dos.writeInt(localPort);
            dos.flush();

            byte buf[] = byteOut.toByteArray();
            int len = byteOut.size();

            dbg("Packet size: " + len);

            DatagramPacket dp = new DatagramPacket(buf, len, addr[0], port);
            dbg("Client sending on port: " + dp.getPort());

            socket.send(dp);

            DatagramPacket recPkt = new DatagramPacket(new byte[128], 128);
            while (true) {
                socket.receive(recPkt);
                dbg("Received " + recPkt.getLength()
                    + " bytes from: " + recPkt.getAddress().toString()
                    + " port number: " + recPkt.getPort());

                byteIn = new ByteArrayInputStream(recPkt.getData());
                dis = new DataInputStream(byteIn);
                n = dis.readInt();
                x = dis.readDouble();

                if (n == -1 && x == -1.0)
                    break;
                System.out.println("\t[ " + n + ", " + x + "]");

            }
            socket.close();
            dbg("Socket closed.");
        } catch (Exception e) {
```

Figure 8.5
(*Continued*).

```
                if (socket != null) {
                    socket.close();
                }
                e.printStackTrace();
            }
        }

    }
```

Figure 8.5
(*Continued*).

Multithreaded Communication

A distinct advantage to writing server applications in Java is that, with its integrated support of multithreading, Java makes it very easy to write efficient, multithreaded servers. In the TCPServer example presented previously, once a connection is received by the server, a socket is created and communication commences with the client over the socket. Once communication terminates, the socket is closed and the server waits for the next connection request. This is not the way servers are usually written. In multitasking environments, once a client connection is received, a new process is created to handle the communication, allowing the server to return to waiting for other clients to connect. A disadvantage to the multitasking model managing client connections is that the overhead for the operating system in creating new processes is usually relatively high. In particular, if the lifetime of the connection is short, the overhead for creating and terminating a new process to handle the connection may outweigh the benefits of quickly freeing the server to wait for new clients.

A multithreaded server model changes the paradigm slightly in that instead of creating a whole new process to manage the communication with the clients, new threads within the existing server process are created. The overhead for creating threads is much less than for creating new processes, so there are fewer concerns about the duration of the connection being too brief to justify the new thread. One thing to be aware of when writing multithreaded servers, though, is that some care must be taken to ensure that thread priorities are managed in a reasonably equitable manner. If all threads are running at the same priority, there is a hazard of some threads not receiving adequate attention by the virtual machine.

Since multithreaded socket servers are so common in Java, and since much of the functionality of each server can be generalized, it is possible to create an abstract multithreaded server class that can be subclassed and specialized for a particular application. The remainder of this chapter presents such a server class.

What follows is actually a framework for creating multithreaded servers. There are two abstract classes in the framework, *ThreadedSocket* and *ThreadedServer*. The ThreadedServer waits for connections from client applications and creates ThreadedSockets to manage the communication when a connection arrives. The ThreadedSocket class is a subclass of Thread and as such has a run() method that encompasses the life cycle of the connection. When the ThreadedSocket is created, the ThreadedServer calls its start() method to initiate communication with the client.

To create an actual multithreaded server, subclasses of the ThreadedSocket and ThreadedServer classes must be created that flesh out the abstract methods of the two classes. The following two sections describe the two abstract classes. After the presentation of the two classes is a section titled "Example: A Simple Multithreaded Server" that shows a multithreaded version of the TCPServer presented earlier in this chapter.

The ThreadedSocket Class

The ThreadedSocket class is an abstract subclass of the Thread class and is shown in Fig. 8.6. As an abstract class, the ThreadedSocket cannot be instantiated and must be subclassed to be used. The constructor for the ThreadedSocket, which should be called from a subclass constructor, takes a Socket object as an argument from which it extracts a reference to the socket's I/O Streams. The only abstract method in the class is the method communicate(), which is called from within the class's run() method. The purpose of the communicate() method is to provide for a customizable communication loop over the socket. Subclasses of Threaded-Socket must provide a communicate() method that can use the instance variables input and output to communicate to the application on the other end of the socket.

The public methods in the ThreadedSocket class are described in Table 8.2.

The ThreadedServer Class

ThreadedServer is the other abstract class in the multithreaded server framework. To create a multithreaded server, both ThreadedSocket and

```
package ajp.net;

import java.net.*;
import java.io.*;

/**
 * An abstract class to provide for the creation of threaded TCP sockets.
 *
 * @version 1.2
 **/
public abstract class ThreadedSocket extends Thread {

    protected boolean debug = false;
    protected InputStream input;
    protected OutputStream output;
    protected Socket socket;

    public ThreadedSocket(Socket sock) throws IOException {
        input = sock.getInputStream();
        output = sock.getOutputStream();
        socket = sock;
    }

    protected void dbg(String str) {
        if (debug) {
            System.out.println(this.getClass().getName() + ": " + str);
            System.out.flush();
        }
    }

    public void setDebug(boolean dbg) {
        debug = dbg;
    }

    public abstract void communicate();

    public void run() {
        communicate();
        try {
            close();
        }
        catch (IOException e) {
        }

    }

    protected void close() throws IOException {
        socket.close();
    }

    public Socket getSocket() {
        return socket;
    }
}
```

Figure 8.6
The ThreadedSocket
class.

TABLE 8.2

Public Methods
of the Abstract
ThreadedSocket
Class

Method signature	Purpose
`void setDebug(boolean dbg)`	If `dbg` is *true,* turns on the generation of debugging messages.
`abstract void communicate()`	The method that must be provided to exchange data over the socket.
`void run()`	Calls `communicate()` then closes the socket.
`void close()`	Calls the actual socket's `close()` method.
`Socket getSocket()`	Returns a handle to the actual Socket object.

ThreadedServer subclasses must be defined. The ThreadedSocket must define the `communicate()` method as described in the previous section. The ThreadedServer subclass must define a `getThreadedSocket()` method which returns a reference to a ThreadedSocket object, usually by simply instantiating the ThreadedSocket subclass. The API to the ThreadedServer class is described in Table 8.3. The full implementation is presented in Fig. 8.7.

TABLE 8.3

Public Methods
of the Abstract
ThreadedServer
Class

Method signature	Purpose
`abstract ThreadedSocket getThreadedSocket(Socket socket)`	Returns a reference to the ThreadedSocket object that will do the actual communication over the socket.
`void setDebug(boolean dbg)`	If `dbg` is *true,* turns on the generation of debugging messages.
`void setup()`	A subclass should override this method to provide a necessary initialization.
`void cleanUp()`	A hook for subclasses to do any needed cleaning up after the server closes down the port it is listening to.
`int getPortNumber()`	Returns the port number the server is listening to.
`void exceptionThrown(Exception e)`	Will print out an exception if debugging is enabled through `setDebug()`.
`void run()`	The body of the server. Creates a ServerSocket and calls `accept()` from a loop, spawning ThreadedSockets to handle the client connections.

```
package ajp.net;

import java.net.*;
import java.io.*;

/**
 * An abstract class to support multithreaded TCP socket servers.
 *
 * @version 1.2
 **/
public abstract class ThreadedServer extends Thread {
    protected boolean debug = false;
    protected int port = -1;

    public ThreadedServer(int port) {
        this.port = port;
    }

    protected void dbg(String str) {
        if (debug) {
            System.out.println(this.getClass().getName() + ": " + str);
            System.out.flush();
        }
    }

    public void setDebug(boolean dbg) {
        debug = dbg;
    }

    public void setup() {
    }

    public int getPortNumber() {
        return port;
    }

    public abstract ThreadedSocket getThreadedSocket(Socket socket)
                    throws IOException;

    public void exceptionThrown(Exception e) {
        dbg(e.toString());
        if (debug)
            e.printStackTrace(System.out);
    }

    public void cleanUp() {
    }

    public void run() {
        setup();
```

Figure 8.7
The ThreadedServer
class.

```
        ServerSocket server = null;
        Socket socket = null;

        // start server socket on HOST at PORT
        try{
            try{
                server = new ServerSocket(getPortNumber());
            }
            catch(IOException e) {
                exceptionThrown(e);
            }

            // now listen for a connection
            while(true) {
                try{
                    // this method will block until a connection is made
                    socket = server.accept();
                    dbg("Got connection " + socket.toString());
                    ThreadedSocket handler = getThreadedSocket(socket);
                    handler.start();
                }
                catch(IOException e) {
                    exceptionThrown(e);
                }
            }

        }
        finally{
            // if there was some error we didn't expect or catch,
            // make sure to close socket
            try{
                server.close();
                socket.close();
                cleanUp();
            }
            catch(Exception e) {
                exceptionThrown(e);
            }
        }
    }
}
```

Figure 8.7
(Continued).

Note that like the ThreadedSocket class, the ThreadedServer class is a subclass of Thread. The run() method of the ThreadedServer creates a ServerSocket on the port that was passed to the constructor, then starts a while loop in which connections are listened for with the ServerSocket's accept() method. Each Socket returned by accept() is passed to the getThreadedSocket() method. The ThreadedSocket returned commences its running as a separate thread, which causes its `communicate()` method to be called. Meanwhile, the ThreadedServer returns to waiting for the next client connection.

Example: A Simple Multithreaded Server

To illustrate the use of the ThreadedServer and ThreadedSocket classes, this section shows a multithreaded version of the TCPServer presented earlier in the chapter. This example illustrates how simple it is to extend these abstract classes to create a multithreaded server. There are two classes in the example: *ThreadedTCPSocket* and *ThreadedTCPServer.*

The ThreadedTCPSocket class is shown in Fig. 8.8. It defines only a constructor and a `communicate()` method. The constructor has the following signature:

```
public ThreadedTCPSocket (Socket socket, int priority,
                          boolean debug)
```

The constructor calls the parent constructor, then sets the `debug` state and the `priority` at which the thread runs.

The `communicate()` method of the ThreadedTCPSocket class is, by and large, the same as the body `while` loop in the `main()` method in the TCPServer class. When `communicate()` is called, the server creates a DataOutputStream, then enters a loop of sending data until an exception is thrown. The only significant difference between the `while` loops in TCPServer's `main()` and ThreadedTCPSocket's `communicate()` is that the ThreadedTCPSocket calls `yield()` at the end of each iteration of the loop to ensure an equitable distribution of virtual-machine time.

The ThreadedTCPServer class shown in Fig. 8.9 defines a constructor and two methods. The constructor is passed a port for listening and a `debug` flag which, in addition to turning debugging statements on or off in the server, is passed to each ThreadedTCPSocket the server creates. The two methods defined by the class are `getThreadedSocket()`, which simply instantiates a ThreadedTCPSocket object and returns a reference to it, and `main()`, which creates a ThreadedTCPServer object and calls its `start()` method. When `start()` is called, the parent class's `run()` method is called, which starts the loop of listening for connections and spawning threads to handle them.

```
import java.net.*;
import java.io.*;
import ajp.net.*;

/**
 * A class to demonstrate the use of the ThreadedSocket class.
 * @version 1.2
 **/
class ThreadedTCPSocket extends ThreadedSocket {
    DataOutputStream out;

    public ThreadedTCPSocket(Socket socket, int priority, boolean debug)
                        throws IOException {
        super(socket);
        setDebug(debug);
        setPriority(priority);
    }

    public void communicate() {
        out = new DataOutputStream(output);
        int count = 1;

        try {
            while (true) {
                out.writeInt(count);
                out.writeDouble(count * 2.0 / 3.0);
                out.flush();
                count++;
                yield();
            }
        }
        catch (Exception e) {
            try {
                dbg("Closing socket: " + getSocket().toString());
                close();
            }
            catch (IOException ex) {
            }
        }
    }
}
```

Figure 8.8
The ThreadedTCP-
Socket class.

Example: Encrypted Socket Communication

A second example of a multithreaded server is the *EncryptedMTServer* class shown in Fig. 8.10. The purpose of the EncryptedMTServer is to multi-thread connections from clients and decrypt the strings they send, reen-crypt them, and send them back. While in general the EncryptedMTServer

```
import java.net.*;
import java.io.*;
import ajp.net.*;

/**
 * A class to demonstrate the use of the ThreadedServer class.
 * @version 1.2
 **/
public class ThreadedTCPServer extends ThreadedServer {

    public ThreadedTCPServer(int port, boolean debug) {
        super(port);
        setDebug(debug);
    }

    public ThreadedSocket getThreadedSocket(Socket socket) throws IOException {
        int serverPriority = Thread.currentThread().getPriority();
        return new ThreadedTCPSocket(socket, serverPriority - 1, debug);
    }

    public static void main(String args[]) {
        int port;
        try {
            port = Integer.parseInt(args[0]);
        }
        catch (Exception e) {
            port = 8765;
        }
        ThreadedTCPServer s = new ThreadedTCPServer(port, true);
        s.start();
    }
}
```

Figure 8.9
The ThreadedTCP-
Server class.

and the EncryptedMTSocket classes are similar to the ThreadedTCPServer and ThreadedTCPSocket classes of the previous example, they do demonstrate how straightforward it is to modify the data streams used by the sockets through the use of filters, as presented in Chap. 7.

The EncryptedMTServer class is almost identical to the ThreadedServer class presented in Fig. 8.9, except that the ThreadedSocket it creates is an EncryptedMTSocket rather than a ThreadedSocket. When the server application is started, it instantiates an EncryptedMTServer object and calls its `start` method.

The EncryptedMTSocket class shown in Fig. 8.11 has a `communicate()` method that is very similar to the ThreadedTCPSocket class. The only difference is that the EncryptedMTSocket reads Strings and writes

```
import java.net.*;
import java.io.*;
import ajp.io.*;
import ajp.net.*;

class EncryptedMTServer extends ThreadedServer {

    public EncryptedMTServer(int port, boolean debug) {
        super(port);
        setDebug(debug);
    }

    public ThreadedSocket getThreadedSocket(Socket socket)
                          throws IOException {
        int serverPriority = Thread.currentThread().getPriority();
        return new EncryptedMTSocket(socket, serverPriority - 1, debug);
    }

    public static void main(String args[]) {
        int port;
        try {
            port = Integer.parseInt(args[0]);
        }
        catch (Exception e) {
            port = 8765;
        }
        EncryptedMTServer s = new EncryptedMTServer(port, true);
        s.start();
    }
}
```

Figure 8.10
The EncryptedMT-
Server class.

them back out again, rather than just writing integers and doubles. The principal difference between the constructors for the two classes is in how they filter the data being passed through the socket's InputStream and OutputStream. The EncryptedMTSocket's constructor passes the Input-Stream through a DecryptedInputStream object before filtering it with a DataInputStream. The OutputStream is prefiltered with a PrintStream and an EncryptedOutputStream:

```
in = new DataInputStream(new DecryptedInputStream(input, key));
out = new PrintStream(new EncryptedOutputStream(output, key));
```

The net effect of the filters is that encrypted data arriving at the socket is decrypted, then converted to a DataInputStream ready for reading. Data being sent to the client is written to a PrintStream and encrypted before being sent to the client.

```
import java.net.*;
import java.io.*;
import ajp.io.*;
import ajp.net.*;

class EncryptedMTSocket extends ThreadedSocket {
    DataInputStream in;
    PrintStream out;

    public EncryptedMTSocket(Socket socket, int priority, boolean debug)
                            throws IOException {
        super(socket);
        setDebug(debug);
        String key = ")P(O*I&U^Y  %T$%R$E#W@#";
        in = new DataInputStream(new DecryptedInputStream(input, key));
        out = new PrintStream(new EncryptedOutputStream(output, key));
        setPriority(priority);
    }

    public void communicate() {
        String str;
        try {
            while(true) {
                str = in.readLine();
                out.println("Server got string: " + str);
                out.flush();
                yield();
            }
        }
        catch (Exception e) {
            try {
                dbg("Closing socket: " + getSocket().toString());
                close();
            }
            catch (Exception ex) {
            }
        }
    }
}
```

Figure 8.11
The EncryptedMT-
Socket class.

The client side of the application, EncryptedClient (shown in Fig. 8.12), performs the same filtering that the server does. Data arrives at the client encrypted and is decrypted before being converted to a DataInput-Stream. Data is encrypted once again before being sent from the client.

As was mentioned in the original discussion of the two encryption filters, because the filtering they do is so simple, they should not be considered secure. However, in the case of socket communications, the primary

```
import java.net.*;
import java.io.*;
import ajp.io.*;
import ajp.net.*;

class EncryptedClient {
    static String strings[] = {
        "dynamic",
        "secure",
        "multithreaded",
        "object oriented",
        "networked",
        "way cool"
    };

    public static void main(String args[]) {
        int port;
        String host;
        DataInputStream in;
        PrintStream out;
        String key = ")P(O*I&U^Y  %T$%R$E#W@#";

        try {
            port = Integer.parseInt(args[0]);
        }
        catch (Exception e) {
            port = 8765;
        }
        try {
            host = args[1];
        }

        catch (Exception e) {
            host = "localhost";
        }

        try {
            Socket socket = new Socket(host, port);
            InputStream input = socket.getInputStream();
            OutputStream output = socket.getOutputStream();
            out = new PrintStream(new EncryptedOutputStream(output, key));
            in = new DataInputStream(new DecryptedInputStream(input, key));

            for (int i=0; i<strings.length; i++) {
                out.println(strings[i]);
                out.flush();
                System.out.println("Client got: " + in.readLine());
                try {
                    Thread.sleep(1000);
                }
                catch (InterruptedException ie) {
```

Figure 8.12
The EncryptedClient
class.

```
            }
        }
    }
    catch (IOException e) {
        }
    }
}
```

Figure 8.12
(*Continued*).

security risk is someone examining packets of data for clear text. Even simple exclusive-or encryption is better than no encryption and is probably enough to encourage the less sophisticated crackers to move on to easier prey.

Passing Object State Between Client and Server

The previous examples in this chapter have all shown client/server applications that passed simple data back and forth, which for many applications is adequate. However, there are times when it is necessary to pass more than just integers, strings, and byte arrays. Sometimes passing an entire object is more appropriate.

Before discussing a technique for passing simple Java objects across the network, it should be pointed out that there are currently available APIs that allow full Java objects to be passed from one application to another across a network. Object serialization in the JavaSoft RMI specification, for example, allows Java objects to be marshaled and transmitted. There are situations, however, when something simpler will suffice. Rather than send an actual object, instead preserve the state of the object, then transmit the state information across the wire, allowing the recipient to instantiate a new object from the state information.

Take, for example, user-defined protocols. Client/server applications often need to pass data that defines a protocol back and forth. For example, if you are creating a client/server shopping application, you will probably define certain operations that will be initiated from the client side—such as *select, buy, return, lookup,* and so on. These actions must be translated into data that can be sent to the server, interpreted, and acted on. These actions could be sent as strings to the server or perhaps translated into integer tokens and sent. In whatever form the actions are transmitted, the relationship between the actions and the data that represents the action must be the same on both sides. One way to keep the relationship the same at both the client and the server is to encapsulate the protocol in a class.

Figure 8.13 presents a simple transaction protocol encapsulated in a class. The Transaction class is a specific protocol class that defines two transactions, *buy* and *return*. Each transaction has associated with it a description of the item being transacted, the quantity, a catalog number, and a unit price. Each attribute of the transaction and the transaction type are stored in instance variables:

```
int transType;
String description;
double price;
int quantity;
int catalog;
```

The Transaction class contains a method, value(), which returns the dollar value of the transaction: price multiplied by quantity, multiplied by –1 if the transaction is a return. There is also a toString() method that will print out the current state of the Transaction's instance variables.

The two most significant features of the Transaction are its constructor and its write() method. The write() method is passed an Output-Stream as an argument, which could be a reference to a socket's output stream or a reference to a FileOutputStream object, for example. The write() method filters the OutputStream through a DataOutputStream and writes the current state of the Transaction object, the values of all the instance variables, to the stream. Each value written is prefixed by an integer token that indicates how the data that follows should be interpreted. For example, the price of the item being transacted is written to a stream as follows:

```
dos.writeInt(PRICE);
dos.writeDouble(price);
```

Prefixing the set of values written to the stream is a token, TRANSACTION, followed by an integer indicating whether it is a SELL or a BUY. Following all the token/instance variable pairs, the token DONE is written, indicating that the complete state of the object has been written to the OutputStream.

```
import java.io.*;

class Transaction {

    public static final int DONE    = 0;
    public static final int BUY     = 1;
    public static final int RETURN  = 3;

    public static final int TRANSACTION = 4;
    public static final int DESCRIPTION = 5;
    public static final int PRICE       = 6;
    public static final int QUANTITY    = 7;
    public static final int CATALOG     = 8;

    int transType;

    String description;
    double price;
    int quantity;
    int catalog;

    public Transaction(int type, String desc, double pri, int qty, int cat) {
        transType = type;
        description = desc;
        price = pri;
        quantity = qty;
        catalog = cat;
    }

    public Transaction(InputStream is) throws IOException {
        DataInputStream dis = new DataInputStream(is);
        boolean done = false;

        while (! done) {
            switch(dis.readInt()) {
            case TRANSACTION:
                transType = dis.readInt();
                break;
            case DONE:
                done = true;
                break;
            case DESCRIPTION:
                description = dis.readLine();
                break;
            case PRICE:
                price = dis.readDouble();
                break;
            case QUANTITY:
                quantity = dis.readInt();
                break;
            case CATALOG:
                catalog = dis.readInt();
                break;
```

Figure 8.13
The Transaction class.

```java
            }
        }
        System.out.print("Created: ");
        System.out.println(this.toString());

    }

    public void write(OutputStream os) throws IOException {
        System.out.print("Writing: ");
        System.out.println(this.toString());

        DataOutputStream dos = new DataOutputStream(os);
        dos.writeInt(TRANSACTION);
        dos.writeInt(transType);
        dos.writeInt(DESCRIPTION);
        dos.writeBytes(description + "\n");
        dos.writeInt(QUANTITY);
        dos.writeInt(quantity);
        dos.writeInt(CATALOG);
        dos.writeInt(catalog);
        dos.writeInt(PRICE);
        dos.writeDouble(price);
        dos.writeInt(DONE);
        dos.flush();
    }

    double value() {
        double tmp = quantity * price;
        return (transType == RETURN) ? tmp * -1.0 : tmp;
    }

    public String toString() {
        String type = "Unknown";
        switch(transType) {

        case BUY:
            type = "Buy";
            break;
        case RETURN:
            type = "Return";
            break;
        }
        return "Type=" + type + ", Item=" + description + ", Cat#=" + catalog
            + ", Price=$" + price + ", Quant=" + quantity;
    }

}
```

Figure 8.13
(*Continued*).

Transaction objects written to a stream can be reconstructed through the class constructor, which has two forms. The first form is not used for recreating Transactions from a stream and requires that values for all the instance variables be passed. This form of the constructor would be used on a client-side application, for example, where a user would select items and quantities from a graphical user interface. Once an item is selected for purchase, the user interface code could instantiate a transaction object to be eventually transmitted to a server. The second form of the constructor takes an InputStream as an argument and creates a transaction object by converting the InputStream to a DataInputStream and parsing the token/value pairs out of the stream, assigning the values to instance variables. When the constructor returns, the newly instantiated Transaction object encapsulates the same transaction as was originally written to the stream.

To illustrate the use of the Transaction class, Figs. 8.14 through 8.16 present a multithreaded client/server application based on the Encrypted-MTServer/EncryptedMTSocket/EncryptedClient example presented in the previous section of this chapter. The purpose of this client/server application is to create Transaction objects on the client side, encrypt them, and pass them to the server side of the application through a socket connection. The server decrypts the input stream and instantiates new Transaction objects from the information passed through the stream.

Figure 8.14 shows the TransactionSocket class and Fig. 8.15 shows the TransactionServer class. The only significant difference between these two classes and the EncryptedMTSocket and EncryptedMTServer classes shown in Figs. 8.10 and 8.11 is in the `communicate()` method of the two ThreadedSocket subclasses. The `communicate()` method of the TransactionSocket class loops continuously, instantiating Transactions objects from the socket's InputStream, which has been passed through the decryption filter. Each new Transaction object is asked to total itself and the result is printed to `System.out`.

The client half of the application opens a socket connection to the server, instantiates several new Transaction objects, and has them write themselves to the socket's OutputStream, which the TransactionClient has placed behind an encryption filter. After sending the Transaction objects, the client closes the socket connection and exits. The source code for the TransactionClient application is shown in Fig. 8.16.

This technique for creating client/server protocols has some advantages over other techniques. First, it is lightweight. The entire protocol and methods for manipulating the data encapsulated in the protocol are

```
import java.net.*;
import java.io.*;
import ajp.io.*;
import ajp.net.*;

class TransactionSocket extends ThreadedSocket {
    DecryptedInputStream in;
    PrintStream out;

    public TransactionSocket(Socket socket, int priority, boolean debug)
                             throws IOException {
        super(socket);
        setDebug(debug);
        String key = ")P(O*I&U^Y  %T$%R$E#W@#";
        in = new DecryptedInputStream(input, key);
        setPriority(priority);
    }

    public void communicate() {
        String str;
        Transaction trans;
        double sum = 0;
        try {
            while(true) {
                trans = new Transaction(in);
                sum += trans.value();
                yield();
            }
        }
        catch (IOException e) {
            System.out.println("Total transation for connection = $" + sum);
            try {
                dbg("Closing socket: " + getSocket().toString());
                close();
            }
            catch (Exception ex) {
            }
        }
    }
}
```

Figure 8.14
The Transaction-
Socket class.

encapsulated in one class file. The mechanism for transmitting the object encapsulating the protocol is simply writing it to an OutputStream and instantiating it from an InputStream. Second, because the protocol is encapsulated in one class, changes to the protocol are localized to one file (unless, of course, parts of the protocol being used by applications are removed, in which case those applications relying on the now-defunct

```
import java.net.*;
import java.io.*;
import ajp.io.*;
import ajp.net.*;

class TransactionServer extends ThreadedServer {

    public TransactionServer(int port, boolean debug) {
        super(port);
        setDebug(debug);
    }

    public ThreadedSocket getThreadedSocket(Socket socket) throws IOException {
        int serverPriority = Thread.currentThread().getPriority();
        return new TransactionSocket(socket, serverPriority - 1, debug);
    }

    public static void main(String args[]) {
        int port;
        try {
            port = Integer.parseInt(args[0]);
        }
        catch (Exception e) {
            port = 42420;
        }
        TransactionServer s = new TransactionServer(port, true);
        s.start();
    }
}
```

Figure 8.15
The Transaction-
Server class.

parts of the protocol will have to be modified). Finally, while the protocols themselves are not necessarily easily reused, they are simple enough
to implement using existing code as a model.

The major disadvantage to this method of transmitting object state is
that it does not provide for writing and instantiating complex classes—
classes that contain Java objects as instance variables rather than just data
types. For example, if a class contained a linked-list object, the linked-list
class would have to support writing its state to the stream in order for
the containing class to be able to write itself. Furthermore, the objects the
linked list contained would have to be able to write themselves to the
stream, as would any objects the contained objects held references to, ad
infinitum. For complex classes, more sophisticated and heavyweight techniques are needed.

```java
import java.net.*;
import java.io.*;
import ajp.io.*;
import ajp.net.*;

class TransactionClient {
    public static void main(String args[]) {
        int port;
        String host;
        EncryptedOutputStream out;
        String key = ")P(O*I&U^Y  %T$%R$E#W@#";
        Transaction trans;

        try {
            port = Integer.parseInt(args[0]);
        }
        catch (Exception e) {
            port = 42420;
        }
        try {
            host = args[1];
        }

        catch (Exception e) {
            host = "localhost";
        }

        try {
            Socket socket = new Socket(host, port);
            out = new EncryptedOutputStream(socket.getOutputStream(), key);
            trans = new Transaction(Transaction.BUY, "Sport Coat",
                                    250.95, 1, 12345);
            trans.write(out);
            trans = new Transaction(Transaction.BUY, "Shirt",
                                    29.95, 4, 54321);
            trans.write(out);
            trans = new Transaction(Transaction.RETURN, "Electric Tie",
                                    8.95, 1, 10101);
            trans.write(out);
            out.close();
            socket.close();

        }
        catch (IOException e) {
        }
    }

    void sleep(int ms) {
        try {
            Thread.sleep(ms);
        }
```

Figure 8.16
The Transaction-
Client class.

```
        catch (InterruptedException ie) {
        }
    }
}
```

Figure 8.16
(Continued).

SUMMARY

The Java environment provides a simple network programming model based on sockets. In the socket model, introduced by the Berkeley versions of UNIX, client and server applications are endpoints on a shared, two-way communications channel. In Java, once the socket is open, client and server read and write to the socket using the classes in the java.io package.

Of the two types of Socket objects supported by the JDK—UDP and TCP sockcts—TCP sockets are the more common and provide a guarantee of delivery of data. Any packet not sent over a TCP socket that is not received will be retransmitted. The delivery of packets sent over a UDP socket, also called a Datagram socket, is not guaranteed. Datagram sockets are useful for applications where it is more important for an application to keep up with the flow of data, rather than to be certain it has received every packet.

Since support for multithreading is built into Java, it is a natural platform for creating socket servers. By utilizing the two abstract classes, ThreadedServer and ThreadedSocket, as a framework for creating servers, much of the repetitive work of creating threaded socket servers can be avoided. The ThreadedServer/ThreadedSocket framework is simple enough to make creating multithreaded servers simple, yet flexible enough to allow extension for specialized applications.

While many heavyweight APIs for sending Java objects over the networks are available or under development, a solution for simple Java objects that don't contain references to other Java objects is to enable them to write their state to OutputStreams and instantiate from Input-Streams. The Transaction class developed at the end of the chapter encapsulates a simple protocol passed from client to server that is used to simulate sales and returns of catalog merchandise. Through encapsulation in a single class file, the protocol is easily shared between client and server applications. Furthermore, the mechanism by which the object reads and writes itself to the I/O streams can be completely hidden from the client and server—classes exchanging a Transaction object can use it without having to know anything about how it is read or written. Encryption could be added directly to the Transaction class, for example, and the encryption techniques modified or replaced without having to change any of the classes that use the Transaction objects.

Interaction
with Browsers

Introduction

Although Java is a full-featured application programming language, it is Java's unique capability for creating applets that has garnered so much attention. Java's core-class packages provide a rich base on which to build applications targeted at the Web. These packages include support for direct interaction with Web browsers, URLs, and protocols.

This chapter describes techniques for applying the classes in the JDK to integrate more seamlessly into the environment of a Web browser. There are four areas of focus:

1. Interaction of applets and browsers
2. Enhancement of the browser environment with reusable applets and AWT extension classes
3. Interaction of applets and CGI programs
4. Introduction and handling of new protocols from downloaded applets

An Overview of Browser Interaction

When an applet is loaded into a browser, the browser provides two interfaces through which the applet can obtain information about, and interact with, its environment. Interaction with the applet's environment is provided through the *AppletContext* interface (introduced in Chap. 5) as a mechanism for providing interapplet communication. Information about the applet's environment is provided through the *AppletStub* interface.

AppletStub

The AppletStub interface is defined in the `java.applet` package and is an abstraction of both the APPLET tag that specifies the applet, and aspects of the Web page that contains the APPLET tag. The AppletStub defines methods that return these specifics:

- The URL of the applet
- The URL of the HTML document

- The parameters specified in the APPLET tag
- The AppletContext associated with the applet

The methods specified by the AppletStub interface are outlined in Table 9.1.*

The Applet class contains wrapper methods that directly call each of the methods in the AppletStub interface. When an Applet is created, the browser in which the applet is running will call the applet's `setStubs()` method, which stores in an instance variable a reference to an AppletStub object supplied by the browser. The wrapper methods in the Applet class call the corresponding methods on the stored AppletStub reference. It is from the AppletStub object that the applet can obtain a reference to its associated AppletContext.

AppletContext

The AppletContext provides interaction with the environment in which the applet is running. As is discussed in Chap. 5, the methods in the

---

* It should be pointed out that although the AppletContext provides an `applet-Resize()` method, browsers are free to, and typically do, ignore this method call. When an applet resizes, there are resizing implications for any HTML text in the document. An applet that continually resizes causes any document it is embedded in to be reformatted with each call to `appletResize()`. To avoid the hazard of creating a continually resizing applet—which could hang the browser—browsers ignore calls to `appletResize()`.

TABLE 9.1	**Method signature**	**Purpose**
Methods of the AppletStub Interface	`boolean isActive()`	Indicates whether the applet is currently active
	`URL getDocumentBase()`	Returns the URL of the HTML file that specified this applet
	`URL getCodeBase()`	Returns the URL of the applet itself
	`String getParameter(String name)`	Returns the value string associated with the named parameter in the applet tag
	`AppletContext getAppletContext()`	Returns the AppletContext for this applet
	`void appletResize(int width, int height)`	Resizes the applet

AppletContext fall into two categories: methods that provide access to other applets running in the same context, and methods that allow interaction with the browser itself. The methods that access other applets, getApplet() and getApplets(), are covered in Chap. 5. The remaining methods in the AppletContext interface, covered here, provide for accessing images and audio through URLs, loading other documents in the browser, and changing the browser's status message. A summary of the methods in the AppletContext that allow for direct interaction with the browser is provided in Table 9.2.

Applet interaction with a Web browser through the AppletContext interface is driven by URL objects instantiated from the java.net.URL class. (The URL class and the related classes in the java.net package will be discussed at the points they are utilized in this chapter, primarily in the sections on interacting with CGI programs and creating protocol handlers.) The URL class is an abstraction of the familiar URL strings used to cause browsers to visit a web page or retrieve an object. There are several forms of the URL class's constructor; the two commonly employed in conjunction with the methods in the AppletContext interface are as follows:

1. `public URL(String url)`

2. `public URL(URL context, String path)`

The first form is used to create URL objects from Strings that contain fully qualified URLs. The latter form creates URL objects from Strings that specify file names relative to existing URL objects.

TABLE 9.2

Methods of the AppletContext Interface That Interact with the Browser

Method	Description
`AudioClip getAudioClip(URL url)`	Returns the audio clip specified by the URL
`Image getImage(URL url)`	Returns an Image object created from the image specified in the URL
`void showDocument(URL url)`	Displays the document specified by the URL in the browser window the applet is running in
`void showDocument(URL url, String target)`	Displays the document specified by the URL in the specified browser window
`void showStatus(String status)`	Displays the string in the browser's status display area

The two methods of the AppletContext class that are utilized in this chapter are the showStatus() and showDocument() methods. The showStatus() method can be used by applets to display strings in the status area the browser may provide. Since it is an independent decision by each browser vendor whether or not to provide a textual status area, requests to setStatus() may be ignored by certain browsers. Furthermore, if a status area is provided, the browser will probably make use of it to display its own status messages. If your applet does indeed share the status area with the browser, it is possible that any status message your applet displays will be overwritten by messages generated by the browser. For this reason, use of the showStatus() method to display critical status or error messages is discouraged. Instead, it is better to create a message area within the applet, in a pop-up window or in another applet elsewhere on the same page, as is discussed in the section titled "A message applet" later in this chapter.

The showDocument() method, described in Table 9.2, provides a hook that allows applets to drive the browser, feeding it a URL to display in one of its windows. There are two forms of the method: one that takes a URL object as an argument, and one that takes a URL object and an optional String argument. The latter form allows the applet to specify the name of the browser window into which the document will be loaded. If supported by the browser, the window name can be used by applets to open multiple browser windows. Valid options for the name of the browser window are described in Table 9.3.

The showDocument() method will be effective only if the applet's AppletContext is active. That is, if the HTML page the applet is embedded in is currently visible in a browser window, the call to showDocument() will cause a URL to be loaded in the appropriate browser window. For example, suppose an applet creates a pop-up window that has buttons which, when pressed, cause showDocument() to be called. If the user

	Name	Description
TABLE 9.3 Valid Browser Window Names for the *showDocument()* Method	_self	The browser window the calling applet is running in
	_parent	The parent window of the window the calling applet is running in
	_top	The topmost window of the window tree the calling applet is running in
	_blank	A new unnamed window
	string	A new window named with the string specified

changes the document in the browser such that the applet is no longer visible, the buttons in the pop-up frame will no longer cause the browser to load new documents. If, however, the user returns to the page containing the applet that created the pop-up, the buttons will once again cause interaction with the browser as expected. To avoid this situation, a well-written applet creates new browser windows so as to display new URLs and to avoid losing its active AppletContext. Furthermore, applets that interact with the AppletContext through a pop-up window will usually hide the pop-up, or disable the controls that cause the AppletContext to be referenced, when the AppletContext becomes inactive. Since the AppletContext becomes inactive when the applet's HTML page is no longer visible in the browser, and since the browser calls the applet's stop() method when the applet's page is no longer visible, disabling or hiding UI objects that show documents should be done in the applet's stop() method.

Adapting Applet Behavior to the Browser Environment

The behavior of any applet is, to a great degree, under the control of the programmer. In Chap. 4, great care is taken when creating extensions to the AWT to ensure that the behavior of custom widgets mirrors the behavior of related widgets. As discussed, the behavior of the ImageButton shown in Fig. 4.26 is modeled closely after that of the AWT Button so that, to the user, there will be no discernible differences; users do not have to use AWT buttons one way and ImageButtons another. When developing applets, it is wise to take the same care in mirroring common browser behavior.

This section presents three examples of applets or AWT extensions that interact directly with the browsers in which they run. Each example has a closely related corollary in the browser environment and, as such, attempts to mirror the behavior of its cousin. These three examples exercise features in the AWT and in the java.net package that can make an applet look more like part of the browser, rather than something completely alien to it, added as an afterthought.

A Message Applet

In the discussion of the AppletContext, shortcomings of the showStatus() method were discussed: the browser might overwrite your status message, or the browser might not even support a status line at all. These limitations of the `showStatus()` method provide the motivation to create an applet designed to display error or status messages. The Message-Applet provides a dynamic text area that is intended to be written to by any applet on the same page, using the interapplet communication techniques described in Chap. 5. The MessageApplet is based on a class called *GraphicText*, shown in Fig. 9.1, that does most of the work for the applet.

The GraphicText class is much like the AWT label class in that it can be passed a string to display and it supports colors and fonts. However, GraphicText objects draw strings into an off-screen image and provide for word wrap if the strings are too long to fit in the horizontal dimension of the image. The class provides a method that returns a handle to the off-screen image, so that the text can be rendered in an applet's paint method, for example.

The MessageApplet instantiates a GraphicText object in its `init()` method and then provides a public method called `getGraphicText()` that returns a reference that other applets can use to change the font or the foreground/background colors. The MessageApplet class provides two other public methods: `setMessage()`, used to change the message it displays, and `setOffset()`, which dictates a vertical offset from the top of the applet, allowing for repositioning of the text in instances where a menu bar or *Untrusted Applet Window* banner would cover the text. Figure 9.2 shows the MessageApplet implementation.

The applet shown in Fig. 9.3, *MessageDriver*, illustrates how the Message-Applet might be used from within another applet. In the MessageDriver's `init()` method, the applet steps through the enumeration returned by the AppletContext's `getApplets()` method and looks for a Message-Applet. Once the MessageApplet is found, its font and foreground/background colors are changed by the MessageDriver through the MessageApplet's GraphicText object. The MessageDriver then creates a new thread that will update the MessageApplet with a new message every two seconds. (A Web page that includes the MessageDriver applet and MessageApplet, as well as Web pages for all the applets described in this section, can be found on the CD-ROM that accompanies the book.)

The message applet provides a mechanism for displaying status messages that is not subject to interference from the browser. In addition, the MessageApplet gives both Web-page designers and Java programmers flexibility over where the status message appears. For example, the MessageApplet as it is can be placed anywhere on an HTML page. With minor modification, it could be made to use static objects for interapplet communication, allowing the MessageApplet to appear in a separate

```
package ajp.awt;

import java.awt.*;
import java.util.*;

/**
 * A GraphicText class.
 *
 * @version 1.1
 */

public class GraphicText {

    // the current text in this object
    private String currentText;

    // the current color to use
    private Color currentColor;

    // the current background color to use
    private Color bgColor;

    // the current Font to use
    private Font currentFont;

    private boolean debug = false;

    /**
     * Create a Graphic Text Object
     **/
    public GraphicText() {
        this(false);
    }

    public GraphicText(boolean debug) {
        this.debug = debug;
    }

    /**
     * Set the text for this object to use
     **/
    public void setText(String someText) {
        currentText = someText;
    }

    /**
     * Get the current text
     **/
    public String getText() {
        return currentText;
    }

    /**
```

Figure 9.1
The GraphicText class.

```
    * Set the drawing color
    **/
   public void setColor(Color someColor) {
        currentColor = new Color(someColor.getRGB());
   }


   /**
    * Set the drawing color
    **/
   public void setBGColor(Color someColor) {
        bgColor = new Color(someColor.getRGB());
   }


   /**
    * Get the current drawing color
    **/
   public Color getColor() {
        return new Color(currentColor.getRGB());
   }


   /**
    * Set the Font to use
    **/

   public void setFont(Font someFont) {
        currentFont = new Font(someFont.getName(), someFont.getStyle(),
                                someFont.getSize());
   }


   /**
    * Get the current Font
    **/
   public Font getFont() {
        return new Font(currentFont.getName(), currentFont.getStyle(),
                        currentFont.getSize());
   }


   /**
    * Get the graphic text as an image
    **/
   public Image getAsImage(Component component, Dimension size) {
        dbg("Width to create: " + size.width);
        Image i = component.createImage(size.width, size.height);
        Graphics g;
        if (i != null) {
            g = i.getGraphics();
            if (bgColor != null) {
                Color tmp = g.getColor();
                g.setColor(bgColor);
                g.fillRect(0, 0, size.width, size.height);
                g.setColor(tmp);
            }
            if (currentColor != null) {
```

Figure 9.1
(*Continued*).

```
                    g.setColor(currentColor);
            }
            if (currentFont != null) {
                g.setFont(currentFont);
                dbg(currentFont.toString());
            }
            String lines[] = breakIntoLines(g.getFontMetrics(), size.width);
            int height = g.getFontMetrics().getHeight();
            int currentY = height;
            for(int x=0; x<lines.length; x++) {
                dbg("Graphic text drawing: " + lines[x]);
                g.drawString(lines[x], 0, currentY);
                currentY += height;
            }
        }
        return i;
    }

    String[] breakIntoLines(FontMetrics metrics, int width) {
        int currentWidth = 0;
        String currentString = new String();
        dbg("Before break: " + currentText);
        dbg("width passed in: " + width);

        StringTokenizer token = new StringTokenizer(currentText);
        Vector lines = new Vector(token.countTokens());
        while (token.hasMoreTokens()) {
            String temp = token.nextToken() + " ";
            dbg("token: " + temp);
            int w = metrics.stringWidth(temp);
            dbg("width: " + w);
            if (w + currentWidth <= width) {
                dbg("Token could be added! ");
                currentString += temp;
                currentWidth += w;
            }
            else {
                dbg("Token could not be added! ");
                lines.addElement(new String(currentString));
                currentString = new String(temp);
                currentWidth = w;
            }
        }
        dbg("currentString: " + currentString);
        // now add last line working on
        lines.addElement(new String(currentString));

        String[] returnString = new String[ lines.size() ];
        dbg("Number of tokes to be pushed: " + lines.size());
        for(int x=0; x < lines.size(); x++) {
            returnString[ x ] = (String)lines.elementAt(x);
            dbg("Adding string: " + (String)lines.elementAt(x));
        }
    }
}
```

Figure 9.1
(Continued).

```
import ajp.awt.GraphicText;

import java.awt.*;
import java.applet.*;

/**
 * A MessageApplet class.
 *
 * @version 1.1
 */
public class MessageApplet extends Applet {

    // the internal GrahpicText object to use
    GraphicText text;

    // how far to move the text down
    private int offset = 20;

    public void init() {
        text = new GraphicText();
        text.setText( "" );
        String fonts[] = Toolkit.getDefaultToolkit().getFontList();
        Font font = new Font( fonts[0], Font.BOLD, 14 );
        text.setFont( font );
        text.setColor( Color.red );
        text.setBGColor( Color.lightGray );

    }

    public GraphicText getGraphicText() {
        return text;
    }

    public void setOffset( int off ) {
        offset = off;
    }

    public void paint( Graphics g ) {
        Dimension size = new Dimension( size().width - 20, size().height - 20 );
        System.out.println( size() + " " + size );
        g.drawImage( text.getAsImage( this, size ), 0, offset, this );
    }

    public synchronized void setMessage( String message ) {
        System.out.println("Text = " + message );
        text.setText( message );
        repaint();
    }

}
```

Figure 9.2
The MessageApplet
class.

```
import ajp.awt.GraphicText;
import java.awt.*;
import java.util.*;
import java.applet.*;

/**
 * A MessageDriver class that writes to a MessageApplet.
 *
 * @version 1.1
 */
public class MessageDriver extends Applet implements Runnable {
    MessageApplet status = null;
    Thread thread;
    Font font;

    static String strings[] = {
        "dynamic",
        "secure",
        "multithreaded",
        "object oriented",
        "networked",
        "Really totally way cool and without peer"
    };

    public void start() {
        thread.resume();
    }

    public void stop() {
        thread.suspend();
    }

    public void showStatus(String str) {
        if (status != null) {
            status.setMessage(str);
        }
        else {
            getAppletContext().showStatus(str);
        }
    }

    public void init() {
        boolean gotMessageApplet = false;
        font = new Font("TimesRoman", Font.ITALIC, 14);

        while(! gotMessageApplet) {
            Enumeration e = getAppletContext().getApplets();
            while(e.hasMoreElements()) {
                Applet a = (Applet)e.nextElement(); .
                if (a instanceof MessageApplet) {
                    status = (MessageApplet)a;
```

Figure 9.3
The MessageDriver
class.

```
                        status.getGraphicText().setFont(font);
                        status.getGraphicText().setBGColor(getBackground());
                        status.setOffset(0);
                        gotMessageApplet = true;
                        break;
                    }
                }
                if (! gotMessageApplet) {
                    try {
                        Thread.sleep(2000);
                    }
                    catch (InterruptedException ex) {}
                }
            }

        thread = new Thread(this);
        thread.start();
    }

    public void run() {
        int count = 0;

        while(true) {
            showStatus(strings[count++]);
            count = count % strings.length;
            try {
                Thread.sleep(2000);
            }
            catch (InterruptedException e) {}
        }

    }

}
```

Figure 9.3
(*Continued*).

frame from the applets that display messages in the MessageApplet. It would also take minimal effort to have the MessageApplet contained in a pop-up window, giving even more flexibility to the Web-page designer.

An AWT HypertextLink Widget

The second example that extends the Java programmer's toolkit for use with the browser is the *HypertextLink* class. The HypertextLink is an AWT extension class that provides the same functionality as do hypertext links in HTML documents. Both provide the following features:

- A link from some text to a URL
- A visual indication of their presence through the use of color
- Visual feedback when the link has been clicked on with the mouse
- Visual feedback to the user when the mouse is over a link
- A visual indication that the new document is being loaded

The implementation of the HypertextLink class is shown in Fig. 9.4. The widget is a subclass of Panel, so it can be easily incorporated into AWT user interface designs. The link to a URL is provided through the class's constructor, which has the following forms:

```
public HypertextLink(URL url, Applet parent)
public HypertextLink(URL url, String frameName, Applet parent)
public HypertextLink(String urlString, Applet parent)
                     throws MalformedURLException
public HypertextLink(String urlString, String frameName,
                     Applet parent) throws MalformedURLException
```

HypertextLink objects can be created by passing either an existing URL object or a string containing a URL specification. When a URL string is passed to the constructor, a URL object is instantiated and passed to one of the other forms of the HypertextLink constructor. The URL, parent applet, and name of the browser frame in which to open the URL are saved in instance variables and used later when the HypertextLink object detects a mouse click. Since the two forms of the constructor instantiate a URL object from the string they are passed, they pass through any MalformedURLException thrown by the URL constructor.

When a user clicks the mouse on the HypertextLink, the widget causes the browser to switch pages by calling one of the two forms of showDocument():

```
if (frameName != null) {
    parent.getAppletContext().showDocument(url, frameName,
                                           parent);
}
else {
    parent.getAppletContext().showDocument(url, parent);
}
```

Visual feedback is provided by the HypertextLink in several ways. First, it provides support for two colors, a *normal* color and a *visited* color, through the methods:

```
void setColor(Color color)
void setVisitedColor(Color color)
```

```
package ajp.awt;

import java.awt.*;
import java.applet.*;
import java.net.*;
import java.awt.event.*;

/**
 * A Hypertext link class.
 *
 * @version 2.1
 **/
public class HypertextLink extends Panel implements MouseListener {

    // the internal GrahpicText object to use
    GraphicText text;
    // the parent applet
    Applet parent;
    // the URL pointed to
    URL url;
    // the URL as a string
    String urlString;
    // the cursors
    Cursor waitCursor;
    Cursor handCursor;
    Cursor defaultCursor;
    // Has the link been visited
    boolean visited = false;
    // Colors to use for the link
    Color visitedColor = new Color(0, 0, 80);
    Color unvisitedColor = Color.blue;
    // frame name if we are displaying in alternate frames
    String frameName = null;
    // the font to use
    Font font = null;

    /**
     * Create a Hypertext link object.
     **/
    public HypertextLink(String urlString, String frameName,
                         Applet applet) throws MalformedURLException {
        this(new URL(urlString), frameName, applet);
    }

    /**
     * Create a Hypertext link object.
     **/
    public HypertextLink(String urlString,
                         Applet applet) throws MalformedURLException {
        this(new URL(urlString), null, applet);
    }
```

Figure 9.4
The HypertextLink
class.

```java
/**
 * Create a Hypertext link object.
 **/
public HypertextLink(URL url, Applet parent)
                                throws MalformedURLException {
    this(url, null, parent);
}


/**
 * Create a Hypertext link object.
 **/
public HypertextLink(URL url, String frameName, Applet parent) {
    super();
    // register for mouse events
    addMouseListener(this);
    // define the cursors
    waitCursor = Cursor.getPredefinedCursor( Cursor.WAIT_CURSOR );
    handCursor = Cursor.getPredefinedCursor( Cursor.HAND_CURSOR );
    defaultCursor = Cursor.getDefaultCursor();
    // port the the server is listening to
    int port;

    // Set up instance variables
    this.url = url;
    this.parent = parent;
    this.frameName = frameName;
    text = new GraphicText();
    text.setText("");
    String fonts[] = Toolkit.getDefaultToolkit().getFontList();
    text.setColor(unvisitedColor);

    urlString = new String(url.getProtocol() + "://" + url.getHost());
    if ((port = url.getPort()) > 0) {
        urlString = urlString + ":" + port;
    }
    urlString = urlString + url.getFile();
}

// set the font and text color
public void addNotify() {
    super.addNotify();
    text.setBGColor(getBackground());
    if (font == null){
        setFont(getFont());
    }
}

/**
 * Set the default color of the link.
 **/
public void setColor(Color color) {
    unvisitedColor = color;
    text.setColor(unvisitedColor);
```

Figure 9.4
(Continued).

```
        repaint();
    }

    /**
     * Set the "visited" color of the link.
     **/
    public void setVisitedColor(Color color) {
        visitedColor = color;
        text.setColor(color);
        repaint();
    }

    /**
     * Set the font used by the link.
     **/
    public void setFont(Font font) {
        this.font = font;
        text.setFont(font);
        repaint();
    }

    // A mouse click happened.  Change the cursor and visit the page.
    public void mouseClicked( MouseEvent evt ) {
        setCursor(waitCursor);

        if (frameName != null) {
            parent.getAppletContext().showDocument(url, frameName);
        }
        else {
            parent.getAppletContext().showDocument(url);
        }
        visited = true;
        setColor(visitedColor);
    }

    // entered the hypertext link
    public void mouseEntered( MouseEvent evt ) {
        setCursor( handCursor );
        parent.getAppletContext().showStatus(urlString);
    }

    // exited the hypertext link
    public void mouseExited( MouseEvent evt ) {
        setCursor( defaultCursor);
        parent.getAppletContext().showStatus("");
    }

    public void mousePressed( MouseEvent evt ){}
    public void mouseReleased( MouseEvent evt ) {}

    public GraphicText getGraphicText() {
        return text;
    }
```

Figure 9.4

(Continued).

```
    public void paint(Graphics g) {
        g.drawImage(text.getAsImage(this, getSize()), 0, 0, this);
    }

    public void setText(String message) {
        text.setText(message);
        repaint();
    }

}
```

Figure 9.4
(*Continued*).

The setColor() method is used to set the color of the text when it is initially displayed. The setVisitedColor() sets the color the text will be drawn in after the user has clicked on the link. This provides a feedback mechanism similar to that supported by hypertext links in browsers.

A second visual feedback provided by the HypertextLink is a change in the mouse pointer or cursor when the mouse is moved over the link. When the user moves the mouse over the HypertextLink, a copy of the current cursor is saved and the cursor is changed to the familiar *hand* cursor. When the user clicks on the link, the cursor is changed again to the *busy* cursor to indicate that a page is being downloaded. This clue is helpful in that not all browsers give direct visual feedback when a URL is being loaded at the request of an applet. When the mouse leaves the region occupied by the HypertextLink, the widget changes the cursor back to the cursor saved at the point the mouse first entered the region.

The third and final piece of feedback the HypertextLink class provides is an indication of the URL to which the object is linked. When the mouse pointer is moved onto a HypertextLink widget, the showStatus() method is called to display the name of the URL in the browser's status area. In spite of the shortcomings of using showStatus() outlined earlier, the status area of the browser is typically used to display the destination of any hypertext link. To remain consistent with hypertext links in HTML, the HypertextLink class emulates that behavior.

The implementation of the HypertextLink, as is the case with the MessageApplet, utilizes a GraphicText object to display the text of the link. The GraphicText object was chosen rather than an AWT Label because the dynamic nature of the GraphicText object provides greater flexibility with respect to resizing, fonts, and changing text. Some details of the implementation warrant discussion.

To facilitate changing the cursor, three Cursor objects are used, `wait-Cursor`, `handCursor`, and `defaultCursor`. The cursors are initialized in the constructor and are changed in the mouse event notification methods.

Since the browser does not provide any direct notification to the applet when the requested URL is actually loaded into the browser, it is impossible to know when to change the cursor from the *busy* cursor back to the default cursor used by the browser.* The HypertextLink changes the cursor to the *busy* cursor in the `mouseClicked()` method. The cursor will remain *busy* until the cursor is moved off the HypertextLink object and `mouseExited()` is called. This design provides a reasonable solution to the lack of notification since, after `showDocument()` is called, either one of the following will occur: the page the applet is on will be unloaded in favor of the new document (else an error message if the document is not found), or when the new page is displayed in a new browser window, the user will likely move the mouse to the new window to interact with the new document.

Figure 9.5 shows a simple Applet called *HypertextLink Test* that is passed a message and a URL via its HTML APPLET tag:

```
<applet code=HypertextLinkTest.class
    codebase="http://www.somehost.com:8888/rice/classes"
    width=300 height=30>
<param name="url" value="http://java.sun.com">
<param name="message" value="Visit the JavaSoft home page!!">
</applet>
```

Since the HypertextLink class utilizes a GraphicText object, altering the applet's width and height will allow the link to appear all on one line or on multiple lines with word wrapping.

URL ImageButtons

The final example of a tool that can be used to integrate applets with the browser is the *URLImageButton* class, which provides the same basic functionality as the HypertextLink class but does so as an extension of

---

* If the page is loaded into the same browser window as the applet, the applet is notified indirectly that the document has been loaded when the applet's `stop()` method is called. If the page is loaded in a different browser window, the applet has no way of knowing when the document has been loaded.

Figure 9.5

The HyperTextLinkTest
applet.

```
import java.applet.*;
import java.net.*;
import java.awt.*;
import ajp.awt.HypertextLink;

public class HypertextLinkTest extends Applet {
    public void init(){

        String url = getParameter("url");
        String message = getParameter("message");

        try{
            setLayout(new BorderLayout());
            HypertextLink i =
                new HypertextLink(new URL(url), this);
            i.setText(message);
            add("Center", i);
        }
        catch(Exception e) {
            e.printStackTrace();
        }
    }
}
```

the ImageButton class described in Chap. 4. Like the HypertextLink, the URLImageButton provides visual feedback to the user when the mouse enters, leaves, or clicks on the button. The URLImageButton also emulates the browser's display of the URL in the status area when the cursor is on a link.

The implementation of the URLImageButton appears in Fig. 9.6. You may also wish to refer back to Chap. 4 for the details of the ImageButton class that the URLImageButton extends. The similarities between the URLImageButton and the HypertextLink should be expected since they provide very similar functionality. This is another case where multiple inheritance, perhaps from an abstract class representing a generic hypertext link, would be convenient. However, since the widgets inherit from different parent classes, functionality must either be copied or delegated to a separate object that can be included as an instance variable. Delegating the interaction with the browser to an included object would only remove the construction of the URL path from the HypertextLink and URLImageButton. Both widgets would still need to have similar code in their event methods; they would just be calling methods of the included object, rather than the AppletContext itself.

Figure 9.7 shows an applet called *SortedButtons* that creates a pop-up window containing several URLImageButtons arranged by a SortedLayout manager. A snapshot of the pop-up window was presented in Fig. 4.32.

```
package ajp.awt;

import java.awt.*;
import java.awt.event.*;
import java.net.*;
import java.net.MalformedURLException;
import java.applet.*;

/**
 * A class for associating images with URLs.  The image is placed in
 * a button, the cursor is changed to give familiar feedback that this
 * is associated with a URL.
 *
 * @version 2.2
 **/
public class URLImageButton extends ImageButton {
    static final long serialVersionUID = 4557746424622281849L;
    private boolean debug = true;
    // The URL the button points to.
    URL url;
    // The Applet the button is owned by.
    Applet parent;
    // Name of the frame to display in.
    String frameName;
    // The string representation of the URL
    String urlString;
    // Cursor to use when the mouse is over the button.
    Cursor handCursor;
    Cursor defaultCursor;

    /**
     * Create a button pointing to a specific URL.
     **/
    public URLImageButton(URL url, Image image, Applet applet) {
        this(url, null, image, applet);
    }

    /**
     * Create a button pointing to a specific URL.
     **/
    public URLImageButton(URL url, String name, Image image, Applet applet) {
        super(image);
        String tmp;
        int port;

        this.url = url;
        parent = applet;
        frameName = name;

        urlString = new String(url.getProtocol() + "://" + url.getHost());
        if ((port = url.getPort()) > 0) {
```

Figure 9.6
The URLImageButton
class.

```
                    urlString = urlString + ":" + port;
            }
        urlString = urlString + url.getFile();
        handCursor = Cursor.getPredefinedCursor( Cursor.HAND_CURSOR );
        defaultCursor = Cursor.getDefaultCursor();
    }

    /**
     * Create a button pointing to a specific URL.
     **/
    public URLImageButton(String urlString, String name, Image image,
                         Applet applet) throws MalformedURLException {
        this(new URL(urlString), name, image, applet);
    }

    /**
     * Create a button pointing to a specific URL.
     **/
    public URLImageButton(String urlString, Image image,
                         Applet applet) throws MalformedURLException {
        this(new URL(urlString), null, image, applet);
    }

    /**
     * Handle the mousde events, trapping MOUSE_ENTERED and MOUSE_EXITED
     * to change the cursor to and from the "hand".
     **/
    protected void processMouseEvent(MouseEvent e) {
        switch(e.getID()) {
        case MouseEvent.MOUSE_ENTERED:

                setCursor(handCursor);
                dbg("Set Cursor to " + handCursor);
                parent.getAppletContext().showStatus(urlString);
                break;
        case MouseEvent.MOUSE_EXITED:
                parent.getAppletContext().showStatus("");
                setCursor(defaultCursor);
                dbg("Set Cursor to " + defaultCursor);
                break;
        }
        super.processMouseEvent(e);
    }

    // The local debug method
    void dbg(String str) {
        if (debug) {
            System.out.println(this.getClass().getName() + ": " + str);
            System.out.flush();
        }
    }
}
```

Figure 9.6
(Continued).

```
import java.applet.*;
import java.awt.*;
import java.util.StringTokenizer;
import java.net.URL;
import java.net.MalformedURLException;
import ajp.awt.*;

/**
 * A SortedButton applet.
 *
 * @version 1.5
 **/
public class SortedButtons extends Applet {
    URLImageButton b;
    Frame frame;

    public void init() {
        String params;
        String imageName;
        String URLName;
        String name;
        StringTokenizer imageURLs;

        frame = new Frame("Image Button Frame");
        frame.setLayout(new SortedLayout());

        params = getParameter("imageURLs");

        if (params != null) {
            imageURLs = new StringTokenizer(params, "|");
            // now parse out the image/URL pairs
            while (imageURLs.hasMoreTokens()) {
                URL url;
                Image im;

                // split the "image|URL" into tokens.
                StringTokenizer nameImageURL
                    = new StringTokenizer(imageURLs.nextToken(), ";");
                name = nameImageURL.nextToken();
                imageName = nameImageURL.nextToken();
                URLName = nameImageURL.nextToken();
                try {
                    url = new URL(URLName);
                }
                catch (MalformedURLException e) {
                    System.out.println("Bad URL: " + URLName);
                    continue;
                }
                im = getImage(getDocumentBase(), imageName);
                b = new URLImageButton(url, im, this);
                frame.add(name, b);
            }
        }
```

Figure 9.7
The SortedButtons
applet.

```
        frame.setSize(new Dimension(200, 450));
        frame.setVisible(true);
    }

    public void start() {
        frame.setVisible(true);
    }

    public void stop() {
        frame.setVisible(false);
    }

}
```

Figure 9.7
(*Continued*).

Each button is linked to a URL that is passed to the applet via the HTML APPLET tag. The APPLET tag specifies a parameter named *imageURLs* that consists of a list of specifications, separated by vertical bars (|), for configuring the URLImageButtons. Each specification consists of a name for the button, a URL to the image that is used on the button, and the URL that is linked to the button. A sample button specification for a single button follows:

```
Rice,J;images/Jeff.gif;http://www.somehost.com/~rice/JeffRice.html
```

Since all the buttons on the SortedButtons applet are specified by one APPLET tag parameter, the list must be broken apart and parsed. The imageURL's parameter is decomposed in the applet's init() method using two StringTokenizers: one to split the list into button specifications and one to split the button specifications into its three constituent pieces.* Each URLImageButton is created using the parsed parameters and added to the applet. The only other methods specified in the applet are the start() and stop() methods, which show and hide the pop-up window when the AppletContext becomes active or inactive.

As with the MessageApplet and the HypertextLink, the URLImage-Button represents a new object designed to integrate smoothly into the Web browser, extending existing and familiar user interface paradigms.

---

* An alternate approach to specifying large numbers of applet parameters is to give each parameter a unique, but related name, such as *button1, button2,* and so on. With parameters specified using a name suffixed by a number, the init() method can programmatically construct the name passed to getParameter() in a while loop and iterate until the first getParameter() call returns a null. An example of this form of parameter passing is illustrated in the ImageMap applet demo in the JDK's demo directory.

Interaction with CGI Programs

The Common Gateway Interface (CGI) is the workhorse of Web sites. The basic idea behind CGI is that an http request is received by a Web server which, in response to the request, runs an application on the server and returns the output of the application to the client. The output is typically a data stream representing an HTML document that is loaded into the client's browser. CGI applications can be any executable programs, written in whatever programming language is supported on the server platform.

This section of the chapter is about interfacing to existing CGI programs, not about writing them.* It is also worth noting, however, that while the Perl language has been the overwhelming language of choice for CGI programming, with the emergence of Java on so many platforms and commitments by so many operating system vendors to support the Java VM directly at the operating system level, Java has much to recommend it as a CGI programming language.

There are so many sophisticated CGI programs in existence, it is almost inevitable that at some point applet programmers will want or need to interact with them. The JDK provides classes that allow for interaction with CGI script using either GET or POST methods of invocation. To demonstrate the interaction between Java applets and CGI programs, a CGI program called *readfile* will be used. The readfile program receives requests via http to read files and passes contents of the files back to the requestor in the form of straight ASCII text. The readfile program is straightforward and can easily be implemented in a variety of programming or scripting languages. A sample implementation of the readfile program is included on this book's companion CD-ROM. Since the focus here is not on CGI programming, those interested in the implementation of the readfile program are encouraged to investigate it on the CD-ROM.

There are two methods for accessing CGI programs via http: *GET* and *POST.* Programs invoked through the GET method have the arguments to the program encoded in the URL through which the program is referenced. The typical syntax of a GET URL follows:

---

* It is far beyond the scope of this book to discuss CGI programming in any detail. Those interested in exploring CGI programming might consider adding Shishir Gundavaram's *CGI Programming* (Sebastopol, Calif.: O'Reilly & Associates, 1996) to their bookshelves. Gundavaram's is one of the few books whose primary focus is CGI programming. While the book uses the Perl language for almost all its examples, the concepts are easily adaptable to other languages.

```
http://host:port/cgi-bin/get_program_name?encoded_arguments
```

The encoded arguments are passed to the CGI program through the environment variable QUERY_STRING. The encoding of the string translates characters—which might carry special meaning as part of a URL—into a hexadecimal representation. GET methods are used to create a one-way flow of data from the CGI program to the browser.

The steps in interacting with a CGI program from a Java applet through the GET method follow:

1. Construct a URL to the program and append the encoded arguments.
2. Open the URL and obtain a handle to an input stream from the URL.
3. Read the output of the program from the stream.

The POST method of invoking CGI programs involves two-way communication between browser and CGI program. The program is invoked with a simpler URL that omits any encoded arguments:

```
http://host:port/cgi-bin/post_program_name
```

Once the program starts, it attempts to read a fixed-length stream of data from standard input; it then writes to standard output any information that is to be sent back to the browser. The data sent to the CGI program typically includes arguments that the application will have to interpret.

Applets accessing CGI programs through the POST method take the following steps:

1. Construct the URL to the CGI program.
2. Open the URL and get a URLConnection from it.
3. Signal that the URLConnection is to be used for output.
4. Extract the output stream from the connection.
5. Write *all* output to the stream.
6. Open an input stream from the connection.
7. Read all input from the stream.

It is important to note that the sequence of opening the streams and writing the data is significant. URLConnections that have been read from cannot be subsequently written to. Applets must do all their writing to the CGI program before attempting to read from it.

Accessing GET Programs

Figure 9.8 shows a snapshot of an applet called *GetApplet* that calls the readfile program through the GET method. The applet constructs a string representing a URL by concatenating the file name provided by the user at the top of the user interface with the URL of the readfile CGI program. The URL of the readfile program is provided through the APPLET tag that specifies the GetApplet applet. When the button at the bottom of the UI is pressed, the URL string is constructed, the readfile

Figure 9.8
An applet that inter-
faces to CGI GET
scripts.

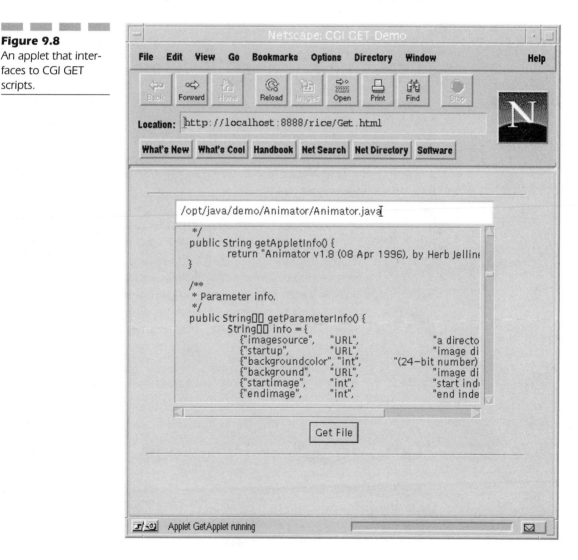

program is called, and the file is streamed back to the applet and displayed in the TextArea in the center of the applet.

The applet creates its connection to the CGI program in its `action-Performed()` method, following the steps outlined previously. When the user presses the button in the user interface, a string is constructed and passed to the URL constructor. The URL object's `getConnection()` method is used to obtain a URLConnection object, from which an input stream is extracted. The input stream is filtered by a DataInputStream so the output of the readfile program can be read a line at a time and copied into the TextArea in the center of the UI. The applet's implementation is shown in Fig. 9.9.

Interacting with POST Programs

An applet similar to GetApplet is shown in Fig. 9.10. This new applet, called *PostApplet,* interacts with the readfile CGI program through the POST method. The user interface it presents is the same as GetApplet, as is most of its source code. The primary differences are in the `actionPerformed()` method. When the PostApplet creates the URLConnection, it first calls connection's `setDoOutput()` method to enable it for writing. Next, an output stream is extracted from the URLConnection and the name of the file to be read by readfile is written to the connection. An input stream is then extracted from the URLConnection and the contents of the file are read as before.

While the two applets, GetApplet and PostApplet, are quite simple, the basic techniques for interacting with CGI programs remain the same regardless of the complexity of the CGI program or of the applet accessing it. It is important to note that the same security restrictions apply to applets communicating with CGI programs as to applets connecting to remote hosts via sockets. Applets can only connect to CGI programs on the same server from which they were downloaded.

Handling New Protocols

A limitation of Web browsers prior to the advent of Java was their inability to dynamically adapt to the introduction of new protocols. Browsers traditionally supported a fixed number of protocols—such as *http, ftp, telnet, gopher, nntp,* and *file*—and could only support new protocols through

```
import java.net.*;
import java.awt.*;
import java.awt.event.*;
import java.util.*;
import java.io.*;

import java.applet.*;

/**
 * A simple applet to demonstrate interation with CGI programs through
 * the GET request method.
 *
 * @version 2.1
 **/
public class GetApplet extends Applet implements ActionListener {
    TextArea textArea;
    Button button;
    TextField textField;
    String urlString;

    public void init() {

        urlString = getParameter("url");

        if (urlString == null) {
            System.out.println("No CGI Program specified.");
            return;
        }
        setLayout(new BorderLayout());
        textArea = new TextArea();
        textArea.setEditable(false);
        add("Center",  textArea);
        Panel p = new Panel();
        p.add(button = new Button("Get File"));
        button.addActionListener(this);
        add("South", p);
        add("North", textField = new TextField());
    }

    public void actionPerformed(ActionEvent ev) {
        DataInputStream dis = null;

        try {
            String data;
            textArea.setText("");

            if ((data = textField.getText()) == null)
                return;
            URL url = new URL(urlString + "?" + data);
            URLConnection conn = url.openConnection();
            dis = new DataInputStream(conn.getInputStream());
            while ((data = dis.readLine()) != null) {
                textArea.appendText(data + "\n");
            }
```

Figure 9.9
The GetApplet class.

```
            dis.close();

    }
    catch (Exception e) {
        e.printStackTrace();
        try {
            dis.close();
        }
        catch (Exception ex) { }
    }
  }
}
```

Figure 9.9
(*Continued*).

new software releases. With the public release of the HotJava browser in 1995, Sun Microsystems changed the rules of the game. HotJava was able to dynamically adapt to new protocols through loadable Java protocol handlers. The dynamic nature of HotJava granted Web developers the freedom to conjure up new ways of communicating data over the Web without having to worry about having enough clout to convince browser vendors to integrate a new protocol into future releases of their browsers.

Although the classes in the JDK's `java.net` package have all the hooks and handles for direct support of adding new protocol handlers, browsers do not allow applets to directly introduce new protocol handlers. Since protocol handlers are shared among all applets running in the browsers, there are obvious hazards in allowing applets to dynamically download a protocol handler that could potentially be used by other applets. At present, the direct support of adding new protocol handlers is limited to HotJava and other stand-alone Java applications, subject to the security policies they implement. (See Chap. 10 for a discussion of security managers.) Rather than discuss how protocol handlers can be added to HotJava, this section presents an alternate mechanism for handling protocols that works in any Java-enabled browser.* Before detailing the specifics of this alternate protocol-handling scheme, however, it is helpful to understand how protocol handlers are supported by the Java networking classes.

---

* For those interested in how to develop protocol handlers for the HotJava browser, or for Java applications, see Dave Brown's homepage at JavaSoft (http://java.sun.com/people/brown). Included on his homepage are links to an example protocol handler for HotJava along with step-by-step instructions on how to build and install it.

```java
import java.awt.*;
import java.awt.event.*;
import java.net.*;
import java.util.*;
import java.io.*;

import java.applet.*;

/**
 * A simple applet to demonstrate interation with CGI programs through
 * the POST request method.
 *
 * @version 2.1
 **/
public class PostApplet extends Applet implements ActionListener {
    TextArea textArea;
    Button button;
    TextField textField;
    String urlString;

    public void init() {

        urlString = getParameter("url");

        if (urlString == null ) {
            System.out.println("No CGI Program specified.");
            return;
        }
        setLayout(new BorderLayout());
        textArea = new TextArea();
        textArea.setEditable(false);
        add("Center",  textArea);
        Panel p = new Panel();
        p.add(button = new Button("Get File"));
        button.addActionListener(this);
        add("South", p);
        add("North", textField = new TextField());
    }

    public void actionPerformed(ActionEvent ev) {
        DataInputStream dis = null;
        PrintStream ps = null;

        try {
            String data;
            textArea.setText("");

            if ((data = textField.getText()) == null)
                return;
            URL url = new URL(urlString);
            URLConnection conn = url.openConnection();
            conn.setDoOutput(true);
            ps = new PrintStream(conn.getOutputStream());
```

Figure 9.10
The PostApplet class.

```
                ps.println(data);
                dis = new DataInputStream(conn.getInputStream());
                while ((data = dis.readLine()) != null) {
                    textArea.appendText(data + "\n");
                }
                ps.close();
                dis.close();
        }
        catch (Exception e) {
            e.printStackTrace();
            try {
                dis.close();
            }
            catch (Exception ex) { }
        }
    }
}
```

▬▬ ▬▬ ▬▬ ▬▬

Figure 9.10
(*Continued*).

Protocol Handling in the JDK

When a string is passed to the URL class's constructor, the constructor attempts to find a handler for the protocol embedded in the URL string. For instance, if the string

```
xyzzy://someserver.com/pathname
```

is passed to the URL constructor, the constructor will try to find a handler for the xyzzy protocol. Protocol handlers in Java are implemented in two classes. The first is a subclass of the *URLStreamHandler* class, which is tasked with establishing a connection to the remote host using the appropriate protocol. The second is a subclass of *URLConnection*, an instance of which can be retrieved from the URLStreamHandler. The URLConnection class provides a getContent() method that uses the connection to retrieve an object appropriate for the protocol.

The task of looking up the appropriate URLStreamHandler for a given protocol falls to the URL class's *URLStreamHandlerFactory* object. There is one stream-handler factory for the URL class; it can be set only once, and only at the discretion of the security manager. Most browsers will already have a URLStreamHandlerFactory object set for the URL class when the browser starts up, and there are no methods in the URLStreamHandler-Factory class for registering new URLStreamHandler subclasses. Without the ability to register new URLStreamHandlers with the URL class's URLStreamHandlerFactory, new protocols cannot be introduced.

If xyzzy were a supported protocol, data could be exchanged using the URL and URLConnection classes, through the xyzzy protocol, with code similar to the following:

```
URL url = new URL("xyzzy://www.somehost.com/something");
URLConnection con = url.openConnection();
Object obj = con.getContent();
```

The alternate protocol-handling scheme discussed in the following section implements a similar programmatic interface.

An Alternate Protocol-Handling Scheme

To start with, it should be pointed out that there is no magic in the protocol-handling scheme described here. It uses standard Java classes and programming techniques. It also requires a reasonable amount of effort to implement the actual classes that perform the data transfer. Nonetheless, this scheme does allow for protocol handling in a way that can be implemented by applet programmers and shared by any applets that use this alternate approach.

Central to this protocol extension is the *ProtocolRegistry* class, which provides a mechanism through which "protocol handlers" can be registered. (These are not protocol handlers in the same sense as the URL-Connection subclasses, but rather are objects which support the Protocol interface, as will be described later in this section.) The ProtocolRegistry class can be used to transfer data based on a particular protocol through its static getContent() method:

```
        Object o =
ProtocolRegistry.getContent("xyzzy://www.somehost.com/something");
```

The registry is implemented such that if a request to getContent() specifies a protocol supported by the browser, the real protocol handler will be used in preference to all others in the registry. This implementation allows any request for a content handler to be filtered through the registry without fear that the http handler will be overridden, for instance.

The implementation of the ProtocolRegistry class is shown in Fig. 9.11. There is no way to instantiate the class since its constructor is declared private. The ProtocolRegistry contains two class variables and two public

```
package ajp.net;

import java.net.*;
import java.util.*;
import java.io.IOException;

/**
 * This class is a purely static class, in the fact that all of its
 * methods are purely static.  It provides a registry for Protocol
 * objects to allow users to define their own protocols and grab
 * objects easily created from the protocols.  Once a person has
 * defined their own protocol, for others to use it, this provides an
 * easy abstract way of doing it with URL like constructs.  This class
 * can be used with built in protocols because it will check the built
 * in ones before the added ones.
 *
 * @version 1.1
 **/
public class ProtocolRegistry {
    private static boolean debug = false;

    // the Hashtable of protocols
    final static Hashtable protocol = new Hashtable();
    // the default protocol handler, which will be tried before others so someone cannot
    // define a new http protocol or ftp or anything built into JVM
    final static DefaultProtocol def = new DefaultProtocol();

    // cannot instantiate this class
    private ProtocolRegistry() {};

    private static void dbg(String str) {
        if (debug) {
            System.out.println("ProtocolRegistry: " + str);
            System.out.flush();
        }
    }

    public static void setDebug(boolean debug) {
        ProtocolRegistry.debug = debug;
    }

    /**
     * Adds a protocol to the list of protocols that this Registry
     * can handle.  IF built in protocols are attempted to be
     * overriden, they will not be used, as built in ones are checked
     * first.
     *
     **/
    public static void addProtocol(String protocolName, Protocol fetcher)
                    throws ProtocolRegistrationException {
        Object p = protocol.get(protocolName);
```

Figure 9.11
The ProtocolRegistry
class.

```
            if (p == null) {
                  protocol.put(protocolName, fetcher);
                  dbg("Added protocol: " + protocolName);
            }
            else {
                  dbg("Protocol already registered: " + protocolName);
                  throw new ProtocolRegistrationException(
                          "Protocol already registered: " + protocolName);
            }

      }


      /**
       * Get the object referred to by the urlString passed in.  This
       * will first try to get the content of the built in protocols,
       * then check for an added protocol.  If there is an error or if
       * the protocol could not be found, the object returned will be
       * null.  The protocol is defined as any text before the first :.
       **/
      public static Object getContent(String urlString)
                              throws IOException, MalformedURLException {
            Object object = null;
            try {
                  dbg("looking in default");
                  object = def.getContent( urlString );
            }
            catch(Exception e) {
                  dbg( "Not found in default looking in registry" );
                  // now parse out protocol myself
                  int index = urlString.indexOf( ":" );
                  String pro = urlString.substring( 0, index );
                  dbg("Looking for: " + pro);
                  Protocol p = (Protocol)protocol.get(pro);
                  if (p == null) {
                        throw new MalformedURLException();
                  }
                  synchronized (p) {
                        dbg("Found it okay");
                        object = p.getContent( urlString );
                        dbg( "Found it okay" );
                  }
            }
            return object;
      }
}
```

Figure 9.11
(*Continued*).

class methods. The class variables are private and reference a hash table, on which the protocol handlers are stored, and a DefaultProtocol object, which is used to access any protocol handler supported directly by the browser. The two class methods are getContent(), which was discussed briefly previously, and addProtocol(), which is used to add new protocol handlers to the hash table.

When the getContent() method calls a protocol handler's getContent() method, it does so in a block synchronized on the Protocol object. The synchronization prevents two applets, which may be using the same protocol handler, from entering the getContent() method at the same time. It should also be noted that since the methods of the ProtocolRegistry are static, they are potentially shared by any applet downloaded from the same host. The implementation of the registry does not allow protocol handlers to replace ones already in the table—the first handler to register a name wins. Subsequent applets will be thrown a ProtocolRegistrationException when attempting to register a protocol name already in the registry.

```java
package ajp.net;
import java.net.*;

/**
 * This class represents the Built in protocols at any time in the VM.
 * This object cannot be overriden and will always be checked before
 * any others in the ProtocolRegistry.
 *
 * @version 1.1
 **/
public final class DefaultProtocol implements Protocol {

    /**
     * Called by ProgramRegistry.getContent before its own registry
     * is looked into.  This is to prevent others from redefining the
     * http protocol etc.
     **/
    public synchronized Object getContent(String unparsedURLString)
                    throws java.io.IOException, MalformedURLException {
        return (new URL(unparsedURLString)).getContent();
    }

    public String getName() {
        return null;
    }

}
```

Figure 9.12
The DefaultProtocol
class.

If the exception is caught and ignored, the second applet will use the first applet's protocol handler when `getContent()` is called.

The `ProtocolRegistry.getContent()` method first attempts to call the `getContent()` method of the DefaultProtocol object. The Default-Protocol class, shown in Fig. 9.12, attempts to construct a URL object from the string it is passed, and then calls the `getContent()` method of the URL object. If either exception is thrown—the MalformedURLException from the URL constructor or the IOException from the URL's `getContent()` method—the ProtocolRegistry will attempt to find an appropriate protocol handler in the hash table.

The DefaultProtocol class, as well as any other class that is to be stored in the registry, must implement the Protocol interface shown in Fig. 9.13. The interface allows protocol handlers to be created and stored in the registry even if they do not inherit from the same base class.

```
package ajp.net;

/**
 * The interface to implement when making your own protocols.  When
 * your object is registered with the ProtocolRegistry under a certain
 * protocol, its getContent method below will be called with the url
 * string that referenced it.  Given a protocol myprotocol, a call
 * such as ProgramRegistry.getContent(
 * "myprotocol://someserver.com/something/else" ) will call the
 * getContent method below with the full unparsed string above.
 *
 * @version 1.1
 **/
public interface Protocol {

    /**
     * This method will be called by ProtocolRegistry whenever the
     * protocol this object is registered under is referenced. Tt io
     * to return the implementation dependent object associated with
     * the protocol.
     **/
    public Object getContent(String unparsedURLString)
                    throws java.io.IOException;

    /**
     * What is the name of the protocol.
     **/
    public String getName();
}
```

Figure 9.13
The Protocol
interface.

```
package ajp.net;
import ajp.util.*;

/**
 * This class is an abstract representation of a TextFile.  It is
 * basically a wrapper around an array of Strings that is appendable.
 *
 * @version 1.1
 **/

public class TextFile {
    private boolean debug = false;

    // the list of my current strings
    LinkedList strings;

    /**
     * Create a TextFile object that is initially empty
     **/
    public TextFile() {
        this(false);
    }

    public TextFile(boolean debug) {
        this.debug = debug;
        strings = new LinkedList();
    }

    /**
     * Appends a line to the end of this TextFile
     **/
    public void addLine(String line) {
        dbg("**Adding line: " + line);
        strings.insertLast(line);
    }

    /**
     * Get the strings that are contained within this TextFile.
     **/
    public String[] getStrings() {
        String[] array = new String[ strings.numItems() ];
        int current = 0;
        try{
            for(strings.goFirst(); !strings.offList(); strings.goForward()) {
                array[ current++ ] = (String)strings.getCurrent();
            }
        }
        catch(OffListException e) {
        }
        return array;
    }

    private void dbg(String str) {
```

Figure 9.14
The TextFile class.

```
        if (debug) {
            dbg(this.getClass().getName() + ": " + str);
            System.out.flush();
        }
    }
}
```

▬▬ ▬▬ ▬▬ ▬▬

Figure 9.14
(*Continued*).

To illustrate the use of the ProtocolRegistry, a protocol handler for a text protocol is presented here. Text files for the purposes of this example are any ASCII files and are specified by URLs of the form:

```
text://hostname/absolute pathname
```

When a text URL is processed by a protocol handler, the object it returns will be an instance of the class *TextFile*. The TextFile class, presented in Fig. 9.14, is an abstraction of multiline ASCII files. The class supports adding lines, which are appended to a LinkedList each time the `addLines()` method is called, and retrieving the lines as an array of Strings through the `getStrings()` method.

The protocol handler whose `getContent()` method returns a Text-File object is implemented in the *TextFileProtocol* class, shown in Fig. 9.15. When a TextFileProtocol object is instantiated, it registers itself with the ProtocolRegistry as a handler for the *text* protocol. The registration is kept inside the constructor, rather than making the programmer register the object, to avoid having the handler registered in the ProtocolRegistry under an accidentally misspelled protocol name. Whenever it is needed, the name of the protocol can be retrieved from any Protocol implementation using the `getName()` method.

The TextFileProtocol class's `getContent()` method does the work of transferring the data according to the text protocol. There are several ways the data transfer can be implemented. For example, it can open a socket connection to an application running on the remote host, providing all the normal security restrictions are met. Another way to implement `getContent()` is to translate the request to a compatible protocol and manipulate the returned object. In this case, the protocol handler uses the readfile CGI program on the remote host to download the file.

The `getContent()` program converts the URL into a CGI GET request and opens a standard URL object. Then, interacting with the CGI script as described earlier in this chapter, the data is transferred and added

```
package ajp.net;

import java.net.*;
import java.io.*;

/**
 * This class implements a protocol that will read in a file given a
 * text://someserver.com/filename url string and fill up a TextFile
 * object with the contents and return that in getContent.  This is a
 * standard thing that is done very often and should prevent it from
 * having to be done again.
 *
 * @version 1.2
 **/
public class TextFileProtocol implements Protocol {
    private boolean debug = false;
    private String name = "text";
    /**
      * Construct a TextFileProtocol object, which will register
      * itself as the "text" protocol.  After constructing this
      * object, any calls to text://myserver.com/filename or the like
      * will result in calls to getContent below.
      **/
    public TextFileProtocol()
                            throws ProtocolRegistrationException {
        this(false);
    }

    public TextFileProtocol(boolean debug)
                            throws ProtocolRegistrationException {
        this.debug = debug;
        ProtocolRegistry.addProtocol(name, this);
    }

    /**
      * What is the name of the protocol.
      * @return a copy of the protocol name.
      **/
    public String getName() {
        return new String(name);
    }

    /**
      * Gets the object created in a call to this protocol.  Will be
      * called when the ProtocolRegistry gets notified that someone
      * wants a text protocol to happen.  Does not need to be called
      * directly, even though you can.  ProtocolRegistry will call it
      * for you.
      **/
    public synchronized Object getContent(String urlString) throws IOException {
        TextFile tf = new TextFile();
```

Figure 9.15
The TextFileProtocol
class.

```
            dbg("Getting: " + urlString);
            try{
                // now parse out protocol myself
                int index = urlString.indexOf(":");
                String file = urlString.substring(index + 3,
                                            urlString.length());
                index = file.indexOf("/");

                String host = file.substring(0, index);
                file = file.substring(index, file.length());

                String newURL = "http://" + host + "/cgi-bin/readfile?" + file;

                dbg("**New URL: " + newURL);
                URL url = new URL(newURL);
                dbg("**Actual getting: " + url);
                DataInputStream in = new DataInputStream(url.openStream());

                String buffer = in.readLine();
                while (buffer != null) {
                    tf.addLine(buffer);
                    buffer = in.readLine();
                }
            }
            catch(Exception e) {
                dbg("Exception in getContent: " + e);
                throw new IOException();
            }
            return tf;
        }

    private void dbg(String str) {
        if (debug) {
            dbg(this.getClass().getName() + ": " + str);
            System.out.flush();
        }
    }

}
```

Figure 9.15
(Continued).

to the TextFile object. After the CGI script completes, the TextFile object is returned by the handler.

Figure 9.16 shows a screen snapshot of an applet similar to the GetApplet and PostApplet, except that it transfers files using the text protocol. In this version of the applet, the TextField is used to specify text protocol URL rather than a path to a file. In all other respects the user interface is the same. The implementation of the applet is shown in Fig. 9.17. The interaction with the ProtocolRegistry is straightforward: the string in the TextField is passed to the registry's `getContent()` method, which will return a TextFile object. The applet extracts the string array from the TextFile object and copies it to the TextArea.

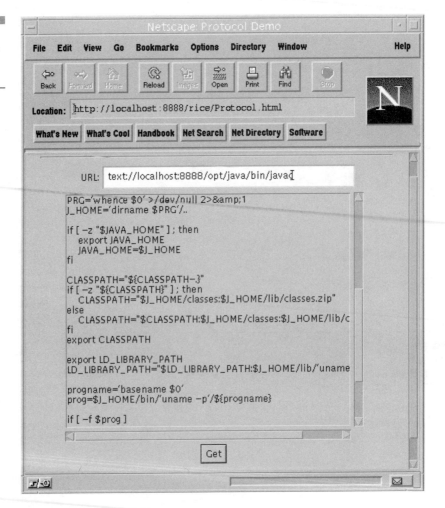

Figure 9.16
An applet that transfers files using a text protocol.

```
import java.net.*;
import java.awt.*;
import java.util.*;
import java.io.*;

import java.applet.*;
import ajp.net.*;
import ajp.awt.*;

/**
 * A simple applet to demonstrate the text protocol using the
 * ProtocolRegistry class.
 *
 * @version 1.2
 **/
public class ProtocolApplet extends Applet {
     TextArea textArea;
     Button button;
     LabeledTextField textField;
     String urlString;

     public void init() {

         try {
             TextFileProtocol fp = new TextFileProtocol();
         }
         catch (ProtocolRegistrationException e) {
             System.out.println(e.getMessage());
             System.out.println("Using existing handler...");
         }
         setLayout(new BorderLayout());
         textArea = new TextArea();
         textArea.setEditable(false);
         add("Center",  textArea);
         Panel p = new Panel();
         p.add(button = new Button("Get"));
         add("South", p);
         add("North", textField = new LabeledTextField("URL:", 40));
     }

     public boolean action(Event ev, Object o) {
         boolean ret = false;

         if (ev.target instanceof Button) {
             String data = null;
             try {
                 textArea.setText("");

                 if ((data = textField.getText()) == null)
                     return true;
```

Figure 9.17
The ProtocolApplet
class.

```
                TextFile tf = (TextFile)ProtocolRegistry.getContent(data);
                String str[] = tf.getStrings();
                for (int i=0; i<str.length; i++) {
                    textArea.appendText(str[i] + "\n");
                }
            }
        catch (Exception e) {
            textArea.setText("");
            textArea.setText("Error with URL: " + data);
            e.printStackTrace();
        }
        ret = true;
    }
    return ret;
    }
}
```

Figure 9.17
(*Continued*).

SUMMARY

The focus of this chapter is on how to better utilize the browser environment from Java applets. The applet's primary interface for interacting with the browser is through URL objects and through the AppletContext interface supplied to the applet by the browser. The AppletContext contains methods for loading pages into the browser and changing the status message the browser displays. These methods, combined with the user interface elements in the AWT, facilitate the creation of applets and AWT extensions that can interact directly with the browser, making applets appear to be more a part of the browser rather than just something the browser displays.

A big part of integrating into the browser is being able to deal with the same types of links and protocols as does the browser. Interacting with CGI programs is a major component. CGI programs are the de facto standard for server-side Web programming today and are the legacy applications of tomorrow. There are an enormous number of CGI programs on the Web today, providing a wide range of services from interfacing with databases that provide shopping on the Web to performing intranet calendar management. With the advent of Java, there is now a facility for moving the processing out of CGI programs, off the Web servers, and into Java applets running on the clients. New features being added to the Java platform—such as the Java Database Connectivity

(JDBC), cryptography, and authentication—add further motivation to move from CGI programs to Java. However, because there are so many CGI programs in existence, most applet programmers will, at some time or another, need to write an applet that must interact with CGI programs. This interaction is provided by the URL and URLConnection classes in the `java.net` package.

The JDK's networking classes provide a model through which protocol handlers can be added such that they are directly supported by the URL class. Unfortunately, there are restrictions on how this model can be utilized. Currently, applets are not able to download their own custom protocol handlers. A ProtocolRegistry class is presented in this chapter that allows applets to create protocol handlers that can be shared among applets downloaded from the same host. This protocol-handling scheme, while not intended as a replacement for the real protocol handlers in Java-enabled browsers, could be used to handle disparity between the protocols that are supported on different browsers. Since the ProtocolRegistry always checks the installed handlers first, an applet running on a browser that supports the text protocol directly will get the browser's implementation. An applet running on a browser that does not support text URLs will get the TextFileProtocol handler downloaded with the applet. The applet will continue to function in either case.

10
Security Managers

Introduction

The Java platform supports a multilayered approach to security. First, there is security built into the language through its bounds checking of arrays, strict typing, method-access restrictions, and lack of pointers. The next layer of security is in the Java runtime, where the bytecode verifier ensures that code being downloaded has not been corrupted, and where the Java class loader segregates downloaded classes into separate name spaces and guarantees that downloaded classes won't replace or "spoof" the built-in classes. The third layer of Java security is within applications and is implemented through security managers.

Security managers implement security policies, which can be defined as the set of well-known operations a Java object is allowed to perform. For example: Is an object allowed to read or write files, can it open socket connections, is it allowed to pass commands to the operating system to execute, and so on. For applets, the security policy is defined by the browser in which the applet is running. For Java applications there is no default security manager—it is up to the application to define what, if any, access controls are appropriate. This chapter targets Java programmers who wish to create applications that define a security policy.

This chapter is divided into two sections. The first section is an overview of the SecurityManager class and the methods it defines. The purpose of the overview is to show how a security manager works and to outline the range of checks that define a security policy. The second section presents an implementation of a SecurityManager that defines a set of file-access restrictions. This security manager is then used in a Java-based CGI program that is the server side of the CGI demonstrations that are presented in Chap. 9.

The SecurityManager Class

The Java SecurityManager class is an abstract class that is a framework for creating security policies. Once a SecurityManager subclass is defined and installed in an application, it acts as a gateway to protected operations. Since the types of operations security managers protect are usually low-level operations implemented in the classes that comprise the Java core-class libraries, programmers don't often encounter the resident SecurityManager directly, but rather see only the side effects of its work through occasional SecurityExceptions that are thrown when they program outside the bounds of the security policy.

Applications may or may not define a security manager. If none is defined, as is the default for Java applications, it is equivalent to giving all classes in an application permission to perform any operation supported by the JDK. If a security manager is installed, the policy it implements will govern the use of protected operations. Before describing what the protected operations are, it will be useful to review an example from the java.io package that is presented in Chap. 7.

The File class provides several methods for interrogating the state of a file. For example, the exist() method returns a boolean indicating whether or not a specified file exists. In order for a Java object to check for the existence of a file, the security manager must first verify that the object has permission to read that file. From the File class, the exist() method reads as follows:

```
private native boolean exists0();
...
public boolean exists() {
    SecurityManager security = System.getSecurityManager();
    if (security != null) {
        security.checkRead(path);
    }
    return exists0();
}
```

A handle to the current SecurityManager object is returned from the getSecurityManager() method in the System class. If no security manager has been set, a *null* is returned by getSecurityManager() and the native exists0() method is called. If, however, a security manager is in place, its checkRead() method is called and is passed the path to be checked. If the security policy allows the object that called exists() to read the file, checkRead() simply returns. If the security policy forbids read access to the file, checkRead() throws a SecurityException object. This example is typical of how security managers are used throughout the Java core classes.

The task of implementing a SecurityManager, then, is to implement the various checks defined in the SecurityManager class. The methods implemented should either simply return if the operation requested is to be permitted, or throw a SecurityException if the operation is to be disallowed. After a SecurityManager subclass has been defined, it can be set for an application using the setSecurityManager() method in the System class. Once a SecurityManager has been set for an application, subsequent calls to setSecurityManager() will cause exceptions to be thrown. Applets, for example, cannot create their own security managers because the browsers they run in already have security managers defined and set.

SecurityManager Class Overview

As was already mentioned, the SecurityManager is an abstract class that must be subclassed to create an implementation. Although Security-Manager is an abstract class, there are no abstract methods in the class; when implementing a SecurityManager subclass, it is necessary to override only those methods that affect the security policy being defined. When deciding which methods to override, however, it is important to note that all the non-native methods in the SecurityManager class throw a SecurityException—by default—blocking all access to privileged operations.

The methods in the SecurityManager class can be divided into five categories:

1. System-access checks
2. File-access checks
3. Network-access checks
4. Utility methods
5. Class-loader interaction

Tables 10.1 through 10.5 present descriptions of the methods in the Security Manager, organized in the tables according to the five categories. Table 10.1 presents the methods that check for permission to access system-level functionality. Loading native methods, passing commands to the operating system, and causing the virtual machine to exit are all examples of operations protected by system-access checks. The methods in Table 10.2 comprise the checks performed prior to allowing file access and are called from various classes in the java.io package. In Table 10.3 is a summary of the methods called from the java.net package that check for permission to perform network operations, such as creating socket servers, handling protocols, or accepting connections from remote hosts. Table 10.4 provides a description of the two utility methods, and Table 10.5 shows the protected methods that interact with the class loader.

TABLE 10.1

SecurityManager
Class System
Checks

Method	Description
void checkCreateClassLoader()	Has the ClassLoader been created?
void checkAccess(Thread g)	Can the given thread modify the thread group being checked?
void checkAccess(ThreadGroup g)	Can the given thread group modify the thread group being checked?
void checkExit(int status)	Can the virtual machine be exited?
void checkExec(String cmd)	Can the specified command be passed to the operating system for execution?
void checkLink(String lib)	Can the given dynamic library be loaded?
void checkPackageAccess (String pkg)	Can classes in the given package be accessed?
void checkPackageDefinition (String pkg)	Can classes be defined in the given package?
void checkPropertiesAccess()	Can the system properties be accessed?
void checkPropertyAccess (String key)	Can the specified system property be accessed?
void checkPropertyAccess (String key, String def)	Can the specified system property and definition be accessed?
void checkAWTEventQueueAccess()	Can the AWT event queue be accessed?
void checkPackageAccess (String pkgName)	Can the package specified be accessed?
void checkPackageDefinition (String pkgName)	Can classes be defined in the specified package?
void checkPrintJobAccess()	Can print jobs be initiated?
void checkSystemClipboardAccess()	Can the windowing system's clipboard be accessed?
boolean checkTopLevelWindow (Object window)	Can the specified window be created without a warning banner?

TABLE 10.2

SecurityManager
Class File Access
Checks

Method	Description
`void checkRead(FileDescriptor fd)`	Can the specified file descriptor be read from?
`void checkRead(String file)`	Can the specified file be read from?

Implementing Access-Control Lists Through a SecurityManager

From just reviewing the SecurityManager class, it may not be obvious why an application other than a browser would be interested in using a security manager. Browsers, after all, must contend with classes of unknown origin that, once running on the same virtual machine as the browser, must be managed and restricted with great care. Other Java applications don't have the same concerns. If we programmers don't want the application to open a socket connection, we probably need not worry about one opening unexpectedly as long as we are writing all the code. File access, on the other hand, is an area where SecurityManagers are quite useful and where the application may not easily be self-controlled.

Access to files in most modern operating systems is managed at two levels. At the operating-system level there are permissions on files—what individuals or groups of people are allowed to read from, write to, execute,

TABLE 10.3

SecurityManager
Class Network
Access Checks

Method	Description
`void checkConnect(String host, int port)`	Can a connection be made to the given host at the given port?
`void checkConnect(String host, int port, Object context)`	Used to check if a connection can be made to a given host and port and to the host and port represented by the given context. Used when server redirection is encountered. Security was checked for the initial connection but must be reassessed for the redirect connection.
`void checkListen(int port)`	Can ServerSocket objects be created?
`void checkAccept(String host, int port)`	Can ServerSockets accept connections?
`void checkSetFactory()`	Can socket, protocol, and content handler factories be created?

TABLE 10.4

SecurityManager
Class Utility
Methods

Method	Description
boolean getInCheck()	Is a security check currently in progress?
Object getSecurityContext()	Gets an object that encapsulates the state of the current security environment. The returned object can be used later on to perform security checks. What this method actually does will depend on the implementation.

or delete files. At a higher level, applications may implement finer-grained access control for specific purposes.

For example, in the UNIX operating system there are well-known files that are used to facilitate system administration. The password file, */etc/passwd,* is one example. Generally, most users on a UNIX system have permission to read the password file, meaning that the applications they run are able to open the password file and read its contents. On the other hand, a particular application may not allow a user to open the password file even if, in general, the user is allowed to access the file.

User access is an important issue when considering the CGI program, *readfile,* mentioned in Chap. 9. When a remote user accesses readfile through an http request, the program determines the filename that is being requested, reads the file, and passes the contents of the file to the remote host via http. The readfile program is able to access and transfer any file that the operating system determines the user ID running the readfile program has permission to read. (CGI programs are typically run

TABLE 10.5

SecurityManager
Class Interface to
the Class Loader

Method	Description
native Class[] getClass Context()	Returns an array of Class objects representing the classes on the current execution stack.
nativeClassLoader currentClassLoader()	Returns a reference to the current class loader.
native int classDepth (String name)	Returns the number of frames deep the named class is on the execution stack.
native int classLoaderDepth()	Returns the depth of the class loader itself in the execution stack.
boolean inClass(String name)	Is the named class anywhere in the class stack?
boolean inClassLoader()	Has the class loader been set?

on UNIX systems with a special user ID that has limited privileges. Even with limited privileges, however, this user ID is able to read most files on the system, including the password file.) While the operating-system restrictions may be sufficient, it is possible to have widely accessible files that should not be read by a program like readfile. To place restrictions on readfile and other CGI programs, the programs themselves could implement some form of access control list (ACL) to identify a small set of directories from which the program is permitted to read.

By creating a security manager that implements file-access restrictions based on an access-control list, any Java application can make use of an ACL. The applications need only create an instance of the security manager and set it through the `setSecurityManager()` method. Once the security manager is set, every file access will be verified against the access-control list before access is permitted.

Implementation

The implementation of a file-access security manager described in this section falls into two classes: a SecurityManager subclass called *FileSecurity* and an auxiliary class called *FileACL*. The FileACL class maintains three lists that define what paths and files are accessible: one list controls *read* access, another controls *write* access, and a third controls *delete* access. When an application calls a method in one of the `java.io` classes that access a file, the access will be checked with the SecurityManager; here it will be an instance of the FileSecurity class. The FileSecurity object will use a FileACL object to check the file name against the appropriate access lists. It is the FileACL class that actually determines if a file may be accessed. Since most of the work is done by the FileACL object, it is reasonable to discuss the implementation beginning with the FileACL class.

When a FileACL object is created, it is typically passed the name of a file from which it is to initialize the access lists it maintains. The file format supported by the FileACL class is that utilized by the `java.util.Properties` class and has the form:

```
# comment
property1=value1
property2=value2
...
```

---

* Note that this ACL implementation is not intended to be conformant to the Java Security API. Thus, it does not implement the `java.security.acl.ACL` interface.

The Java Properties class provides methods for reading and writing files of this format and is an extremely useful class for creating, storing, and reading initialization files. Once a property file is read by a Properties object, the values contained in the file can be accessed programmatically through the getProperty() method as follows:

```
Properties props = new Properties();
props.load(pathToPropertiesFile);
String value1 = props.getProperty("property1", "Not found");
```

If "property1" was specified in the file, its associated value is assigned to the string value1; otherwise the string "Not found" is assigned to value1.

The actual properties file used by the FileACL class specifies three properties, READ_PATH, WRITE_PATH, and DELETE_PATH, each of which can be assigned a File.pathSeparator separated list of directories and file names. The permissions for any directory specified in one of the lists apply as well to all directories below the one specified. Thus, if a directory /usr is specified on the READ_PATH list, read access would apply to /usr/local/bin as well. Similarly, on the Windows platform, specifying C:\USR implies equal permission is granted to C:\USR\LOCAL\BIN. The FileACL class also allows the character * to be used to mean all directories and – to mean no directories. On a UNIX platform, a typical FileACL properties file might read:

```
#
READ_PATH=/tmp/greeting.txt:/home/rice:/home/igs
WRITE_PATH=/tmp:/var/tmp
DELETE_PATH=-
```

The FileACL object that is initialized with the preceding file would approve read access to the file greeting.txt in the directory /tmp, and would allow any file in /home/rice or /home/igs or any of their sub-directories to be read. Write access would be allowed in /tmp, /var/tmp, and any directory below them. Delete access is disabled, meaning that the FileACL will not approve any request for delete access.

The constructor for the FileACL class, as can be found in the full source listing shown in Fig. 10.1, performs two tasks. First, it initializes the Properties object, *props*, from the file name passed to the constructor. Second, it initializes the three hash tables, *readTable*, *writeTable*, and *deleteTable*, from the values that were stored in the properties file. The hash table initialization is performed by the private method initTable(), which parses the list of paths and stores each directory and file name it finds into the hash table as keys that can be queried later on.

```
package ajp.security;

import java.io.*;
import java.util.*;

/**
 * A class for creating access control lists
 *
 * @version 1.6
 **/
public class FileACL implements PathChecker {
    private boolean debug = false;
    Hashtable readTable;
    Hashtable writeTable;
    Hashtable deleteTable;
    Properties props = null;

    /**
     * Create an access control list from the properties file specified.
     **/
    public FileACL(String filename) throws IOException {
        this(filename, false);
    }

    /*
     * A debug version of the constructor.
     */
    public FileACL(String filename, boolean debug) throws IOException {
        this.debug = debug;
        readTable   = new Hashtable();
        writeTable  = new Hashtable();
        deleteTable = new Hashtable();
        props = new Properties();

        // load the properties from the file
        props.load(new FileInputStream(filename));

        // initialize each of the acls.  they default to "no restrictions"
        initTable(readTable, props.getProperty("READ_PATH", "*"));
        initTable(writeTable, props.getProperty("WRITE_PATH", "*"));
        initTable(deleteTable, props.getProperty("DELETE_PATH", "*"));
    }

    /**
     * Initialize the specified table with the elements of the specified
     * colon separated parameter string.
     **/
    private void initTable(Hashtable hash, String params) {
        StringTokenizer st = new StringTokenizer(params, File.pathSeparator);
        String spec;
        // iterate across the list adding to the table
        while(st.hasMoreTokens()) {
            spec = st.nextToken();
```

Figure 10.1
The FileACL class.

```
                    hash.put(getPath(spec), getUsers(spec));
        }

    }

    /**
     * Parse out the path part of the string.
     **/
    protected String getPath(String spec) {
        return spec;
    }

    /**
     * Parse out any users, if desired.  For example creating a
     * protocol of path,+user1,+user2 to allow only user1 and user2
     * to access the path, or path,-user3,-user4 to allow all users
     * except user3 and user4 to access the path.
     **/
    protected String getUsers(String spec) {
        return "*";
    }

    /**
     * Checks a given path against the specified hash table.  Starts
     * with the full path name and successivly removes components
     * from the end of the path, checking each one until either a
     * match is found or the path is fully disassembled.
     **/
    private boolean checkTable(Hashtable hash, String path) {
        String pathToCheck = path;
        boolean okay = false;
        boolean done = false;
        int index;

        // immediately drop out if permissions are disabled
        if (hash.containsKey("-"))
            return false;
        // immediately drop out if permissions are wide-open
        if (hash.containsKey("*") || hash.containsKey(File.separator))
            return true;

        dbg("Checking: " + pathToCheck);
        okay = hash.containsKey(pathToCheck);
        while(((index = pathToCheck.lastIndexOf(File.separatorChar)) >= 0)
                && !okay ) {
            //trim last component off path
            pathToCheck = pathToCheck.substring(0, index);
            dbg("Checking: " + pathToCheck);

            okay = hash.containsKey(pathToCheck);
        }
        if (okay) {
            dbg("Okay");
```

Figure 10.1

(Continued).

```
            // now check user...
            okay = checkUser((String)hash.get(pathToCheck));
        }
        else {
            dbg("Not found.");
        }
        return okay;
    }

    /**
     * Check the list of users to see if current user, returned by
     * System.getProperty(user.name) for example, is on the list.
     **/
    protected boolean checkUser(String userList) {
        return true;
    }

    /**
     * Is the path or one of its parent directories specified on the
     * read access list.
     **/
    public boolean canRead(String path) {
        return checkTable(readTable, path);
    }

    /**
     * Is the path or one of its parent directories specified on the
     * write access list.
     **/
    public boolean canWrite(String path) {
        return checkTable(writeTable, path);
    }

    /**
     * Is the path or one of its parent directories specified on the
     * delete access list.
     **/
    public boolean canDelete(String path) {
        return checkTable(deleteTable, path);
    }

    void dumpTable(PrintStream out, Hashtable hash) {
        Enumeration e;
        String s;
        e = hash.keys();
        while(e.hasMoreElements()) {
            s = (String)e.nextElement();
            out.println("\t[" + s + "," + (String)hash.get(s) + "]");
        }

    }
    /**
     * Dump the ACL to the specified output stream.
```

Figure 10.1
(Continued).

```
    **/
public void dump(PrintStream out) {
    Enumeration e;
    String s;
    if(props != null)
        props.list(out);

    out.println("\nRead Table");
    out.println("-----------");
    dumpTable(out, readTable);

    out.println("\nWrite Table");
    out.println("-----------");
    dumpTable(out, writeTable);

    out.println("\nDelete Table");
    out.println("-----------");
    dumpTable(out, deleteTable);

}
// local debug method.
protected void dbg(String str) {
    if (debug) {
        System.out.println(this.getClass().getName() + ": " + str);
        System.out.flush();
    }

}

}
}
```

Figure 10.1
(*Continued*).

Once access lists are extracted from a properties file and stored in hash tables, an FileACL object is ready to verify pathnames. There are three methods specified by the PathChecker interface (see Fig. 10.2) that the FileACL class implements:

1. `public boolean canRead(String path)`

2. `public boolean canWrite(String path)`

3. `public boolean canDelete(String path)`

As implemented in the FileACL class, each of the three access-checking methods is a wrapper around the private method `checkTable()`, which takes as arguments a reference to the table to be checked and the pathname to be looked up in that table. If the path or one of its parents is found, `checkTable()` will return *true;* otherwise it returns *false,* indicating that the type of access being checked is denied. The results of calling check-

```
package ajp.security;

/**
 * An interface for checking read/write/delete permissions on paths.
 *
 * @version 1.1
 **/
public interface PathChecker {
     /**
      * Is the path readable by the caller?
      **/
     public boolean canRead(String path);

     /**
      * Is the path writeable by the caller?
      **/
     public boolean canWrite(String path);

     /**
      * Is the path deletable by the caller.
      **/
     public boolean canDelete(String path);

}
```

Figure 10.2
The PathChecker
interface.

Table() are passed back to the caller by canRead(), canWrite(), and canDelete.

The checkTable() method is responsible for examining each component of the pathname and determining if that component of the path is in the hash table. First, the full path is checked using the Hashtable.containsKey() method. Then, if the path is not found in the table, each component of the path is removed, one by one, and the remaining path is checked until either the path is found in the table, or no more paths remain to be checked. For example, given a READ_PATH of

```
READ_PATH=/usr/local:/tmp
```

when asked to check the paths /usr/local/bin/xpilot and /home/rice/foobar, the debugging output from the checkTable method appears as follows:

```
Checking: /usr/local/bin/xpilot
ajp.security.FileACL: Checking: /usr/local/bin/xpilot
ajp.security.FileACL: Checking: /usr/local/bin
```

```
ajp.security.FileACL: Checking: /usr/local
ajp.security.FileACL: Okay

Checking: /home/rice/foobar
ajp.security.FileACL: Checking: /home/rice/foobar
ajp.security.FileACL: Checking: /home/rice
ajp.security.FileACL: Checking: /home
ajp.security.FileACL: Checking:
ajp.security.FileACL: Not found.
```

Although they are not implemented here, user IDs could be added to this ACL implementation via hooks that are already in place. By overriding the getPath(), getUsers(), and checkUser() methods, a subclass can create a mechanism for adding lists of user names to the properties file. For example, a modified READ_PATH might be changed to have each element of the list conform to this format:

```
path,[+/-]username1,[+/-]username2,...
```

such that an element of the READ_PATH that was set to

```
/usr/local/bin/xpilot,+rice,+igs
```

would imply that users rice and igs were the only users allowed to read the file /usr/local/bin/xpilot. On the other hand, a READ_PATH element that was set to

```
/home/rice,-guest
```

would mean that any user except the user guest was permitted to read files under the directory /home/rice.

In the initTable() method, each element of the READ_PATH, WRITE_PATH, and DELETE_PATH lists is passed to the getUsers() method. The result of the getUsers() method call is stored as the object in the table under a key which is returned from the getPath() method. The idea is that a string like

```
/usr/local/bin/xpilot,+rice,+igs
```

would be passed to getUsers() and getPath(), and the string returned by getUsers(), +rice,+igs, would be stored under the key /usr/local/bin/xpilot.

After the checkTable() method verifies that a path, or a component of a path, is in the appropriate hash table as a key, the string stored by that key is retrieved and passed to checkUser(). The checkUser() method can be overridden and could verify that the user of an application, as returned by `System.getProperty(user.name)`, for instance, is on the list of authorized users.

The existing implementation of `getUsers()`, `getPath()`, and `check-User()` doesn't perform any checking of user lists. If a path being checked is found as a key in the hash table by `checkTable()`, the application is allowed to access the path. Adding the user-list verification is left as an exercise for the reader.

The security manager that makes use of the FileACL class is called *FileSecurity* and is shown in Fig. 10.3. The constructor for the FileSecurity class is passed an object that implements the PathChecker interface, which will perform the actual access checks. By allowing the object that will perform the path verification to be passed to the security manager's constructor, any PathChecker object—perhaps a subclass of FileACL which implements user lists—can be used with the FileSecurity class with no changes to the security manager.

The most significant aspect of the FileSecurity class is in the `check-Read()`, `checkWrite()`, and `checkDelete()` methods. Each method is overridden to call the appropriate method from the PathChecker interface. If the PathChecker's method returns *false*, the FileSecurity will instantiate and throw a SecurityException object. All but one of the other public methods in the SecurityManager class are overridden to do nothing. Since the default behavior of almost all the methods in the SecurityManager class is to throw a SecurityException, subclasses must override this behavior to allow applications to access the network, files, and the protected methods of the System class. The FileSecurity class limits only file access; all other methods in the Java core classes, subject to security manager approval, are allowed.

The other public method previously mentioned is `checkTopLevel-Window()`, which is overridden to return *true*. If the `checkTopLevel-Window()` method were to return *false*, as is the default, any Window objects created by the application would have a banner placed in the window reading "Warning: Applet Window"—clearly not desirable.

Using Access-Control Lists

To illustrate the use of the FileSecurity class, the Java application behind the readfile CGI program utilized in Chap. 9 will now be examined. The readfile program consists of two pieces, a Java application called *ReadFile*, and a UNIX Bourne-shell script called *readfile*. The readfile script is a wrapper around the command that passes the ReadFile class name along

```
package ajp.security;

import java.io.IOException;
import java.io.FileDescriptor;

/**
 * A file security manager that utilizes a customizable access control
 * list to define which files and directories are accessible.
 *
 * @version 1.3
 **/
public class FileSecurity extends SecurityManager {

    // the abstract representation of the access control list
    // that will be used as needed
    private PathChecker checker;

    /**
     * Construct a new FileSecurity object.
     *
     **/
    public FileSecurity(PathChecker checker) {
        super();
        this.checker = checker;
    }

    /**
     * Get the security context.  Not needed since nothing is done
     * with the context in the checkRead() and checkWrite() methods.
     *
     **/
    public Object getSecurityContext() {
        return null;
    }

    /**
     * Checks to see if the specified filename can be read
     * This will check the FileACL object to see if
     * it can be accessed or not
     **/
    public void checkRead(String file) {
        if (!checker.canRead(file)) {
            throw new SecurityException("Cannot read file: " + file +
                                        " it is not on the access list."
                );
        }
    }

    /**
     * Checks to see if the Object can read the specified file
     * or not.  This will call the above method, for access
     * applies to all objects, not on a discriminating basis.
     **/
```

Figure 10.3
The FileSecurity class.

```
    public void checkRead(String file, Object context) {
        checkRead(file);
    }

    /**
     * Checks to see if the specified filename can be written
     * This will check the FileACL object to see if
     * it can be accessed or not
     **/
    public void checkWrite(String file) {
        if (!checker.canWrite(file)) {
            throw new SecurityException("Cannot write file: " + file +
                                        " it is not on the access list."
                );
        }
    }

    /**
     * Checks to see if the Object can write the specified file
     * or not.  This will call the above method, for access
     * applies to all objects, not on a discriminating basis.
     **/
    public void checkWrite(String file, Object context) {
        checkWrite(file);
    }

    /**
     * Checks to see if the specified filename can be deleted
     * This will check the FileACL object to see if
     * it can be deleted or not
     **/
    public void checkDelete(String file) {
        if (!checker.canDelete(file)) {
            throw new SecurityException("Cannot delete file: " + file +
                                        " it is not on the access list."
                );
        }
    }

    /**
     * Check to see if a top-level window can be created.
     * This method returns true becuase we want to let
     * windows be created, and we want no warning message to
     * be placed on the window.
     **/
    public boolean checkTopLevelWindow(Object o) {
        return true;
    }

    /**
     * Once the SecurityManager is set, it defaults to not
     * letting objects do much of anything.  Therefore, to
     * get the work done that our project will need, the
```

Figure 10.3
(Continued).

```
     * methods following need to be overridden to allow for
     * access to sockets, etc.  By making these methods do
     * nothing, the objects that are asking think it is OK
     * to do their respective actions
     **/

    public void checkPackageDefinition(String pkg) {}
    public void checkConnect(String host, int port) {}
    public void checkConnect(String host, int port, Object context) {}
    public void checkAccept(String host, int port) {}
    public void checkPropertiesAccess() {}
    public void checkPropertyAccess(String key) { }
    public void checkPropertyAccess(String key, String def) {}
    public void checkPackageAccess(String pkg) {}
    public void checkLink(String lib) {}
    public void checkListen(int port) {}
    public void checkAccess(Thread g) {}
    public void checkAccess(ThreadGroup g) {}
    public void checkRead(FileDescriptor f) {}
    public void checkWrite(FileDescriptor f) {}
}
```

Figure 10.3
(*Continued*).

with some command-line parameters to the Java interpreter.* The command line parameters, with one exception, correspond to environment variables that the httpd program, the program that services http requests on a Web server, sets before calling readline. When the Java interpreter is invoked, the command line looks something like:

```
java -DREQUEST_METHOD=$REQUEST_METHOD -DPROPS_FILE=$PROPS_FILE \
  -DCONTENT_LENGTH=$CONTENT_LENGTH -DQUERY_STRING=$QUERY_STRING
  ReadFile
```

Each variable following an equal sign in the command line will be replaced with parameters provided by httpd—except the variable PROPS _FILE, which is set in the readfile script itself and indicates where the properties file used by the FileACL class is stored.

The source code for the ReadFile class is shown in Fig. 10.4. As is discussed in Chap. 9, the purpose of the readfile program is to open files and

---

* The readfile script could easily be rewritten as a Perl script or batch file to be run on non-UNIX operating systems. In fact, the basic functionality that readfile provides, exclusive of the file-access protection, can be implemented in a single line of code in most scripting languages. This implementation is what some might refer to as *a bazooka for swatting flies*. Keep in mind that: (1) This is a book about Java, and (2) readfile is only an example.

```
import ajp.security.*;
import java.io.*;

/**
 * A simple CGI program in Java
 *
 * @version 1.3
 **/
public class ReadFile {

    public static void main(String args[]) throws Exception {
        FileACL facl;
        String propsFile = System.getProperty("PROPS_FILE");
        facl = new FileACL(propsFile);
        FileSecurity sm = new FileSecurity(facl);

        System.setSecurityManager(sm);

        //facl.dump(System.err);

        String line;
        String method = System.getProperty("REQUEST_METHOD");

        if (method == null) {
            System.exit(1);
        }
        else if (method.equals("GET")) {
            printFile(System.getProperty("QUERY_STRING"));
        }
        else {
            int length = 0;
            try {
                length = Integer.parseInt(System.getProperty("CONTENT_LENGTH"));
            }
            catch (Exception e) {
                System.out.println("Error, could not determine CONTENT_LENGHT");
                System.exit(1);
            }
            byte arr[] = new byte[length];

            System.in.read(arr);
            System.in.close();
            DataInputStream dis =
                new DataInputStream(new ByteArrayInputStream(arr));

            while((line = dis.readLine()) != null) {
                printFile(line);
            }
        }
    }

    static void printFile(String filename) {
        String line;
```

Figure 10.4
The ReadFile class.

```
        try {
            FileInputStream fis = new FileInputStream(filename);

            DataInputStream dis = new DataInputStream(fis);

            while((line = dis.readLine()) != null) {
                System.out.println(line);
            }
        }
        catch (Exception e) {
            e.printStackTrace();
        }
    }
}
```

Figure 10.4
(Continued).

relay their contents to the remote browser via http. As a CGI program, readfile must simply open the file and echo its contents to the standard output device. Thus, the ReadFile class must open the filename passed to the readfile script by httpd, open the file, and print it to System.out.

The ReadFile class consists of two static methods: main() and print-File(). The task performed by main() is to extract the command-line parameters and call printFile(), passing it the name of the file to read. The printFile() method opens the file as a DataInputStream and then enters a while loop, reading a line from the file and echoing it to System.out with each iteration of the loop.

In the main() method, the ReadFile class first determines the location of the ACL properties file, then instantiates a FileSecurity object, passing it a FileACL object that is initialized from the properties file. The security manager is set with a call to System.setSecurityManager(), after which all protected methods in the JDK are subject to the security policy implemented by the FileSecurity and FileACL classes.

For those interested in the details of implementing a CGI program in Java, some CGI-related details of the ReadFile are worth pointing out. First, ReadFile works with both GET and POST request methods. The type of request is stored in the environment variable REQUEST_METHOD, which is relayed to ReadLine through a property of the same name. If called through a GET request, ReadLine calls the printFile() method, passing it the name of the file, which httpd sets in the QUERY_STRING environment variable. If the request method is POST, things get a bit more complicated.

In a POST request, arguments are passed to the CGI program through standard input—System.in for Java applications. The httpd program sets the environment variable CONTENT_LENGTH to indicate how many bytes of data are being sent to the program through its input stream. The ReadLine application reads the specified number of bytes into an array and then closes System.in. Next, the byte array is converted into a ByteArrayInputStream filtered by a DataInputStream. The filenames to be read are pulled out of the byte array using readLine(), then passed to printFile() to be streamed back to the client.

What is significant about the ReadLine program is that it basically takes two lines of code to incorporate the security manager into the application: one to instantiate the FileSecurity object and one to set it as the security manager for the application. The same two lines of code can be used in any other Java application to obtain identical functionality.

SUMMARY

Security managers in Java are often thought of as "that thing" that keeps applets from doing all the things applets aren't supposed to do. Every Java-enabled browser implements a security policy through a SecurityManager object. Once the security manager has been set for the browser, it cannot be changed. Therefore, applets work within the bounds of the security policy set forth by the browser in which they are running.

Java applications, by default, run without a security manager. Any method call that would otherwise be checked by a resident security manager is allowed to execute unchecked. Since most applications do not dynamically download classes from unknown or untrusted sources, it is reasonable to assume that security managers are a browser-only tool. Security managers, however, can be useful in any context where limitations to file, network, or system resources are needed.

The example presented in this chapter—a security manager that implements access control lists—is applicable to many applications where file system access controls are insufficient to guarantee file integrity and security. By applying ACLs to CGI programs, for example, security beyond that provided by the file system or the HTTP server software alone can be obtained. While ACLs are not unique to Java and could, in fact, be implemented in any language, the security-manger model in Java allows ACLs to be implemented in a portable, object-oriented, and highly reusable way.

APPENDIX A

SOURCES FOR THE LED CLASS

LEDPanel Supporting Code

Presented in this appendix are the three classes that are used to create a seven-segment LED object used by the LEDPanel class in Chap. 4. These classes are presented here with minimal explanation, strictly as a convenience. The base class for creating LEDs is the *LEDSegment* class shown in Fig. A.1. The abstract class *LED* is used to represent a single LED, as shown in Fig. A.2. An LED comprised of seven LEDSegments, the *SevenSegment-LED* class, is shown in Fig. A.3.

```
package ajp.awt;

import java.awt.*;

/**
 * A class to represent the individual segments of a LED
 */
class LEDSegment {
    public static final int HORIZONTAL = 0;
    public static final int VERTICAL   = 1;

    // The current state: on of off
    private boolean on = false;

    // Has this been draw yet?
    private boolean drawnYet = false;

    // The polygon that holds the points
    private Polygon poly;

    // Orientation of the segment: HORIZONTAL or VERTICAL
    private int orientation;

    // Length in pixels
    private int length;

    // Width in pixels
    private int width;

    // Coordinates of the segment
    private int x;
    private int y;

    // Color when on (green and red are nice)
    private Color onColor;

    // Color when off.  Calculated from background color of parent LED
    private Color offColor;

    /**
     * Create a LEDSegment with the given orientation, width and length
     */
    public LEDSegment(int direction, int width, int length) {

        /*
         *    1----------------2 ------
         *     /                \   |
         *0,6/----------+        \3 width
         *   |\          tip    /|   |
         *   | \          |    / |   |
         *   | 5---------+------4 +-----
         *   +------length--------+
         */
```

Figure A.1
The LEDSegment
class.

```
            int tip =  (int)(width/2.0 + 0.5);
            int x[] = new int[7];
            int y[] = new int[7];

            orientation = direction;
            this.width = width;
            this.length = length;

            if (direction == HORIZONTAL) {
                 x[0] = 0;
                 x[1] = tip;
                 x[2] = length - tip;
                 x[3] = length;
                 x[4] = x[2];
                 x[5] = x[1];
                 x[6] = x[0];

                 y[0] = 0;
                 y[1] = - tip;
                 y[2] = - tip;
                 y[3] = 0;
                 y[4] = tip;
                 y[5] = tip;
                 y[6] = 0;
            }
            else {
                 y[0] = 0;
                 y[1] = tip;
                 y[2] = length - tip;
                 y[3] = length;
                 y[4] = y[2];
                 y[5] = y[1];
                 y[6] = y[0];

                 x[0] = 0;
                 x[1] = - tip;
                 x[2] = - tip;
                 x[3] = 0;
                 x[4] = tip;
                 x[5] = tip;
                 x[6] = 0;
            }
            // create the Polygon to hold the points
            poly = new Polygon(x, y, x.length);

        }

        /**
         * Create a LEDSegment rotated to the given angle, with the given width
         * and length.
         */
        public LEDSegment(double angle, int width, int length) {
            this(HORIZONTAL, width, length);
```

Figure A.1
(Continued).

```
            Geometry.rotatePolyPoint(poly, new Point(0, 0), angle);
    }

    /**
     * Set the "on" color to <tt>c</tt>
     */
    public void setOnColor(Color c) {
        onColor = c;
    }

    private static final double FACTOR = 1.25;

    /**
     * Set the "off" color.  The actual color is a bit lighter than
     * the color passed.  This gives a realistic LED look.
     */
    public void setOffColor(Color c) {
        offColor = new Color(Math.min((int)(c.getRed()   * FACTOR), 255),
                             Math.min((int)(c.getGreen()* FACTOR), 255),
                             Math.min((int)(c.getBlue() * FACTOR), 255));
    }

    /**
     * Move the LEDSegment to the specified coordinates
     */
    public void moveTo(int x, int y) {
        int deltaX = x - this.x;
        int deltaY = y - this.y;
        this.x = x;
        this.y = y;
        moveRelative(deltaX, deltaY);
    }

    /**
     * Move the LEDSegment relative to its current position.
     */
    public void moveRelative(int deltaX, int deltaY) {
        for (int i = 0; i < poly.npoints; i++) {
            poly.xpoints[i] += deltaX;
            poly.ypoints[i] += deltaY;
        }
    }

    /**
     * Turn the LEDSegment off. Draws the segment in the passed <tt>Graphics</tt>
     * object using the "off" color.
     */
    public void off(Graphics g) {
        if (on | !drawnYet) {
            g.setColor(offColor);
            g.fillPolygon(poly);
            on = false;
            drawnYet = true;
```

Figure A.1
(*Continued*).

```
            }
      }

      /**
       * Turn the LEDSegment on. Draws the segment in the passed <tt>Graphics</tt>
       * object using the "on" color.
       */
      public void on(Graphics g) {
            if (!on) {
                  g.setColor(onColor);
                  g.fillPolygon(poly);
                  on = true;
            }
      }

      /**
       * The location of the LEDSegment.
       */
      public Point location() {
            return new Point(x, y);
      }
}
```

Figure A.1
(*Continued*).

```
package ajp.awt;

import java.awt.*;

/**
 * A abstract class for drawing LED objects.
 */
abstract class LED {
    // The X and Y coordinates
    protected int x;
    protected int y;

    // The dimensions of the LED
    protected int height;
    protected int width;

    /**
     * The segments that make up the LED
     */
    protected LEDSegment seg[];

    // The background color (foreground color saved in the segments)
    protected Color bgColor;

    // The selected color (foreground color saved in the segments)
    protected Color selectedColor = Color.red;

    /* Has the LED been painted yet? Used to determine whether or not
     * to paint the LED's background.
     */
    private boolean painted = false;

    // Is the LED selected
    private boolean selected = false;

    protected LED() {
    }

    /**
     * Intialize the segment array and move the segments to their
     * appropriate position.
     */
    protected abstract void createSegments();

    /**
     * Set the foreground color of the LED. This corresponds to the
     * "on" color of the segments.
     */
    public void setForeground(Color fg) {

        for (int i = 0; i < seg.length; i++) {
            seg[i].setOnColor(fg);
```

Figure A.2
The abstract LED
class.

```
        }
    }

    /**
     * Set the selected color of the LED.
     */
    public void setSelectedColor(Color color) {
        selectedColor = color;
    }

    /**
     * Get the size of the LED.
     */
    public Dimension size() {
        return new Dimension(width, height);
    }

    /**
     * Sets the background color of the LED.  The segments will get a
     * slightly lighter version of this for a realistic effect.
     */
    public void setBackground(Color bg) {
        bgColor = bg;

        for (int i = 0; i < seg.length; i++) {
            seg[i].setOffColor(bg);
        }
        /* flag to repaint the background of the LED since we changed
         * the color.
         */
        painted = false;
    }

    /**
     * Draw the segments of the LED.
     */
    protected abstract void drawSegments(Graphics g);

    /**
     * Draw the LED. Clears the LED the first time it is called.  It
     * allways calls </tt>drawSegments()</tt>.
     */
    public void draw(Graphics g) {
        /*
         * Just draw the background once since the individual
         * segments will do all the drawing.
         */
        if (!painted) {
            g.setColor(bgColor);
            g.fillRect(x, y, width, height);
            painted = true;
        }
        if (selected) {
```

Figure A.2
(Continued).

```
                    g.setColor(selectedColor);
        }
        else {
            g.setColor(bgColor);
        }
        g.drawRect(x, y, width, height-1);
        drawSegments(g);
    }

    /**
     * Move the LED to the specified coordinates
     */
    public void moveTo(int x, int y) {
        Point p;
        int deltaX = x - this.x;
        int deltaY = y - this.y;
        this.x = x;
        this.y = y;

        moveRelative(deltaX, deltaY);
    }

    /**
     * Move the LED relative to its current position.
     */
    public void moveRelative(int deltaX, int deltaY) {
        // move the segments
        for (int i = 0; i < seg.length; i++) {
            seg[i].moveRelative(deltaX, deltaY);
        }

    }

    /**
     * Get the current location of the LED.
     */
    public Point location() {
        return new Point(x, y);
    }

    /**
     * Is the LED selected.
     */
    public boolean isSelected() {
        return selected;
    }

    /**
     * Select the LED.
     */
    public void select() {
        selected = true;
    }
```

Figure A.2
(Continued).

```
    /**
     * Deselect the LED.
     */
    public void deselect() {
        selected = false;
    }

    /**
     * Checks whether a specified x, y location is "inside" this LED.
     */
    public boolean inside(int x, int y) {
        return (x >= this.x && x <= this.x + width
            && y >= this.y && y <= this.y + height);
    }

}
```

Figure A.2
(Continued).

```
package ajp.awt;

import java.awt.*;

/**
 * A class for drawing 7 segment LED objects.
 */
class SevenSegmentLED extends LED {
    public static final int MINUS    = -1;
    public static final int OFF      = -2;
    public static final int LETTER_E = (int)'E';
    public static final int LETTER_r = (int)'r';
    public static final int LETTER_o = (int)'o';

    private static final int PAD      = 5;

    // The current value 0-9, OFF or MINUS
    private int value = 0;

    /* Has the LED been painted yet? Used to determine whether or not
     * to paint the LED's background.
     */
    private boolean painted = false;

    private int segLength;
    private int thick;

    /**
     * Create the LED at the default thickness.
     */
    public SevenSegmentLED(int x, int y, int width) {
        this(x, y, width, 3);
    }

    /**
     * Create the 7-segment LED at the specified  thickness.
     */
    public SevenSegmentLED(int x, int y, int width, int thick) {

        this.thick = thick;
        // segment length
        segLength = (width - 2 * PAD - 2 * thick);

        this.x = x;
        this.y = y;
        this.height = 2 * (segLength + PAD) + 3 * thick;
        this.width = width;

        createSegments();

    }
```

Figure A.3
The SevenSegment-
LED class.

```
    protected void createSegments() {
        int halfThick = (int)(thick/2.0 + 0.5);
        seg = new LEDSegment[7];

        // Create the segements and move them to position
        seg[0] = new LEDSegment(LEDSegment.HORIZONTAL, thick, segLength);
        seg[1] = new LEDSegment(LEDSegment.VERTICAL, thick, segLength);
        seg[2] = new LEDSegment(LEDSegment.VERTICAL, thick, segLength);
        seg[3] = new LEDSegment(LEDSegment.HORIZONTAL, thick, segLength);
        seg[4] = new LEDSegment(LEDSegment.VERTICAL, thick, segLength);
        seg[5] = new LEDSegment(LEDSegment.VERTICAL, thick, segLength);
        seg[6] = new LEDSegment(LEDSegment.HORIZONTAL, thick, segLength);

        seg[0].moveTo(x + PAD + thick,
                      y + PAD + halfThick);
        seg[1].moveTo(x + PAD + halfThick,
                      y + PAD + thick);
        seg[2].moveTo(x + PAD + thick + segLength,
                      y + PAD + thick);
        seg[3].moveTo(x + PAD + thick,
                      y + PAD + thick + halfThick + segLength);
        seg[4].moveTo(x + PAD + halfThick,
                      y + PAD + 2 * thick + segLength);
        seg[5].moveTo(x + PAD + thick + segLength,
                      y + PAD + 2 * thick + segLength);
        seg[6].moveTo(x + PAD + thick,
                      y + PAD + 2 * (thick + segLength) + halfThick);

    }

    /**
     * Set the value of the LED.  Valid numbers are 0-9,
     * OFF and MINUS.
     */
    public void setValue(int val) {
        value = val;
    }

    /**
     * Gets the value of the LED.
     */
    public int getValue() {
        return value;
    }

    /**
     * Draw the LED.
     */
    public void drawSegments(Graphics g) {

        switch(value) {
        case 0:
            seg[0].on(g);
```

Figure A.3

(*Continued*).

```
                seg[1].on(g);
                seg[2].on(g);
                seg[3].off(g);
                seg[4].on(g);
                seg[5].on(g);
                seg[6].on(g);
                break;
        case 1:
                seg[0].off(g);
                seg[1].off(g);
                seg[2].on(g);
                seg[3].off(g);
                seg[4].off(g);
                seg[5].on(g);
                seg[6].off(g);
                break;
        case 2:
                seg[0].on(g);
                seg[1].off(g);
                seg[2].on(g);
                seg[3].on(g);
                seg[4].on(g);
                seg[5].off(g);
                seg[6].on(g);
                break;
        case 3:
                seg[0].on(g);
                seg[1].off(g);
                seg[2].on(g);
                seg[3].on(g);
                seg[4].off(g);
                seg[5].on(g);
                seg[6].on(g);
                break;
        case 4:
                seg[0].off(g);
                seg[1].on(g);
                seg[2].on(g);
                seg[3].on(g);
                seg[4].off(g);
                seg[5].on(g);
                seg[6].off(g);
                break;
        case 5:
                seg[0].on(g);
                seg[1].on(g);
                seg[2].off(g);
                seg[3].on(g);
                seg[4].off(g);
                seg[5].on(g);
                seg[6].on(g);
                break;
```

Figure A.3
(*Continued*).

```
            case 6:
                  seg[0].on(g);
                  seg[1].on(g);
                  seg[2].off(g);
                  seg[3].on(g);
                  seg[4].on(g);
                  seg[5].on(g);
                  seg[6].on(g);
                  break;
            case 7:
                  seg[0].on(g);
                  seg[1].off(g);
                  seg[2].on(g);
                  seg[3].off(g);
                  seg[4].off(g);
                  seg[5].on(g);
                  seg[6].off(g);
                  break;
            case 8:
                  seg[0].on(g);
                  seg[1].on(g);
                  seg[2].on(g);
                  seg[3].on(g);
                  seg[4].on(g);
                  seg[5].on(g);
                  seg[6].on(g);
                  break;
            case 9:
                  seg[0].on(g);
                  seg[1].on(g);
                  seg[2].on(g);
                  seg[3].on(g);
                  seg[4].off(g);
                  seg[5].on(g);
                  seg[6].off(g);
                  break;
            case MINUS:
                  seg[0].off(g);
                  seg[1].off(g);
                  seg[2].off(g);
                  seg[3].on(g);
                  seg[4].off(g);
                  seg[5].off(g);
                  seg[6].off(g);
                  break;
            case LETTER_E:
                  seg[0].on(g);
                  seg[1].on(g);
                  seg[2].off(g);
                  seg[3].on(g);
                  seg[4].on(g);
                  seg[5].off(g);
                  seg[6].on(g);
                  break;
```

Figure A.3
(Continued).

```
            case LETTER_r:
                seg[0].off(g);
                seg[1].off(g);
                seg[2].off(g);
                seg[3].on(g);
                seg[4].on(g);
                seg[5].off(g);
                seg[6].off(g);
                break;
            case LETTER_o:
                seg[0].off(g);
                seg[1].off(g);
                seg[2].off(g);
                seg[3].on(g);
                seg[4].on(g);
                seg[5].on(g);
                seg[6].on(g);
                break;
            case OFF:
            default:
                seg[0].off(g);
                seg[1].off(g);
                seg[2].off(g);
                seg[3].off(g);
                seg[4].off(g);
                seg[5].off(g);
                seg[6].off(g);
                break;

        }
    }

}
```

Figure A.3
(*Continued*).

INDEX

Index

Exhibit A
Java™ Development Kit
Version 1.1
Binary Code License

This binary code license ("License") contains rights and restrictions associated with use of the accompanying software and documentation ("Software"). Read the License carefully before installing the Software. By installing the Software you agree to the terms and conditions of this License.

1. Limited License Grant. Sun grants to you ("Licensee") a non-exclusive, non-transferable limited license to use the Software without fee for evaluation of the Software and for development of Java™ compatible applets and applications. Licensee may make one archival copy of the Software. Licensee may not re-distribute the Software in whole or in part, either separately or included with a product. Refer to the Java Runtime Environment Version 1.1 binary code license (http://www.javasoft.com/products/JDK/1.1/index.html) for the availability of runtime code which may be distributed with Java compatible applets and applications.

2. Java Platform Interface. Licensee may not modify the Java Platform Interface ("JPI", identified as classes contained within the "java" package or any sub-packages of the "java" package), by creating additional classes within the JPI or otherwise causing the addition to or modification of the classes in the JPI. In the event that Licensee creates any Java-related API and distributes such API to others for applet or application development, Licensee must promptly publish an accurate specification for such API for free use by all developers of Java-based software.

3. Restrictions. Software is confidential copyrighted information of Sun and title to all copies is retained by Sun and/or its licensors. Licensee shall not modify, decompile, disassemble, decrypt, extract, or otherwise reverse engineer Software. Software may not be leased, assigned, or sublicensed, in whole or in part. **Software is not designed or intended for use in on-line control of aircraft, air traffic, aircraft navigation or aircraft communications; or in the design, construction, operation or maintenance of any nuclear facility. Licensee warrants that it will not use or redistribute the Software for such purposes.**

4. Trademarks and Logos. This License does not authorize Licensee to use any Sun name, trademark or logo. Licensee acknowledges that Sun owns the Java trademark and all Java-related trademarks, logos and icons including the Coffee Cup and Duke ("Java Marks") and agrees to: (i) to comply with the Java Trademark Guidelines at http://java.com/trademarks.html; (ii) not do anything harmful to or inconsistent with Sun's rights in the Java Marks; and (iii) assist Sun in protecting those rights, including assigning to Sun any rights acquired by Licensee in any Java Mark.

5. Disclaimer of Warranty. Software is provided "AS IS," without a warranty of any kind. ALL EXPRESS OR IMPLIED REPRESENTATIONS AND WARRANTIES, INCLUDING ANY IMPLIED WARRANTY OF MERCHANTABILITY, FITNESS FOR A PARTICULAR PURPOSE OR NON-INFRINGEMENT, ARE HEREBY EXCLUDED.

6. Limitation of Liability. SUN AND ITS LICENSORS SHALL NOT BE LIABLE FOR ANY DAMAGES SUFFERED BY LICENSEE OR ANY THIRD PARTY AS A RESULT OF USING OR DISTRIBUTING SOFTWARE. IN NO EVENT WILL SUN OR ITS LICENSORS BE LIABLE FOR ANY LOST REVENUE, PROFIT OR DATA, OR FOR DIRECT, INDIRECT, SPECIAL, CONSEQUENTIAL, INCIDENTAL OR PUNITIVE DAMAGES, HOWEVER CAUSED AND REGARDLESS OF THE THEORY OF LIABILITY, ARISING OUT OF THE USE OF OR INABILITY TO USE SOFTWARE, EVEN IF SUN HAS BEEN ADVISED OF THE POSSIBILITY OF SUCH DAMAGES.

7. Termination. Licensee may terminate this License at any time by destroying all copies of Software. This License will terminate immediately without notice from Sun if Licensee fails to comply with any provision of this License. Upon such termination, Licensee must destroy all copies of Software.

8. Export Regulation. Software, including technical data, is subject to U.S. export control laws, including the U.S. Export Administration Act and its associated regulations, and may be subject to export or import regulations in other countries. Licensee agrees to comply strictly with all such regulations and acknowledges that it has the responsibility to obtain licenses to export, re-export, or import Software. Software may not be downloaded, or otherwise exported or re-exported (i) into, or to a national or resident of, Cuba, Iraq, Iran, North Korea, Libya, Sudan, Syria or any country to which the U.S. has embargoed goods; or (ii) to anyone on the U.S. Treasury Department's list of Specially Designated Nations or the U.S. Commerce Department's Table of Denial Orders.

9. Restricted Rights. Use, duplication or disclosure by the United States government is subject to the restrictions as set forth in the Rights in Technical Data and Computer Software Clauses in DFARS 252.227-7013(c)(1)(ii) and FAR 52.227-19(c)(2) as applicable.

10. Governing Law. Any action related to this License will be governed by California law and controlling U.S. federal law. No choice of law rules of any jurisdiction will apply.

11. Severability. If any of the above provisions are held to be in violation of applicable law, void, or unenforceable in any jurisdiction, then such provisions are herewith waived to the extent necessary for the License to be otherwise enforceable in such jurisdiction. However, if in Sun's opinion deletion of any provisions of the License by operation of this paragraph unreasonably compromises the rights or increase the liabilities of Sun or its licensors, Sun reserves the right to terminate the License and refund the fee paid by Licensee, if any, as Licensee's sole and exclusive remedy.

SOFTWARE AND INFORMATION LICENSE

The software and information on this diskette (collectively referred to as the "Product") are the property of The McGraw-Hill Companies, Inc. ("McGraw-Hill") and are protected by both United States copyright law and international copyright treaty provision. You must treat this Product just like a book, except that you may copy it into a computer to be used and you may make archival copies of the Products for the sole purpose of backing up our software and protecting your investment from loss.

By saying "just like a book," McGraw-Hill means, for example, that the Product may be used by any number of people and may be freely moved from one computer location to another, so long as there is no possibility of the Product (or any part of the Product) being used at one location or on one computer while it is being used at another. Just as a book cannot be read by two different people in two different places at the same time, neither can the Product be used by two different people in two different places at the same time (unless, of course, McGraw-Hill's rights are being violated).

McGraw-Hill reserves the right to alter or modify the contents of the Product at any time.

This agreement is effective until terminated. The Agreement will terminate automatically without notice if you fail to comply with any provisions of this Agreement. In the event of termination by reason of your breach, you will destroy or erase all copies of the Product installed on any computer system or made for backup purposes and shall expunge the Product from your data storage facilities.

LIMITED WARRANTY

McGraw-Hill warrants the physical diskette(s) enclosed herein to be free of defects in materials and workmanship for a period of sixty days from the purchase date. If McGraw-Hill receives written notification within the warranty period of defects in materials or workmanship, and such notification is determined by McGraw-Hill to be correct, McGraw-Hill will replace the defective diskette(s). Send request to:

Customer Service
McGraw-Hill
Gahanna Industrial Park
860 Taylor Station Road
Blacklick, OH 43004-9615

The entire and exclusive liability and remedy for breach of this Limited Warranty shall be limited to replacement of defective diskette(s) and shall not include or extend to any claim for or right to cover any other damages, including but not limited to, loss of profit, data, or use of the software, or special, incidental, or consequential damages or other similar claims, even if McGraw-Hill has been specifically advised as to the possibility of such damages. In no event will McGraw-Hill's liability for any damages to you or any other person ever exceed the lower of suggested list price or actual price paid for the license to use the Product, regardless of any form of the claim.

THE McGRAW-HILL COMPANIES, INC. SPECIFICALLY DISCLAIMS ALL OTHER WARRANTIES, EXPRESS OR IMPLIED, INCLUDING BUT NOT LIMITED TO, ANY IMPLIED WARRANTY OF MERCHANTABILITY OR FITNESS FOR A PARTICULAR PURPOSE. Specifically, McGraw-Hill makes no representation or warranty that the Product is fit for any particular purpose and any implied warranty of merchantability is limited to the sixty day duration of the Limited Warranty covering the physical diskette(s) only (and not the software or in-formation) and is otherwise expressly and specifically disclaimed.

This Limited Warranty gives you specific legal rights; you may have others which may vary from state to state. Some states do not allow the exclusion of incidental or consequential damages, or the limitation on how long an implied warranty lasts, so some of the above may not apply to you.

This Agreement constitutes the entire agreement between the parties relating to use of the Product. The terms of any purchase order shall have no effect on the terms of this Agreement. Failure of McGraw-Hill to insist at any time on strict compliance with this Agreement shall not constitute a waiver of any rights under this Agreement. This Agreement shall be construed and governed in accordance with the laws of New York. If any provision of this Agreement is held to be contrary to law, that provision will be enforced to the maximum extent permissible and the remaining provisions will remain in force and effect.